THE INTERNATIONALIZATION OF CURRICULUM STUDIES

PETER LANG
New York • Washington, D.C./Baltimore • Bern
Frankfurt am Main • Berlin • Brussels • Vienna • Oxford

THE INTERNATIONALIZATION OF CURRICULUM STUDIES

Selected Proceedings
from the LSU Conference
2000

EDITED BY

Donna Trueit, William E. Doll, Jr.,
Hongyu Wang, & William F. Pinar

PETER LANG
New York • Washington, D.C./Baltimore • Bern
Frankfurt am Main • Berlin • Brussels • Vienna • Oxford

Library of Congress Cataloging-in-Publication Data

The internationalization of curriculum studies: selected proceedings from the LSU Conference 2000 / [edited by] Donna Trueit ... [et al.].
p. cm.
Papers from the conference held at the Louisiana State University, Apr. 27–30, 2000.
Includes bibliographical references and index.
1. Curriculum planning—Cross-cultural studies—Congresses. 2. Education—Curricula—Cross-cultural studies—Congresses. 3. Education—International cooperation—Congresses. I. Trueit, Donna.
LB2806.15.I597   375' .001—dc21   2002156037
ISBN 0-8204-5590-3

Bibliographic information published by **Die Deutsche Bibliothek**.
Die Deutsche Bibliothek lists this publication in the "Deutsche Nationalbibliografie"; detailed bibliographic data is available on the Internet at http://dnb.ddb.de/.

Cover design by Lisa Barfield

The paper in this book meets the guidelines for permanence and durability of the Committee on Production Guidelines for Book Longevity of the Council of Library Resources.

© 2003 Peter Lang Publishing, Inc., New York
275 Seventh Avenue, 28th Floor, New York, NY 10001
www.peterlangusa.com

All rights reserved.
Reprint or reproduction, even partially, in all forms such as microfilm, xerography, microfiche, microcard, and offset strictly prohibited.

Printed in the United States of America

CONTENTS

Preface:
Democracy and Conversation
Donna Trueit • Canada...ix

Introduction:
Toward the Internationalization of Curriculum Studies
William F. Pinar • United States..1

1 Poaching: Sanctifying Time
 Peter Appelbaum • United States...15

2 WES: A Theory and Framework for an International Curriculum
 Keith Bookwalter • Colombia..35

3 Technology Unmasked?
 Kevan Brewer • Canada..51

4 Bernstein *avec* Lacan: Desire, Jouissance, and Pedagogic Discourse
 Zain Davis • South Africa...71

5 Re-constituting Pedagogies: The (Im)possibilities for
    Inter/nationalizing Curriculum Studies
 Aristides Gazetas • Canada..103

6 Reflections on a Dialogue about Education for the Future
 Urve Läänemets • Estonia...117

7   What Knowledge Is of Most Worth?
    Ajeet Mathur • India...137

8   Curriculum Reforms in Norway:
    "To Change in Order to Preserve?"
    Lars Monsen • Norway...179

9   Co-operative Education, the Curriculum, and Working Knowledge
    Hugh Munby, Peter Chin, and Nancy L. Hutchinson • Canada......205

10 Creating a Dialogue with Difference
    Antoinette Oberg • Canada..219

11 The Project and Vision of Transformative Learning
    Edmund O'Sullivan • Canada..233

12 The Globalization of the World and the Need for the
    Internationalization of Curriculum Studies:
    A Change for the Future
    Sid N. Pandey • Botswana...249

13 Teacher Identity and the Ideologies of Teaching:
    Some Remarks on the Interplay
    Eero Ropo and Veli-Matti Värri • Finland..................................261

14 Action Competence as an Educational Ideal
    Karsten Schnack • Denmark..271

15 The Specific Challenges of Globalization for
    Teaching...and Vice Versa
    David Geoffrey Smith • Canada..293

16 Creation of Participatory Public Spaces
    Judith J. Slater • United States..319

17 "El sueño de razón produce monstruos," or Deconstructing the
    Curriculum of Philosophy
    Tuukka Tomperi • Finland..337

18 The Politics of Moral Education: A Cross-Cultural Analysis
    Tianlong Yu • People's Republic of China................................359

Index..377

PREFACE

Democracy and Conversation

Donna Trueit • Canada

For several years prior to the 2000 LSU Internationalization of Curriculum Studies Conference, the proceedings of which appear here, I was privy to conversations in which William Pinar talked passionately about the possibilities for conversation—and the possible pitfalls, including the intrusion of global politics.[1] For him, internationalization is about learning—about curriculum scholars meeting to talk about issues in curriculum, hearing what people do, how they do it, how they think about things—in the hope that we can learn from each other. But his concerns about the likelihood of such meaningful discussions could be heard when he asked, in the introductory address to the conference, "Given the cultural and linguistic complexity of the world, how can *democratic dialogue* possibly proceed?" The emphasis in the question is clear. When we come together from such diverse backgrounds, with international histories that involve colonization, occupation, political ignorance, and arrogance, how can we speak with each other in such a way that the past does not overshadow the present encounter? Can we speak as scholars in ways that honor democratic ideals? In this collection of essays, which intends to provide a historical record of the internationalization movement in the year 2000, it seems appropriate to ponder the possibility of curriculum theory as a "complicated conversation" (W. Pinar, in Pinar, Reynolds, Slattery, Taubman 1995: 848).

It seems obvious to me that in the Western/Anglo-American tradition, curriculum theory in the twentieth century was profoundly affected, perhaps even spawned, by *The Linguistic Turn* that Richard Rorty (1967) outlined in the discipline of philosophy. Before the linguistic turn, philosophy was the authority on all knowledge—moral, political, epistemological. Theories of knowledge sat within the realm of philosophy, which directly influenced education. Philosophers were the teachers of teachers. But with Peirce and Putnam, Quine and Wittgenstein, the discipline fractured into groups that talked about knowledge being constructed through language, the role language plays in meaning, and the way we think and speak about *everything*.[2] Philosophy questioned its methods of inquiry and representation, the so-called correspondence theory of truth. The credibility of philosophy's traditions crumbled as the foundations of positivism, empiricism, and rationality gave way, and in the disjunctures, crevices, and faults there started to emerge a new field—curriculum theory—positioned between philosophy and education. Curriculum theorists make inquiries into and critiques of both fields with a view to understanding and improving the processes of teaching and learning. They draw upon such diverse fields as anthropology, political and cultural theory, gender theory, history, and the arts to inform their activities—because, as Clifford Geertz (2000) says (and Ludwig Wittgenstein would agree), "the answers to our most general questions—why? how? what? whither?—to the degree they have answers, are to be found in the fine detail of lived life" (xi).

In considering curriculum as a complicated conversation, it is on the fine detail of everyday speech and its relation to thought that I focus, from a cultural anthropological approach to oral/folkloric traditions, à la Richard Bauman, Walter Ong, Eric Havelock, Richard P. Martin, Gregory Nagy. Foregrounding speech in this way, "conversation," becomes *marked*,[3] elevated to a special significance allowing us the opportunity of "seeing" speech as speeches, a historical, cultural phenomenon. Conversation is seen as the expression of a very different thought process than that shaped—disciplined—by the philosophical/academic tradition which chooses argumentation to express itself.

As Richard Rorty (1979) explains in *Philosophy and the Mirror of Nature,* the traditional discourse of intellectual (philosophical, metaphysical) thought is argumentation. Rorty's repeated call for conversation, echoed by Pinar (1995, 2000, 2002), is a demand that we examine the linguistic foundations of "knowledge." By calling attention to the terms "argumentation" and "conversation," Rorty metonymically contrasts schools of thought about "knowledge"—and the processes of its construction.[4] There is, he suggests, a political aspect to the "discourse." Language is a tool and we may use tools to conquer or to cultivate. Do we pound home our point, or do we question, wonder, suggest, and persuade? Rorty wants us to understand the Anglo-American philosophical tradition as one that puts stock in the linguistic skill of the discussants as much as in their ability to find Truth. From his perspective, the linguistic turn in philosophy attends to the fallibility of language, to the idea that meaning (truth) is discovered, represented in words, and passed from my lips to your ears.

Academia was, perhaps still is, characterized by *certain* discourses: research-based certainty, empirical certainty and logical certainty. The tradition of academic discourse,[5] written or spoken, is to make a clear strong case coming out of the philosophical tradition—to speak with certainty, logic, and rationality; to speak in such a way that opportunities for further discussion are limited, such as argumentation. More recently, however, academic thought was influenced by Western (Euro-American) modernity with its focus on scientific methods and underlying Judeo-Christian values. The resulting spoken discourse often sounds like the speaker is not only right, but *he* is the only one who can be right and has God on *his* side (sic—with a nod to the patriarchal canon). The intent of this discourse is cogency and power.

Dialogue has an etymological and cultural history beyond just (some assume, two) people talking together. That history involves the shaping of academic and philosophical speech and thought based on "Platonism" and captured in representational language. (For more on this point, see Tuukka Tomperi, this volume). Rorty explains,

> "Platonism" in the sense in which I use the term does not denote the (very complex, shifting, dubiously consistent) thoughts of the genius who wrote the *Dialogues*. Instead, it refers to a set of philosophical distinctions (appearance—reality, matter—mind, made—found, sensible—intellectual, etc.): what Dewey called "a brood and nest of dualisms." These dualisms dominate the history of Western philosophy, and can be traced back to one or another of Plato's writings. (Preface 1999: xii)

To go back then, to Pinar's question to the conference participants, "How can democratic dialogue possibly proceed?"—the answer is, to use Rorty's metaphor, dialogue will not work to achieve democracy because, like argument, dialectic, and rhetoric, it is the wrong tool. Dialogue is a modernist discourse of representationalism and Platonist dualisms—as Dewey says, either/or's. With these forms of speech, the one with the most truth/power and argumentative skill wins. With these ways of speaking, these tools, so tied to a modernist vocabulary, there is little room for conceiving possibilities. A shovel is very useful for digging a hole. For other purposes we can use other tools. Rorty might say that that is why we have poetic ways of speaking. Regarding language and inquiry in a biologistic way, i.e., outside of representationalism, Rorty (1999: 39) says, "The right question to ask is, For what purposes might it be useful..."—and I fill in the blank with "to use this tool." Dialogue as a way of speaking and a process of thinking, leads to what Gadamer describes, in its gentlest and most ideal form, as a "fusion of horizons." A point. A truth. There is no tolerance for difference or dissent. And there is no room at the table for those who do not have the cultural capital, the academic background, or the "vocabulary." It is an exclusionary discourse and is coercive. For Rorty, democracy is about freedom and justice, or, if you like, self-creation and human solidarity, but always about incommensurable ideals. Could dialogue ever be a democratic way of speaking? Witness the political strife of the Middle East. Meaning does not reside in words. Meaning arises from action.

Rorty says, "Our efforts at persuasion must take the form of gradual inculcation of new ways of speaking, rather than straightforward argumentation within old ways of speaking" (1999: 34). What does he mean by *conversation*? He characterizes conversation several ways: abnormal discourse, edifying discourse, poetic and descriptive discourse. For him the difference between argument and conversation is synonymous with the difference between Cartesian thought and Darwinian thought.[6] He says, "we need to stop thinking of words as representations and to start thinking of them as nodes in the causal network which binds the organism together with its environment" (Niznik and Sanders 1996: 38). *Nodes in the causal network*...what kind of thinking is that? Metaphorically, instead of the cogency of the argument, one thing following from the other leading down the singular path, the words (nodes) of conversation create connections (causal networks)—places where we touch. The difference is between argument/rationality and conversation "something else." That something else is the presence of the person(al)—the *engagement* of the speaker—the speaker is fully present to the conversation.[7]

What are the "fine details" of conversation that make it appropriate for "democratic" discourse? There are two performative characteristics of conversation that are necessary—essential—to democratic process: the first I will call *praxis,* the second is inquiry. Praxis is the ancient (pre-literate) Greek notion concerning the virtue of word and deed—thought and action. In primarily oral cultures, truth was constituted by the coherence between speech and actions. Praxis is the element of conversation that accounts for the active presence of "self"—in Rorty's terms, the organism bound together with its environment. The self is present through, and engaged with, the word. Praxis is the key to one having a sense of one's self as a "knower," as someone who *can* participate in the conversation which does not require a special "vocabulary."

The second aspect of conversation that relates to democratic process is the mode inquiry—just "finding out about," as Rorty says in *Philosophy and Social Hope* (1999), or *edification,* as he says elsewhere (1979: 360). Conversation is not only an opportunity for us to voice our thoughts, often understanding them only when they are heard, when *we* hear them. It is also a chance to hear the thoughts of others—*nodes in the causal network,* making connections with others, because, Rorty says, it "takes us out of ourselves by the power of strangeness, to aid us in becoming new beings" (1979: 360).[8] We are changed. Conversational discourse, to go back to the idea of language as a tool, is used to cultivate, generate ideas, to make connections. These two elements of conversation, praxis and inquiry, make conversation uniquely appropriate as the discourse of democracy—social action which arises out of the engagement of one with the other.

Curriculum studies is an evolving field of inquiry whose history differs from country to country, but in light of both the obvious and yet unknown effects of globalization, the move to advance the field in the area of internationalization is crucially important politically and ethically. As the essays in this volume indicate, this is a time of political, economic, and educational reformation. In this transforming world, as the field comes to maturation, it is timely to take action to understand what is occurring within and beyond national borders and to support others as they do the same. To do this we must talk. Recognizing speech as related to thought, attending to the history of oral discourses and the influences that have shaped them, one may be able to move beyond the nationalistic, colonizing, and imperialistic values and tendencies that persist in modernist speech genres and practices. To honor difference, to learn from each other, we need to attend to ways to keep the conversation going, to work toward understanding incommensurabilities, even, as Rorty says, to *play,* to keep from imposing our values and beliefs on others. I would suggest that the *interplay,* the back-and-forth, adds complexity and generativity to the talk.

The essays in this collection reflect just such differences as one might expect when scholars from such varied circumstances come together. There are twenty essays by authors from fourteen countries, written by teacher-educators, philosophers, students of curriculum theory—one principal in Colombia, and a business administration and economic relations specialist. This volume intends to (re)present the author's voice as much as possible, and to that end there are inconsistencies between chapters that reflect the differences between American and British systems of written English. References are provided but also reflect the international flavor of the collection. Not all books are available at the local library or available in English. Looking beyond those superficialities, the essays represent the struggles of individuals to work within the constraints of their locale, bureaucracies, institutions, and cultures to improve education. Often this is a lonely and thankless task. The movement toward the internationalization of curriculum studies hopes to provide support for those heroes. As William Pinar said, addressing the AAACS conference in New Orleans (2002), "Let us, together, in conversation with colleagues worldwide, construct an increasingly sophisticated field of curriculum studies, one worthy of those schoolteachers and students who, each day nearly everywhere on the globe, labor to understand themselves and the world they inhabit."

The first Internationalization of Curriculum Studies Conference held at Louisiana State University was filled with exciting discourses, and if it was to be judged by the volume of the talk, the conference was a raging success. The joy for the organizing committee was in receiving strongly positive feedback from the participants. The reward was in hearing people's stories of the work they do and the conditions under which they work. In the spirit that the conference was conceived, understanding curriculum as a complicated conversation, in the hope that we can speak democratically—in spite of, in full recognition of, rejoicing in!—incommensurabilities, this book is offered as the first of a series of Internationalization records. The conversations have begun.

Notes

1. These conversations took place with William E. Doll, Jr., from Louisiana State University, co-chair of Curriculum Theory Project, and co-organizer of the LSU Internationalization of Curriculum Studies Conference, who has been advocating conversation as an aspect of a post-modern curriculum since 1993. See his book, *A Post-Modern Perspective on Curriculum* (1993).
2. Rorty outlines a parallel shift in philosophical thinking in continental Europe, following Neitzsche and Heidegger, to Derrida, Foucault, and other poststructuralist philosophers.
3. The irony here is that although I suggest distancing from a linguistic analysis, I use a

term and technique "borrowed" from the Prague School of Linguistics, as demonstrated by Richard P. Martin, in *The Language of Heroes* as a method of highlighting certain "ways of speaking" so that they may be characterized and distinguished from other ways of speaking. Linguistics as a science tends to analyze speech atomistically, methodically, and in the tradition of modern science rather than as contextual and historically situated. Rorty says, "The idea that philosophy might make progress through 'linguistic analysis' was, as Wittgenstein and Quine have helped us see, a dead end" (Niznik and Sanders, 1996: 62).

4. Rorty objects to the term "social construction of knowledge" on the basis of being an "anti-dualist." The term social construction would be the other part of the discovery of the dualism of knowledge. He says, referring to Platonist or Kantian "opponents": "I think it is important that we who are accused of relativism stop using the distinctions between finding and making, discovery and invention, objective and subjective. We should not let ourselves be described as social constructionists. We cannot formulate our point in terms of a distinction between what is outside us and what is inside us. We must repudiate the vocabulary our opponents use and not let them impose it upon us" (Niznik and Sanders 1996: 33).

5. This point is confirmed by Walter Ong (1981: 29) who says: "Although the fact has been almost entirely overlooked in cultural history, the academic world itself has in the past been conspicuously dominated by agonistic activity and structures—from its beginnings in the ancient rhetorical and dialectical tradition in the West and comparable traditions elsewhere through later academic and other educational practices dominant until the advent of the Romantic movement, which reduced or masked the agonistic mind-set in academia but did not eliminate it."

6. Habermas (Niznik and Sanders 1996: 19) reminds us not to mistake "Rorty's utterances as truth-vehicles or expressions of veridical beliefs…[but to] recognize them as rhetorical devices…." Rorty's contrast of Darwin to Descartes highlights speech (and inquiry) as "biologisitic" compared to the Cartesian mind which sees words as representational and "which somehow swings free of the causal forces on the body." (Rorty 1999: xxiii). He explains the same point more fully this way: "My references to Darwin are simply devices for directing your attention to the existence of a nondualist, non-Platonist, non-Kantian, naturalistic description of the human situation. They suggest a way of thinking of culture as continuous with biology by thinking of the development of language as an event in nature requiring no special magic, no foot in another world" (Niznik and Sanders 1996: 123). Regarding the differences between Habermas and Rorty (according to Rorty) concerning their views on "conversation" and "dialogue," one might position Habermas in relation to globalization (due to his universalizing language) compared with Rorty in relation to internationalization (with his preference for the local). Rorty states: "There is considerable convergence between Habermas's substitution of communicative reason for subject-centered reason and what I am calling the Protagorean/Emersonian tradition. The principal differences between Habermas and myself concern the notion of universal validity" (Niznik and Sanders 1996: 28). Both are strong proponents of democratic action and/through discourse.

7. By "fully present" I am emphasizing a difference in relation to Cartesian mind/body rationality.
8. Rorty pragmatically reframes what I call the self-other relationship in terms of self-creation and justice: "self-creation is necessarily private, unshared, unsuited to argument" and "the vocabulary of justice is necessarily public and shared, a medium for argumentative exchange" (1989: xiv), thereby allowing that more than one type of discourse is necessary for a "just and free society."

References

Bauman, R. (1986). *Story, performance and event. Contextual studies of oral narrative*. Cambridge, MA: Cambridge University Press.

Doll, W. E. Jr. (1993). *A post-modern perspective on curriculum*. New York: Teachers College Press.

Gadamer, H. (1998). *Truth and method*. 2nd revised edition. Translation revised by Joel Weinsheimer and Donald G. Marshall. New York: Continuum.

Geertz, C. (2000). *Available light. Anthropological reflections on philosophical topics*. Princeton, NJ: Princeton University Press.

Havelock, E. (1986). *The muse learns to write. Reflections on orality and literacy from antiquity to the present*. New Haven, CN: Yale University Press.

Martin, R. P. (1989). *The language of heroes. Speech and performance in the Iliad*. Ithaca, NY: Cornell University Press.

Nagy, G. (1996). *Poetry as performance: Homer and beyond*. Cambridge, MA: Cambridge University Press.

Niznik, J. and J. T. Sanders (Eds.) (1996). *Debating the state of philosophy: Habermas, Rorty, and Kolakowski*. With contributions by Ernest Gellner and others. Westport, CT: Praeger.

Ong, W. (1981). *Fighting for life. Contest, sexuality and consciousness*. Ithaca, NY: Cornell University Press.

────── (1982). *Orality and literacy: The technologizing of the word*. London and New York: Methuen.

Phillips, J. (1996). Hermeneutics. *Philosophy, psychiatry, & psychology 3.1*: 61–9. Johns Hopkins University Press. Internet: http://muse.jhu.edu/demo/philosophy_psychiatry_and_psychology /3.1phillips.html

Pinar, W. (2000). Address to the 1st Internationalization of Curriculum Conference. Baton Rouge, Louisiana. April, 2000.

Pinar, W. (2002). Paper presented to the 1st Annual Meeting of the American Association for the Advancement of Curriculum Studies. New Orleans, Louisiana. April 2, 2002.

Pinar, W. F., W. M. Reynolds, P. Slattery, and P. Taubman (1995). *Understanding curriculum: An introduction to the study of historical and contemporary curriculum discourses*. New York: Peter Lang.

Rorty, R. (Ed.) (1967). *The linguistic turn: Recent essays in philosophical method*. With introduction by Richard Rorty. Chicago: University of Chicago Press.

Rorty, R. (1979). *Philosophy and the mirror of nature*. New Jersey: Princeton University Press.

——— (1989). *Contingency, irony and solidarity*. Cambridge, MA: Cambridge University Press.
——— (1991). *Objectivity, relativism and truth. Philosophical papers, Vol.1*. Cambridge, MA: Cambridge University Press.
——— (1999). *Philosophy and social hope*. New York: Penguin.
Vygotsky, L. (1997). *Thought and language*. Translation, revised and edited by Alex Kozulin. Cambridge, MA: MIT Press.

INTRODUCTION

Toward the Internationalization of Curriculum Studies

William F. Pinar • United States

We convened this conference to encourage the internationalization of curriculum studies, that is, to contribute to the formation of a worldwide field of curriculum studies, institutionally supported by an International Association for Curriculum Studies. Why should anyone be interested in such a possibility? Are there not already too many conferences, too many organizations? Are we not already overwhelmed by the demands of our local situations? Is this project simply another American effort to expand its market for intellectual property, in this instance the global market for its conceptual products in education? While this "call for conversation" is sincere, given the cultural and linguistic complexity of the world, how can democratic dialogue possibly proceed without the dry formalism of those diplomatic exchanges associated with, say, representatives to the United Nations, or with the more nakedly political manipulations associated with cultural and economic imperialism? While it is I who have raised these questions, it will be each of us who must answer them for himself or herself. We will meet again to report to each other our answers, including our answer to the question: Shall we start an international association for curriculum studies? What a "worldwide" field would look like we shall decide together.

We may well decide, of course, not to meet again, may decide not to pursue the possibilities of a worldwide field with an international association of curriculum scholars. More than other fields, perhaps, curriculum studies tend to be explicitly situated within the national borders in which they are conducted, although this may be more true for some nations—like the United States—than it is for others, like Canada or China or Japan or Korea. This fact is why I chose the word "internationalization" for the conference—rather than, say, "globalization" or simply "worldwide"—even though, as Tony Whitson pointed out at last year's meeting (focused on the intersections between curriculum studies and philosophy of education internationally), the term for some may imply endorsement of the notion of nationalism, at the least a problematical historical and political phenomenon. Certainly I share Whitson's worry over nationalism, but that seems to me to be work for another day. What I mean by the term in the conference title—a term to which, by the way, I'm hardly wedded—is the simple acknowledgment that for most of us our work is very much situated within, linked to, sometimes even dictated by the political and educational (overlapping terms to be sure) issues that preoccupy the nations in which we do our work.

Given this national character of much curriculum work, what can be the benefit of meeting with others whose work is so focused? I take this question to be an open one. We may decide that it is not worthwhile at this time, despite the hype about "one world" and "globalization," a complex economic, cultural, and political phenomenon which, as David G. Smith made clear at last year's meeting, is hardly to be greeted uncritically. It is a question each of us must answer for her- and himself. Permit me to speak with you for the next few minutes about how I think about that question, including its genesis in my work which, as you realize, takes place in the United States.

It is in chapter 14 of *Understanding Curriculum* (a survey of the American curriculum field I wrote with William Reynolds, Patrick Slattery, and Peter Taubman), a chapter entitled "Understanding Curriculum as International Text," that, I confess, I first seriously grappled with the subject. Actually, it was my co-author Patrick Slattery who grappled with the subject, at my request. He found that there had been relatively little done in the United States on internationalization, at least published in mainstream curriculum journals. There is of course an extant field—comparative education—which has labored for decades to understand education across national borders. Because of time limitations (it was chapter 14 out of 15, and the book was overdue at the publisher), we did not do a systematic search of that field for information specific to curriculum. I still hope to encourage graduate students and colleagues to undertake a systematic search of the field of comparative education, to summarize scholarship in that field we might find useful to an internationalized field of curriculum studies. But the project of internationalization, while it can no doubt profit from comparative education, is, from the point of view of American curriculum studies at least, relatively recent, and needs to be constructed from the ground up, as it were. Tonight we're on the ground floor.

There is, if I'm compelled to stay with this metaphor, at the very minimum a basement already constructed, provided primarily (although not exclusively) by the Canadians and the British. I am thinking, for instance, of the work of Ivor Goodson, Terry Carson, John Willinsky, David G. Smith, and especially Ted Aoki. In addition to the international character of his intellectual and pedagogical work, Ted has long been involved in the World Council for Curriculum and Instruction, still an ongoing organization, whose members we might invite to join us, should we proceed with an organization of our own.

A small section of the "basement" may be the international handbook of curriculum research I am editing, the first volume, I believe, of its kind. While there have been numerous handbooks focusing on various specializations and topics within educational research and practice, this is, I believe, the first international handbook reporting curriculum theory, inquiry, and research in the various nations and regions. Another small section of this "basement" might be the book series I edit at Lawrence Erlbaum Associates (LEA) and Peter Lang, for which I encourage international book projects. For instance, I have invited Shigeru Asanuma to edit a collection reporting the state of curriculum studies in Japan and Hongyu Wang to participate in a volume reporting the state of curriculum studies in China, and last year LEA published a volume on the German tradition of *didaktik* edited by Ian Westbury, Stefan Hopmann, and Kurt Riquarts. The idea for that volume began in August 1995, in Oslo, Norway, during the conference on *didaktik* and curriculum studies held at the University of Oslo, directed by Professor Bjorg Gundem.

That 1995 conference—the proceedings of which are available from Peter Lang (who, like Lawrence Erlbaum, are sponsors of this conference)—I regard as the direct antecedent of this meeting. Under Professor Gundem's deft leadership, the Oslo meeting encouraged a conversation between North American and European traditions. If there develops someday a worldwide field of curriculum studies, it can be said to have been conceived in Oslo in August 1995.

Permit me to point out that I am hardly the only member of LSU's Curriculum Theory Project who has been working internationally, as co-director Bill Doll's *A Post-Modern Perspective on Curriculum* has been translated into, among other languages, Spanish and Chinese and his new collection entitled *Curriculum Visions* has involved collaborations with Australian and Canadian scholars. Moreover, Bill has lectured in Finland and Russia, and this fall is set to visit China; Petra Munro's research on engendering curriculum history has taken her to England and Germany; Denise Egéa-Kuehne studies and translates French theorists such as Derrida and works closely with French officials and scholars and participates regularly in international conferences; Nina Asher participated in an international conference in Bombay last winter and works in the area of post-colonialism; and Claudia Eppert's work on historical trauma will take her to Germany and eastern Canada this summer. Other faculty affiliated with the Project have also been working internationally: Ron Good and Jim Wandersee participate regularly in international science education meetings; Nancy Nelson's current research on critical literacy took her to New Zealand last year; Ann Trousdale is studying the Celtic warrior Boadicea; and David Kirshner spent much of his last sabbatical in Korea. My colleagues are not simply traveling abroad; their intellectual interests and research projects often require it. For me, I work in Canada as often as circumstances permit, and in 1997 I spent six weeks in Japan. But it was a 1993 conference on curriculum decentralization, sponsored by UNESCO and held in Santiago, Chile, at which I represented the United States, which emphasized to me (again) how problematical the position of the American is in international events.

I would say I have become rather self-conscious of my problem as an American. There is a confidence bordering on narcissism which accompanies coming of age here, at least at this time, for my generation, despite the lessons of the Vietnam War, despite our—I am referring to those of us on the political left—defeat in 1968 and the humiliations and horrors of the decades that have followed and haunt us still. Despite that bitterness and our despair over developments in the schools, many of us Americans still exude a naïve, if more than occasionally imperialistic, confidence that "the world is ours." Of course this is nonsense, but somewhere in the American unconscious such nonsense is, it seems, always at work.

In this regard, in addition to supporting the emergence of an international field, one of my motives for this conference is to contest the sometimes unbelievable narcissism of American curriculum studies. Probably it is not a special fault of those who work in the field; it seems to come with citizenship. One way we Americans can work through that narcissism is to become more aware, in fact to regard it as part of our professional responsibility, to keep track of what others interested in the concept of curriculum (or its equivalent) are doing around the world. Another way is to heighten our awareness of the international origins of many of our intellectual sources and influences. For example, many of us working at the theoretical end of the American field rely very much on a number of French scholars and theorists, from Derrida, Lyotard, Latour, and Foucault, to Lacan, Wittig, Cixous, Kristeva, and others. To underscore our awareness of these theorists' situatedness in France cannot but help increase our awareness of the relations of ideas to national settings, including national histories and politics, not to mention the profoundly multicultural and international character of the American nation itself. The curriculum field as we Americans know it is a rather American affair, although I doubt few of us have spent much time dwelling on that fact. Even if an international conversation—a worldwide field—fails to develop at this time, if this conference could contribute, however modestly, to Americans' realization that our own field is profoundly international and multicultural, the labor would be, in my judgment, well justified.

So when I propose a "worldwide" field of curriculum studies, I do not mean "uniform," nor do I expect that it would resemble the American field. To repeat, I acknowledge—and not as a problem to overcome—that at this stage of things and for the foreseeable future, curriculum inquiry occurs within national borders, often informed by governmental policies and priorities, and is thereby nationally distinctive. I do not secretly dream of a worldwide field of curriculum studies mirroring the standardization and uniformity that the larger phenomenon of globalization threatens. Certainly I am not looking—allow me to emphasize—for new "markets" for American conceptual products. More than anything else, I recognize, it is the fact of American economic and cultural imperialism that leaves many scholars suspicious about this meeting and the larger project of internationalization. It is this fact that makes problematical Americans taking leadership in the formation of a worldwide field, and this is why, while I may seem to be belaboring this issue, I decline to set an agenda aside from the democratic idea of "conversation," why I insist each of us must pose questions and answer them, together and separately.

Comments on the American Scene

Of course there is no way for me to escape being an American, and my definition of curriculum as a "complicated conversation" (Pinar, Reynolds, Slattery, Taubman 1995: 848) is thoroughly (although hardly exclusively) an American idea. In the "paradigm shift" that occurred in American curriculum studies almost thirty years ago, we left a more narrowly institutional (some would say bureaucratic) conception of our work as "curriculum development" for a more scholarly effort to understand curriculum. By enlarging and complicating our conception of curriculum—yes, it still includes objectives, course syllabi, etc., but it is now a highly symbolic concept as well in which curriculum debates are understood, for instance, as debates over the identity of the nation—we hope to protect, at least conceptually, American teachers' still-shrinking space of intellectual freedom, professional autonomy, and personal creativity, and, in so doing, support the intellectual freedom and creativity of the students they teach. (I realize that American public education is judged by some scholars and critics—from both within and outside the United States—as suffering from too much "freedom," from insufficient standardization and supervision. I do not share that judgment.)

The discursive reformulation of our work as curriculum theorists from "curriculum development" to "understanding curriculum" represents, in part, a sober acknowledgment of the triumph in the schools of "business thinking"—an insistence that educational achievement be quantified, and that all engaged in the process of education must focus on the "bottom line," i.e., test scores. We in the university are left trying to protect and create spaces of intellectual freedom and professional autonomy "behind enemy lines," as it were. In another sense, the American curriculum field—in general, as there is hardly a consensus—represents an effort to revitalize the old Progressive project associated with Dewey, Counts, Kilpatrick, and others who struggled to make the public school a laboratory for democracy. Ours, like theirs, is a "rear-guard" action, compensatory, partial, and—yes—doomed, but it is an action we are ethically and professionally obligated to take.

The pressure upon us is enormous. Students, teachers, administrators, and education professors as well are pressed to work harder, to achieve more, to raise those test scores. While sometimes accompanying this political pressure are calls for increased teacher autonomy, such autonomy is always relative, performed in the shadow of standardized examinations. By test scores schools will be compared; those that fail are threatened with closure. What is operative today in the politics of American school reform is an accountant's concept of education, higher figures (i.e., higher test scores) indicating the accumulation of knowledge, which presumably translates into increased gross national product.

That the American school reform movement is dominated by business thinking and is thereby obsessed with the "bottom line" comes as no surprise to any serious student of American curriculum history. Despite progressive fantasies of the school as a laboratory for democracy, the truth is that America's public schools were established to make immigrants into "Americans" and to prepare all citizens for jobs in an industrial economy. The private sector did not want to pay for this job preparation, and so it persuaded the public sector to pay. On this issue, little has changed in the last one hundred years. The schools are still assumed to exist for the sake of job preparation, despite continuing (if largely empty) rhetoric linking education with democracy and a politically engaged citizenry.

While the point of the American public schools has not changed much, the economy they were designed to support has. The consensus is that the American economy is less and less industrial and more and more "service oriented," strongly "information based," increasingly organized around technological developments, including the Internet. It is said to be international or global in character. Rather than the assembly line of the early automobile factory, the major mode of economic production today is semiotic (i.e., production of signs, symbols, and other information), and it occurs not in factories but in committees and in front of computer screens in corporate offices. Most American schools, however, still tend to be modeled after the assembly-line factory. Modeling schools after contemporary corporations would represent an improvement. So-called "smart schools" tend to be versions of the corporate model (Fiske 1991). Even in this corporate model, however, the economic function of schools remains unchallenged, and the modes of cognition appropriate to even corporate schools are fewer and narrower than intelligence more broadly understood.

Because the organization and culture of the school are linked to the economy and dominated by "business thinking," the school and the American curriculum field have traveled different paths over the past thirty years. For the foreseeable future, teachers will be trained as "social engineers," directed to "manage" learning that is modeled loosely after corporate work stations. Certainly some segment of the American curriculum field will devote itself to assist in the design and implementation of this corporate school curriculum. However, those of us who labored to reconceptualize the atheoretical, ahistorical field we found in 1970 have always seen a more complex calling for the field. The theoretical wing of the reconceived field aspires to ground itself not in the pressured everyday world of the corporate classroom but in worlds not present in the schools today, in ideas marginal to the maximization of profits, and in imaginative and lived experience that is not exclusively instrumental and calculative.

In its press for efficiency and standardization, the factory model tends to reduce teachers to automata. In designing and teaching the curriculum in units that presumably "add up" to a logical, even disciplinary, "whole" (like products on an assembly line), the factory-model school achieves social control at the cost of intelligence, intelligence broadly understood as including problem-solving, critical thinking, and creativity as well as memorization and calculation. Those students who tolerate the routinized, repetitious nature of instruction that is only teacher and textbook centered and relies upon recitation and memorization sometimes are able to perform reasonably well on similar tasks, although the "transferability" of these task-specific skills has remained a problem for the factory model.

The corporate model accepts learning the "basics" as the goal of the school. However, this model permits a variety of instructional strategies to be employed in its attainment. Peer teaching, small-group work, other forms of so-called cooperative learning, even minor curriculum changes are permitted to allow students and teachers to find their own ways to learn what is demanded of them. Moreover, the corporate model tends to acknowledge that intelligence is multiple in nature and function and includes aesthetic, intuitive, and sensory elements as well as linear, logical, narrowly cognitive ones. The social character of intelligence is also acknowledged, as corporate classroom organization often permits the use of dyadic and small-group activities. The teacher in this scheme is a manager or, in Theodore Sizer's (1984) image, a "coach." These images are considerably less authoritarian than those associated with the teacher in the factory school.

Even in the corporate model, the goal of instruction—the acquisition of that knowledge and the cultivation of those skills deemed necessary for productivity in a post-industrial economy—is not in question. Intelligence is viewed as a means to an end, the acquisition of skills, knowledge, and attitudes utilizable in the corporate sector. The maximization of profits remains the "bottom line" of the corporation as well as that of its earlier version, the factory. I am not suggesting that schools should have no relationship to the economy. Capitalism does require forms of knowledge and intelligence that the corporate model of schooling is more likely than the factory model to produce. Nor am I suggesting that we could have publicly supported schools in the United States that might have non-economic goals, at least for the imaginable future.

What I do want to do is to remind those of us committed to the project of education (which, of course, does not always coincide with what goes on in the schools) that for intelligence to be cultivated in fundamental ways, it must be set free of even corporate goals. Such an idea hardly excludes instrumental reason, calculation, and problem-solving as major modes of cognition. Intellectual freedom must allow, however, for meditative, contemplative modes of cognition, and for exploring subjects—those associated, for instance, with progressive forms of the arts, humanities, and social sciences—that have no immediate practical payoff and might not be evaluated by standardized examinations.

Intelligence is made narrow, and thus undermined, when it is reduced to answers to other people's questions, when it is only a means to achieve a preordained goal. This instrumental and calculative concept of intelligence, while useful to the present form of economic organization—the corporation—is less helpful in investigations of more fundamental questions of human experience, experience that might not lead directly to economic development and increased productivity. To study these questions is to "ride" intelligence to destinations perhaps not listed in the present economic and political agenda. Such a view of curriculum inquiry and research is akin to what in the natural sciences would be termed basic research, wherein destinations are not necessarily known in advance. For us, it might be theoretical research freed of the taken-for-granted demands of everyday problems in schools. To suggest one form such research in the United States might take, allow me to discuss very briefly an emergent category in American curriculum theory. This category—identity—emerged in debates over multiculturalism, but it promises to take us other places as well, including investigations of what it means educationally to be conceived by others (see Pinar 1994, 1998).

Identity

The category of identity organizes educational investigations of political, racialized, and gendered experience around questions of self. This "self" is not the bourgeois individual decried by the various Marxisms and embraced by conservatives, but rather the vortex of psychosocial and discursive relations theorized by Lacan, Freud, and Foucault. The study of identity enables us to portray how the politics we had thought were located "out there," in society, are lived through "in here," in our bodies, our minds, our everyday speech and conduct. The political status quo is not simply "reproduced," of course. Even when we resist social trends and political directives, we are reconstructing ourselves in terms of those trends and debates and our resistance to them. In studying the politics of identity, we find that who we are is invariably related to who others are, as well as to who we have been and want to become.

Currently, the American teacher's identity is being reconceived from factory supervisor to corporate manager. It is a promotion. However, if loyal to the cultivation of intelligence and the democratic project of education, teachers still face the challenge to become more than they have been conceived and conditioned to be. If we are submerged in identities conceived by others, the cultivation of intelligence is necessarily restricted and undermined. Of course, we teachers must meet contractual obligations regarding curriculum and instruction. However, we need not necessarily believe them or uncritically accept them. Curriculum theorists might assist teachers to avoid the disappearance of their ideals into the maelstrom of daily classroom demands. We might support teachers' identities apart from those constructed by corporatism by proclaiming the existence of other ways of conceiving education, non-instrumental ways of speaking and being with children.

Understood from a social psychoanalytic perspective, we teachers are conceived by others, by the expectations and fantasies of our students and by the demands of parents, administrators, policymakers, and politicians, to all of whom we are sometimes the "other." We are formed as well by their and our own internalized life histories. These various spheres or levels of self-constitution require investigation. Locating the process of knowing in the politics of identity suggests escaping the swirling waters created by the demands and pressure of others. The capacity to stand calmly in a maelstrom can come only with knowledge of other worlds, with living in other realities, not split off or dissociated from the world of work. "Separate but connected" permits us to enter the work world in larger, more complex roles than those prescribed for us, making it less likely that we will collapse upon the social surface, reduced to what others make of us.

We Americans might then model to our children how we can live in this society without succumbing to it, without giving up our dreams and aspirations for education. Teachers can become witnesses to the notion that intelligence and learning can lead to other worlds, not just the successful exploitation of this one. Knowledge need not be regarded as a sacred text (as in fundamentalist religions) or an inviolate procedure (as on the assembly line); nor is it only the more complex, sometimes even creative means to an end (as it is in the corporate model). Rather, knowledge and intelligence as free exploration become wings by which we take flight, visit other worlds, and return to this one to call others, especially our children, to futures more life-affirmative than the world we inhabit now. When we sink, submerged in those roles conceived by others, we become aborted possibilities, unable to realize in everyday life, in our relations with others, the politics of our individual and civic identities, the educational dynamics of creation and birth.

What value is American curriculum theory to the American schoolteacher? To those teachers hardened by thirty years of conservative reaction, it may well seem pointless. To the novice teacher eager to "learn the ropes," it might seem fanciful, interesting perhaps, but to be reserved for later. The constituency of American curriculum theorists may not be in schools at this time. However, if we can teach, if we can make friends with our colleagues struggling in the schools, build bridges between the realms of theory and practice, create passages—to borrow Jacques Daignault's (1992) phrase—to travel from here to there and back again, broadened, deepened, enlivened by the voyage, then we theorists might participate with subtlety and acumen in school reform. Being a theorist, after all, does not mean being dissociated or inefficient. Being a theorist does not mean being a celibate in terms of everyday practice. It does not mean one cannot function successfully in the corporate school, providing advice and assistance. Being a theorist *does* mean that the contemporary curriculum organization and the modes of cognition it requires must be bracketed, situated in history, politics, and our own life histories. Such understanding might allow us to participate in school reform in ways that do not hypostatize the present, but rather, allow our labor and understandings to function as do those in psychoanalysis, to enlarge the understanding and deepen the intelligence of the participants.

Conclusion

Of course, other American scholars regard the situation differently. I make this brief commentary on the American scene to suggest one way an international conversation might begin, one value it might have. In explaining to colleagues outside our specific national situations, we are encouraged to distance ourselves from our situations, enabling us to reflect more critically upon them and what they demand of us. Links among various curriculum inquiries in various national settings might be elaborated, differences clarified and explored. But I'll stop here. I am hesitant to proceed in making too many suggestions, as a conversation requires collective participation. Each of us must decide for ourselves if there is potential value in a worldwide field of curriculum studies.

If you decide the project of internationalization is worthwhile, I propose the formation of a Committee of One Hundred: one hundred scholars from around the world who would form the core of an International Association for Curriculum Studies. In the course of everyday correspondence, members of the committee might mention to those they think would be interested that the association is in formation. My thought—everything is up for discussion, allow me to emphasize—is that such a group would organize meetings at various locations every three to five years, with local affiliates meeting annually (perhaps not in the years the international conferences are held; here, of course, the local affiliate would be the American Association for Curriculum Studies). An association journal is certainly a possibility; while I am not assuming it would be housed in the United States, I do want to report that Lawrence Erlbaum has already expressed an interest.

Please know that I am grateful you have come here. For us at LSU, this conference is an unusual and important opportunity for students and faculty to learn from you. Many of you have traveled great distances to engage us and others in conversation over the curriculum, reporting its import for your own nation and locale, but as well—by virtue of the global character of the conference—to think about its import for the world, a concept to which we all must contribute our culture, our history, and our hopes for our children and theirs. When we welcome you tonight to LSU and to Baton Rouge, we are not only welcoming you to a specific university and city in North America, but, this weekend, to a university that is a worldwide one, in which scholars from all continents and twenty-seven nations will engage in a uniquely international conversation. You come from Argentina, Australia, Botswana, Brazil, Canada, China, Colombia, Costa Rica, Denmark, Estonia, Finland, Germany, India, Israel, Japan, Korea, Malaysia, the Netherlands, Nigeria, Norway, the Philippines, Poland, Romania, Sweden, South Africa, Turkey, and the United States. (Have I inadvertently omitted anyone?) Welcome!

Note: My thanks to Bill Doll, Donna Trueit, and Hongyu Wang for your helpful suggestions in the revision of this chapter, and for your leadership and labor in the production of this conference.

References

Daignault, J. (1992). Traces at work from different places. In *Understanding curriculum as phenomenological and deconstructed text,* pages 195–215. Edited by W. Pinar and W. Reynolds. New York: Teacher's College Press.

Fiske, E. (1991). *Smart schools, smart kids.* New York: Simon & Schuster.

Pinar, W. F. (1994). *Autobiography, politics, and curriculum.* New York: Peter Lang.

——— (Ed.) (1998). *Curriculum: Toward new identities.* New York: Garland.

Pinar, W. F., W. Reynolds, P. Slattery, and P. Taubman (1995). *Understanding curriculum.* New York: Peter Lang.

Sizer, T. (1984). *Horace's compromise: The dilemma of the American high school.* Boston, MA: Houghton Mifflin.

CHAPTER ONE

Poaching: Sanctifying Time
Peter Appelbaum • United States

The elevator in Raubinger Hall is very slow. Everyone is always waiting, waiting. Will it come? Why does it take so long between each floor? More than anything else in my work these days, this elevator dominates most every experience. If it's not just slow but out of service, I will have to trudge up and down two flights of stairs, lugging a cartload of manipulatives to each class. If it's merely taking its time again, I'll spend several minutes complaining with the rest, sharing impatience and anger. I find myself repeating advice that I heard back when I was an undergraduate music major; then, too, there was a frustratingly slow elevator. Alvin Lucier, a professor and composer, would wait with us and suggest that we celebrate our technology: accept this treasure that the elevator gives us, of time. Time to relax, to think, to not have to be doing anything else but waiting and then riding the elevator. The elevator experience was a musical composition, a pattern of pauses and movements in time and space. A delicious opportunity to experience. So now I find myself talking to students I have not yet met, other faculty racing late to class on the third floor. Take this treasure, I say; enjoy this moment in time. We're all crazed with speed and things we have to do, but here we have something that we can take as ours, a time away from all else and all the demands of others that encroach on our peace, a time that is only for us. By taking the elevator in this way, it is no longer an eternal wait; it is a moment that we cherish.

Some years after that music phase of my life, as I was a graduate student in mathematics searching for meaning and purpose in my efforts and life's work, I had possibly my first and only genuinely religious experience. Reading Abraham Joshua Heschel's (1951) *The Sabbath,* I was not only reading about the Sabbath as a place in time, as a treasure waiting for me to seize and enjoy, but was transported to another space thoroughly removed from my everyday life's thrills, fears, and obligations. We seem to need these kinds of oases these days. Indeed, many educators have suggested that schools can and should be such oases from the ennui or violence of everyday life (Greene 1982).

Heschel offers us the Sabbath, and many people do find this place in time serves a unique purpose, while others pursue meditation, aerobic exercise, and so on. The interesting thing about these "treasures" is that they are not gifts or possessions: they are unowned objects waiting to be seized. And it is not enough just to take them. It takes a lot of effort to find them, even though they are there always to be seized. And we must put in an enormous amount of effort in order to seize them. It is as if something is holding us back, as if we are always acting not to find them until we do; and then we know they were always there. Looking back, it was not the Sabbath that I took, but Heschel's beautiful meditation on the Sabbath. The Sabbath is not something we receive as a gift but something we must pursue as a treasure. Heschel's book is the treasure I possess, and I "own" the experience of reading this book; the Sabbath itself is something that must be embraced on my own through my own efforts.

This issue of "property," and of the need for serious labor in order for property to be recognized as owned, is deeply entrenched in Ameroeuro culture. And the idea that it is the basis for education has a long tradition as well. Rousseau (1979) recognized this for his education of *Emile.* For Emile to be happy, he must learn over time that "the best way to provide oneself with the things one lacks is to give up those that one has" (81). Early in life, writes Rousseau, a child reaches out toward objects. A child is stretching "his" hand well before "he" can say anything, not yet comprehending the distance. At first the lack of comprehension is like an error of judgment.

> But when he complains and screams in reaching out his hand, he is no longer deceived as to the distance; he is ordering the object to approach or you to bring it to him. In the first case carry him to the object slowly or with small steps. In the second act as though you do not even hear him. The more he screams, the less you should listen to him. (66)

In this parable of the object, Rousseau asks us to recognize the essential link between the labor of seizing objects and the ownership of the object. He believes it is important to accustom a child not to give orders either to people (to establish a taboo against owning people as objects to seize) or to things (for things cannot hear, can only be taken by one's own serious efforts).

> Thus, when a child desires something that he sees and one wants to give it to him, it is better to carry the child to the object than to bring the object to the child. He draws from this practice a conclusion appropriate to his age, and there is no other means to suggest it to him (66).

Hence my theoretical leap that a teacher should never give the knowledge and skills to a student as a gift. If school is a place in time, then this place can not be owned in this way unless it is taken as such an object. We can carry children to the space, but they themselves must take it. It turns out in the end that it was always there, and that we just did not see it yet. But it is in another real sense only there when we take it.

In my family these days, the Sabbath occasionally takes on this role. More routinely, however, our "Sabbath" is found in the evening ritual of reading before bedtime. We read every night with both of our children, Noah, almost eleven, and Sophia, who is six. We have been reading for as long as I can remember. This is not bedtime reading, although it may have started out that way, and it does continue to be part of a slow winding down toward sleep. Rather, it is a time outside of time. All four of us are all together, in one bed, and we take turns reading a book ostensibly for one child and then the other. All four of us read and listen to all of the reading together. As parents, we bring our children and ourselves to the reading. Each of us on our own, however, must "take" the reading for ourselves; it is at this point that the reading is there.

Rousseau does not share our enthusiasm for reading together. He warns that it is the "companion of his games" (159) that the child approaches. It is instead the "severe and angry man" who takes him by the hand, speaks gravely, and takes him away into a room of books.

> What sad furnishings for his age! The poor child lets himself be pulled along, turns a regretful eye on all that surrounds him, becomes silent, and leaves, his eyes swollen with tears he does not dare shed, and his heart great with sighs he does not dare to breathe. (159)

But perhaps he thinks we parents are trying to teach a love of books, rather than merely allowing the books to be taken together, as Rousseau and Emile are together, "never depend[ing] on one another, but [always agreeing]" (159). He warns us that "Our didactic and pedantic craze is always to teach children what they would learn much better by themselves and to forget what we alone could teach them" (79). In this spirit our reading books is one of our games; our love of books is what we parents alone could teach our children about who we are.

But what can the child learn about herself? What is hers and hers alone? Rousseau notes for us how difficult this is, because so very little of what is around a child genuinely belongs to the child. A child can not understand her clothing, her furniture, her toys, as property in the sense that Rousseau means, because she can not fully comprehend how they came to be clothing, furniture, toys, or how they came to be "hers." To say that they were given to her and that is why they are hers is no better, since in order to give one must already have; besides, a gift is a form of convention, something only learned through years of enculturation. Property, thus, is something exterior or anterior to a child.

Therefore, Emile, and all children by extension, need to learn about property. Emile is encouraged to see himself in the garden he has created. He has taken possession of the earth by planting a bean, by returning every day to care for his garden, by investing his time and labor, his effort, and finally his person there.

> There is in this earth something of himself that he can claim against anyone whomsoever, just as he could withdraw his arm from the hand of another man who wanted to hold onto it in spite of him. (98)
>
> ...
>
> One fine day he arrives eagerly with the watering can in his hand. O what a sight! O pain! All the beans are rooted out, the plot is torn up, the very spot is not to be recognized. O, what has become of my labor, my product, the sweet fruit of my care and my sweat? Who has stolen my goods? Who took my beans from me? This young heart is aroused. The first sentiment of injustice comes to shed its sad bitterness in it. Tears flow streams. The grieving child fills the air with moans and cries. I partake of his pain, his indignation. We look; we investigate; we make searches. (99)

It turns out that the gardener did it! But he, too, is furious. He had planted his melons on this land, had come back after investing labor and time to see his melon patch ripped asunder and some beans there instead. This was his property and should not have been taken by anyone else. "In this model of the way of inculcating primary notions in children one sees how the idea of property naturally goes back to the right of first occupancy by labor" (99).

I want to tie all of this together. On the one hand, something is ours when we take it through labor and not when it is given to us. This is what constructivists mean when they say that learners need to construct their own knowledge. A child takes objects, both physical and symbolic, and in the process takes ownership of these objects; at the moment of taking, the child owns knowledge that has always been there but was not "real" to her before the taking. On the other hand, the very place in which such labor unfolds is not a place of learning until it is taken as such. This is what Herb Kohl (1991) means when he writes about the role of assent in learning. A student is not in school until the moment in which she takes a place at school. When an adult and a child together take a place as theirs, danger lurks in the adult's first occupancy by labor. The property belongs to the adult.

Rousseau negotiates a deal for Emile. He can work the land as "his" garden in return for sharing half of the produce with the farmer and, more importantly, for making sure that he respects the farmer's labor and thus ownership of the melon crop. He must set aside his garden in a space not yet worked by the farmer. The labor in the taking of the land is, in the end, more important than the right of first occupancy. And it is upon this principle that modern pedagogy is based. As long as the child labors herself, we trust that she can take possession of knowledge. Still, we come back to the notion that the earth is not a garden until one takes it as a place in which to make a garden. Just as Emile gets the idea for taking a space as a potential garden from noticing farmers already working the soil around him, so do we hope that our students will get the idea of taking a place as school by watching others. Here is the principle that guides all barriers to modern pedagogy: What happens if Emile never thinks it interesting that farmers are doing all this plowing and sowing and watering and harvesting? What happens if a child does not take school as a place for learning?

In our nightly reading at home there is no such issue, I believe. This is because we are in a place where people do not 'not take' "sitting around with books and decoding the words and talking about what they mean" as reading. Now this reading is not always the object that I describe above. Sometimes we are merely going through the motions, and this special place in time is lost, we can't find it anymore. But at other times we know it is there, and it has always been there. There are special books that have been the focus of these times, maybe because of their special-ness or maybe because of what we came to the reading with at that time. It will be hard to know why they are special. However, I can recall two books that seemed to resonate particularly well, and also seem—probably without randomness—to speak to the issue of property and ownership and, in the end, how our relationship with the taking of objects is intimately bound to who we are and how we learn. They speak as well to the issue of losing that place and finding our way back—our way back home.

For Sophia and me, the book is Roald Dahl's (1982) *The BFG,* a story about a little girl named, coincidentally, Sophie, who meets a big, friendly giant, and how they together save the world from bigger, evil giants and make it possible for all the boys and girls to have beautiful dreams. For Noah and me, the book is another work by Dahl (1975) that includes a cameo appearance by the BFG, *Danny, the Champion of the World.* In this one, a boy named Danny finds out that his wonderful father is even "sparkier" than he thought when his father teaches him the beauty of poaching that he can share with him. Of course, I believe these books are about more than these brief descriptions. They are first of all about my relationship with my children. How Sophia loved to listen to me reading *The BFG;* how the BFG may or may not caricature a father, every girl's big, friendly giant who towers over her and frightens her at first but quickly comes to be known as a protector against scarier, more menacing giants, and then to be the provider of all good dreams. How Noah didn't want me to stop reading *Danny, the Champion of the World,* and I, in cahoots, stayed up with him past midnight (on a schoolnight!) to finish it; how the father in the story fulfilled his destiny as teacher for his son according to Rousseau's prescription (this one didn't hire out a philosopher like Jean-Jacques, relishing his own responsibilities); how my son read the last page, that every boy deserves a father who is sparky, and then declared, "Like my dad's sparky!" How poaching is not the violation of labor Emile learned from Rousseau but instead an essential challenge of life requiring careful and skillful planning, analysis, and problem-solving skills; how poaching is in fact the "spark" of life.

We need to unpack a lot of what these books are about, including the problematic gendering of these images, of the role of girls and boys and who does the poaching, who is the listener and who the actor. For now, I want to ask, what is it that enables us to read Dahl as a shift in our taking of poaching? As Alan Block (1999) writes, "The space—seemingly an objective locus—itself has been redefined by the entrance into it by someone whose action changes the potentialities of the space" (23). Block quotes the Mishnah: "If one sees an ownerless object and falls upon it and another person comes and seizes it, he who has seized it is entitled to its possession." The landowner in Danny's world takes some pheasants as his own; Danny, his father, and it turns out most everybody in town lay claim to these pheasants because they come along and seize them. Hadn't Emile's farmer earned his garden by seizing the land, working it with his labor? Danny, our modern Emile, lives in a place where the landowners no longer work their land but merely fall upon it. Danny's (and our) classed society understands poaching in a new light. The Mishnah, according to Block, had it right all along: a field may not acquire absolutely for the owner; what is left must be considered unowned and so findable, available for the taking. Gleaning is what Danny does, and in gleaning he avoids the plight of the sharecropper Emile, who no longer owns half of what he makes.

Sophie, too, is a new kind of poacher. Her name, synonymous with Emile's lover, the everywoman for Rousseau, evokes true wisdom—(just this year, my Sophia noted in her "Proud to Be Me" book that she's "special" "because my name means wisdom")—and genders this wisdom in its juxtaposition with Danny, the new Emile. She's the companion for the BFG, poacher and giver of beautiful dreams.

Reading Poaching

Ordinary usage of the word "poaching" carries a bad connotation. Crafty thieves who have no respect for wildlife, poachers are typically represented as disregarding licensing fees, ignoring wildlife and its habitat, and thieving for profit or ego (National Anti-Poaching Foundation 2001). Law enforcement agencies go to elaborate lengths to capture poachers (Tisch 1997, Bartz 1999). Yet beneath the rhetoric of sportsmen as the true conservationists and poachers as destructive criminals lurks a romantic intrigue of squirrelly, outrageously clever artists of camouflage, deception, and ingenuity. "I've seen animals stuffed in hubcaps—turkey breasts, stuff like that," said Jeff Babauta, a wildlife office with the Florida Game and Fresh Water Fish Commission (GFC). "I've found hogs and deer underneath the hoods" (Tisch 1997).

It is this romantic aspect of poaching that Michel de Certeau (1984) captures in *The Practice of Everyday Life:*

> Far from being writer-founders of their own place, heirs of the peasants of earlier ages now working on the soil of language, diggers of wells and builders of houses—readers are travellers; they move across lands belonging to someone else, like nomads poaching their way across fields they did not write, despoiling the wealth of Egypt to enjoy it themselves. (174)

When Sophia, Noah, Belinda, and I are reading together, suggests de Certeau, we are "not here or there, one or the other, but neither the one nor the other, simultaneously inside and outside, dissolving both by mixing them together, associating texts like funerary statues" that we awaken and host but never own. Far removed from the bricolage of constructivism, welding conceptual bridges and monuments to our masters, we poachers—crafty as ever—take ownership of things that have been withheld and locked away in others' fields and forests; we carry these things to new places, to new contexts.

In *Danny, the Champion of the World*, nasty Mr. Hazell stocks his woods with pheasants in preparation for hosting a fancy hunting party for his rich, important friends. As a single parent, Danny's father hasn't gone poaching for years, staying home with his son instead. But one day, the yearning is too great, and he walks the six and a half miles to Hazell's wood.

> "I have decided something," he said. "I am going to let you in on the deepest, darkest secret of my whole life."
> "Do you know what is meant by poaching?"
> "Poaching? Not really, no."
> "It means going up into the woods in the dead of night and coming back with something for the pot. Poachers in other places poach all sorts of different things, but around here it's always pheasants."
> "You mean stealing them?" I said, aghast.
> "We don't look at it that way," may father said. "Poaching is an art. A great poacher is a great artist."
> "Is that actually what you were doing in Hazell's wood, dad? Poaching pheasants?"
> "I was practicing the art," he said. "The art of poaching." (28–29).

Danny's granddad was a "splendiferous" poacher who "studied poaching the way a scientist studies science" (33). Back in those days, people poached not only because they loved the sport but because they needed food for their families. "There was very little work to be had anywhere, and some families were literally starving. Yet a few miles away in the rich man's wood, thousands of pheasants were being fed like kings twice a days" (30). But to say that people poach for food is to miss the point. "Poaching is such a fabulous and exciting sport that once you start doing it, it gets into your blood and you can't give it up."

A thief would go into the woods with a gun, shoot some pheasants, and drag them home. A poacher practices elaborate schemes, perfecting strategies and techniques for months and years, experimenting on roosters and calculating the interests and fears of the pheasants themselves. Danny's father inherited a number of these intricately developed secrets from his own dad. Danny's father inherited a number of these intricately developed secrets from his own dad. One such legacy, the "Horsehair Stopper" is completely silent:

> There's no squawking or flapping around or anything else with The Horsehair Stopper when the pheasant is caught. And that's mighty important because don't forget, Danny, when you're up in those woods at night and the great trees are spreading their branches high above you like black ghosts, it is so silent you can hear a mouse moving. And somewhere among it all, the keepers are waiting and listening. They're always there, those keepers, standing strong stony still against a tree or behind a bush with their guns at the ready. (35)

We'll come back to this image of the "keepers," like the real thieves with their guns, working for Mr. Hazell, and ask who or what the keepers might be for education and reading. For now, though, let's stick to the elaborate art of poaching:

> "What happens with The Horsehair Stopper?" I asked. "How does it work?"
> "It's very simple," he said. "First, you take a few raisins and you soak them in water overnight to make them plump and soft and juicy. Then you get a bit of good stiff horsehair and you cut it up into half-inch lengths"
> "Here's what my dad discovered," he said. "First of all, the horsehair makes the raisin stick in the pheasant's throat. It doesn't hurt him. It simply stays there and tickles. It's rather like having a crumb stuck in your own throat. But after that, believe it or not, the pheasant never moves his feet again! He becomes absolutely rooted to the spot, and there he stands pumping his silly neck up and down just like a piston, and all you've got to do is nip out quickly from the place where you've been hiding and pick him up."
> "Is that true, dad?"
> "I swear it," my father said. "Once a pheasant's had The Horsehair Stopper, you can turn a hosepipe on him and he won't move. It's just one of those unexplainable little things. But it takes a genius to discover it."
> My father paused, and there was a gleam of pride in his eyes as he dwelt for a

moment upon the memory of his dad, the great poaching inventor.

Such storied convey the thrills of poaching. Although the "horsehair Stopper" is an amazing technique, Danny used yet another one that special evening, an ingenious set-up called the "Sticky Hat." Laying a trail of raisins to a little paper hat in a small depression in the ground, he smeared it with glue and filled the hat with more raisins. The old pheasant was supposed to some along, pop his head inside to gobble up the raisins, and find a hat over his eyes, so that he couldn't see a thing. Here too the pheasant would not move and could be gently collected on the way out of the woods. As with any art, the technique takes practice, and this night, the first in many years, Danny's dad was out of practice.

A bricoleur is given a toolbox out of which she fashions new uses for the tools. Schools drill us in skills and intellectual tools, hoping that some day a few of us may use them in new ways. Instead, most of us leave disaffected yet master our bricolage in the realm of popular and consumer culture (Fiske 1989, Appelbaum 1995); like the affichist artists of the 1920s, we scavenge the worthless trash of popular capital and retool our clothes and images to meet the crises of our culture. We buy things to make a statement and use these things we buy to make new statements. What would our lives be like if schools were places that fostered poaching? There would be no buying and selling, no consumer culture. Students would take as theirs the knowledge and skills that adults immorally safeguard for their own pleasures. Instead of waiting around for small gestures of generosity, waiting for paralled gifts of knowledge, students would be refining and extending their crafts of poaching, of taking as their own these knowledges and skills.

Indeed, people are poachers. Poaching makes life "sparky." The keepers of knowledge protect that knowledge from students as Mr. Hazell's keepers guard his pheasants. And those keepers hide this knowledge so that it's hard to find; like the pheasants who disappear into the trees after twilight, knowledge in the classroom is made invisible by the rules and regulations of the school, the curriculum standards, and school expectations. Students and teachers play elaborate, intricate games in order to poach a place in these classrooms, and the playing out of these games becomes the fun of being there, indeed becomes the "real" curriculum of the school. Resistance theorists have presented a less optimistic view of these games. Here I offer a potentially more positive interpretation of resistance as poaching. The basic idea is that the treasure cannot be given to another person, because it is in the taking of that treasure that the spark is found, in the poaching that the meaning of the encounter is manifested.

A generous teacher tells students what they need to know. Then they know. Is it surprising if the students mock or dismiss what the teacher offers? Is it surprising if the child does not take what the teacher offers? If the child cannot take what the teacher offers? Danny learns that Mr. Hazell's token generosity is unwanted, because with it come disrespect and physical threats. There is no need to serve him at the filling station, despite the family's plight of poverty. Rather than take his money, Danny and his dad will take the pheasants he so unjustly keeps in his wood. They will take the pheasants Mr. Hazell is fattening up for entertainment and use them for a good purpose. In the process, however, the purpose is immediately transformed away from stealing or redistribution of resources toward the art of poaching itself, the process and method as opposed to the result. It is like the difference between "fandom" (Jenkins 1988) and "social activism." Fans buy mass culture products and may even reclaim in a bricolage the shards of popular culture, salvaging pieces of found material in making sense of their own social experience. In fandom, marginalized subgroups of a culture re-read texts and rewrite texts in ways that pry open spaces for (women's, gay, bisexual) voices. Fans often cast themselves as loyalists, rescuing essential elements of the primary texts misused by those "keepers" who police the copyrights. Social activists, on the other hand, trespass the terrains of consumer culture and its keepers, not to reassert a fundamental truth or preexisting nostalgia but to glean what can be taken for parallel purposes.

We know that Danny attends school. Indeed, his father walks him all the way to town to get there (two miles each way). Yet it is Dad who is Danny's teacher. By the age of eight he was a master mechanic. Now it is the walk to school that is Danny's real education, a time for looking and talking and learning about nature and, now, planning an extensive new method of poaching pheasants. Until now, Danny gleaned from the fields along the road things to take and study; he asked questions, and his father answered. Now he asks questions for which nobody knows the answer ("Why does the skylark make its nest on the ground where the cow can trample it?"), and this only piques his interest more. His questions take on a new role he takes on the aura and excitement of a poacher. Before Dad let Danny in on poaching, he merely led his son to places of freedom where unowned objects could be seized. This alone made Danny's education special in its possibilities. But now there is the pleasure of the game: Danny can't just seize; he has to come up with a clever way to do it without being caught. It is Danny who comes up with a really big plan for poaching a really big number of Mr. Hazell's pheasants in a really great way.

Boys and Girls

In *The BFG*, it is Sophie who comes up with the big plan after her surprising initiation into something that might be poaching. But for Sophie, it is a Big Friendly Giant, not her dad, who carries her off into her new state of awareness. This BFG spends his days catching dreams and bottling them up. At night he blows them into the heads of sleeping boys and girls. We originally meet the BFG in *Danny*, in a bedtime story Danny's dad tells as they are going to sleep in the old caravan behind the filling station. There is no Sophie in that version, but of course Danny doesn't know her. Here we learn that the BFG enters a silent twilight very much like Hazell's Wood: swirling mist and ghostly vapors, "It was ashy grey. There was no sign of a living creature and no sound at all except for the soft thud of the BFG's footsteps as he hurtled on through the fog" (80). The BFG, too, has mastered the art of poaching. He waits, quietly, a long net in his right hand. His colossal ears swivel out from his head and gently wave to and fro.

> Suddenly the BFG pounced. He leaped high in the air and swung the net through the mist with a great swishing sweep of his arm. "Got him!" he cried. "A jar! A jar! Quick quick quick!" (81)

He catches both the good dreams, the "winksquifflers," and the bad ones, "frightsome trogglehumpers"; the former to give someone, the latter to bottle up so that nobody will ever have it. The difference between these dreams and Mr. Hazell's pheasants is that nobody is keeping these dreams from the BFG; he keeps them for the children. Sophie is not capable of catching dreams, and she never learns how. This really isn't poaching, and Sophie is not an initiated comrade. She's merely a companion. Unlike Danny, who asks more and more questions, and finds an increasingly sparkier life with his father, Sophie is constantly confronted with her narrow-minded presumptions as a "human bean," and her need to practice polite acceptance.

But Sophie's destiny is not a sparky life. She has the loftier role of helping the BFG save all humanity from other giants, the ones who aren't friendly. Sophie gets him to mix up a special dream for the Queen of England, a dream designed to help her majesty understand what's behind the large numbers of missing children. She can talk to scary giants and queens, and she knows how they think. She is pleasant and inoffensive and can talk about anything; she is an effective go-between for those who act, even as she helps to define their actions. Like Rousseau's Sophie—and I claim the common name is no accident—this one wields power through her femininity, manipulating the big friendly giants (men) behind the scenes, and accomplishing her work through them, using their brute powers and public images. She is a poacher of male public power in this respect, but not a public male. The BFG is likable while Mr. Hazell is not. The BFG is his own keeper and he is generous with his dreams, unlike mean Mr. Hazell, hoarding pheasants for the big showy shoot. The irony is that mean Mr. Hazell makes it possible for poaching to exist, whereas the benevolent BFG, doling out the right dreams and locking away the bad ones, winds up being the creepier of the two. Docile folks need to poach, and never learn what they are missing. And who provides the oversight for the BFG? Who decides which dreams are winksquifflers, and which are togglehumpers?

Sophie's world and Danny's world are not the same. Yet they share the BFG. In both worlds, dreams are not constructed out of objects related to one's life. Dreams for these children are not the result of poaching but are breathed in as they sleep; dreams are gifts from a benevolent giant. What a creepy image! And this image is not at all the stuff of good dreams that I bring with me from my reading of Winnicott; dreams should be the creative use of objects to evoke the self (Winnicott 1984: 95). It seems that dreaming as poaching is a critical piece of the life project, and this lovable BFG has taken that project away.

The child who can manage dreams is becoming ready for all kinds of playing, either alone or with other children (60). "It is in the use of objects," writes Alan Block (1995), "that playing occurs; it is in playing that creativity is realized"(23). Block, too, quotes Winnicott (1971: 101): "Every object is a 'found' object. Given the chance, the [child] begins to live creatively, and to use actual objects to be creative into and with."

Block (1995: 59) again: "The child must be able to use the dream creatively; it must be available for play." Sophie loves the BFG "as she would a father" (207). This "father" is the keeper of dreams, her dreams, and, since she cannot poach dreams, she cannot evoke a self. In the end she teaches the BFG to write not only stories but the story of her life from the beginning: she herself, in a grand twist of irony, is merely the dream of the BFG, as we see on the very last page:

> But where, you might ask, is this book that the BFG wrote?
> It's right here. You've just finished reading it. (208)

But of course! We know from the beginning that the BFG poached Sophie. He plucked her out of bed through the window and used her to dream his own new life.

Danny has a different fate. The specter of the BFG haunts his dreams too. Luckily, however, he has learned the practical, poaching art of play. He is therefore able to write his own life. "It is not play to do with the object what it has been ordered to do; rather playing is to do with the object what we will because it is available for use" (Block 1995: 60). This is poaching. This is Danny's life experience. "The power to endow our world with our dreams is creativity. Our action creates the world, and then it is our world and not that of common sense" (Block 1995: 170). We leave Danny and his dad, two poachers together, in the middle of their dreams, and we know, with Danny—the narrator of his own life story—that, after they buy just two knives and two forks, they will buy two more of each.

And after that,

> We would walk home again and make up some sandwiches for our lunch.
> And after that, we would set off with the sandwiches in our packets, striding up over Cobbler's Hill and down the other side to the small wood of larch trees that had the stream running through it.
> And after that?
> Perhaps a big rainbow trout.
> And after that?
> There would be something else after that.
> And after that?
> Ah, yes, and something else again. (204–205)

Everything is in place: I just know that Danny grows up to marry Sophie, exactly like Emile and Rousseau's Sophie. The poacher writes his life as a tribute to his dad. The daughter's life is written by her Big, Friendly Giant.

Should we try, as others have done using different terms in different contexts, to just say that poaching can and must be practiced as an art, studied as a science, by both boys and girls? This is first-stage feminism: poaching the male public presence. And it is not enough. It is little better for Sophie to live the BFG's dreams than it was to have him give her her dreams. It is crucial that her life story stopped, was arrested at this young age, before she could learn that what she dreams will change the world. She does not yet learn from her dreams. Only when she poaches to dream—what Danny has been given the opportunity to do all of his life—when she dreams as opposed to breathing in the BFG's dreams, will she evoke her self.

Time

At its best, our family reading is a place in which we each dream. It is a place in time during which we craftily take what is being kept by the keepers as our own, and in doing so evoke our selves. And when we're done with this book? We'll read another book. And after that some other one. And yes, something else again. As I said, this is our Sabbath in our secular life. Why should the keepers of the Sabbath guard it for the traditionally observant Jew? We've poached it. And in it we poach our dreams.

But we have a lot of work to do if we are to take this into the schools, if we are to explicate more carefully what it means to poach as a learner. Who, exactly, are the keepers? The adults? Do we paint school as children ingenuously strategizing ways to poach the knowledge that adults guard from them to no purpose? This indeed is the life project of children. We are always keeping things from them: she's not ready for this; he's not going to understand that. And in the end our most cherished treasures—our anxieties, our phobias, our prejudices and hubris—are taken to new places to be used in new ways.

Poaching opportunities have been reduced to resistance in our schools, telescoped into the poaching of space, turning time into an object that can be given or taken. Teachers and students take sick days, leave early, and arrive late. Students devise elaborate schemes for seizing school as a place in which they evoke their selves: they pass notes, plan their weekend, disseminate important information (where and when certain drugs are on sale, whether or not a hallway will be safe from violence after school). Students and teachers perform, take the stage to be seen possessing the space: they become a person when they have taken the space. It is in the playing that the creative use of objects occurs. It is not enough to release all control, to remove the keepers. In the end, we need to sanction the playing around the rules and regulations.

What all of these have in common is that they move away from people jockeying for space toward the possibility of poaching time. We know from Danny's book that you cannot just poach at any time of the day. One must wait for twilight, when the keepers will have a hard time seeing you but the pheasants are still on the ground and poachable. Even trout must be poached at a certain time—in the morning, when they are visible but still asleep, is the carefully developed time for tickling them so that they can be seized. Poaching is not just taking things; it is playing, developing elaborate games for seizing things that are guarded and protected. But poaching is not just playing to poach what the keepers are guarding; it is doing this at the time that poaching is possible; it is the waiting for this time and then taking it. I don't just take the elevator in Raubinger Hall; I anticipate the elevator ride in my car on the way to campus, as I walk from my parking space to Raubinger, as I push the button and still don't know how long I will wait. I can't just go to the elevator and ride it for fun. The slowness of the elevator must be important at the time I am racing to class, at the time when I am planning my busy day at the office, at the moment when I want to hold time in my grasp as a thing in space. It is just when I am wanting to take time as my own thing, to spend it as I wish, that this treasure can be embraced. The ride is a treasure at this moment, when I can take it as a thing in time.

To gain control of the world of space is certainly one of our tasks. The danger begins when in gaining power in the realm of space we forfeit all aspirations in the realm of time. There is a realm of time where the goal is not to "have" but to "be," not to own but to give, not to control but to share, not to subdue but to be in accord. Life goes wrong when the control of space, the acquisition of things of space, becomes our sole concern (Heschel 1951: 3).

And this is a lot of what is wrong with many of the schools I work in. "Reality to us is a thinghood, consisting of substances that occupy space" (Heschel 1951: 5). Blind to "all reality that fails to identify itself as a thing, as a matter of fact," we build school as a place in space and knowledge as things to collect, receive, stick together. We don't see "time, which being thingless and insubstantial, appears to us as if it had no reality" (Heschel 1951: 5). Instead we are always grasping at time as a thing to have. We say, "If only I had more time. There's not enough time for that." That kind of education, in which I let kids seize what Block calls "un-owned objects" and in which they choose these objects in the way that they themselves choose, takes "too much time." There's not enough time in the day, in the year, to cover all the things I am supposed to cover: we cover, we keep these things hidden, because we can't grab time.

But we also say that this taking of un-owned objects is the stuff of creativity, the stuff of dreams, the evocation of self. Creativity is playing in a realm of time. We should not go to school but wait for, anticipate, and cherish the time of school, regardless of where it is in space: it is a realm of time.

Poaching is about time. It is not about getting the pheasants but about doing it in the "best" way, the cleverest way, and doing it without getting caught. "When looking at space," writes Heschel, "we see the products of creation" (100). This is why we think school is about the products. This is why we list objectives to catch and collect. Heschel continues: "when intuiting time we hear the process of creation."

A New Sophia, A School of Time

> So after four years of classroom research in which I had to continually throw over what I thought I had known about gender, in walks Sophia, who, with the help of her friends, lays down a new layer of complexity to the subject. In effect, Sophia enters and claims territory for herself. She prevents me from making the issue of what it means to be a girl in a primary classroom in any way static. She throws in my face what I thought I had known about girls in public. She reclaims the territory of her social world as unique aboriginal territory, and my place as a tribal member alters once again as I am forced to consider how our lives and our awareness of the world do and don't match. (Gallas 1998: 146–7)

Another Sophia? This is no coincidence that Karen Gallas has brought to our attention. This Sophia is a poacher, not a woman educated for a male poacher. Where did she come from, and why is this teacher able to find her? I believe Karen Gallas can write about her because Gallas's classroom is a place where children can poach. It is a place where the teacher is not so sure that she can give anything to her children, a place where the teacher knows that children need to take things from those who keep the stuff of meaning and learning and use it for themselves.

Gallas writes:

> As the years progressed, my concept of 'teaching well' altered and good teaching became more than believing that I was covering important curricula and that children were mastering subject matter. I wondered what was the most important part of my work. Was it to get the content across, or to get out of the way of the very serious work that children do below the surface?...The classroom is like perishable art. It has an evanescence that makes it, for me at least, energizing and joyful, but also bittersweet, because the events are impossible to hold in time as a complete entity. Being a teacher researcher, however, has given me some capacity to grab onto fragments of the life that is streaming by me. (Gallas 1998: 2, 146).

Here she is beginning to articulate the problems that emerge when we think that time is evanescence, temporality. Heschel tells us that the fact of evanescence flashes upon us when we pore over things of space. But it is the world of space, he writes, that communicates to us a sense of temporality. Time is everlasting, as it is beyond and independent of space: it is a space that is perishable. I learn from Heschel that things perish in time, whereas time itself does not change. Instead of coveting cultural capital, things in space that I can collect and hoard to be spent in the market of space, I should covet the things of time (Heschel 1951: 90).

> We cannot solve the problem of time through the conquest of space, through either pyramids or fame. We can only solve the problem of time through sanctification of time. (101)

So if we could sanction poaching in school, we would sanctify time. We could say: these are the rules. Now, how do you want to get these things of space? You have to do it cleverly, and you may not get caught. The cleverer the better. Watch out! It's dangerous. You could get shot from behind, peppered in the legs at fifty yards, like Danny's granddad:

> You could go to prison for poaching," my father said.
> There was a glint and a sparkle in his eyes now that I had not seen before. (31)

And be careful: there will be traps set to catch you. If you are out of practice you may wind up like Danny's dad, with a broken foot at the bottom of a deep, dark hole. But, if poaching is sanctioned, the poacher feels like she is champion of the world, and she will never have to fear giants among the giants coming to eat her up. She will write a different life, of her own, of eagerly hiking to new things in time.

The tricky thing is that evocation of self is not the same thing as self-expression. It is not as simple as making it possible for people in school to "be themselves." Heschel tells us that "the self gains when it loses itself in the contemplation of the nonself" (228). In terms of sanctifying time by means of poaching, I take this to mean that it is in the art of poaching that the self is in contemplation of the world. It is found in the pleasure of the poaching. And, in order to be ready to guide students into poaching, like Danny's dad, the teacher must have been there before, by which we mean, he or she must be at heart a poacher.

Thanks to Sophia and Noah Appelbaum; to Leif Gustavson, Mark Rodriguez, Bette Goldstone, and Burt Weltman; and special thanks to Alan Block: the best parts of this essay grew out of our conversations.

References

Appelbaum, P. (1995). *Popular culture, educational discourse, and mathematics.* Albany, NY: SUNY Press.

Bartz, D. (1999). *Father and son face $3,276 in fines for turkey poaching.* WON Richland Center. http://www.up-northoutdoors.com/outdoornews/WI/5-19-99/poaching.html (last visited 12/2001).

Block, A. (1995). *I'm only bleeding: Education as the practice of violence against children.* NY: Peter Lang.

——— (1998). Curriculum as affichiste: Popular culture and identity. In *Curriculum: toward new identities,* pages 325–341. Edited by William Pinar. New York: Garland.

——— (1999). Curriculum from the back of the bookstore. *Encounter 12* (4): 17–27.

Dahl, R. (1975). *Danny, the champion of the world.* New York: Puffin Books.

——— (1982). *The BFG.* New York: Puffin Books.

De Certeau, M. (1984). *The practice of everyday life.* Translation by Steven Rendall. Berkeley, CA: University of California Press.

Fiske, J. (1989). *Understanding popular culture.* Boston: Unwin Hyman.

Gallas, K. (1998). *Sometimes I can be anything: Power, gender and identity in a primary classroom.* New York: Teachers College Press.

Greene, M. (1982). Public education and the public space. *Educational Researcher 11* (6): 4–9.

Heschel, A. J. (1951). *The Sabbath: Its meaning for modern man.* New York: Farrar, Straus and Giroux.

Jenkins, H. (1988). Star Trek rerun, reread, rewritten: Fan writing as textual poaching. *Critical Studies in Mass Communication 5* (2): 85–107.

Kohl, H. (1991). *I won't learn from you: The role of assent in learning.* Minneapolis, MN: Milkweed Editions.

National Anti-Poaching Foundation. *Sportsmen aren't poachers, poachers aren't sportsmen.* http://colorado.on-line.com/ogt/naws.htm (last visited 12/2001).

Rousseau, J. (1979). *Emile: Or, on education.* Translation, introduction, and notes by Allan Bloom. New York: Basic Books.

Tisch, C. (1997). *Crafty animal poachers now going to the dogs.* Bradenton Herald Internet Plus. http://www.bhip.com/news/9dogs.htm (last visited 12/2001).

Winnicott, D. (1971). *Playing and reality.* New York: Routledge.

——— (1984). Aggression and its roots. In *Depression and delinquency.* Edited by C. Winnicott, R. Shepherd, and M. Davis. London: Tavistock Publications.

CHAPTER TWO

WES: A Theory and Framework for an International Curriculum

Keith Bookwalter • Colombia

Basic Principles and Components

The Wholistic Educational System (WES) is a comprehensive, systemic, research-based approach to education which can be characterized as being religious in its inspiration,[1] organismic in its philosophic orientation, and scientific in its method. Drawing upon three corresponding bodies of knowledge and human experience—religion, philosophy, and science—a theory of development and learning was derived which posits the interdependence of the actualization of human potentiality and the acquisition of knowledge. From this theory three others were derived: a theory of curriculum, a theory of teaching, and a theory of administration and institution-community relations. From these three theories practical applications were generated. A fifth theory, the theory of evaluation, completes the educational system and assures that inductive knowledge gained from praxis and research will continually renew all of the constituent components of the System. (figure 1 shows the relationship of these various aspects of the Wholistic Educational System.)

The philosophical foundations of WES draw most heavily from the work of Alfred North Whitehead (1917/1967a, 1925/1967b, 1929/1978, 1933/1967, 1938/1966) and Abraham Maslow, and, to a lesser extent, from Henri Bergson and Charles Pierce. However, in the formulation of its theory of curriculum, WES is also informed by two other branches of knowledge—

religion and science. Religion, like philosophy, has always helped to answer the fundamental questions which are beyond the scope of science: What is the essence of reality? What is the purpose of the universe? What is the destiny of human life on this planet? What are the spiritual truths which can illumine our understanding of human nature? and others.[2] Historically, religion was the mother of philosophy. And philosophy, in turn, was the mother of science, mathematics, and other branches of knowledge (Conow 1990: 15–16).

Because educational curricula and teaching methods are strengthened by a deeper understanding of the nature of the learner, WES has formulated a theory of development and learning which draws upon the branches of science which directly or indirectly impact human health and well-being and the educational enterprise, e.g., genetics, neurobiology, neurolinguistics, and other branches of brain research; agriculture; nutrition; medicine; ecology; social-economic development; and many others. Unfortunately, it is beyond the scope of this chapter to present the religious notions, philosophical principles, and scientific tenets which undergird the Wholistic Educational System.

The Historical Roots of WES

The Wholistic Educational System represents the author's attempt to recast, elaborate, and refine the ANISA Model of Education which was developed by the late Rhodes scholar, Daniel C. Jordan, his close colleague Donald T. Streets (1973a), and their associates.[3]

The Theory of Development and Learning

Because the WES theory of curriculum is derived from its theory of development and learning, the basic principles of the latter have been included in this discussion. However, due to the intimate connection between development, learning, and curriculum, it is recommended that the reader refer to the curriculum summary chart (figure 2) during the exposition of the theory of development and learning.

The theory of development and learning of the Wholistic Educational System has drawn on the work of Jordan and Kalinowski (1973), Gardner (1983), Piaget (1972), and others such as Goleman (1995), Werner, Erikson, Gesell, Epstein, Baldwin, Hunt, Havinghurst, Mussen and Langer, Harris, Buhler, Bonner, and Scott. As it stands at this point in time, the theory of development and learning of WES upholds the following principles:[4]

Figure 1: Model of the Wholistic Educational System

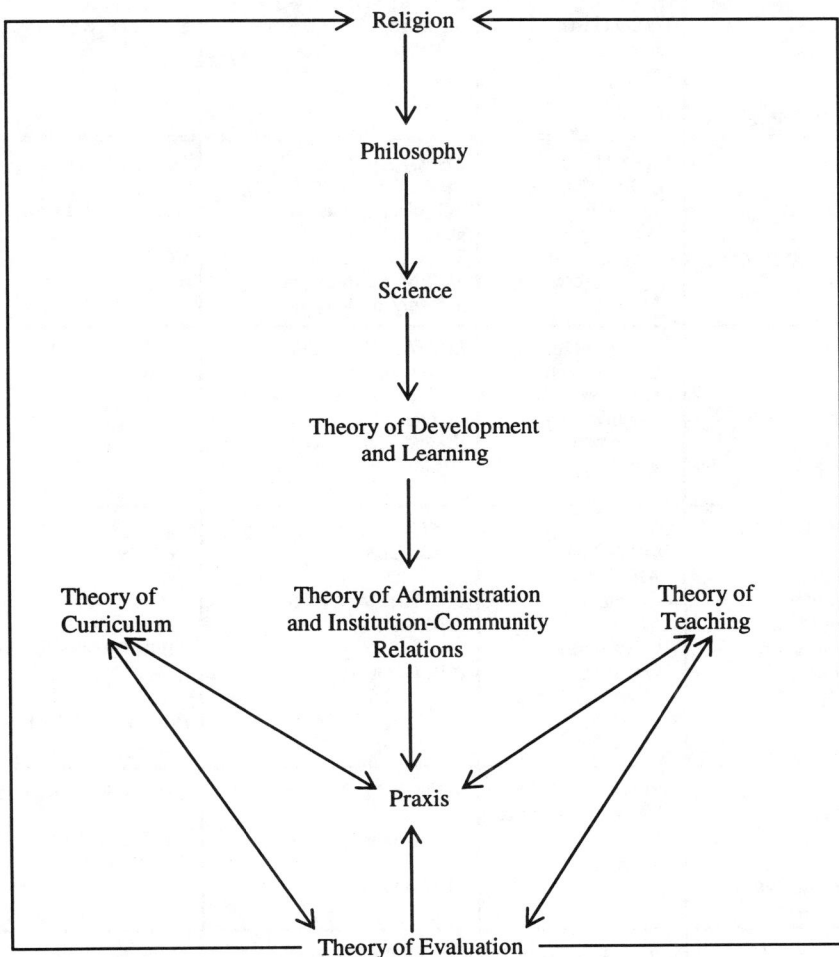

Note: Top-to-bottom arrows indicate lines of deductive generation of the system components. Bottom-to-top arrows originating from praxis and evaluation indicate lines of inductive development of the system, thereby guaranteeing the perpetual renewal of the System. (Actually, bottom-to-top arrows should be drawn to all components but, for the sake of visual clarity, this was not done.) Also, it should be noted that the evaluation of religion does not mean the assessment of God's Revelations but rather the continual reconsideration of our understanding of the Revealed Word and its implications for education, the results of which will be different from one generation to the next.

Figure 2: WES: Curriculum Summary Chart

The person(s) interact(s) with the known, unknown but knowable, & unknowable aspects of these ENVIRONMENTS:	thereby actualizing these basic POTENTIALITIES (process):	assimilating these bodies of basic KNOWLEDGE (content):	by utilizing these higher-order SYMBOL SYSTEMS:
PHYSICAL: -Mineral -Botanical -Zoological -Human (Body[ies]) -Human-made	PHYSIO-ORIENTED: - Biological - Perceptual - Psychomotor - Spatial/Temporal - Musical	THEORETICAL PHYSICAL SCIENCES (physics, chemistry, geology, etc.) THEORETICAL LIFE SCIENCES (biology, anatomy, ecology, etc.)	MATHEMATICS SYMBOLIC LOGIC CODES
SOCIAL: -Partnership -Family -Community -Culture -Humankind	SOCIO-ORIENTED: - Communication - Imitation - Identification - Reciprocity - Altruism	SOCIAL SCIENCES: -Communications -Human Relations -Sociology -Law & Human Rights -History, etc.	LANGUAGE(S): - writing - reading

PSYCHOLOGICAL:
 - Feelings
 - Questions
 - Ideas & Images
 - Aims & Ideals
 - Symbols
 - Memories, etc.
	PSYCHO-ORIENTED:
	 - Affective
	 - Cognitive
	 - Volitional
	 - Cross-domain:
	   - memory
	   - learning, & others
		PSYCHOLOGICAL SCIENCES
		
		 THE HUMANITIES
		 THE ARTS
		
		 PHILOSOPHY
			PROFESSIONAL TERMS
			
			 LITERARY ELEMENT
			 ART FORMS/ ELEMENT
			
			 PHILOSOPHICAL TERMS

SPIRITUAL: - Souls - Prophets & Word of God - The Holy Spirit - The Deity	SPIRIT-ORIENTED: - Virtues acquisition - Faith - Worship	SPIRITUAL SCIENCES RELIGION THEOLOGY	Most of the above plus RELIGIOUS SYMBOLISM
All of the above combined into the ENVIRONMENT OF THE SELF: -Physical self -Social self -Psychological self -Spiritual self	All of the above oriented to the Self: -Personal health care - Self-percept - Body awareness - Self as companion - Self-esteem - Self-concept - Self-determination -Respect divine in self	All of the above applied to the SCIENCE OF THE SELF: vital information about one's - Biological health, - Social health, - Psychological health, - Spiritual health	All of the above applied to SELF-SYMBOLIZATION: - Self-measurement - Self-definition - Self-dialogue - Self-expression

Figure 2: (Continued horizontally)

thereby forming these VALUES/ VIRTUES (content fused with process):	which are "lured" from potentiality into actuality by these IDEALS:	and on which these HIGHER-ORDER COMPETENCIES are based:
MATERIAL VALUES/ VIRTUES	TECHNOLOGICAL EFFECTANCE ECOLOGICAL BALANCE SUSTAINABLE DEVELOPMENT HIGH QUALITY SURVIVAL	TECHNOLOGICAL COMPETENCE (applied science: technology, agriculture, animal husbandry, medicine, etc.)
SOCIAL VALUES/ VIRTUES	SOCIAL EFFECTANCE JUSTICE COOPERATION SERVICE TO HUMANITY WORLD UNITY UNIVERSAL PEACE HAPPINESS	MORAL COMPETENCE (applied social sciences: law, social work, education, business & organizational administration, etc.)
AESTHETIC VALUES/ VIRTUES PHILOSOPHICAL VALUES/ VIRTUES	PSYCHOLOGICAL EFFECTANCE UNITY TRUTH BEAUTY	CREATIVE COMPETENCE SPECULATIVE COMPETENCE (applied fields: arts, crafts, think tanks, etc.))
SPIRITUAL & RELIGIOUS VALUES/ VIRTUES	SPIRITUAL EFFECTANCE LOVING & KNOWING GOD PURITY OF HEART KINGDOMS OF GOD: ON EARTH & IN HEAVEN	FIDUCIAL COMPETENCE SPIRITUAL COMPETENCE (applied fields)

All of the above combined into
 	
SELF-IDENTITY or
 	
CHARACTER
	All of the above combined into
	SELF-EFFECTANCE & the IDEAL SELF:
	  (as a vision
	    of the attributes of God
	    reflected in
	    the Possible Self:
	    the potential
	    "image of God")
		All of the above & to the left as they apply to
		SELF-COMPETENCE which is sustained by:
		-Learning competence
		-Self-teaching
		-Self-actualization
		
		(applied in field of self-help practices)

Based on the ANISA Model of Education
Copyright 1999, by Keith Bookwalter

- Development means the translation of potentiality into actuality, the process of which can be equated with creativity in its broadest sense.
- Interaction with the environment is the means by which development is sustained.
- There are five basic categories or aspects of the environment.[5] (See figure 2.)
- The five aspects of the environment are organized hierarchically. (See figure 3.)
- All environments contain entities which have aspects that are known, unknown but knowable, and ultimately unknowable.
- The perpetual introduction of some novelty[6] into the environment is a primary means of creating disequilibrium (or disparity) between a person's developmental level and experience, thereby compelling new patterns of interaction, which, in turn, facilitate the actualization of potentialities.
- Environments and interactions are categorized and evaluated in terms of their power to facilitate the maintenance of biological integrity (that is, safety must be paramount), the actualization of all categories of potentiality, the acquisition of knowledge, competence in the corresponding symbol systems, the formation of character, and the enhancement of higher-order competencies, especially the development of learning/self-teaching competence.
- Although the number of human potentialities is infinite and the finitude of their actualization is impossible to establish, they can be categorized into domains, each of which can be analyzed and improved in relative isolation to the others.
- There are five broad categories or domains of potentiality, the actualization of which is oriented toward effectance with a particular environment. (White, 1959)[7] (See figure 2.)
- There are five subcategories of physio-oriented potentiality. (See figure 2.)
- Proper nutrition is the essential element in the development of biological potentialities. Other important elements include: hygiene (physical health, freedom from illness, cleanliness of physical environment—clean air, clean water, clean food, etc.), exercise (fitness of muscular, cardiovascular, and respiratory systems), leisure (as of muscular, cardiovascular, and respiratory systems), leisure (as a means of re-energizing the system for further service to God and His creation), and rest (especially sleep, but also mind control and other techniques for revitalization).
- There are five subcategories if socio-oriented potentiality. (See figure 2.)

- Communication—body language, social gestures such as gift-giving, listening, and speaking (lower-order symbol systems)—is the key process in the release of socio-oriented potentialities.
- There are four subcategories of psycho-oriented potentiality. (See figure 2.)
- Learning is the key cross-domain, psychological process involved in the release of psychological potentialities;
- There are three subcategories of spirit-oriented potentiality. (See figure 2).
- Worship is the primary process for the release of spiritual potentialities. Subprocesses of worship include: prayer, meditation, service and work (as devotion to God via helping others), group worship (the traditional idea of worship), fasting, tithing, and scripture study.

Note: All of the above potentialities, which are actualized as processes [or powers] are brain-connected. Hence, the argument can be made that they are all processes which are highly mental or psychological in nature. In order to accommodate this truth while maintaining a pentamerous categorization of processes for practical purposes, the term "-oriented" is used to indicate the primary, though not exclusive, realm of utilization of the process in the person's quest for effectance with a particular environment.

- There are eight subcategories of processes oriented to the Self. (See figure 2.)
- There are five value/virtue subsystems. (See figure 2.)
- Self-identity (character development) emerges in terms of value/virtue formation. Values are defined as relatively enduring structurings of actualized potentialities (patterned uses of energy available to the organism), and virtues are defined as values, the formation of which is guided by universal ideals which seek the highest good for all things everywhere.
- The structural and functional reality of self-identity (the Self) is comprised of the four value/virtue systems combined into an integrated totality, on which depends the personal effectance of the self—"self-competence"—analogously defined as the combination of the higher-order competencies.
- Because of the hierarchical context of development, personality formation cannot be fully understood independently of the culture as transmitted by parents, family, and society.
- Information about the environments, held as beliefs, whether error free or error ridden, affects the structuring of values and virtues.
- Psychological processes such as feelings, perceptions, and intentions af-

fect attitudes, which are fused with beliefs in the structuring of values and virtues.
• In correspondence with the five sets of values/virtues there are five supplementary sets of ideals which lure their development forward. (See figure 2.)
• There are five sets of analogous higher-order competencies. (See figure 2.)
• Learning how to learn (learning competence) is the ultimate source of effectance—the ability to bring about intended effects in relation to any targeted entity, whether it be physical, social, psychological, spiritual, or personal in nature.
• Learning competence means the conscious ability to differentiate aspects of experience, integrate them into novel patterns, and generalize them to other situations. Differentiation, integration, and generalization constitute the trio of interrelated processes that define a developmental unit of change—a stage (sequences of stages being the primary means by which increasing complexity of function and structure is built up and integrated through hierarchical organization).
• Early experience is important in the shaping of subsequent developmental phenomena. The concepts of critical or sensitive periods, stages, and sequences within each category or domain of potentiality have heuristic value.
• Developmental universals provide a framework for the planning and implementation of educational programs cross-culturally, provided that cultural and personal uniquenesses are accounted for and encouraged.
• The WES theory of development and learning also provides a general scheme for understanding the nature of pathology and its etiology, sets forth the conditions for the prevention of mental illness, character disorders, delinquency, and criminality, and is generative of testable propositions concerning therapy and rehabilitation.

The Theory of Curriculum

The theory of curriculum of the Wholistic Educational System, in its present form, has drawn on the work of 'Abdu'l-Bahá[8] (1922–1925/1982), Jordan and Streets (1973b), Doll (1993), Oliver and Gershman (1989), Taba, McDonald, Goodlad, and Tyler. At the present time, the basic principles as illustrated in figure 2 are as follows. Curriculum is defined in terms of educational goals as determined by society and the learner[9] and what learners do (with or without the assistance of teachers) to achieve them. The overarching goal of the curriculum (and the aim of education in general) is to enable the person, through a personalized approach which accommodates his/ her uniqueness, to consciously and continuously:

1) discover, actualize, expand, and refine, at an optimum rate and in constructive directions, his/ her potentialities and special, God-given talents, which are physical, social, psychological, and/ or spiritual in nature;

2) structure these potentialities into a self-identity or character around universal ideals which seek the highest good for all things everywhere and which perpetually improve their well-being;

3) acquire and generate beneficial knowledge;

4) know and love the Creator and His/ Her creation;

5) actualize the potentiality of society (e.g., families, organizations, nations, and humankind as a whole;

6) carry forward an ever-advancing civilization toward ever-wider, ever-more-evolved circles of unity; and

7) prepare his/ her soul for the afterlife.

There are six curricular strands or sets of objectives: 1) process, 2) content, 3) higher-order symbol systems, 4) values/ virtues and their related ideals, 5) higher-order competencies, and 6) the Self.

Just as the five environments are related hierarchically (figure 3), so, too, are the six strands of the curriculum. Each higher strand builds upon, fuses, and subsumes the lower strands with the Self being the highest level, the embodiment of the sum total of all other curricular strands. (See figure 4.)

The main goals and sub-goals of all of the curricular strands are differentiated into process goals and content goals.[10]

1. The Process Curriculum

There are five categories of process goals aimed at the actualization of potentialities. (See figure 2.)

2. The Content Curriculum

There are five categories of content goals analogous to the process goals. (See figure 2.)

The content curriculum at all levels and the logical thinking portion of the cognitive process curriculum give importance to the acquisition of a continuously deepening understanding of all forms of causality and regulatory systems governing the various aspects of the environment. (There is a supplementary curriculum for these aspects.)

Figure 3: Hierarchical Ordering of the Environments

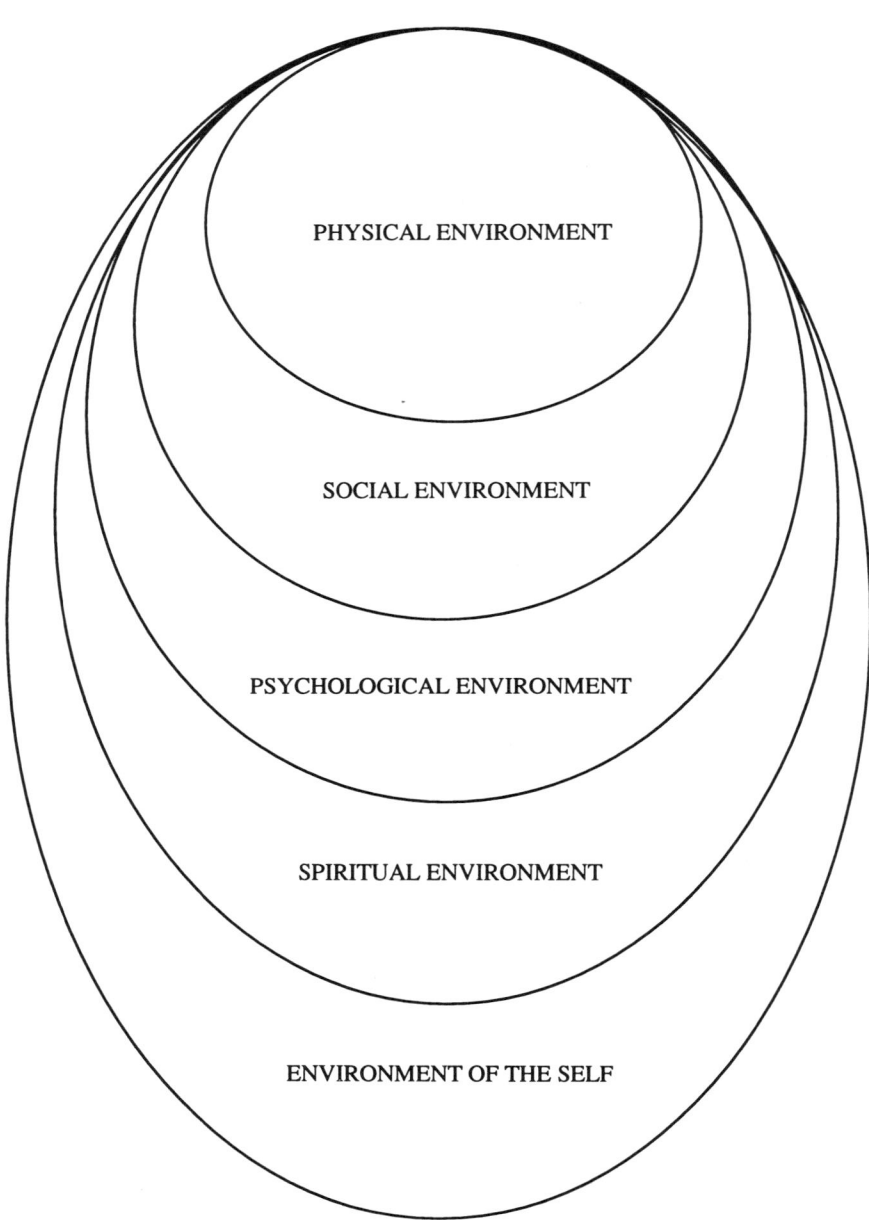

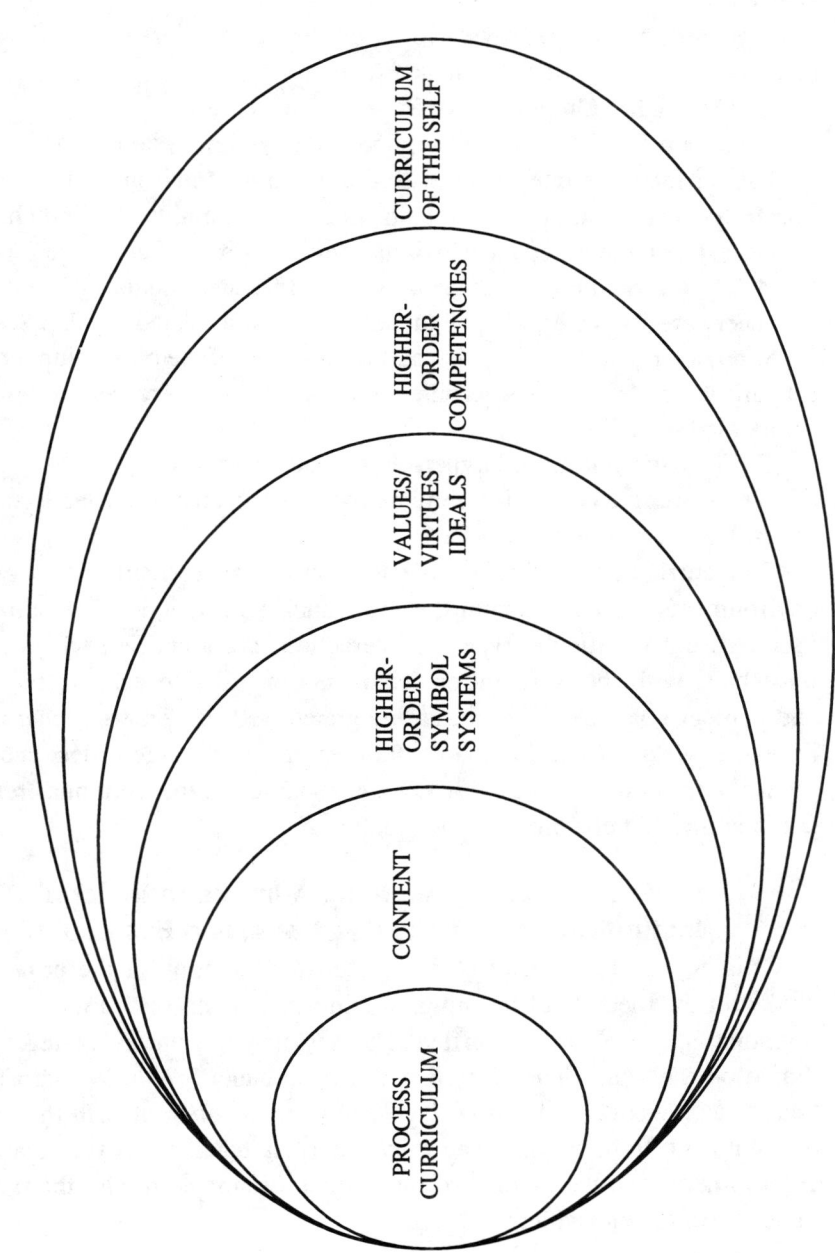

Figure 4: Hierarchical Ordering of the Curricular Strands

Cognitive processes (especially logical and critical thinking) should be as the means for reducing error in the knowledge (content) assimilated, and accumulated content should be applied to render cognitive processes more efficient.

Content knowledge is viewed as consisting of hierarchically organized bodies of concepts, information, and facts.

3. The Higher-Order Symbol Systems Curriculum

There are five categories of higher-order symbol systems[11] which help to mediate or facilitate interaction with the five basic environments, give direction to the structuring of the actualization of potentiality, and heighten consciousness of the entities for which the symbols stand. (See figure 2.)

4. The Curriculum of Values/Virtues and Related Ideals

There are five categories of values/ virtues and related ideals. (See figure 2.) Supplementing the value-virtues-ideals strand of the curriculum are five sets of role models, heroes/heroines, and leaders who serve as exemplars and "embodied lures."

5. The Curriculum for Higher-Order Competencies

There are five categories of higher-order competencies. (See figure 2.)

6. The Curriculum of the Self

The curriculum of the Self is based on the microcosm of the four main environments enfolded within the individual, and includes five sub-strands. (See figure 2.) Particular types of interactions are identified which a person must have with the different environments in order to achieve the process and content goals. As a result, an integrated Self can emerge, characterized by values/virtues (actualized potentialities of a mid-range order) and related higher-order competencies that not only guarantee the continual release of potentialities but also improve the quality of survival.

The Theories of Teaching, Administration and Institution-Community Relations, and Evaluation

It is beyond the scope of this chapter to present all of the principles included in the theories of teaching, administration and institution-community relations, and evaluation. Suffice it to say that the theory of teaching has drawn on the work of Bruner, Broudy, B. Othanel Smith, Woodruff, Gage, Glaser, and Moore, and it is derived from and is coherent with the theory of development and learning. The theory defines teaching as the arranging of environments and the guiding of the learner's interaction with them to attain the goals of the curriculum.

The theory of administration and institution-community relations has been influenced by the work of Barnard, Follett, Argyris, Hershey and Blanchard, and Jordan and Streets. It places administrators in the role of "ministers," whose services include the management of the school's accumulated resources (as an expression of immanence) and leading the actualization of the potentiality of students, teachers, parents, and the school as a whole (as an expression of transcendence). Consultation is utilized as the principal decision-making process, which seeks to draw input from those persons with expertise in the topic at hand and from those persons who will be most affected by the decision. The theory also specifies the need for administrators to lead the process of working with parents to lessen the disparity between the student's experience at school and the home environment.

The theory of evaluation was developed from the work of Cronbach, Hambelton, and Swaminathan. The role of evaluation in relation to the curriculum and teaching is to relate the degree of goal achievement to particular interactions prescribed, encouraged, or permitted. The theory of evaluation emphasizes the importance of not only assessing the students' attainment of both the process and content goals of the curriculum but also the assessment of each component of WES, the related programs which support the components, and the system as a whole. (See figure 1.)

Conclusion

This chapter has briefly discussed the religious, philosophical, scientific, and theoretical foundations of the Wholistic Educational System and has emphasized the theories of development, learning, and curriculum and how they were generated. Unfortunately, due to limitations of scope, it was not possible to include a more detailed history of the development of the ANISA Model and WES, to present an example of a curricular unit based on this theory, nor to convey the sheer excitement of learners when such a system (even just a few components of it) are implemented.

Notes

1. By disregarding the components of WES which refer to religion and spirituality, users who are atheistic or who are working in a country which separates church and state, thereby making it difficult to incorporate the spiritual aspect of reality into educational practices, will still find that this is a very powerful and useful system.
2. WES has drawn upon all of the major religious traditions—the common heritage of the entire human race—such as Hinduism, Judaism, Taoism, Zoroastrianism, Native American religious traditions, Buddhism, Christianity, Islam, and the Bahá'í faith. WES views

the Great Revealed Religions as being hierarchically organized according to the chronological order of their appearance, each one embracing those which have come before while adding to their richness and complexity—like the cardinal nature of numbers in which each successive number contains the previous numbers while adding one to their value. Hence, the greatest source of inspiration for WES has been the Bahá'í faith—the most recent of the Great Revealed Religions.

The relevance of Bahá'í concepts for the post-modern age was attested to by Ervin Laszlo (1989), the foremost exponent of systems philosophy and member of the Club of Rome, who credited Bahá'u'lláh, the Prophet-Founder of the Bahá'í faith with having anticipated the current theory of non-linear evolutionary development in human history (122).

3. The interested reader is referred to the summary statement of the ANISA Model available via the ERIC system (Document Reproduction Service No. ED 110387).
4. Some of these principles are the same as those of the ANISA Model, some are extrapolations of ANISA principles and others are new (see note 3). It is beyond the purpose of this chapter to document and explain exactly where ANISA leaves off and the WES upgrade begins. However, this author wants to give due credit to the original work of the founders of the ANISA Model of Education.
5. The "environment" is one, single and seamless; that is, reality is one. However, for conceptual and practical purposes, its various aspects are differentiated (see figures 2 and 3). This aspect of WES then represents a fundamental ontological analysis of reality—the backbone of the System—from which all other major categories have been generated or organized.
6. Novelty can be physical, social, psychological, or spiritual in nature. For example, asking intriguing questions or using a familiar object in a new way can be considered as the introduction of novelty.
7. Robert White's concept of effectance motivation has been applied in WES to all categories of higher-order competence; the idea being that one of the strongest intrinsic motivators to be harnessed by educators is the learner's desire to achieve intended outcomes in his/her interactions with all aspects of the environment.
8. Abdu'l-Bahá was the eldest son of Bahá'u'lláh (see note 2) and is one of the three Central Figures of the Bahá'í faith.
9. WES seeks to strike a balance between self-chosen goals and society-chosen goals. It is assumed that the accumulated experience of a culture knows better than the child what knowledge and skills are needed for high-quality survival. Yet, within the broad expectations of society, there needs to be room for individuals to pursue their own interests which often reflect their latent talents and future area of contribution to society.
10. Every curriculum topic in any of the six strands (process, content, symbol systems, values/virtues, higher-order competencies, and the Self) will always contain a process and a content aspect. It is impossible to teach process without content, and even the dullest content lesson contains some process, for even rote memorization and recall require certain cognitive processes (Ginsburg and Opper 1988).
11. The higher-order symbol systems (Gardner 1983) are closely related to the content areas and are nearly impossible to separate from them. Their assimilation appears to require di-

rect teaching. That is, they do not develop naturally by themselves (given a normal environment minus a teacher). Hence, mathematical logic, which is possessed by people in cultures that have no math symbol system or who have not learned the system, must be differentiated from the mathematical symbol systems which have a written form. Also, speaking and understanding the spoken word (lower-order symbol systems), which develop in all cultures (some cultures' knowledge has been passed on exclusively by oral tradition), must be distinguished from reading and writing. (For example, the parents on the American frontier sent their children to school to be taught only how to read and write because this knowledge could not be transmitted under normal living conditions in the home). Natural musical creativity, too, must be differentiated from the ability to read and write music. The former can develop naturally but the latter requires a specially arranged learning environment. (In WES, development and learning are viewed as two, interactive aspects of a whole. Each can constrain and/or facilitate the other.)

References

'Abdu'l-Bahá (1922–25/1982). *Promulgation of universal peace*. 2nd edition. Compiled by Howard MacNutt. Wilmette, IL: Bahá'í Publishing Trust.

Conow, B. (1990). *The Bahá'í teachings: A resurgent model of the universe*. Oxford: George Ronald.

Doll, Jr., W. (1993). *A post-modern perspective on curriculum*. New York: Teachers College Press.

Gardner, H. (1983). *Frames of mind: The theory of multiple intelligences*. New York: Basic Books.

——— (1993). *Multiple intelligences: The theory in practice*. New York, Basic Books.

Ginsburg, H. P., and S. Opper (1988). *Piaget's theory of intellectual development*. 3rd edition. Englewood Cliffs, NJ: Prentice Hall.

Goleman, D. (1995). *Emotional intelligence*. New York: Bantam Books.

Jordan, D. C., and M. F. Kalinowski (1973). Being and becoming: The ANISA theory of development. *World Order 7* (4): 17–26.

Jordan, D. C., and D. T. Streets (1973a). The ANISA model: A new basis for educational planning. *Young Children 28* (5): 289–307.

Jordan, D. C., and D. T. Streets (1973b). Guiding the process of becoming: The ANISA theories of curriculum and teaching. *World Order 7* (4): 29–40.

Laszlo, E. (1987). *Evolution: The grand synthesis*. Boston: New Science Library.

——— (1989). *The inner limits of mankind*. London: Oneworld.

Oliver, D., and K. Gershman (1989). *Education, modernity, and fractured meaning*. Albany, NY: SUNY Press.

Piaget, J. (1972). *The principles of genetic epistemology*. London: Routledge.

White, R. W. (1959). Motivation reconsidered: the concept of competence. *Psychological Review 66* (5): 297–333.

Whitehead, A. N. (1967a). *The aims of education*. New York: Free Press (original work published chapter 2, 1922; remainder, 1917).

——— (1967b). *Science and the modern world*. New York: Free Press (original work published 1925).

———— (1978). *Process and reality. An essay in cosmology* (Corrected edition). Edited by David R. Griffin and Donald W. Sherburne. New York: Free Press (original work published 1929).
———— (1967). *Adventures of ideas.* New York: Macmillan (original work published 1933).
———— (1966). *Modes of thought.* New York: Free Press (original work published 1938).

CHAPTER THREE

Technology Unmasked?

Kevan Brewer • Canada

Information pours in on us, instantaneously and continuously. As soon as information is acquired, it is very rapidly replaced by still newer information. Our electrically configured world has forced us to move from the habit of data classification to the mode of pattern recognition. We can no longer build serially, block-by-block, step-by-step, because instant communication insures that all factors of the environment and of experience co-exist in a state of active interplay. (McLuhan and Fiore 1967: 63)

I would like to open some questions regarding technology in education. In particular, I am interested in the ways in which computer-related technology masks its own essence—how it covers at the same time as it reveals—and the danger of this masking.

I run up the stairs two at a time, and weave my way through a maze of bodies until I reach my office. I practically leap into my seat at the computer terminal, and with a couple of clicks of the mouse, I finally fix the printer problem that has been plaguing me all morning. My head is buzzing with caffeine—I've had six cups of coffee so far—and it's only ten o'clock. I look up from the terminal as a student enters the room to tell me that her computer is not working. I follow her into the main computer lab and spend the next ten minutes or so trying to track down the reason that her computer won't log on to the local network. Unsuccessful and frustrated, I move on to help a student who has been waiting with an algebra problem.[1]

This is part of my reality as a technology teacher. I spend more time in service to the machines than I do serving the needs of my students. My teaching job, loosely described as "science, math, computers," has come to include previewing software, ordering software and hardware, maintaining the school's software and hardware inventory, troubleshooting software, hardware, and networking problems, and helping students and staff with computer-related questions. In a school with forty computers, this tends to take up much of my day. If these machines are supposed to be labour-saving devices, I would like to know whose labour is being saved. By the time the school day is done, I don't have the time, energy, or inclination to question technology or anything else.

Technological change, particularly in computer-related areas such as communications and media, is occurring at an ever-increasing pace. Although these changes have been likened to those that occurred during the Industrial Revolution, there is one important difference. The changes wrought by the Industrial Revolution took almost one hundred years, while the technological changes we are experiencing have occurred in less than half that time. We have reached the point where our ability to deal with such change and its consequences is compromised.

This is no accident; it is a direct consequence of what Martin Heidegger calls technological enframing. I have to keep on top of the problems, stay in control, or be controlled. The fast pace of technological development in this "information age" in which we are constructed and construct ourselves does not give us the free time that was promised and actually makes matters worse, giving us less and less time to think or act. As Jacques Ellul says:

> The interval which traditionally separates a scientific discovery and its application in everyday life has been progressively shortened. As soon as a discovery is made, a concrete application is sought. Capital becomes interested, or the state, and the discovery enters the public domain *before anyone has had a chance to reckon all the consequences or to recognize its full import.* (1973: 10; emphasis added)

It is ironic to me that it is this very lack of time for questioning that first draws me into an engagement with technological questions. Somehow, the way in which the essence of technology is masked is also the process which draws it into the open, makes me sit up and take notice. It is this putting-upon, this technological time demand, that forces me to stop and ask: "What is going on here? What is at work?"

However, the pace of technological change is not the issue. It is more a symptom of a problem than a problem in and of itself. I am concerned, not so much with technology but with what moves through it—with how we are through and with technology. In other words, I am concerned with the relationships that we enter into with technology. The traditional view is to look upon technologies as tools that we can use. Our interaction with technology is thought of as value-neutral; technologies can be put to good or evil ends but are themselves neither good nor evil. However, as Heidegger notes, "…we are delivered over to [technology] in the worst possible way when we regard it as something neutral; for this conception of it, to which today we particularly like to do homage, makes us blind to the essence of technology" (1954/1977: 287–88). What is wrong with viewing technologies as mere tools? What does this instrumental view of technology hide? For me what is missing is the recognition that technologies are a part of life, not apart from life. Technologies participate in socio-cultural relations—they are produced by and produce them to such an extent that early in his essay, Heidegger makes the startling assertion that "the essence of technology is by no means anything technological"(287).

In my questioning concerning our relationships with technology, I will draw on a number of philosophical explorations of technology, with a particular focus on two: Martin Heidegger's 1954 essay, "The question concerning technology," and Jacques Derrida's writing concerning the relationship between technology and responsibility in *The Gift of Death*. These writings will be used as a jumping-off point for my own inquiry.

In his essay, Heidegger carefully leads us along a way built through questioning (287). Like me, he is not so much concerned with technological things but with an essence of technology that is nothing technological. To clearly see where Heidegger is taking us, I think we need to be careful to understand what he means by essence. He explains that "[t]hus far we have understood 'essence' in its current meaning." This meaning of essence is what something is, or its *whatness*. For Heidegger, this does not adequately describe essence as it pertains to technology. For him, technology makes us think of essence more as a process than as a fixed state. He wants us to think of essence as the Greeks did, as that which "essences, what comes to presence, in the sense of what endures." And, he adds, "only that which is granted endures" (312). Two questions immediately arise for me here: What is the nature of this process-essence, and what does he mean here by *granted?* It may be tempting to think of this essencing as a linear, cause-and-effect, predictable, controllable process. But I do not think this is what Heidegger has in mind.

Heidegger tells us that "Technology is not equivalent to the essence of technology. When we are seeking the essence of 'tree,' we have to become aware that what pervades every tree, as tree, is not itself a tree that can be encountered among all the other trees" (1954/1977: 287). From my chaos-informed perspective, the essence of a tree, its *treeness,* is not something buried deep within the tree. Nor is it something belonging to trees in the sense of what a tree is. Rather, the essence of the tree is more an effect than a cause. And effects occur at the surface rather than being hidden away. Because technology is not a thing in the same way a tree is, it is necessary to think in terms of a larger-scale system—a system that is in-process with multiple layers of interactions. For purposes of analogy, it is more appropriate to speak of a forest, rather than an individual tree. In this sense, I should add that the essence of a forest is not found in any one species or in any one group of organisms. Rather, the essence of a forest is found in the in-between. "Everything happens at the boundary between things and propositions" (Deleuze 1964/1990: 8). The essence of a forest is an emergent property of the interactions within it and between the forest and us. In order for there to be an essence, there must be an observer, an engagement. In the same way, the essence of technology is not in some primal, core, hidden aspect of technology, but at its emergent surface, and is an effect of our relationship with it. Our relationship with it becomes part of the essence of technology. The essence is not some property of technological things or even of the system itself. The essence of technology is the name we give to the nature of our interaction with technology—what happens between technology and us.

Heidegger himself starts us on this path when he says that essences must be granted. In order to be granted, there must be a granter, an observer. For Heidegger, the granter would be man. But his use of the term man, rather than mankind or men, obscures the plural and relational nature of the term. It hides the radical subjectivity of the essence at which Heidegger is trying to get. If I open up the question of essence to the plurality of the human condition, it quickly loses both its universal character and its rootedness within technology. Instead, essence is forced into the open, into the in-between, exposed in the boundary regions.

Now just because it is a surface effect, out there, visible, staring us in the face if you will, does not mean it is obvious. Sometimes the best place to hide something is in plain view. Derrida refers to this when he speaks of "a logic of secrecy. It is never better kept than in being exposed" (1995: 38).

When I think of essence in a non-linear, chaotic way, something strikes me. The essence of technology is not fixed or permanent; it is relational in nature. If I then go on to search for "that which essences...in the sense of what endures," I have to be very careful. Careful that I am not trying to get at some fixed, unitary core of technology—what it is deep down.

Heidegger has already moved away from essence as referring to a unitary core *whatness* of something. I want to continue this move and return to the Latin root of essence, from *esse,* for "to be." Here, rather than what it is, essence refers to how it is what it is—its being. Or perhaps its becoming, since what is referred to is a process, always in motion—never complete, rather than a final or fixed state. If I think of essence in a relational way, then a number of things happen. The question of essentialism, of essence preceding existence, ceases to make sense. Essence and existence are inextricably linked—woven into and of the same fabric. I also become more aware of the social nature of essences, and what becomes important is our relationship with technology and what technology becomes with and through us rather than some essence that technology has on its own. Essences seem more an emergent property of a dynamical system of interactions, arising from the surface, than from deep within. The essence of technology is the result, in a way, of the interaction of multiple changing factors. It is not a fixed, quantifiable, encompassable, graspable whole, but the being of a fluid, amorphous, in-process, changing relation. If I can keep the essence of essence in play, perhaps I can be more aware of the covering that occurs every time something is revealed.

At this point I think it is important to make several things clear. I want to backtrack for a moment and be more careful, because the terms cause and effect that I have been using belong to a Cartesian, linear viewpoint. I am not saying that cause and effect are no longer important, only that, in non-linear terms, cause and effect are inseparable, and effect may even precede cause. It may be more proper to say that the essence of a tree or a forest or technology is both cause and effect, and at the same time it is neither.

Second, when I speak of technology as a non-linear dynamical system, I am speaking metaphorically. I do not suggest that technology belongs to or is such a system, although it may well be. For my purposes, however, it does not matter. I am using the language and concepts of chaos and complexity theory to give myself different ways to think and speak about technology and essences. I am hoping that this will lead me to fresh insights. I want to avoid shutting down the process of inquiry and keep the questions open. As

Gadamer suggests, "against the solidity of opinions, questioning makes the object and all its possibilities fluid" (1998: 330). In naming the essence of technology, indeed, in searching for the essence of technology, we are in danger of closing ourselves off to other possibilities, much in the same way that Heidegger says that technology closes off all other ways of being.

For Heidegger, our problem with technology begins with conceiving of it in an instrumental way. Then everything depends on how we use technology, on our mastering technology.

> Everything depends on our manipulating technology in the proper manner as a means. We will, as we say, 'get' technology 'spiritually in hand.' We will master it. (Heidegger 1954/1977: 289)

Heidegger traces the essence of technology through the instrumental and arrives at revealing, where technology "is the realm of revealing, i.e., of truth" (294). For him what is new in modern technology is that the revealing is a challenge upon nature. That all of nature becomes a "standing-reserve," waiting on-call for duty (298). He names this "challenging claim which gathers man thither to order the self-revealing as standing reserve: 'Gestell'[enframing]" (301). For Heidegger this destining of revealing is the supreme danger. It forces everything to come to presence as standing-reserve, even man himself. As we are threatened with becoming ourselves standing-reserve, our essence is transformed into a desire for mastery and control. Control becomes our way of being-in-the-world, and we act as though we are "lords of the earth" (308). The real threat is that this mode of being blocks all others, that it transforms the world and our relationship to the world.

> Things are endangered even if the bomb is not dropped, [Heidegger] said, endangered in their "essence," in the way they come to presence, namely, as the raw material of technical power. Things are put upon by man because man is himself put upon by the way technology comes to presence, by its essence as Gestell. (Caputo 1987: 232)

I want to return for a moment to the word "essence." Heidegger has traced an answer to his question of the essence of technology, but I would like to reopen the question of essences. The question of the essence of technology as enframing brings to the front the question of the essence of self. Technical power endangers man in his essence, in the way he comes to presence. For me, though, the question is whether or not there is an essential self, or better: how can we think of the essence of self in a process way? Heidegger claims that we are "endangered in our essence" by the essence of technology. Technology and self are firmly intertwined, in that self comes to presence under the spell of technology. And the reverse is also true—technology comes to presence under the spell of the technical self. Another way to think about this is to say that technology and self are linked in that they are both socially constructed.

I do not believe that there is a unitary, core, essential self any more than I believe that there is a core essence of technology. There is not some part of me that remains unchanged throughout my life and my experiences, a central overseer that simply wears different masks—the teacher mask, the father mask, the son mask, the husband mask. I think that the masks are all there is, that if you succeeded in removing them all there would be nothing left. And yet, that is not the whole story. My experience is of a seemingly coherent self. I would prefer to envision an emergent self, a self that arises from within and without the complex dynamical system that is us.

Unmasking selves seems very much like peeling off the layers of an onion. As each layer or mask is removed there is another to take its place. And like an onion, when the final mask is removed, there is nothing there. There is, it would seem, no core essence—if there is an essence at all it must be found in the pieces of the onion and not the empty core. But the pieces cannot be reassembled, and the onion cannot be reanimated. Something intangible is gone—it is dead. In the same way, the reassembled masks do not equal the persona or self. The whole is more than the sum of the parts.

What is the beauty that a man of erudition sees as he holds a fine pot in his hands? If he picks a flower to pieces, petal by petal, and counts them, and tries to put them together again, can he regain the beauty that was there? All the assembly of dead parts cannot bring life back again. It is the same with knowing (Yanagi 1972: 110).

How do I have a cohesive experience of a self and yet, at the same time, recognize the multiplicity in selves/masks? Is the cohesive self illusory? Or real? Or both and neither? The spark of self seems to emerge from the constant cross-talk in the in-between, in the interaction or dialogue between various selves, and between the body and the outside.

In the Santiago theory of cognition, consciousness is viewed as a whole-body experience—it is not confined to the brain. Humberto Maturana and Francisco Varella identify "cognition with the full process of life—including perceptions, emotions, and behavior—and understand it as a process that involves neither the transfer of information nor mental representations of the outside world" (Capra 1996: 286). There is a lot that goes on inside my body and brain that is not directly accessible to my consciousness. In fact, most brain processes are subconscious and are inaccessible to introspection. It appears that "many different brain processes function in parallel—independently of each other, and simultaneously" (Cohen & Stewart 1994: 176). In a sense, the brain is more like a committee, say, the Academy Awards committee, with each member acting as an independent unit until a decision must be made. The workings of the committee are hidden to us; all we see is the group decision, which makes it appear that only one person was involved. Similarly, the actions that emerge from the chaos operating within the brain and body make it appear as if a coherent, unified self is at work rather than numerous fragmentary, independent selves. As human beings, we exist in a "semantic domain" created by our languaging. The key feature of language, according to Maturana and Varella, is "that language enables those who operate in it to describe themselves and their circumstances," to generate a self by using the notion of an object and the associated abstract concepts (1998: 210). To be human is to exist in language. In language we coordinate our behavior, and together through language we bring forth our world. "The world everyone sees is not the world, but a world, which we bring forth with others" (245).

Self-awareness and human consciousness can only be understood through language and the whole social context in which it is embedded, and an ever-increasing part of our social context is technology. So much so, that Jacques Ellul (1973) has argued that we live in a

> technical civilization...that our civilization is constructed by technique (makes a part of civilization only what belongs to technique), for technique (in that everything in this civilization must serve a technical end), and is exclusively technique (in that it excludes whatever is not technique or reduces it to technical form). (128)

Computers, like any tool, are extensions of the tool user. However, it is important to remember that the tool itself determines to a large extent what it can be used for and how—and in that sense it, or rather our relationship with it, begins to control and fashion the user. It is worth repeating the saying often attributed to Abraham Maslow: "When the only tool you have is a hammer, every problem begins to resemble a nail." Technologies begin to limit the way that we respond to problems and to the world. If we are not careful, we begin to see only technical solutions. Other possibilities are obscured and closed off to us.

Computers are extensions of us, and we are extensions of them, and in this two-way interrelationship it becomes more and more difficult to find where technology ends and "man" begins. The edges are fuzzy, and as we move in with our microscope for a closer look, we see increasingly more complex patterns in the boundary region but never a clear boundary. When we look at technology, we are looking at ourselves. The computer screen is much like the eyes Caputo describes:

> The eyes of the other lure us into mystery and confusion, shadows and dark recesses; they are not windows of the soul but a house of mirrors. They are soft spots where the ground gives out beneath us and we plunge downward, unable to touch bottom, black holes trapping light. Who is speaking here? What looks out upon us from these eyes? What strange powers inhabit this look? (1987: 275)

The house of mirrors reflects multiple changing selves back at us from the computer as it does from the other. We are seeing ourselves, but we do not recognize the blank and vacant stare. We who have never known who we are. "The mystery consists not in a self-transparent Cartesian ego hiding behind the cloak of the body, but in the mystery that the other is to himself, that all of us are to ourselves" (Caputo 1987: 275). What is being created and recreated in Artificial Intelligence programs and so-called "smart systems" and computer networks is ourselves. In a society that is fast becoming almost exclusively technological, technology takes on an increasingly important role in the complex interactions in which self is formed.

> The individualism of technological civilization relies precisely on a misunderstanding of the unique self. It is an individualism relating to a *role* and not a *person*...modern individualism...concerns itself with the *role that is played* rather than with this unique person whose secret remains hidden behind the social mask. (Derrida 1995: 36)

We who fashion and are fashioned by technology have rarely really understood it. It seems there was never a time when we were outside it, apart from it for long enough to question it. Its grasp can be traced all the way back to the first toolmaker, when we first began to transform a cooperative relationship with nature into one of domination. And yet, technology has not caused these changes. It is not an independently operating entity, so we need to think about self as well as technology for a better grasp of what is at work here. As we in the West have moved from an agrarian society to an information age, the concept of self has been placed in an ever-larger arena. "Today that arena is global in size and the multitude of selves crying out for space produces a cacophony of sounds—one can hardly hear oneself think, one hardly knows who one is" (Doll 1997: 2).

Heidegger would say that this is the challenge of coming to presence under the force of technology. That technology obscures all other modes of being. What happens to a coherent sense of self in this environment? What about children and adolescents, who are often said to be in a process of establishing a self? Where do they turn? If we do come to self interactively, between self and other, then what happens to this process when the other becomes a computer? When reality becomes virtual reality?

> Terry and I are talking about some recent upgrades that have been done on the school's computer network. He is sitting in a grey, high-backed chair at the server—the main computer in the network. "So how did it go?" I ask. The question is bit loaded, because we have had a history of difficulties associated with any changes made to the system.
>
> "Actually, it was surprisingly smooth," he answers, "except...." He pauses for a moment and grabbing the mouse he turns to face the screen. As he moves the mouse, intently watching the pointer on the screen, his face begins to develop a frown. Then he mutters a curse under his breath.
>
> And suddenly he is laughing. Laughing so hard that he can't even tell me why. He finally regains his composure and begins:
>
> "I've been working on computers for too long," he says, "You know how I'm in the habit of using the mouse to point out things on the screen to students?" I nod and he continues, "Well, I was trying to use the mouse to point at this," he says, starting to laugh again. And then I'm laughing with him. The thing he was trying to point at was a yellow sticky-note stuck to the side of the terminal.

What happens when the reality on the screen becomes continuous with or indistinguishable from the reality outside of the screen? When the boundaries become permeable and fluid? When we further sever our ties with concrete reality? If it is possible to get confused between a computer screen and "reality," then what kind of crossovers and confusions are we going to experience as virtual reality becomes more realistic?

Marshall McLuhan and Quentin Fiore argue that youth had little difficulty with new technologies, that "[y]outh instinctively understands the present environment—the electric drama. It lives mythically and in depth" (1967: 9). Although it seems to me that there is truth in this statement, I am still concerned that we are distancing ourselves from lived experience in what might be called the "real world."

> In the line that runs from orality to literacy to the printed book to the computer, we find the computer bringing to near completion the severing of the world from its live source in the individual. (Talbott 1995: 22).

Precisely because we come to presence under its spell, it becomes difficult to think outside of technology. I cannot say exactly what technology is, or what its essence is, in part because I cannot say exactly where technology begins and ends or where I begin and end. When I focus in on the border regions, the areas between technology and myself, meanings explosively multiply, and I am quickly lost in ever-increasing fractal complexity. Heidegger's all-pervasive technological essence flows about, becoming intertwined and woven into everything. In education, it is not sufficient to ask if we should have computers in the classroom or even remove computers from classrooms (which probably isn't possible anyway). Technology has invaded our psyche; it is a part of us, and much that we do in education is colored by it. We use the computer as a metaphor for the mind and computer processes as a metaphor for learning. We think of the brain as an information processor, and this all serves to reinforce mechanistic concepts of thinking, knowledge, and communication. We speak of learning objectives as technicians and pre-plan the outcomes of activities.

This transfer of metaphors occurs in the other direction as well. Language formerly reserved for human beings is used to refer to machines. We talk of computers as thinking, learning, and creating. We talk about computer intelligence, write programs in computer languages, and check our computers' memory.

> I walk into the computer room, and pause for a minute to watch a student working on Data Processing 11. He is slumped down in his chair, staring blankly at the CD-ROM instructional material being presented on the computer screen. One hand is ready, gripping his mouse, but all of the action is taking place on the monitor. In a small window, an instructor explains how to select a block of text. Then the computer demonstrates the action. After about ten minutes of similar explanations and demonstrations, the student gets a chance to practice. His hand barely moves as he copies the procedures, pointing and clicking his mouse. This is called interaction.

Computers seem to privilege abstraction over the concrete, and in this move away from the "real world," some strange transformations in meaning and language use occur. Interaction becomes pointing and clicking with a mouse. Conversation is reduced to contact via e-mail. Community becomes the Internet. Research becomes Internet search. Questioning becomes finding answers (and unquestioning acceptance of the computer's authority). Education becomes information transfer—but not transformation. And the self becomes increasingly more fractured as it tries to find some grounding in this increasingly groundless domain.

At this point, I want to stop and ask a different question: How do I respond to the essence of technology as enframing?

> It is precisely in enframing, which threatens to sweep man away into ordering as the supposed single way of revealing, and so thrusts man into the danger of the surrender of his free essence—it is precisely in this extreme danger that the innermost indestructible belongingness of man within granting may come to light, provided that we, for our part, begin to pay heed to the essence of technology.... Thus, the coming to presence of technology harbors in itself what we least suspect, the possible upsurgence of the saving power. (Heidegger 1954/1977: 313–14)

Heidegger shows us the paradoxical double character of enframing, that enframing itself also holds the "upsurgence of the saving power." Everything depends on our "paying heed to the essence of technology." If we are vigilant and attentive, if we are ready and waiting, then we may yet save ourselves.

I want to be vigilant here, for just as Heidegger makes a show of unmasking technology, another bit of slight of hand is occurring. Is Heidegger really unmasking technology? Has he shown us the real essence of technology, the ultimate danger? Is there really some kind of *saving power?* Or is Heidegger's unmasking an "inauthentic dissimulation" that consists of exposing the saving power of technology as one thing, all the while covering up other possibilities?

As Heidegger delves into this question of the "saving power," there is a strange omission—a concealment in his writing. Heidegger, like technology, both conceals and reveals, has a surprising double character. In his genealogy of technology as a tool, as the instrumental, he introduces *poiesis* and *techne* as "the bringing-forth of the true." In this discussion, he also talks of the Greek word *aletheia* for revealing, and he refers specifically to Aristotle's *Nicomachean Ethics* (Heidegger 1954/1977: 314–15). As Richard Bernstein

(1995) points out, the problem is not in what he says but in what he does not say, in what he leaves out.

Aristotle does indeed distinguish between *episteme* and *techne* and then relates these terms to *aletheia*. But Aristotle does not stop there. Indeed, Aristotle's main point is to distinguish *phronesis* from the other intellectual virtues. *Phronesis* is the intellectual virtue or state of the soul that pertains to *praxis,* just as *techne* relates to *poiesis*. This is one of the classic texts in which Aristotle carefully distinguishes *praxis* (the subject matter of *Ethics*) from *poiesis* (Bernstein 1995: 120–1).

Why are *praxis* and *phronesis* absent from Heidegger's discussion? What possibility is being covered over? Heidegger's "saving power" is to be found in *poiesis,* in the "poetic revealing" which he tentatively locates in the arts. For Heidegger, the question "What am I to do?" is the wrong question, since it encourages one to think she or he can control or master the danger, try to find a technical solution to the problem. My true response to this "supreme danger," my response, my action, is, essentially, inaction. My work is to think and question, to reflect and wait. My work is to prepare for "the possible upsurgence of the saving power" (Heidegger 1954/1977: 316). Bernstein (1995) suggests:

> Heidegger seduces us into thinking that the only possible response (the highest possibility) to the supreme danger of Gestell is poetic revealing...Heidegger himself conceals what needs to be unconcealed—"the possible upsurgence of the saving power" may be revealed in action (praxis) and not only in "poetic dwelling." (127–28)

In a very real sense, Heidegger's focus on the heights of true, genuine, authentic thinking, on *poiesis,* takes his work out of the realm of the human—it becomes disconnected from lived experience. By spending so much time pursuing the highest mode of action, thinking, we risk disengaging from the world, from other people, and from practical action. I am not suggesting that Heidegger is wrong in what he suggests, but I am suggesting that *praxis*—that action—is also a valid course.

I am going to return to essences one last time, because there is one problematic aspect of essence that I have not yet raised. I think we need to think of essences more in personal terms rather than in a universal or essential way. Each person's experience of a thing or an idea will be unique, and while there may be some connection between different people's experiences, e.g., shared cultural context, I do not think there is a universal experience or essence involved. It is also important to note again that essence, in these terms, is not a property of the thing or idea itself, independent of a subject, but is an interaction between the subject and the object—it is a process negotiated between the two. Subject and object are not really distinct, disconnected, clearly delineated things but are instead different aspects of the same process. This is true also when I am speaking of technology using chaos metaphors. In a sense a thing's essence is fractal, with each person's experience of the essence being unique and yet somehow echoing the experiences of others. I am suggesting that what we think of as the essence of something is negotiated and renegotiated within a group through shared cultural, social, economic, and historical experiences. So we can reasonably expect that people in the "same" group should have a more similar experience of, say, the essence of technology than those of different groups. And if we are not careful, we may mistake this shared relationship for an essence belonging to the thing itself.

I also believe we have to be careful to not think that the essence of technology is something completely outside of our control or domain. That it somehow arises and exists independently from us. While I think control itself is often an illusion, I think that changing our relationship with technology is within the realm of possibility. The danger in the alternative lies in the lack of responsibility that this view can encourage. If this essence of technology is not our creation, we may be tempted to think it is not our problem, and we need do nothing about it. Derrida (1995) was right when he said that our relationship with technology creates "indifference and boredom" and a return to "demonic" (35) irresponsibility. And this is exactly what we risk if we unquestioningly follow Heidegger's poetic way of revealing as the *only* way. There is nothing that can be done except to watch and think and to be prepared. But at no time are we to act. In fact action leads us into the hands of technology. We are already under its spell, and practical action is exactly the wrong response.

So the questions are now: "What is my responsibility in this?" and "What should I do?" For me, being responsible means being fully present in the situation and acting despite incomplete information. I can not possibly know all of the contingencies and possibilities that are open in this action, but this is the nature of action.

> The activating of responsibility (decision, act, praxis) will always take place before and beyond any theoretical or thematic determination. It will have to decide without

it, independently, from knowledge; that will be the condition of a practical idea of freedom. (Derrida 1995: 26)

So if I accept action as an addition to "poetic dwelling," what next? I said earlier that removing computers from the classroom is not enough, and it is probably at best futile, and at worst exactly the wrong move. As educators, we need to realize that we cannot protect children or ourselves from technology simply by ignoring it or removing it. "Everywhere we remain unfree and chained to technology whether we passionately affirm or deny it" (Heidegger 1977: 287). Technology may be the most important curricular issue facing today's students and educators, and with the introduction of Technology Education, and Information Technology curricula in the Canadian Province of British Columbia at all grade levels, it is evident that the B.C. government shares this sentiment.

> [Technology] provides the tools to extend our vision, to send and receive sounds and images from around the world, and to improve health, lifestyle, economies, and ecosystems. As technology assumes an increasingly dominant force in society, technological literacy is becoming as essential as numeracy skills and the ability to read and write. (Ministry of Education 1996a: 2)

> To be responsible members of society, students must be aware of the ever-growing impacts of information technology. They need to reflect critically on information technology's role in society and consider its positive and negative effects. The information technology curriculum fosters the development of skills and attitudes that increase students' abilities to address the social and ethical issues of technological advancements. (Ministry of Education 1996b: 1)

However, it is also clear that the Ministry of Education has adopted an instrumental view of technology as a tool—a tool that students must learn to use in a responsible manner. This instrumental point of view has led many of us as educators to ask the wrong kinds of questions concerning technology. The questions that do get asked are almost exclusively of the means or "how-to" variety—how to make the machine work or, at best, how should we teach this or that technology. The more serious value questions as to the nature of technology and of our social-ethical relationship with it have not been raised. When the assumptions that lie hidden within the technological revolution are brought to light, we see not only the means technological schools can provide but also the social ends which become affected as we use these means. Technology is not value neutral. As a tool it controls us as much as we control it. To ignore this truth delivers us over to technology "in the worst possible way" (Heidegger 1977: 287–288).

Perhaps the move that needs to be made here is to change the nature of technology education. In too many schools, technology education consists of learning how to use the technology. In the Integrated Resource Package (IRP)s for Technology Education and Information Technology, I notice several things. First, as I have already said, the view of technology is overwhelmingly instrumental and positive. This view is echoed throughout the IRPs, whether I look at the intended learning outcomes or the suggested teaching strategies. Second, the talk is mainly of technological literacy. And while the goals sound good on paper, when I think of what the term literacy means, I get suspicious. The English literacy students whom I teach are learning the basics of how to use the language. Some of the more advanced literacy students may critique literary works, but at this level, they never critically examine the English language itself. In the same way, teaching technological literacy does not equip students to question technology itself, only its application. The question is never, "Should technology be used to solve this problem?" but is rather, "What technology should be used to solve this problem?" Within this instrumental curriculum, "[e]verything depends on our manipulating technology in the proper manner as a means." Everything depends on mastery and control. But, as Neil Postman says, "[W]hat we needed to know about cars—as we need to know about computers, television, and other important technologies—is not how to use them but how they use us" (1996: 44).

I think we need to look at what technology education should be. Do we need to teach students how to use computers? Perhaps. But more importantly in our classrooms, we should be exploring the ethical/political/personal implications of technology. Not just the use of technology but technology itself and the underlying assumptions that make these implications a reality. And even though the curriculum is provincially mandated, I can still take action. For me, this action, this praxis and poiesis, takes on a variety of forms in my practice. For example, it is my job to interpret the intended learning outcomes that the ministry gives me. I can interpret "It is expected that students will identify and analyze legal, ethical, social, and security issues related to network systems and stand-alone computer systems" (Ministry of Education 1996b: 15) to mean "students will learn to question technology." I do not need to be limited by the narrow realm of technological literacy that seems to be envisioned by the government. With any luck at all, I can give the government what they claim they want in their general goals—students with the ability "to reflect critically on technology's role in society and consider its positive and negative effects" and who have increased "abilities to responsibly address the social and ethical issues of technological advancements" (Ministry of Education 1996b: 1).

I believe that students need to be aware of and explore the interconnectedness of technology and society and self. They need to question the nature of these connections/relationships and not just accept them as natural. They need to be aware that technologies shape us as we shape them and to be aware of what emerges from our interactions with and through technologies.

What is the nature of these emergent essences of self and technology that seem to spring spontaneously into being out of the complex interactions and interrelationships between the various interconnected elements? How can we understand emergent essences? How does this apply to curriculum?

Do we, perhaps, need some sense of spirit here? A sense of spirit that does not come out of religion but that emerges more from an understanding of and reverence for the world. A sense of spirit that comes out of awe. An openness to the mystery. A shaking in the face of the *mysterium tremendum*. The realization that we do not and cannot know everything or know it with certainty. An understanding that we must tread carefully, because we don't know if our next step will be just another step or our last. We don't know whether or not our "next footstep is the one that will unleash the landslide of the century" (Kauffman 1995: 29).

So the question that I began with has been transformed from "What is the essence of technology and what is the danger associated with it?" to "What is my relationship with technology?" and "Can I speak of this relationship in any larger or more general sense?" In the end, I agree with Heidegger. I am not sure that we can solve this problem of our relationship to technology. There is no clear answer to the questions concerning technology just as there are no clear answers to any of our problems. I think that as Stephen Talbott says, "no genuine social problem has ever been solved by a program of action. Or even that no problem has ever been solved at all. As we slowly change, we eventually transcend old problems, simply leaving them behind in order to face new ones. Or, you might say, old problems simply assume new forms" (1995: 380). This, however, does not absolve me or any of us of our responsibility. It does not mean that I simply do nothing. Our world is human-made, and technology as part of that world has only the metaphysical character that we have granted it. As I realize that there is a very real danger in our "technical civilization," that there is no easy way out, that a technical answer is probably not going to save us, the more open I am to "an altogether different level of response" (Talbott 1995: 400). What this response might be is still unclear to me, but I believe that in some sense, I am already in the middle of it.

Note
1. The narratives were written from experiences I noticed as I was preparing the paper. The narratives are used to ground the theory in experience and to give the reader a more visceral sense of my experience with technology.

References

Bernstein, R. J. (1995). *The new constellation: The ethical-political horizons of modernity/postmodernity.* Cambridge: MIT Press.

Capra, F. (1996). *The web of life: A new scientific understanding of living systems.* New York: Doubleday.

Caputo, J. D. (1987). *Radical hermeneutics: Repetition, deconstruction, and the hermeneutic project.* Bloomington: Indiana University Press.

Cohen, J., and Stewart, I. (1994). *The collapse of chaos: Discovering simplicity in a complex world.* Toronto: Penguin.

Deleuze, G. (1990). *The logic of sense.* Translation by Mark Lester with Charles Stivale. edited by Constantin V. Boundas, 1964. New York: Columbia University Press.

Derrida, J. (1995). *The gift of death.* Translation by David Willis. Chicago: The University of Chicago Press.

Doll, Jr., W. E. (1997, August 1). Questions concerning technology. Unpublished paper. University of Victoria, Victoria, BC, Canada.

Ellul, J. (1973). *The technological society.* 6th edition. Translation by John Wilkinson, with introduction by Robert K. Merton. New York: Alfred A. Knopf.

Gadamer, H. (1998). *Truth and method.* New York: Continuum.

Heidegger, M. (1977). The question concerning technology. In *Basic writings from Being and Time.*Translation by William Lovitt. Edited, with general introduction and introduction to each selection, by David Farell Krell. Trans.. New York: Harper & Row. (original work published 1954).

Kauffman, S. (1995). *At home in the universe: The search for the laws of self-organization and complexity.* New York: Oxford University Press.

Maturana, H., and Varella, F. J. (1998). *The tree of knowledge: The biological roots of human understanding.* Boston: Shambahla Publications Inc.

McLuhan, M., and Fiore, Q. (1967). *The medium is the massage.* New York: Bantam Books.

McLuhan, M., and Eric McLuhan (1988). *Laws of media: The new science.* Toronto: University of Toronto Press.

Ministry of Education (1996a). *Technology education K to 12: Integrated resource package.* Victoria: Queens Printer.

―――― (1996b). *Information technology K to 12: Integrated resource package.* Victoria: Queens Printer.

Postman, N. (1996). *The end of education: Redefining the value of school.* New York: Alfred A. Knopf.

Talbott, S. L. (1995). *The future does not compute: Transcending the machines in our midst.* Sebastopol, CA: O'Reilly & Associates.

Yanagi, S. (1972). *The unknown craftsman: A Japanese insight into beauty.* Tokyo: Kodansha International.

CHAPTER FOUR

Bernstein avec *Lacan:*
Desire, Jouissance, and Pedagogic Discourse

Zain Davis • South Africa

The seminal work of sociologist Basil Bernstein has been invaluable in educational research that attempts to grasp the internal mechanisms of the production and reproduction of specialised knowledge.[1] Our contention here, though, is that his theory of the *pedagogic device* and *pedagogic discourse* is largely underdeveloped on those elements of the formation of consciousness that are seen as central in another domain of intellectual practice: Freudian/Lacanian psychoanalysis. Since Bernstein's theory is sociological, this is, of course, hardly surprising, and pointing out an absence which derives from elsewhere is no criticism. However, we believe that, today, pedagogy and curriculum cannot be addressed satisfactorily by drawing only on sociological accounts of education. We should put our cards on the table at the outset and say that the compelling work of Sigmund Freud and Jacques Lacan informs our view of education in general and provides us with an initial, though vague, orienting statement:

> Education can be described without much ado as an incitement to the conquest of the pleasure principle, and to its replacement by the reality principle; it seeks, that is, to lend its help to the developmental process which affects the ego. To this end it makes use of an offer of love as a reward from the educators; and it therefore fails if a spoilt child thinks that it possesses that love in any case and cannot lose it whatever happens. (Freud 1995: 304–5; italics in the original)

Freud does not provide us with a theoretical language of sufficient precision to deal with education as a specialised field; that was not his concern. We can see Bernstein's specialised theory of education as going some way towards filling out the nature of the "conquest of the pleasure principle." What is necessarily absent in Bernstein is an explicit account of the libidinal economy of the production and reproduction of knowledge. In pursuing such a development—that is, which takes into consideration a libidinal economy—we also have to take into account the development of Freud in Jacques Lacan's "return to Freud." As with Freud, Lacan provides little in the way of a coherent, specialised theoretical language for describing and analysing schooling, while Bernstein offers a sophisticated theoretical apparatus for doing just so. We shall, therefore, move among the work of Bernstein, Lacan, and Freud in discussing our position.

Before dealing with Bernstein, Lacan, and pedagogic discourse proper, we take a detour through the recent work of Rob Moore and Johan Muller, who published an important, hard-hitting critique of what they term the "Discourse of 'Voice'" and, more generally, of postmodern accounts of knowledge (Moore and Muller 1999). In the elaboration of their argument, following Émile Durkheim, they generate a description of their object of analysis as a central element of critique and appeal to the recent work of Basil Bernstein (Bernstein 1996; see also Bernstein 1999) as a source of theoretical tools, principally his notions of *horizontal* and *vertical discourse* and *horizontal* and *hierarchical knowledge structures*.[2] As in other recent work that in various, diverse ways argues that specialised knowledge (esoteric/vertical discourse) and everyday knowledge (mundane/horizontal discourse) are incommensurable,[3] Moore and Muller dismiss the "Discourse of 'Voice'" as inadequate: for them, as essentially a position-taking strategy that undermines not only the (re)production of erudite knowledge when it is taken seriously but also, for that very reason, itself! Their initial description of this "Discourse" aligns it with

> approaches that question epistemological claims about the objectivity of knowledge (and the status of science, reason and rationality, more generally) [and which] adopt, or at least favour or imply, a form of perspectivism which sees knowledge and truth claims as being relative to a culture, form of life or standpoint and, therefore, ultimately representing a particular perspective and social interest rather than independent, universalistic criteria. They complete this reduction by translating knowledge claims into statements about knowers. Knowledge is translated into knowing and priority is given to experience as specialised by category membership and identity. [...] Today, the most common form of this approach is that which, drawing on

postmodernist and poststructuralist perspectives, adopts a discursive concern with the explication of 'voice.' (Moore & Muller 1999: 189–90)

Moore and Muller state that the episodic recurrence of "voice discourse" and its apparent resilience, despite the death of its *bête noire*—"a simplistic and positivistic caricature of science"(189)—as well as continued criticism against it, demands explanation and suggest explaining voice discourse by way of a description of the structuring of the intellectual field. What they end up doing, using Bernstein, is producing a structural description of voice discourse that demonstrates its inadequacy with respect to the production and reproduction of vertical discourse. The description they generate constitutes, at one and the same time, the diagnosis and treatment of the intellectual malady they term voice discourse—not unlike Freud's approach to hysterical symptoms in which diagnosis and treatment constitute a single path. Unfortunately, unlike hysterical symptoms which dissolve as a consequence of their description, "voice discourse" proves to be much more resilient.

Moore and Muller convincingly demonstrate that voice discourse is ultimately a moral discourse that undermines the idea of knowledge by reducing epistemology to morality (192). The theory of vertical and horizontal discourse that they draw on foregrounds the structuring of discourse and is not immediately concerned with the moral dimension of the pedagogizing of knowledge in the transmission and acquisition of culture even though the theory is used in the description and analysis of pedagogic discourse (see Bernstein 1996, 2000). We should not succumb to the argument of the proponents of voice discourse by reproducing the message of that discourse in its converse form: since the attack on knowledge by voice discourse is motivated by a moral/political concern with the differential acquisition of legitimated, high-status knowledge, *what is immediately at stake is the moral order of the pedagogizing of knowledge* and not knowledge structure. This is not to deny that the proponents of voice discourse produce a solution to a moral/political question by ignoring the structuring of different categories of knowledge and so are rightly criticised on the basis of differences in structure.

What the work of Moore and Muller begins to make apparent is an impasse in curriculum theory in which the central antagonism that inheres in the (re)production of knowledge is crystallised—the Universal/Particular dialectic—in the form of an opposition between knowledge (as it is concerned with the production of universal statements) and morality (as it is concerned with the existential specificity of individuals), and it is the earlier Bernstein of the *pedagogic device* and *pedagogic discourse* rather than the more recent Bernstein of horizontal and vertical discourses who might prove more productive in addressing such issues. A centring on the theory of vertical and horizontal discourses without placing it in the context of Bernstein's earlier work runs the risk of aligning vertical discourse with the universal and horizontal discourse with the particular. In other words, the opposition *context independent/context dependent* cannot be translated into an opposition of the form *universal/particular*.

Pedagogic Discourse and the Moral Order

The problem of the relation between the universal and particular is pertinent to all discourse, to all knowledge and truth claims, to all language. To demonstrate that Bernstein's earlier work maintains rather than avoids the problem of the relation between the universal and particular we start with an examination of his discussion of *recontextualising rules* of the pedagogic device, and specifically, what he calls the *imaginary* in the production of pedagogic discourse:

> Pedagogic discourse is a principle for the circulation and reordering of discourses [...] for delocating a discourse, for relocating it, for refocusing it, according to its own principle....Now in this process of delocating a discourse (manual, mental, expressive), that is, taking a discourse from its original site of effectiveness and moving it to a pedagogic site, a gap or rather a space is created....As the discourse moves from its original site to its new positioning as pedagogic discourse, a transformation takes place. The transformation takes place because every time a discourse moves from one position to another, there is a space in which ideology can play. No discourse ever moves without ideology at play. As this discourse moves, it is ideologically transformed; it is not the same discourse any longer. I will suggest that as this discourse moves, it is transformed from an actual discourse, from an unmediated discourse to an imaginary discourse. As pedagogic discourse appropriates various discourses, unmediated discourses are transformed into mediated, virtual or imaginary discourses. From this point of view, pedagogic discourse selectively creates imaginary subjects. (Bernstein 1996: 47; italics in the original.)

In the constitution of pedagogic discourse, however, the signifiers of a specific discourse are brought into relations with signifiers from other discourses (e.g., developmental psychology, theories of instruction) which necessarily effects a measure of reordering, indicated by Bernstein as the relation between an *instructional discourse* (ID) and a *regulative discourse* (RD):

> What is pedagogic discourse? [...] a rule which embeds two discourses; a discourse of skills of various kinds and their relations to each other, and a discourse of social order. Pedagogic discourse embeds rules which create skills of one kind or another and rules regulating their relationship to each other, and rules which create social order.
>
> We shall call the discourse which creates specialized skills and their relationship to each other *instructional discourse*, and the moral discourse which creates order, relations and identity *regulative discourse*. We can write it as follows:
>
> $$\frac{\text{INSTRUCTIONAL DISCOURSE}}{\text{REGULATIVE DISCOURSE}} \quad \frac{ID}{RD}$$
>
> This is to show that the instructional discourse is embedded in the regulative discourse, and that the regulative discourse is the dominant discourse. Pedagogic discourse is a rule which leads to the embedding of one discourse in another, to create one text, to create one discourse. (Bernstein 1996: 46; italics in the original)

We can understand the Lacanian subject as that which, while "represented" by the signifier, is produced by the *failure* of representation: the subject is the excess which escapes signification, and this excess is produced by the very attempt at signification.[4] It follows that the subject is never a "subject position," which is instead an attempt to deal with the trauma of the alienation of being that inheres in language. The positioning of the subject is therefore always "imaginary." We should not fail to notice the extension of the range of Bernstein's "imaginary" beyond pedagogic discourse implied here: the existence of the signifier supposes the subject and so *all* discourse, whether construed as mediated or not, produces "imaginary subjects" as "subject positions." Conceived of in this way, Bernstein's argument apropos the production of "imaginary subjects" in pedagogic discourse links with the Lacanian notion of symbolic identity (the multitude of "subject positions") produced by fantasy. In other words, Bernstein's *imaginary* points to Lacan's *fantasy*, where fantasy is the mediator between the "formal symbolic structure and the positivity of the objects we encounter in reality" (Žižek 1994: 7). It follows from this that pedagogic discourse always relies on a phantasmatic background. In order to explicate this thesis we need to further fill out the features[5] of the Lacanian notion of fantasy, and we shall begin by way of a consideration of the concept of *boundary* in Bernstein:

If the categories of either agents or discourse are specialised, then each category necessarily has its own specific identity and its own specific boundaries. The speciality of each boundary is created, maintained and reproduced only if the relations between the categories of which a given category is a member are preserved. What is to be preserved? The insulation between the categories. It is the strength of insulation that creates a space in which a category becomes specific. (Bernstein 1990: 23; italics in the original)

What is the structural effect of a "boundary"? Let us approach this question by way of reference to popular culture, the 1998 film version of Nabokov's *Lolita:* the illicit love affair between Humbert and Lolita is apparently sustained only by their use of the automobile as a prosthesis that enables the suspension of the public Law.[6] What is of primary interest here, however, is the disproportion between *inside* and *outside,* in the surplus of the inside with respect to the outside. To see this clearly we should attend to the automobile as that which enables the constitution of a boundary apparently separating the lovers from the Symbolic Order, from the big Other. In what does the excess of the inside consist? Precisely in the *fantasy space* in which the lovers can be lovers, like a dream in which the constraints imposed by the big Other are suspended. In the case of *Lolita* the automobile is apparently the materialisation of the boundary, but we should not miss the more important point that it is precisely the fantasy that produces the automobile as boundary. This phantasmatic excess is not the excess of the material over the discursive, but an excess that is generally absent from post-structuralist accounts of ideology in which the rejection of the notion of boundary is correlative to the occulting of fantasy as productive of reality. The inadequacy of the boundary metaphor criticised by Dowling (1998) is precisely the index of its theoretical truth, for the boundary and its maintenance show the way to the phantasmatic support of ideology.

The phantasmatic mediation is nothing other than the teaching of what and how to desire; in Bernstein's terms, the transmission and acquisition of recognition and realisation rules. This brings us to another feature of fantasy—its thoroughly *intersubjective structure.* "Desire is the desire of the Other" since the fundamental question regarding desire is not "What do I want?" but "What does the Other want from me?" and it is fantasy that provides an answer to this question.[7] We can now see how Bernstein's imaginary pedagogic subject is the desiring subject bound to the moral Law, and consciousness is embedded in conscience as expressed in Bernstein's discussion of pedagogic discourse, and that such an operation requires phantas-

sion of pedagogic discourse, and that such an operation requires phantasmatic mediation (Bernstein, 1990: 185).

Figure 1: Pedagogic Discourse

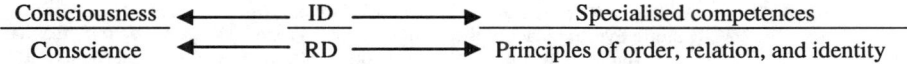

The "embedding" referred to by Bernstein is nothing other than the production of a hegemonic particular that stands in for the universal since universal is always "in-itself" empty. We can see this by taking an example from the recent developments in mathematics education in South Africa: tracking the changing conceptions of the "teacher"—a central agent of symbolic control as subject-supposed-to-know—from so-called "traditional teaching" to a neo-Piagetian "constructivist" pedagogy called the "Problem-Centred Approach," to Curriculum 2005 (see Figure 2). Here the signifier /teacher/ functions as an empty universal that achieves a semblance of positivity only as an effect of the operation that produces it as identical to a particular hegemonic content. That is, from the field of particular contents contesting the conception of /teacher/, a particular content emerges as the universal. It follows that there is always a gap between the particular hegemonic content and the field of particular contents. However, this is not sufficient for the realisation of hegemony because

> [...] every hegemonic universality has to incorporate at least two particular contents: the 'authentic' popular content and its 'distortion' by the relations of domination and exploitation. (Žižek 1999: 184; italics in the original.)

How is the incorporation of an "authentic" popular content into a hegemonic universality? By means of a common element against which the field of particular contents rails. In other words, by means of a coherence around the disavowal of a symptomatic excess that threatens to subvert the universal. In the case of the mathematics education "community" in South Africa, at present it is the notion of the "traditional teacher" that functions as the symptomatic excess that makes possible a political alliance that would have been unheard of in the recent past. In this instance, it is explicit teaching that is under attack, and, in a sense, it is teaching itself that comes to be disavowed as indexed by its replacement with so-called "facilitation."

Figure 2: Different Pedagogies as Hegemonic Pedagogic Discourse

	Empty UNIVERSAL: *Teacher*		
	"Traditional Teaching"	Problem-Centered Approach	OBE (Outcomes-based Education)
PARTICULAR hegemonic content = UNIVERSAL	Subject-supposed-to-know is "mature": Moral, authoritative, upholder of the law; student text constrained to mathematics and must exhibit standard forms of expression. [Teaching≡Demonstration of disciplinary practice; devotion to a discipline (mathematics) within the confines of the Law]	Subject-supposed-to-know is "rational": non-egocentric and non-sociocentric; student texts constrained to mathematics, but idiosyncratic expression is encouraged. [Teaching ≡Rational practice; i.e, the apparent absence of intellectual constraint]	Subject-supposed-to-know the *democratic practitioner/* "facilitator"; student texts are not constrained to mathematics. [Teaching≡Managing democratic access to "relevant" knowledge for all irrespective of race, sex, religion, class....]
GAP			
FIELD OF particular contents	Problem-Centred Approach, People's Mathematics, Critical-Mathematics Education, Humanistic Mathematics Education, Realistic Mathematics Education, Montessori Education...., "traditional teaching"	Problem-Centred Approach, People's Mathematics, Critical-Mathematics Education, Humanistic Mathematics Education, Realistic Mathematics Education, Outcomes-based Education, Montessori Education...., "traditional teaching"	Problem-Centred Approach, People's Mathematics, Critical-Mathematics Education, Humanistic Mathematics Education, Realistic Mathematics Education, OBE, Montessori Education...., "traditional teaching"
GAP			
INDIVIDUAL symptomatic excess	Anti-teaching≡All pedagogies that challenge the Law or do not maintain insulation	Anti-teaching ≡ "Traditional teaching" and any other pedagogy that effects intellectual constraint	Anti-teaching≡ "Traditional teaching" and any other pedagogy that attempts to insulate disciplines
	Subject-supposed-to-know permissive and potentially lawless: anti-social subversive	Subject-supposed-to-know caught up in ideology: egocentric and sociocentric	Subject-supposed-to-know authoritarian, anti-democratic

Now, considering that we are dealing with pedagogic discourse which, by definition, takes as its other ignorance (the subject-supposed-not-to-know), we should consider the relation between ignorance and enjoyment. In

Lacanian terms ignorance is intolerable to the public Law (the moral order) because it conveys a hidden dimension of illicit enjoyment and so cannot function as a sufficient reason for forgiveness of the violation of prohibitions: where we don't know, we enjoy, escaping the Name-of-the-Father. In other words, what we have in Lacanian terms is a split in ideology between the public Law and the illegal enjoyment which emerges from the incomplete character of the public Law.

In order to maintain its semblance of consistency, to guard itself against disintegration, the public Law has to rely on the support of a supplement which is the *cohesion of the community* for which the Law operates. However, while the "community" defines itself formally in the public Law, that is not its point of cohesion, for to be "one of us" is a relation, or social bond, predicated on specific forms of enjoyment, and the intriguing aspect of this enjoyment is that it need not be legal.[8] The form of the Law realised in an enjoyment which acts as the necessary supplement of the public Law is the *superego,* and it is from the superego that the injunction to enjoy issues. Ideological "meaning" is expressed in the public Law which guarantees meaning; enjoyment issues from the superego, the unacknowledged support of meaning. So, when considering the relation between ignorance and enjoyment with respect to pedagogic discourse we should take these two, apparently antithetical, aspects together: on the one hand, ignorance is the index of an intolerable illegal enjoyment escaping the public Law, while on the other hand the public Law requires support in an enjoyment that is at once its Other. Apropos of pedagogic discourse we should, therefore, extend Bernstein's definition: yes, the regulative discourse—in which the instructional discourse is embedded—is the dominant discourse, but it is not sufficient; it must be supplemented by enjoyment. ID/RD should be transformed into the instructional discourse embedded in the public regulative discourse supplemented by a superegoic regulative discourse:

$$\frac{ID}{RD_{public} \wedge RD_{superego}}$$

A difficulty for the reproduction of specialised knowledge is the location of libidinal satisfaction for, in some way, pedagogic discourse must effect a transference of libidinal satisfaction from the specific practices through which the subject derives enjoyment to the reproduction of specialised knowledge. Our discussion of the relation between the public Law and enjoyment now begins to illuminate the ongoing concern of voice discourse with the quotidian in a new way, and it also suggests a possible reconfiguration of our understanding of the relation between Bernstein's vertical and horizontal discourses (Bernstein 1999). Since the superego injunction to enjoy can be realised only in terms of particularities of the subject's everyday activity, it intersects with horizontal discourse, and it is precisely the elements of horizontal discourse that voice discourse takes as the apparent content of the "relevant" specificity of the subject's being in the world. In other words, the "modality" of enjoyment apparently staged in voice discourse is extra-disciplinary but in order to effect a transference of libidinal satisfaction to the practising of school knowledge.[9] Of course there is no way in which the particular relevance of a task can capture exactly the enjoyment of the student; at best the extra-disciplinary "contexts" that voice discourse exploits can be evocative. It follows that relevance creates a space in the structure for a content that cannot be specified—namely, those forms of enjoyment evoked rather than signified directly. In this way relevance circulates around a hole, or empty place, in the structure of pedagogic discourse, which is precisely the place of *jouissance,* of *objet petit a,* of the subject.[10] And it is this aspect of the empty place at the heart of pedagogic discourse that is not explicitly accounted for in Bernstein's theory of the pedagogic device. In other words, the play of ideology in Bernstein's discursive gap is not all; the play of *jouissance*, and, therefore, of the (Lacanian) subject, must also be considered. It is Lacan's discussion of the "four discourses" that provides us with a description of discourse that explicitly includes a consideration of *jouissance* and the subject, and it is to that discussion that we now turn.

The Structure of the Four Discourses

We recall the Lacanian "formulae" for the four discourses as they appear in *Le seminaire, livre XVII: L'envers de la psychanalyse* (See figure 3).

In his account of the four discourses, Lacan seeks to combine what he considers the fundamental relations in which discourse subsists—the intrasubjective relations, the intersubjective relations and the relations, with nonhuman phenomena—into a single model.[11] The different discursive structures produce four intrasubjective factors—knowledge, values, alienation, and *jouissance*—in a manner that produces four intersubjective effects: educating, governing, desiring, and analysing. The latter production is effected through the intrasubjective factors taking up of different positions in the fundamental relational matrix:

$$\frac{\text{Agent}}{\text{Truth}} \rightarrow \frac{\text{Other}}{\text{Production}}$$

The structure of the matrix can be grasped by viewing it as a description of a message passing between a sender and a receiver. For our purposes, we are ultimately concerned with the messages produced by and constituting pedagogic discourse. Of course, Bernstein's *pedagogic device* is already, like Lacan's fundamental matrix, a description of the *carrier*, or *relay*, of discourse. The difference between the two is that Lacan, perversely for post-)structuralists, includes both "structure" and "agency" in his model—in other words, he is already "beyond structuralism and hermeneutics"!—while Bernstein focuses largely on structure. In still other words, the Lacanian formulation attempts to grasp the paradoxical relationship between "structure" and "agency" rather than attempting to dissolve either one or both of them and in which the subject is "the empty place in the structure." What Lacan produces, then, is a third way in which contradiction is the very index of theoretical truth: at the heart of structure Lacan inserts the Cartesian *cogito*.[12]

Figure 3: Lacan's Four Discourses

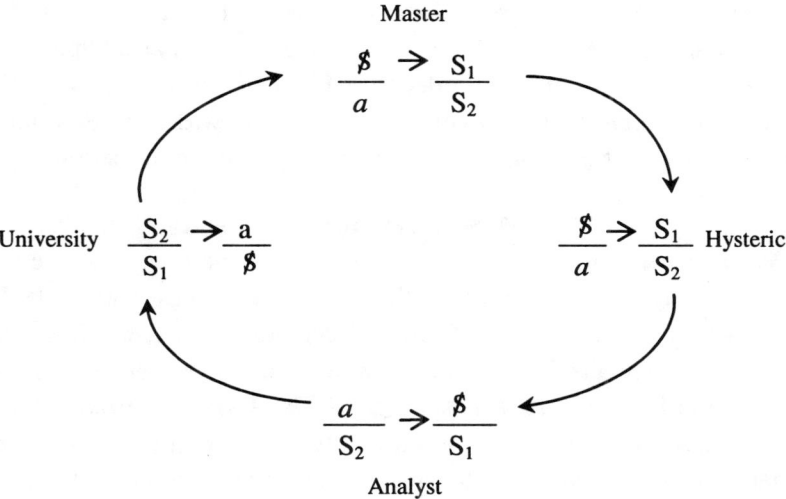

In the fundamental matrix the top position is manifest and the bottom covert (or repressed). More specifically the four positions should be understood as follows:

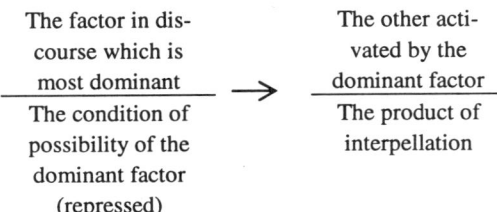

The four factors, written as Lacanian mathemes,[13] are:

S_1: the master signifier(s)
S_2: the system of knowledge (chain of signifiers)
$\$$: the split (alienated) subject
a: *plus-de-jour* (*objet petit a*)

Master signifiers which play a constitutive role in discourse, are essentially secondary identifications and registers of the subject's identifications, be they positive or negative identifications. For Lacan, master signifiers are what produce meaning for the subject, structuring both the subject and discourse. The *system of knowledge* is the chain of signifiers. The *split subject* is an effect of S_1 because identification can never be total and also because identifications do each other collateral damage; they are antagonistic. The subject is, however, also an effect of S_1 in another way: as a hypothesis—the subject has to be assumed in order to explain the very existence of master signifiers. *Objet petit a* is produced simultaneously with $\$$ as S_1 structures S_2 and is that which is both produced by and left out of identification.

The Master and the University

We can begin to explicate the central difference between the two discourses of immediate interest at this point—the Master and the University—by way of an example from popular culture: a scene from the film version[14] of Peter Shaffer's *Amadeus,* where we witness the response of Emperor Joseph II to the first performance of *The Abduction from the Seraglio.* After hearty congratulations, significantly first offered to the soprano, Katharina Cavalieri, and then to Mozart, the emperor proceeds to elaborate a "critique" of the work:

JOSEPH: Brava, Madame! You are an ornament to our stage.

CAVALIERI: Majesty!

All are applauding Cavalieri. The Emperor turns to Mozart.

JOSEPH: Well, Herr Mozart! A good effort. Decidedly that. An excellent effort! You've shown us something ... quite new today.

Mozart bows frantically: he is over-excited.

MOZART: It is new, it is, isn't it, Sire?

JOSEPH: Yes, indeed.

MOZART: So then you like it? You really like it, Your Majesty?

JOSEPH: Of course I do. It's very good. Of course now and then—just now and then—it gets a touch...

MOZART: What do you mean, Sire?

JOSEPH: Well, I mean occasionally it seems to have, how shall one say? (He stops in difficulty; to Orsini-Rosenberg) How shall one say, Director?

ORSINI-ROSENBERG: Too many notes, Majesty?

JOSEPH: Exactly. Very well put. Too many notes.

MOZART: I don't understand. There are just as many notes, Majesty, as are required. Neither more nor less.

JOSEPH: My dear fellow, there are in fact only so many notes the ear can hear in the course of an evening. I think I'm right in saying that, aren't I, Court Composer?

SALIERI: Yes! yes! er, on the whole, yes, Majesty.

MOZART: (to Salieri) But this is absurd!

JOSEPH: My dear, young man, don't take it too hard. Your work is ingenious. It's quality work. And there are simply too many notes, that's all. Cut a few and it will be perfect.

MOZART: Which few did you have in mind, Majesty?

Pause. General embarrassment.[15]

So, the opera, according to Joseph, contains "too many notes," and the perplexed Mozart cannot understand the criticism or the consoling advice: "Just cut a few notes and it will be perfect." His sarcastic retort, "Which few did you have in mind, Majesty?" is the only adequate response: the emptiness of the Master gesture is brilliantly exposed by taking the Master at his word.[16] Here we have the mastery of the subject confronted by the ignorance of the Master, and this is the central distinction: Mozart is bound to the Discourse of the University in which performance and critique are legitimated by reference to the field of knowledge; the Discourse of the Master, on the other hand, is a discourse of ignorance. However, for Lacan the Discourse of the University constitutes a rationalisation (in Freud's pejorative use of the term) of the Master's gesture in which the chain of signifiers (knowledge, S_2) confronts the *plus-de-jouir,* the potentially destructive enjoyment of the subject (*objet petit a, a*); what is suppressed by presenting knowledge as rational and neutral is the gesture of the Master (the operation of power, S_1), and what is produced is a split, alienated subject ($\$$).

$$\frac{S_2}{S_1} \rightarrow \frac{a}{\$}$$

We witness an attempted rationalisation of the Master's gesture in the same scene from *Amadeus:* when needing to elaborate his "critique" of the opera, Joseph turns to Orsini-Rosenberg and Salieri—those who hold the symbolic mandate of the Discourse of the University as it pertains to music—for a suitable rationalisation: "Too many notes" is the response, and one must assume that while Orsini-Rosenberg and Salieri probably *could* produce a more erudite response to the opera, their being bound to the Master's ignorance forces upon them idiocy as well.

The Master gesture should be grasped as both a constitutive and (apparently) excluded element of the Discourse of the University.[17] The academic strategy today, especially in the social sciences, arts, and humanities, is to mask the Master gesture by incorporating it as an object of study, for example, in the form of the study of *power* and *ideology*. Another strategy is the attempt to proceduralise all human activity, to transform social interaction into a set of communicable rules that hold for all participants, which is precisely about avoiding a traumatic encounter with the *jouissance* of the Other by bureaucratising life. For Lacan, the "purest" realisation of the Discourse of the University is in the form of bureaucratic systems: with bureaucracy the question of being is entirely removed from consideration—all events and phenomena are referred to and structured by a closed chain of signifiers, S_2, in which all (potential) events can be exhausted and responded to, even prior to their actual occurrence.

One of the most significant problems for pedagogic discourse, in Lacanian terms, is how to deal with the "uncivilised" enjoyment (a) it is confronted with because, by ignoring the problem of *jouissance,* the phantasmatic background of pedagogic discourse fails to function as required with the consequence that that which must remain repressed, S_1, returns to spark resistance. The same position was already formulated in part, as we saw earlier, by Freud in his remarks on education, albeit in somewhat different terms: that of the curious relationship between the *pleasure* and *reality principles*.

With respect to the superego and its relation to *jouissance* and the public law, we encounter an interesting inversion that emerges from the antagonism between the quotidian and the academic in late capitalism. Should we always view the irruption of the apparent horizontalising effect of the everyday in the domain of academic practices as merely *that?* Are things not substantially more complex? What we might instead do is take into account the effects of liberal democracy on curricula; that is, we should take into account the most general principle of liberal democracy and late capitalism which is realised in the injunction, "Be yourself!" This injunction is, of course, the peculiar con-temporary realization of the superego imperative "Enjoy!" But what effect does this contemporary modality of "Enjoy!" have on the manner in which the discourses of the Master and the University articulate? In short, the effect is the apparent disappearance of the discourse of the Master *by means of its very generalisation*. In other words, by apparently distributing the performative power of the Master gesture to everyone as a *right,* we attempt to produce (to effectuate) the death of the Master. What happens at this point is an implosion of the performative into itself, and, passing in this way through its inner limit, it mutates into the constative to reveal a locally positive world of viral metonymic movement unobstructed by the (paternal Master) gesture of metaphor.[18] We can now see how the generalisation of the Master gesture functions as the operation that distorts the particular popular content of a hegemonic universal and aligns it with the forces of domination these two demands come together in a transformation that produces a demand for the removal of all boundaries.[19] The effect of such a demand is precisely the refusal of "repressive sublimation," of reigning in the drive in the interest of some greater social good *and also* the transformation of a pedagogic discourse into a bureaucratic discourse that lacks support in S_1, and so is left to itself. Indeed, the matheme for voice discourse is really not the usual one for the Discourse of the Master but instead one from which both S_1 and $\barS$ have been evacuated:

$$\frac{S_2}{a}$$

which is none other than the matheme for a totalitarian subject—what is produced is a thoroughly superegoic discourse.

The Hysteric and the Analyst

The hysterical stance in the intersubjective relation between the subject ($\barS$) and the Other ($\barA$) apropos of separation is one characterised by the (hysterical) subject's constitution of him/herself as the lost object of the other, as that which is missing in the other.[20] It follows that the hysteric, in order to secure a space in the Other, always searches for the points of incompleteness in the Other and offers him/herself as the stop that cancels the lack. We can represent the hysteric-Other relation diagrammatically as in figure 4. It is therefore a structural necessity that the hysteric *always fails* to complete the Other and in that way keeps desire unsatisfied, refusing to be an object of the Other's *jouissance*. So, while the hysteric confronts the Other with a question of Being—"Who am I?"—s/he is doomed to meet any answer with what amounts to the same question once again: "Why am I what you say I am?" The fundamental fantasy of the hysteric, which is a response to separation, has the subject identifying with *objet petit a,* and the position of the object in the structure is assumed by the Other who displays an incompleteness ($\barA$). The Lacanian matheme for the fundamental fantasy of the hysteric is therefore $a \lozenge \barA$, rather than the usual $\barS \lozenge a$. The hysterical subject, in relation to the Other, is a failed prosthetic—a paradoxical object that is both the lack and that which fills the lack.

Figure 4: The Hysteric-Other relation

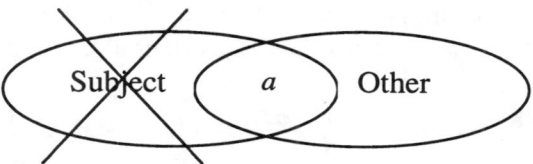

Let us now consider the Discourse of the Hysteric in some detail. Here the split subject ($), is traumatised by the enigma of the other's desire, and demands knowledge (S_2) of her/his status as an object (a) from the other, who s/he addresses as a master (S_1):

$$\frac{\$}{a} \rightarrow \frac{S_1}{S_2}$$

However, the knowledge the hysteric extracts from the other is always met with doubt; that knowledge is always treated as incomplete, provisional, as not quite "It."[21] The hysteric therefore constantly seeks to (re)produce the lack in the Other, homing in on the inconsistencies, slips, pauses in the discourse of the Other. If we accept the Freudian/Lacanian thesis that the real of the unconscious is indicated in the misfiring of the Symbolic Order, then we must conclude that the hysteric ends up seeking encounters with the Real—or, at least, fails to avoid encounters with the Real. The hysteric is the subject who constantly approaches the gap between the ontic and the ontological, which is none other than Bernstein's "potential discursive gap."[22]

When considering the *production* of (erudite) knowledge we should not miss the transformation that occurs when a hysterical stance is adopted towards the gap: the initial "answer" received by the subject adopting such a stance is an enigmatic silence, an empty space which is the object cause of desire: *a*. This is so because the subject approaches the gap by way of the inconsistencies in the Symbolic Order, which means that the Symbolic *cannot*, strictly speaking, answer back other than with silence. The discursive structure that now pertains is that of the Discourse of the Analyst:

$$\frac{a}{S_2} \rightarrow \frac{\$}{S_1}$$

The Symbolic Order takes the position of Agent but in the form of an enigmatic silence (a) confronting the split subject ($\$$) as Other. What gets suppressed in this structure is extant knowledge (S_2), and what gets produced is a new Master-Signifier (S_1), that is, a reconfiguration of the Symbolic Order.

$$\frac{\$}{a} \rightarrow \frac{S_1}{S_2} \Rightarrow \frac{a}{S_2} \rightarrow \frac{\$}{S_1}$$

Of course a shift to the Discourse of the Analyst need not occur. The subject might find a release from the hystericising silence confronted in the gap by reverting once again to the Discourse of the University or the Discourse of the Master, but such a move represents a retreat from the gap rather than a "passing through" it. It should be apparent from the discussion so far that the (academic) subject cannot live in the gap, that it is either passed through or retreated from but never occupied save in psychosis: the Discourses of the University and the Master are precisely those modalities of discourse saving us from abyssal life in the gap, from living in the Real. The ideological battle for control of the gap (Bernstein 1996) can be understood as a battle over the symbolising of the Real. Voice discourse, in effect, forecloses the gap and in that way is apolitical: it replaces the politics of education proper with a battle for cultural recognition.

At the level of the *reproduction* of knowledge, however, things are substantially different. The field of the reproduction of knowledge, within which schooling is situated, exhibits a complex division of labour which should be taken into account in a fuller discussion.[23] For now we shall restrict ourselves to the primary site of transmission and acquisition in schooling: the classroom and the lecture hall. In this site, the "Why ... ?" of the hysterical stance is not directed at the gap but rather at the subject holding the symbolic mandate of the big Other (the-subject-supposed-to-know) because it challenges the interactional practice of the pedagogic context (see figure 5 [Bernstein 1996:31]).[24] In other words, what pertains is a classic transference relation (cf. Salecl 1994). We need to complicate matters a bit by introducing Bernstein's notions of *classification* and *framing* at this point. Briefly, classification refers to the *what* and framing to the *how* of pedagogic discourse, and both are aligned with *power* and *control*, respectively: classification is an effect of power; framing, of control (Figure 6 lists Bernsteinian theoretical concepts in relation to power and control; see Bernstein 1990, 1996).[25] With reference to Bernstein's account of the pedagogic device, the hysterical

"Why ... ?", in confronting the subject-supposed-to-know, must confront both the *what* and the *how* of pedagogic discourse; that is, the policing of both classification and framing.

Figure 5: Pedagogic Context

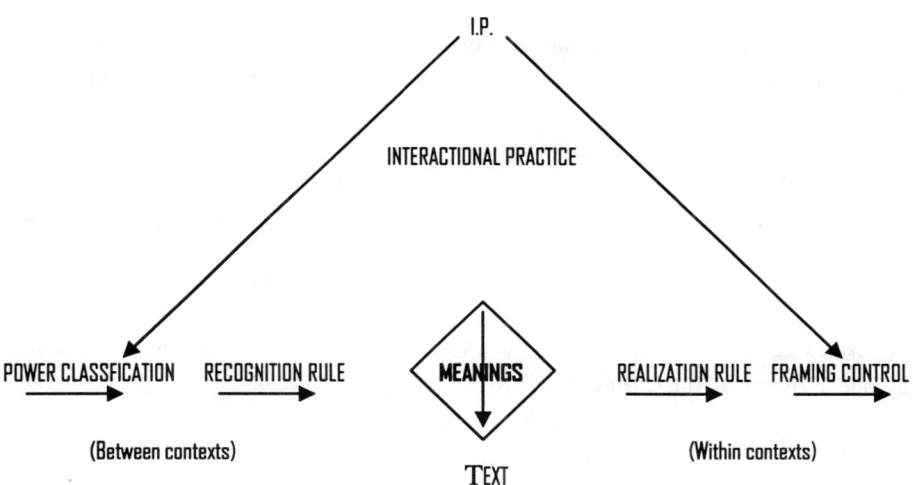

Now, to make things even more complex, we recall that Bernstein defines pedagogic discourse as a discourse of skills and their inter-relations embedded in a discourse of social order (ID/RD), and that the "values" of classification and framing can vary over both the instructional discourse *and* the regulative discourse (Bernstein 1994, 1996).

The hysterical "Why ... ?" therefore addresses classification and framing in both the ID and RD, and since we are dealing strictly with *reproduction* rather than the production of knowledge, it follows that the hysterical gesture should have little or no direct impact on the *classification value of the ID*. In other words, the *what* of the ID of pedagogic discourse—power—is largely unaffected, because if the *what* is impacted on we do not have reproduction but rather *the production of something different*. The space of play for the hysterical gesture in the field of the reproduction of knowledge at the moment of schooling is therefore framing.

Figure 6: Theoretical Concepts Related to Power and Control in Beinstein

Power	Control	
Voice	Message	
Relations between	Relations within	
Structural relations	Interactional practices	
What	How	
Recognition rules	Realisation rules	
Classification	Framing ⇔	• selection of communication
		• its sequencing
		• its pacing
		• the criteria
		• control over the social base that makes communication possible

We can now see why Bernstein (1996: 28) curiously identifies framing as pedagogic discourse in the equation:

$$\text{framing} = \frac{\text{instructional discourse}}{\text{regulative discourse}} \quad \frac{ID}{RD}$$

So, since pedagogic discourse is concerned with the reproduction of knowledge/culture, it generally tends not to disturb the classification value in schooling in order to meet the reproductive imperative with respect to erudite knowledge—a result also captured in Lacan's matheme for the Discourse of the University in which the operation of power, S_1, is masked.[26]

Now, what often appears as merely a weakening of framing is really a change in the external values of both classification and framing. Often pedagogies that claim to be "progressive"—irrespective of their political referents (liberalism, socialism, populism)—apparently relax framing so that the pedagogy is more "participatory," but on closer examination we find that the proponents of such pedagogies enforce *even stricter framing in the form of more detailed and precise rules for social relations and interactions*[27] while actually weakening the insulation between disciplines (the external value of classification) and between disciplinary knowledge and the quotidian (the external value of framing). Where "progressive" pedagogies do not weaken the external value of classification they are forced to resort to teaching techniques that enable teachers to transmit the contents of a discipline while appearing not to do so, as in, for example, the Problem-centred Approach.[28] Both varieties of "progressive" pedagogy referred to here are examples of what Bernstein (1990, 1996) calls "invisible pedagogies" and operate on the guilt of the student. Students are not given explicit access to the recognition and realisation rules of the pedagogic discourse, and this *manufactured ignorance* of the students is used as a marker of their even greater guilt, of their being immersed in a clandestine enjoyment that escapes the Law: the student knows s/he is *a priori* guilty but not what s/he is guilty of.[29] What is produced is an even more terrifying form of control because it references that which does not appear in the public Law but which is its obscene supplement: the superego.[30] The more the students succumb to their guilt, the more guilty they *must* become precisely because, in succumbing to the superego, they give up on their desire. We can see in this, once again, how voice discourse tends towards a totalitarian discourse, one that exerts even greater control over the student than the so-called "authoritarian" pedagogic discourses it seeks to displace.[31] Ironically, from a Lacanian perspective, the signifier /voice/ in "voice discourse" is rather apt in a negative sense: the superego is often conceived of as a disembodied voice searching for a body to which it can attach itself.[32] What voice discourse apparently invokes is the "authentic" voice of "difference," but what it ends up doing is producing a hysterical discourse *that demands the voice of a Master*. This is an entirely different modality of the hysterical gesture in that it is never sustained but instead retreats from the gap in its celebratory narration of self—"Yes! I am indeed It!"—and into the social bond Lacan calls the Discourse of the Master.[33]

Pedagogic discourses that refuse to weaken the external classification value of the ID, like the Problem-centred Approach,[34] attach the guilt of the student to their *ignorance of erudite knowledge which they should already possess without having received explicit instruction:* they are *a priori* guilty because they do not know what they have not yet been taught! Here the extra-school lives of students, of their families and communities, are constructed as risky and/or incoherent and the particular discipline (mathematics, in this case) as a set of techniques that enables the overcoming of risk and incoherence (Davis 1995)—a celebration of "expert systems" in the sense of Beck (1992) and Giddens (1991). Self, family, and community are potentially threatened by the student's ignorance of erudite knowledge: the student's *a priori* guilt is exploited to install the Discourse of the University as social bond—all are bound to erudite knowledge here, teachers as well as students, and neither can appeal to ego- or sociocentrism ("It is so because I say so"; "It is so because that's what people like us believe") because all utterances must refer to the "rational" as it is represented in disciplined argument. In the context of official curriculum production of mathematics curricula in South Africa, we might refer to the Problem-centred Approach as the "vanishing mediator"[35] of the transition from mathematics education under apartheid to "mathematical literacy" in C2005.

Conclusion

It seems clear that, today, under conditions of late capitalism and liberal democracy (sometimes triumphantly declared the age of the decline of Oedipus), curriculum design and policy increasingly have to take into account the vicissitudes of the *jouissance* of the subject in an effort to realise the Discourse of the University, and this is so because of the distortion (by liberalism and late capitalism) of an authentic popular demand for access to erudite knowledge into a demand for the dissolution of all boundaries (which is really a necessary demand of capital). One effect of such a demand is the irruption of *jouissance*. Here we have been discussing two responses to the "problem" of the irruption of *jouissance* for the (re)production of erudite knowledge: one is the attempt to assert ever more firmly and eloquently that the quotidian and specialised knowledge are incommensurable; the other is an attempt to bureaucratise the subject's *jouissance* via discourses of "authenticity" and "voice"; and we have introduced a third response. All the positions—in different ways—recognise the inherent antagonism between desire and *jouissance* and the problems that arise for the Discourse of the University when *jouissance* is apparently allowed (even encouraged) to explode.[36] The first two positions, however, potentially transform pedagogic discourse from being aligned with the Discourse of the University to being aligned with the Discourse of the Master: the first by, ultimately, having to rely on strong assertion in the face of popular demands for access and thereby having to reveal what must remain hidden in the Discourse of the University; the second by pretending that we are all masters and in that way also disrupting the Discourse of the University.[37] The third position is the vanishing mediator that indexes the moment of transformation from the first to the second.

We can also describe the problem in terms of desire and drive. First, we recall that desire and drive are radically antagonistic: desire derives its coordinates from the Law, circulates in the field of castration, and attempts to deal with the renunciation of *jouissance;* the drive is indifferent to prohibition and operates in the field of *jouissance*. The drive is, strictly speaking, lawless and always finds satisfaction, even if it is a painful satisfaction. It is desire that attempts to reign in the drive and protect the subject from the terrible *jouissance* attached to it. In Lacanian terms, the three modalities of the hysterical gesture—which always addresses the enigma of the desire of the other—with respect to the modalities of pedagogic discourse discussed above, might be viewed as follows: first, at the level of the production of erudite knowledge, the hysterical gesture flip-flops into the Discourse of the Analyst *if the subject does not retreat from the gap,* and the hysteric confronts the abyss of the Real and attempts to symbolise it. Second, in those varieties of voice discourse that attempt to solve the moral/political problem of access to knowledge for all by weakening the external values of classification and framing, the subject inhabits the Lacanian Imaginary and is the subject as demand—what results is a Discourse of the Master. Third, the pedagogic discourses that do not disturb the external values of classification and framing but do countenance the changing of their internal values attempt to reproduce the subject as desire and, in that way, to reproduce the Discourse of the University, but they do run the risk of weakening the external values.

These three modalities of the subject correspond to the Lacanian categories of *traversing the fantasy*, *alienation*, and *separation,* and the registers of the Real, the Imaginary, and the Symbolic, respectively (see figure 7). Under alienation, the subject is dominated by the demand of the Other and demands that the Other demand: "Tell me what you want of me!" Under separation, the subject is dominated by the enigma of the Other's desire: "I know what you say, but what do you *really* want?" For the subject as drive, the enigma of desire gives way to the *jouissance* of following the path of desire which is never terminated; that is, the *path itself* becomes the object. In other words, the subject turns away from the demand of the Other and from the enigma of the Other's desire. The problem for curriculum and pedagogy is how to return to desire after *jouissance* has been encouraged to explode. What we are suggesting here is that it is the hysterical stance towards knowledge, especially towards the ID of pedagogic discourse as realised in the Discourse of the Hysteric, at both the levels of the production and the reproduction of knowledge, that ultimately serves the Discourse of the University and guards against the transformation of pedagogic discourse into a Discourse of the Master, which is a discourse of ignorance. Approaching pedagogic discourse by way of the Discourse of the Hysteric in educational research and pedagogic practice opens a space for a more explicit consideration of the *why* of pedagogic discourse, which is backgrounded in Bernstein's focus on the *what* and the *how*.

Figure 7: The Subject as Demand, Desire, and Drive

Alienation	Separation	Traversing the fantasy
Subject as demand (Imaginary)	Subject as desire (Symbolic)	Subject as drive (Real)
$\dfrac{\text{Other}}{\$}$	$\dfrac{\textit{Object petit a}}{\$}$	$\dfrac{\$}{\textit{Objet petit a}}$

Notes

1. Education is a relay for power relations external to it. The degree of success of the relay is not here the point. The pedagogic system's communication in the school, in the nursery, in the home, is the relay for class relations; the relay for gender relations; the relay for religious relations, for regional relations. Pedagogic communication is a relay for patterns of dominance external to itself. I am certainly not denying that this is the case, that it is not true. But if this is what is relayed, what is the medium which makes the relaying possible? It is as if this medium were somehow bland, neutral as air.

    Think of a carrier wave. One can distinguish between the carrier and what is carried. What is carried depends upon the fundamental properties of the wave. Think of hi-fi (assuming you have a hi-fi system). When the tuner is activated, what is heard is a function of the system carrying the signal. What of pedagogic communication? We all know what it relays, but what is the relay? We all know what it carries, but what is the structure that allows, enables it to be carried? This is very similar to a distinction between language and speech. It is as if when we study pedagogic communication we study only the surface features, only its message, not that structure which makes the message possible. At the same time, as with others, when I read (but more often when I travel) it occurrs to me that what we have to account for about educational systems, educational practices, is not how different they are from one society to another but their overwhelming similarity. The most outstanding feature of educational principles and practices is their overwhelming and staggering uniformity independent of the dominant ideology. The question here is, what is it that is generating this stability?" (Bernstein 1990: 168–69)

2. Bernstein on *horizontal* and *vertical discourses:* "A horizontal discourse consists of local, segmentally organised, context-specific and dependent strategies for maximising encounters with persons and habitat" (Bernstein 1996: 171). Also: "A horizontal discourse entails a set of strategies which are local, segmentally organised, context specific and dependent, for maximising encounters with persons and habitat" (Bernstein 1999: 159). And: "Briefly, a vertical discourse takes the form of a coherent, explicit, and systematically principled structure, hierarchically organised, as in the sciences, or it takes the form of a series of specialised languages with specialised modes of interrogation and specialised criteria for the production and circulation of texts, as in the social science and humanities" (ibid.).
3. See Bernstein 1996, 1999; Davis 1995; Dowling 1998; Ensor 1997; Muller & Taylor 1995; and Taylor 1999, for example.
4. This description of the subject is at the same time that of the *objet petit a*, the object-cause of desire—that object which is in the subject more than itself addressed by the chain of signifiers (knowledge) in the Discourse of the University.
5. Here we rely on Žižek's excellent discussion, "The Seven Veils of Fantasy," in Žižek (1997).
6. This, of course, relates precisely to the gaze: today we imagine that the gaze of the public Law can be elided as long as we remain in motion; the gaze not only produces mortification as an effect but requires an acceptance of mortification by that which it seeks to mortify. Disruptions of the love affair in *Lolita* enter when the lovers are stationary—when they pause so that they experience the grasp of the big Other firmly once again.
7. Why fantasy? Because of the enigma of the Other's desire: the Other is unable to tell us what s/he wants. In other words, it is the *lack* in the Other that demands the operation of fantasy.
8. This aspect comes out clearly in instances of legalised discrimination: think, for example, of the relation between the activities of the Ku Klux Klan and the public Law; the night pogroms of the Nazi party and the public Law; the interrogation of dissidents under apartheid and the public Law.
9. Dowling (1998), for example, has brilliantly demonstrated how "relevance" in school mathematics texts used in UK schools does violence to everyday practices and ends up producing "contents" that are *irrelevant* with respect to the everyday. In other words, the "relevance" is produced by and for *school mathematics* and has little to do with the particularities of the extra-school lives of students. But Dowling also shows how, more often than not, such a move backfires in that the "contents" that are produced *are also irrelevant with respect to mathematics*. At the end of the day what is (re)produced is neither mathematics nor the everyday.
10. Here, again, as we shall see below, the structure of Discourse of the University always confronts *objet petit a* as ignorant enjoyment and attempts to civilise it.
11. I rely here on Mark Bracher's (1994) discussion of the four discourses.
12. To conceive of Lacan as a postmodern or poststructuralist misses the point: the Lacanian "subject" is not to be confused with the "subject-positions" of post-moderism/post-structuralism.
13. A *matheme* is the term used for the most basic units of psychical structure.

14. The screenplay was written by Shaffer and is, in places, substantially different from the original play.
15. The extract used here is from the screenplay, which is published on the Internet at http://www.godamongdirectors.com/scripts/Amadeus.txt; slight changes have been made where necessary so that what appears here is the actual dialogue of the film.
16. In a later scene, that of the rehearsal of the *Marriage of Figaro,* Orsini-Rosenberg rips out sections of the score devoted to the dance at Figaro's wedding because "the Emperor has forbidden ballet in his opera." Mozart's strategy is to continue to include the dance, but without music, transforming the sublime into ludic and so demonstrating the vacuity of the Master's edict. Joseph's response is to insist that the music be reinserted, in contradiction of his own law.
17. Perhaps the position of the gesture of the Master in the Discourse of the University can be grasped by way of an example of transference in love. Think of the situation, for example, in which a man spends a great deal of time with a woman, treating her as a very dear friend: he assists her with mundane tasks, acts as her confidant, goes out with her, shares celebratory moments with her, perhaps even sleeps over at her home—in short, he does almost everything a lover would—but resists, for whatever reasons, giving her an unambiguous indication that he wishes to be her lover. When the woman falls in love with someone else, the man suffers a rage of disillusionment, wailing about betrayal: he complains that he has been a "perfect gentlemen" and has been repaid for his sexual restraint with rejection. The point, of course, is that he has received his own message back in inverse form, but we should not miss a more interesting feature: the notion of the "perfect gentleman" employed here is one who relegates sex to the margins, as something alien to that notion "in-itself." When, however, the prospect of sexual union is apparently removed, when the sexual stain is blotted out and the "perfect gentleman" *can* be fully realised, the man's self-description in terms of the category "in-itself" dissolves because its (silent) constitutive element has been subtracted. In a similar way, the erudite neutrality of reason is exploded when the gesture of the Master is recognised in the Discourse of the University, when the stain of the *jouissance* of the Master is apparent—suddenly Universal reason becomes infected with the smutty specificity of self-interest. This is why the hand of the Master must remain hidden in the Discourse of the University.

    In the matrix of the four discourses the position of *truth* is always related to the particular discourse in the manner described here—that is, as necessary yet disavowed: in the Discourse of the Master, it is the truth of the split subject ($\$$); in the Discourse of the University, the truth of the Master gesture (S_1); in the Discourse of the Hysteric, the truth of the object cause of desire and drive (*objet petit a*); and in the Discourse of the Analyst, it is the truth of the chain of knowledge (S_2).
18. The mutation of the performative into the constative is already there in Spinoza: the (divine) Law is only such because of our ignorance; what God is really on about for Spinoza is the description of things *as they are,* rather than the enunciation of the Law (see Spinoza 1989).
19. The injunction to "be oneself," or "know oneself," is also an injunction to be "normal" everywhere. Now, however, "normality" is indexed by the celebration of "difference," of singularity, rather than of commonality. One can see now how to be "everywhere nor-

mal" today demands the apparent suspension of the big Other and its replacement by a series of "small Others" (cf. Žižek 1999c).
20. The three main clinical categories are *neurosis, perversion,* and *psychosis. Hysteria,* along with *obsession* and *phobia,* are the subcategories of *neurosis.*
21. We see here the inherent antagonism between the hysteric and the pervert: the pervert is precisely "It," s/he for whom the *jouissance* of the other is transparent; i.e., s/he who possesses certain knowledge. The perverse stance has, of course, long reflected in advertising: "Coke is it!" and "Just do it!," for example. Indeed, the subject of market relations in late capitalism is a perverse subject (see Žižek 1999b, 1999c).
22. I want to suggest that this gap itself can become (not always) a site for alternative possibilities, for alternative realisations of the relation between the material and the immaterial. The gap itself can change the relation between the material and the immaterial. This potential gap or space, I will suggest, is the site for the unthinkable, the site of the impossible, and this site can clearly be both beneficial and dangerous at the same time. This gap is the meeting point of order and disorder, of coherence and incoherence. "It is the crucial site of the *yet to be thought.*" (Bernstein 1996: 44; italics in the original)
23. See Bernstein (1990), chapter 5, for a detailed discussion of the social construction of discourse.
24. Since both transmitter and acquirer assume the pedagogic relation, by definition, we have both a subject-supposed-to-know and a subject-not-supposed-to-know. See Salecl (1994) for an extended discussion of this point.
25. Classification (C) and framing (F) have both *internal* (i) and *external* (e) values which can be strong (+) or weak (-): C_i concerns the arrangement of space and objects in it; C_e concerns the relations between categories; F_i concerns relations within categories; and F_e concerns control over communications from outside the pedagogic practice entering the pedagogic practice.
26. Rotman (1993), in his discussion of the "constructivist" turn in mathematics, makes the interesting point that all the hullabaloo about the anti-Platonic gesture of constructivism amounts to nothing unless the construction of the counting numbers is disturbed; that is, unless counting can be constructed differently, the constructivist will not (cannot) produce a different mathematics. It would seem that this is precisely what, in school mathematics, for example, the pedagogic constructivists (mistakenly) rely on: we can play around with the internal values of classification and framing because the conditions of possibility for disturbing the external value of classification do not pertain.
27. This is usually not explicitly stated because to do so would again be an "imposition" and therefore potentially authoritarian. What emerges are sets of rules for social interaction that allow all, in principle, to express their own, unique "voice." These rules should not be confused with ritualised practices because ritual is always about the legitimate means, according to our station, for entering the sacred place of the leader or community. In fact, we do not have a unique "voice" in ritual—we approach the sacred along a certain legitimated path, the terminus of which is fully established in advance of the sacred journey. The rules to which we refer constitute instead a bureaucratic mechanism saving us from immersion in a psychotic universe in which the ideal of a polyphonic symphony of "voices" has collapsed into a cacophonic babble of incoherence.

28. See Davis (1996) for a discussion of some of the strategies employed in such pedagogies.
29. That is, a prolongation of the moment of interpellation captured in Althusser's "hailing" metaphor: prior to identification, there is a moment of "pure," abstract guilt in which subjects experience their *a priori* guilt when confronted by the Law (see Althusser 1994).
30. Such forms of control are, of course, common in love relationships. Often one partner is positioned as *a priori* guilty and if s/he succumbs, the other is able to take on the position of Master. In schooling, the student who refuses to confess guilt by "sharing" with others is pathologised, often as someone unable to "risk"—we should point out that when "risking" is the norm, a refusal to "risk" is undoubtedly very risky!
31. It is therefore not surprising that "voice discourse" and so-called "progressive" pedagogic discourses require increasingly sophisticated techniques and apparatuses to extract confessions from students: journal writing, "personal narratives," and public "risking," to name a few. Another important technique is that of "questioning" that apparently reveals "what students always already knew." Yet, as Bernstein (1990, 1996) demonstrates, it is precisely through questioning that the evaluative criteria of pedagogic discourse are transmitted. For Bernstein, at the level of classroom practice, the whole of pedagogic discourse is condensed in the evaluative rules of the pedagogic device.
32. See Žižek (1994) for an extended discussion of this point—specifically his discussion of the mother's voice in relation to the body of Norman Bates in Alfred Hitchcock's *Psycho*.
33. The hysterical discourse that is now produced is one in which the student is hystericised by the teacher in order to produce the student's demand, "Tell me who I am!," which is nothing but the trap of a false promise of the realisation of the self-identical subject, if ever there was one. It matters little whether the answer comes from the teacher or the students themselves—the result is the same. The transference relation is maintained through the foreclosure of the student's potential hystericising of the interlocutor: "Why am I what you say I am?"
34. Even though the PCA texts directed at students make substantial use of extra-mathematical "contexts" without any explicit instruction in how they should be read, the teacher's guides (in which the central elements of the teaching methodology are mapped out for teachers) prescribe that "contexts" are to be redescribed and interpreted in terms of mathematics, and such redescription is modelled for teachers for all the tasks that appear in the texts for student use. When we consider the value of the classification, we should not commit the error so common to postmodernism/poststructuralism of failing to recognise the distinction between the *rule for determining mean* and a *determined meaning*. The "rule of reason," in Saussurian terms, produces an antinomy: on the one hand, the chain of signifiers is inexhaustible—there is always another signifier (unlimited semiosis); on the other hand, the value of any signifier is given by its difference from *all* the other signifiers. The former requirement asserts the necessary *incompleteness* of language (and so of meaning), while the latter asserts the necessary *completion* of language/meaning. What postmodernist/poststructuralist discussions of "deconstruction" often ignore is the latter requirement, that of completion, and end up assuming an absence of stability (see Copjec 1994 for a more detailed discussion). Saussure dealt with his own traumatic rediscovery of the antinomy at the heart of language/meaning by fixing on the synchronic (the complete) aspect, abandoning the diachronic (incompleteness). The

postmodernist/poststructuralist solution is to celebrate the diachronic aspect, ignoring the necessity of maintaining the antinomy. Is the practice of attempting to capture in writing and speech the incompleteness of language/meaning, its instability, not a hankering after that which has been excluded? Since *all* discourse is unstable for poststructuralism/postmodernism, the attempted demonstration of this instability in the form of an aesthetic "style" is unnecessary and, in any event, requires the completion of meaning to be intelligible.

35. See Jameson (1988), especially the chapter, "The Vanishing Mediator; or, Max Weber as Storyteller," and Žižek (1991) for a discussion of the notion of the *vanishing mediator*. The interesting work of Galant (1997) provides an account of the displacement of the principles underpinning the South African school mathematics curriculum under apartheid by principles more compatible with liberalism. What remains to account for is how it is that the new liberal principles contained the means of their own displacement by the principles underpinning "mathematical literacy" in OBE. For the moment we will merely point out that with the dissolution of apartheid, those wielding the political power to redefine the curriculum simply refused to allow the *empty gesture* of liberalism—we are all free to choose—to function as empty and, subversively, took it at its word.

36. The antagonism between desire and *jouissance* is nothing other than the antagonism between desire and drive.

37. Another way of describing the antagonism between the two positions is as follows: the former asserts the impotence of "voice discourse" to generalise, while "voice discourse" asserts the impossibility of producing universal statements about the particular.

References

Althusser, L. (1994). Ideology and ideological state apparatuses (notes towards an investigation). In *Mapping Ideology*. Edited by S. Žižek. London: Verso.

Beck, U. (1992). *The risk society: Towards a new modernity*. London: Sage.

Bernstein, B. (1990). *The structuring of pedagogic discourse. Class, codes, and control*. Vol. 4. London: Routledge.

——— (1996). *Pedagogy, symbolic control, and identity: Theory, research, critique*. London: Taylor & Francis.

——— (1999). Vertical and horizontal discourse: An essay. *British Journal of Sociology of Education* 20 (2): 157–73.

——— (2000). Symbolic control: Issues of empirical description of agencies and agents. Mimeo.

Bracher, M. (1994). On the psychological and social functions of language: Lacan's theory of the four Discourses. In *Lacanian theory of discourse: Subject, structure and society*. Edited by Mark Bracher, Marshall W. Alcorn, Jr., Ronald J. Corthell, and Francoise Massardier-Kenney. New York: New York University Press.

Copjec, J. (1994). *Read my desire*. Cambridge: MIT Press.

Davis Z. (1995). Myth and mathematics: an analysis of the IEB ABE Level 2 Guide In *Exploring Mathematics Teaching & Teacher Education*. Edited by Z. Davis. Cape Town: Mathematics Education Project, University of Cape Town.

────── (1996). *The problem-centred approach and the production of the vanishing pedagogue*. Paper presented to the Kenton–at–Wilgespruit Conference.

────── (1999). *Pedagogy, fantasy and enjoyment in mathematics education:A case study with special reference to the problem-centred approach*. School of Education Seminar Series, University of Cape Town.

────── (2000). *Desire and "jouissance" in pedagogic discourse*. Paper presented to the First Internationalization Curriculum Conference. Louisiana State University, Baton Rouge.

────── (2001). School mathematics as useful pleasure; or, even farther uses of Jeremy Bentham to the living. *Pythagoras 54:* 6–16.

Dowling, P. C. (1998). *The sociology of mathematics education: Mathematical myths/ pedagogic texts*. London: Falmer.

────── (1999). Basil Bernstein in frame: "Oh dear, is this a structuralist analysis?" Located at http://www.ioe.ac.uk/ccs/dowling/kings1999/index.html.

Ensor, P. (1997). School mathematics, everyday life and the NQF: A case of non-equivalence? *Pythagoras 41*: 36–44.

────── (1999). *A study of the recontextualising of pedagogic practices from a South African university preservice mathematics teacher education course by seven beginning secondary mathematics teachers*. Ph.D. diss. Institute of Education, University of London.

────── (1999) The myth of transfer? Teacher education, classroom teaching, and the recontextualising of pedagogic practices. *Pythagoras 50*: 2–14.

Fink, B. (1995a). Science and psychoanalysis. In *Reading seminars XI: Lacan's four fundamental concepts of psychoanalysis*. Edited by Richard Feldstein, Bruce Fink, and Maire Jaanus. Albany: SUNY Press.

────── (1995b). *The Lacanian subject: Between language and jouissance*. Princeton: Princeton University Press.

────── (1997). *A clinical introduction to Lacanian psychoanalysis: Theory and technique*. Cambridge, MA: Harvard University Press.

Freud, S. (1991). *The interpretation of dreams*. London: Penguin (original work published 1913).

────── (1995). An autobiographical study. In *The Freud reader*. Edited by Peter Gay. London: Vintage (original work published in English 1935).

────── and J. Breuer (1974). *Studies on hysteria*. Translation by James Strachey and Alix Strachey. Edited by J. and A. Strachey, assisted by Angela Richards. London: Penguin.

Galant, J. (1997). *Teachers, learners, and mathematics: an analysis of HSRC research reports on mathematics education, 1970–1980*. M. Ed. thesis. School of Education, University of Cape Town.

Giddens, A. (1991). *Modernity and self-identity: Self and society in the late modern age*. Stanford: Stanford University Press.

Holland, J. (1981). Social class and changes in orientation to meaning. *Sociology 15* (1): 1–18.

Jameson, F. (1988). *The ideologies of theory. Vol. 2*. London: Routledge.

Lacan, J., (1977). *The four fundamental concepts of psycho-analysis*. London: Penguin.

────── (1977a). The agency of the letter in the unconscious or reason since Freud. In *Écrits: A selection*. Translation by Alan Sheridan. London: Routledge.

——— (1977b). The subversion of the subject and the dialectic of desire in the Freudian unconscious. In *Écrits: A selection*. London: Routledge.
——— (1982). *Feminine sexuality*. Translation by Jacqueline Rose. Edited by Juliet Mitchell and Jacqueline. Rose London: Norton.
——— (1988a). *The seminar of Jacques Lacan. Book I: Freud's Papers on Technique, 1953–1954*. London: Norton.
——— (1988b). *The seminar of Jacques Lacan, Book II: The ego in Freud's theory and in the technique of psychoanalysis, 1954–1955*. London: Norton.
——— (1992). *The seminar of Jacques Lacan, Book VII: The ethics of psychoanalysis, 1959–1960*. London: Norton.
——— (1993). *The seminar of Jacques Lacan, Book III: The psychoses, 1955–1956*, London: Norton.
——— (1998). *The seminar of Jacques Lacan, Book XX, encore: On feminine sexuality, the limits of love and knowledge, 1972–1973*. London: Norton.
Moore, R., and J. P. Muller (1999). The discourse of "voice" and the problem of knowledge and identity in the sociology of education. In *British Journal of Sociology of Education* 20 (2): 189–206.
Muller, J. P., and N. Taylor (1995). Schooling and everyday life: Knowledges sacred and profane. *Social Epistemology* 9: 257–75.
Republic of South Africa (1997). *Government Gazette 384:* (18051). Pretoria: Government Printer.
Rotman, B. (1993). *Ad Infinitum: The ghost in Turing's machine*, Stanford: Stanford University Press.
Salecl, R. (1994). Deference to the Great Other: The discourse of education. In *Lacanian theory of discourse: Subject, structure and society*. Edited by Mark Bracher, Marshall W. Alcorn, Jr., Ronald J. Corthell, and Francoise Massardier-Kenney. New York: New York University Press.
Shaffer, P. (1980). *Amadeus*. London: Penguin.
Spinoza, B. De (1989). *Ethics:Including, the improvement of understanding*. Translation by R. H. M. Elwes. Buffalo: Prometheus.
Taylor, N. (1999). Curriculum 2005: Finding a balance between school and everyday knowledges. In *Getting learning right: Report of the President's Education Initiative Research Project*. Edited by Nick Taylor and Penny Vinjevold. Johannesburg: Joint Education Trust.
Taylor, N., and P. Vinjevold (1999). Teaching and learning in South African schools. In *Getting learning right: Report of the President's Education Initiative Research Project*. Edited by Nick Taylor and Penny Vinjevold. Johannesburg: Joint Education Trust.
Žižek, S. (1989). *The sublime object of ideology*. London: Verso.
——— (1991). *For they know not what they do: Enjoyment as a political factor*. London: Verso.
——— (1994). *The metastases of enjoyment: Six essays on women and causality*. London: Verso.
——— (1997). *The plague of fantasies*. London: Verso.

——— (1998). Four discourses, four subjects. In *Sic 2: Cogito and the unconscious*. Edited by Slavoj Žižek. Durham: Duke University Press.
——— (1999a). The undergrowth of enjoyment. In *The Žižek Reader*. Edited by Elizabeth Wright and Edmond Wright. London: Blackwell.
——— (1999b). *The ticklish subject: The absent centre of political ontology*. London: Verso.
——— (1999c). "You may!" In *London Review of Books 21* (6), March 18. Also located at http://www.lrb.co.uk/v21.

CHAPTER FIVE

Re-constituting Pedagogies: The (Im)possibilities for Inter/nationalizing Curriculum Studies

Aristides Gazetas • Canada

A new mode of historical study is marked as part of the post-structural movement, mainly as a result of concepts and procedures that it has assimilated from various literary theories and writings of Foucault, Derrida, and Lacan. This (new) historical mode is grounded on the concepts that history itself is not a set of fixed, objective facts but, like the literature with which it interacts, a text which needs to be interpreted; that a text, whether literary or historical, is a discourse which, although it may seem to present or to reflect an external reality, in fact consists of what are called representations, that is, verbal or visual information—or both—which are the "ideological products" or "cultural constructs" of a particular era; and that these cultural and ideological representations in texts (and film narratives) serve mainly to reproduce, confirm and propagate the power structures of domination and subordination which characterize a given modern society (Abrams 1993: 249).

With the rise of global telecommunications and information networks, a desire for an international accord between nation-states is on the horizon. How such space technologies, associated with satellites, will foster a desire for an internationalization of curriculum studies is problematic. On cultural grounds a postmodern sensibility resists this new global system of symbolic interaction and exchange, for while this international system allows for the pursuit of global markets by transnational corporations, it also exposes other nation-states to a new form of media colonialism in which advertising agencies transform "the media and its contents into opportunities to sell ideas, values, products, in short, a consumerist worldview" (Sklair 1991: 76).

Since the Western nation-states control access to the technologies that disseminate information worldwide, the impact on different indigenous cultures becomes a contested cultural space for these people. A "politics of difference" arises with a crisis in representation of cultural identities that are re-positioned by a global economy structured toward the prevailing belief systems and dominant ideologies of the Western world. Here, globalization through space technology advances humankind into an international electronic age now defined as "late capitalism" or "postmodernism." This chapter addresses the concept of cultural pedagogy embedded in a growing "crisis in representation" and knowledge as set forth by Jean-Francois Lyotard in *The Postmodern Condition* (1984). Here, Lyotard argues that science does not simply consist of a neutral body of knowledge claims about the world but rather "produces a discourse of legitimation with respect to its own status, a discourse called philosophy." Lyotard states that the postmodern involves "an incredulity toward metanarratives" and conceives of knowledge as paralogical: that is, as searching for and creating instabilities in the dominant perspectives of the world (xxiii–xxiv). This challenge to the positivist paradigm will be considered within the cinematization of contemporary Western societies. Here I will attempt to determine how the concept of narrative or historical discourse attempts to constitute a cultural pedagogy that operates on two levels: (1) as a communication phenomenon that pedagogically and culturally constructs human identities and role-playing and (2) as a social phenomenon that reinforces or challenges the social order (Mumby 1993: 2). Thus each narrative discourse is "double coded." The new historicism becomes part of the postmodern voice that orientates itself through "little narratives" (*petit recits*) as an alternative way of making knowledge claims about the social world in which we live. Accordingly, Lyotard conceives of "a postmodern sensibility" as one which continually critiques any foundational conception of knowledge. Moreover, it challenges the economic global narrative that is secured through the "logic" of modern education. Further, narrative theory also recognizes the open-ended nature of knowledge claims. It examines the shifting terrain of meaning that makes up the social/political world and acknowledges the difficulty of making any universal claims concerning the nature of the human condition. It also acknowledges that as researchers and educators we are never neutral observers of behavior because of the role we play in the construction of the social reality in any narrative, large or small (Mumby 1993: 3). Today, the postmodern world is caught up within a constant profusion of images produced through film/video by numerous television channels that inform and persuade us about our "imaginary" selves in multiple forms of representation. This new world of the electronic image transmission becomes directly linked to the way motion pictures mediate information about the world out there while advancing discourses about the need for Western transnational companies to be involved in a postwar global economy. By employing the power of the visual media in television broadcasts, every advertisement is a short film narrative making a connection between the reality of the image (mimesis) and the cultural constructs of our society. Therefore, each narrative (diegesis) contains within its illusionistic framework a convincing power to reconstitute reality based upon actual happenings/events. When asked why some people believe in the power of cinema, the producer in Peter Weir's film, *The Truman Show* (1998), responded, "We accept the reality of the world as it is presented to us. It is as simple as that." The implication of this cinematic situation should cause the viewer/spectator to realize that illusions are part of our reality. This becomes the political condition of our lives, as Bertolt Brecht, the German playwright and essayist, declared during the 1920s (Wright 1989: 21).

Before the 1960s, little was written about films that related motion pictures to a broader cultural pedagogy or historical context. Yet, reconsideration of the medium as a valid and respectable subject for research in media studies has been confirmed by the sociological writings of Norman K. Denzin (1991). Denzin's research distinguishes three features of "the cinematization of contemporary life" upon which our visual culture is grounded:

- "Reality" is now a staged, social production.
- The "real" is now judged against its staged cinematic-video counterpart involving cultural formations through mass media.
- The postmodern society "becomes a cinematic, dramaturgical production transformed by representations of the 'real' through the images and meanings that flow from cinema and TV." Hence, the theatrical metaphor that "art not only mirrors life, it structures and...reproduces it" (Denzin 1991: x) has taken over everyday life. He thus concludes the postmodern society is a dramaturgical society.

As part of any analysis or interpretation of the knowledge and power of these film narratives, it is important to identify the social-political discourses that carry the formative ideological frameworks governing the communication and exchange of ideas. The reason for "unmasking" these ideas reflects my assumption that most cultural constructs operate in the society as a way of assigning predetermined social discourses over time. As stated by Bill Nichols, "Ideology uses the fabrications of images and the processes of representation to persuade us that how things are is how they ought to be and that the place provided for us is the place we ought to have" (Nichols 1981: 1).

In the 1990s, Hollywood produced a number of film narratives that undertook to deconstruct the power of cinema to "construct reality" for viewers. First on the scene was Lawrence McTiernan's *Last Action Hero* (1993) starring Arnold Schwarzenegger, who played a superhero who deconstructs his own film persona. Then James Cameron directed *True Lies* (1994), also starring Arnold Schwarzenegger, Bond-like action-adventure that deconstructs the hero when the narrative doubles as a romantic comedy. *The Truman Show* (Weir 1998), convinces us that a television show houses a real-life community, while in *Pleasantville* (1999) two teenagers leave the 1990s and enter the world of the 1950s through a TV situational comedy. Being teenagers, they decide to help the people in this strictly black-and-white small town discover the joys of living out their lives in full colour. Barry Levinson's *Wag the Dog* (1997) is a postmodern parody satirizing the power of television that stars Robert De Niro as a political consultant who creates a television war with Albania to divert media attention from a presidential indiscretion with a young woman in the Oval Office.

These films become part of *The Politics of Postmodernism* (1989). The author, Linda Hutcheon, asserts that "postmodern fiction often thematizes this process of turning events into facts through the filtering and interpreting of archival documents. In 'historiographic metafiction' the very process of turning events into facts through the re-interpretation of archival evidence is shown to be a process of turning the traces of the past (our only access to those events today) into new historical representations." She continues to argue that "in a very real sense, post-modernism reveals a desire to understand present culture as the product of previous representations. The representation of history becomes the history of representation" (58). We can easily view this on television through the History Channel, a station that deliberately broadcasts film narratives to present a "historical event" as if it were a true history. The programming is called "History on Film." Thus, film narratives play a large part in the images and identities of ourselves and our world that are constantly saturating the environment through the news media, television sitcom, and the computer networks on the "information highway" of the Internet.

In "Simulations" (1983), Jean Baudrillard views these images as cultural constructs by the media and not reflective of real "lived experiences" of our world. He has already predicted that the Western world has reached the saturation point and suggests that the "mirror of production" has replaced our understanding of ourselves or our knowledge of "reality" since we entered the era of the "simulacra." Henceforth, in this world of simulacrum, Baudrillard states that when the "map engenders the territory" in which everything is a generational copy of everything else, we find "a proliferation of myths of origin and signs of reality...a panic stricken production of the real and the referential" (10–12). This is the space of the "hyperreal." It breaks down the interconnectedness of humankind with their own perceptions of themselves in the modern world, creating a "political unconscious," that, according to Frederic Jameson (1982), raises the individual to the collective level where narrative discourses operate to repress change, opposition and, most of all, revolution. Knowledge as power now functions as a form of social control in diverse communication contexts in which images of identity conceal the discourses of a late capitalist, postmodern global world of endless production and consumption.

A poststructural movement in philosophy, history, and psychology has surfaced to challenge all "master narratives" of this "late modern" society through a deconstruction of the "regimes of truth" and their focus on reason, objectivity and certainty by foregrounding ambiguity, contingency, and pluralism that break open the binary systems of Western rationality.

Further, authors diverse as Wittgenstein, Kuhn, and Foucault argue that objects of knowledge are locally and historically specific, and that they become available for human understanding only within certain "language games," "paradigms shifts," and "discursive formations." Speaking from these different positions, postmodernism contains multiple histories that attempt to seek out and destroy the dominance of any unitary linear historical narrative that functions as the foundation of Western thought. This notion suggests that our identities, beliefs, and practices are culturally "contingent" upon such construction of paradigms or models, subject to revisions or paradigm shifts but not tied to any single historical determinism. Foucault calls these measures part of a disciplinary society where all future conflicts appear already won in advance by this cultural society since the exercise of power and the forces policing this power are no longer visible. They are now hidden, diversified, and strong enough to avoid battle.

Commenting upon a postmodern approach to modern curriculum, Henry Giroux states in his foreword to David Trend's book *Cultural Pedagogy* (1992):

> the new work on pedagogy instead views the practice as a form of political and cultural production deeply implicated in the construction of knowledge, subjectivities and social relations....Increasingly, the link between education and cultural work has been viewed in light of recent developments in feminism, cultural studies, deconstruction postcolonialism, and the new historicism....In part, this means taking up pedagogy as a form of cultural politics that addresses how art get produced and how it comes to function in the broader community. Trend wants art and pedagogy to refigure [or re-constitute] a variety of human experiences within a discourse in which diverse political views, sexual orientations, races, ethnicities and cultural differences can coexist amid social relations that support free expression and uninhibited debate. (1992: vii)

However, Trend's new discourse on pedagogy has not been able to develop a theory of articulation that links or connects the work of cultural workers in a variety of public spheres. What, asks Giroux, is the relationship then, between pedagogical practice and cultural production which links education in the broader sense to the relevancies shared by diverse cultural workers that would bring about a postmodern democracy? (Giroux, cited in Trend 1992: viii)

Yet, Trend's cultural pedagogy demonstrates the multiple connections that film narratives serve to open up as possibilities for an international curriculum. As educative yet subversive art forms, many Euro-American and Latin American film narratives afford educators a perspective implicated in the production of and support for different cultural discourses. These film narratives provide a dramatic rendering in the relation of the "self" and "other" within the dynamics of Western hegemonic thought. A group of different film narratives of the 1970s and 1980s, now broadcast over television, are international in scope, ranging from Coppola's *Apocalypse Now* (1979), Fassbinder's *Ali: Fear Eats the Soul* (1973), Bertolucci's *The Conformist* (1970), Peter Weir's *Gallipoli* (1981), Antonioni's *The Passenger* (1975), to Von Trotta's *Marianne and Juliane* (1982).

Marianne and Juliane is a film narrative that constructs identities of women within a "disciplinary society" based upon a reconstruction and remembrance of the past. Von Trotta's film is a modern re-presentation of the Sophoclean drama *Antigone* adapted to modern times, in which the central conflict emerges between the political tactics of an "urban terrorist" the hidden powers of a police state. More in keeping with the Sophoclean tragedy, Von Trotta shows the effects of such power on the body of the victim in episode after episode and declines to represent the power that inflicts such punishment on her "crime." The film narrative "doubles" then, both as a critique on the roles played by women in film narrative and on the surveillance and identification of a subversive group of terrorists in protest against the abuses of power by a totalitarian German government. Seen through the perspective of Foucault's writing of history as "genealogy," the film depicts the rise of fascism in Germany in the 1930s and its impact upon two young women to illustrate how a "disciplinary regime…brought individuality into the field of observation through a vast meticulous documentary apparatus" (Dreyfus & Rabinow 1982: 122).

In many ways, the critical writings of Michel Foucault address the different effects of the power/knowledge connection as reconstituted in these film discourses. Foucault claims a new type of power and control came into existence in Europe at the end of the nineteenth century that he designates as "disciplinary power." It is concerned with the regulation and surveillance of the human species and the governance of the individual through the mind and the body. It is sited in the new institutions of the modern world, from schools and hospitals to workshops and prisons, etc., infiltrating and shaping what is said and done. Its purpose is to produce human beings as "docile bodies" through the power of administrative regimes and the expertise of the professional (Foucault 1980: 104–108). Foucault's writings, moreover, illustrate an ironic discourse describing how power relationships are historically reconstructed in the serious theatre of discipline and surveillance played out in a series of petty, melodramatic theatres hiding behind moral-political, legal and philosophical justifications and ideals. However, the "great, tragic theatre" of the past no longer survives. As Foucault describes in *Discipline and Punish* (1977), the theatre of public torture and execution allowed the public to act as participants in the public ritual where the execution could be resisted and possibly reversed. Foucault states that this public theatre, where power is seen face to face, has been displaced by the theatre of discipline and surveillance. Now, any intervention by the public is neutralized, and, as if they were watching the event unfold on the TV screen, the public are only spectators to the interrogations and are silenced by being kept in their own place. All that remains in the theatre of surveillance and discipline are "thousands of tiny theatres of punishment" (Foucault 1977: 113) that provide for a regulating form of interrogation in a hazardous play of dominations to produce "docile bodies."

Power and authority remain invisible, masked by various discourses in education, knowledge, humanist ideology, judicial reform, etc., as is the case with different TV programs on "Law and Order." This is "serious theatre with its multiple and persuasive scenes," which is more absolute and is all the less successfully combated by the public. If there is, indeed, a rupture between modern society and what has begun to be called the postmodern sensibility, what are the characteristic features of this critical antifoundational culture? Moreover, what is significant in the intellectual refusal to respect traditional hierarchies, transgress high culture, blur boundaries of authority, and challenge the dominant discourses on the way the Western world has been structured? What changes are now underway to reorganize and restructure capitalism and the global economy within a new model of commodification known as the "Free Market"? And can the cultural diversity of a global economy prepare for a new history based upon a global democracy that will survive the fragmentation, de-centering, and inequalities of opportunities created by the revolution in telecommunications?

From an adult learner's perspective, this chapter leads to an acknowledgment that any discourse is a conceptual framework for purposes of power and control. Education has been part of this modernist construction, appearing as "a politics of representation" between self and other, fact and fiction, power and knowledge in verbal and visual narratives. Within the development of these modern pedagogies, education served as a rational feature in the regulatory practices of schools. It is through the power of such educational techniques that one's identity and subjectivity are produced and organized. Representations of learners/educators, readers/spectators are part of a planned outcome in which "modernity's grand narratives, the Enlightenment ideals of critical reason, individual freedom, progress, and benevolent change, are substantiated and realized" (Usher and Edwards 1994: 2). By inherently accepting the modernist discourse on education the possibilities of a more open inter/nationalized study of curriculum would be constrained by an "already given" self/Other dichotomy.

However, in a study of ways to internationalize curriculum within different world cultures, educational theorists may wish to explore the nature of hybridity (Bhabha 1994) and how the "floating signifier" of identity activates a metonymic contiguity against the repressive "force of logic" and institutional "conventions and fetishes." As part of the language games played by educators on students within a "reality" existing as a "staged, social production," such reexaminations of educational theory and practice allow for a space in between master narratives. In this space of hybridity, opportunities are established for a disengagement and disruption of these narrative codes of language, cultural values, and ideological goals of modernism. Here an irony emerges which neither attacks nor mocks but irritates "because it denies us certainties by unmasking the world as ambiguity" (Kundera 1986: 134).

As a manifestation of today's information society and its popular culture, contemporary film narratives act as persuasive historical documents that introduce social and political realities into our educational systems. These narratives, in turn, influence our notions of identity and place with regard to the means in which ideas and power relations pervade institutions of government and their educational institutions. Today, in fact, with the emergence of global communications, all areas of our social-political life are under the mediation and surveillance of such technologies. I might even suggest that such film narratives function pragmatically as political myths about fashioning imaginative selves that challenge or justify the contemporary conduct and actions of people operating in the tensions of a space of ambiguity and uncertainty, designated by Homi Bhabha as the "Third Space." And as cultural artifacts, these film narratives let us play with multiple identities within an imaginative world of cinema.

In *The Location of Culture* (1994), Homi Bhabha advances the concept of a "politics of difference" by creating what he terms a Third Space, a space for translation and negotiation where hybridization can be constructed. The formation of any narrative thus contains both the cultural story and the transformation of the story simultaneously. This strategy emphasizes alterity and otherness in a sharing of self with the Other. It emphasizes the linguistic notion of metonymy rather than metaphor as its dominant trope. In practice, cultural differences become frames of reference that drive a desire to fill the void. This desire emphasizes "a process of political articulation and political negotiation across a whole range of contradictory social sites" (Bhabha, quoted in Rutherford 1990: 220). Then, a cultural hybridity arises in this in-between space and taps into a translation of what is actually happening in the world. The process of cultural hybridity thus can give rise to something different, something new and unrecognizable, a new area of negotiation of meaning and representation (211).

By eschewing polarities, a Third Space induces a hybrid moment of political change. A new area of meaning and representation proceeds from imaginary and symbolic forms of the contact with the narrative through a conflictual identification with the object of otherness, a psychoanalytical process of identifying with and through another object, with the differences of the Other. In the interview, "The Third Space," conducted by Jonathan Rutherford (1990), Bhabha is asked to explain his notions of the terms "translation" and "hybridity." Bhabha replies that translation is a form of cultural translation "both as representation and reproduction" insofar as "all cultures are in the process of hybridity." Thus we can speak of translation not in a strictly linguistic sense, "but as a motif or trope," which is:

> also a way of imitating, but in a mischievous, displacing sense—imitating an original in such a way that the priority of the original is not reinforced but by the very fact it can be simulated, copied, transferred, transformed, made into a simulacrum and so on....What this really means is that cultures are only constituted in relation to that otherness internal to their own symbol forming activity which makes them decentered structures—through that displacement or liminality opens up the possibility of articulating different, even incommensurable cultural practices and priorities. (210–11)

Bhabha uses the notion of hybridity as the Third Space which he claims allows the position of cultural difference and translation to emerge. In response to the question, "Is the Third Space an identity as such?" Bhabha replies:

> No, not so much identity as identification (in the psychological sense). I try to talk about hybridity through a psychoanalytical analogy so that identification is a process of identifying with and through another object, an object of otherness, at which point the agency of identification—the subject—is itself always ambivalent, because of the intervention of that otherness. (211)

In Bhabha's contestation with standard practices of interpretation on a literal level, he challenges the preemptive knowledge accorded to empiricism and its rationality that "writers say what they mean and mean what they say." But the effect of writing, warns Minh-ha T. Trinh in *Framer Framed* (1992), is that it challenges "the direct relationship between the reader's reading and the text's telling" (230). The "question of belief" is raised when doubting the authenticity of the image/word and the veracity of the writer. As a writer and Third Cinema filmmaker, Trinh attempts to articulate this Third Space as an

> always-emerging-already-distorted place that remains so difficult, on the one hand, for the Western World even to recognize, and on the other, for our own communities to accept to venture into, for fear of losing what has been a costly gain through past struggles. (Trinh 1992: 139)

The Third Space is a hybrid reality where "the metaphysics of presence" offered by the Enlightenment finds itself confronted by its Other—or the negativity of space—the absence of presence—The Void. In her film, *Surname Viet Given Name Nam* (1989), Trinh understands this negative space as one "that makes both composition and framing possible, that characterizes the way an image breathes" (1992:142). Further, this space is a generative space since it is the relationship between I and the Not-I. Its vitality is produced by the tensionality "in this site that makes forms and contents possible but also inseparable." In her own poststructural film ethnographies, Trinh observes play within the paradox of the true and the false, between "imagined selves" and their counterpart, thus between the real and the staged, or "necessary illusions."

In *Surname Viet Given Name Nam* Trinh juxtaposes a series of "real" interviews with the women in the first part with a re-enactment of the same interview with the same women in a different time and place. Trinh is working to achieve a critical space in the viewing of her film. This process of recognition, of the form and content of her work, produces an uncomfortable uncertainty between performance and non-performance in each narrative. The illusion/reality paradox enforces a *Brechtian distanciation* rather than *an Aristotelian empathy*. Once a reader or viewer is located in the space in between presence and absence, illusion and reality, fact and fiction, power and knowledge, the reader/viewer is more cognizant that film is more readily the place where Derrida's "absence of a presence" can more easily be contemplated. In conclusion, we can understand both Bhabha and Trinh as they move beyond the fixed spaces of modernity's "cultural binaryism" in order for both student and teacher alike to enter(tain) a Third Space "eluding the politics of polarity." It is a generative space in between different cultures that recognizes the power of cultural translation "as a politics of constructing meaning" (Trinh 1992: 127–8). This poststructural approach may also allow for the reconstituting of new pedagogies in the interstices between different cultural worlds in the manner Trinh has developed in her own ethnographies. It also may provide possibilities for links to and connections with alternative ways of negotiating differences. All this is to remind educators that the postmodern age is both playful and paradoxical, where the power of late capitalism attempts to turn all cultural constructs into perpetuating myths or master narratives (Denzin 1991: 151). The globalization of the economy, using the hi-tech forces of the Internet, implicates everyone with forms of cultural hybridity.

References

Abrams, M. H. (1993). *A glossary of literary terms*. 6th ed. New York: Harcourt, Brace, Jovanovich.

Bhabha, H. K. (1990). Interview with Homi Bhabha: The Third Space. In *Identity: Community, culture, difference*. Edited by J. Rutherford. London: Lawrence & Wishart.

———— (1994). *The location of culture*. London: Routledge.

Baudrillard, J. (1975). *The mirror of production*. St. Louis, Miss.: Telos.

———— (1983). Simulations. In *Semiotext(e)*. Translated by Paul Foss, Paul Patton, and Philip Beitchman. New York: Columbia University Press.

Denzin, N. K. (1991). *Images of postmodern society: Social theory and contemporary cinema*. London: Sage.

Dreyfus, H., and P. Rabinow (1982). *Michel Foucault: Beyond structuralism and hermeneutics*. Brighton: Harvester.

Foucault, M. (1970). *The order of things: An archaeology of the human sciences*. Translation by Alan Sheridan. New York: Random House (French edition 1966).

———— (1972). *The archaeology of knowledge*. Translation by Alan Sheridan. New York: Pantheon.

———— (1977). *Discipline and punish: The birth of the prison*. Translation by Alan Sheridan. New York: Pantheon.

———— (1980). *Power/knowledge: Selected interviews & other writings, 1972–1977*. Translation by Colin Gordon. Edited by C. Gordon et al. New York: Pantheon.

———— (1984). *Nietzsche, genealogy, history*. In *The Foucault Reader*. Translation by Donald F. Bouchard and Sherry Simon. Edited by P. Rabinow. New York: Pantheon.

Freire, P. (1972). *Pedagogy of the oppressed*. New York: Herder & Herder.

———— (1985). *The politics of education: Culture, power, and liberation*. With an introduction by H. A. Giroux. New York: Bergin & Garvey.

Hutcheon, L. (1989). *The politics of postmodernism*. London: Routledge.

Jameson, F. (1982). *The political unconscious: Narrative as a socially symbolic act*. Ithaca, New York: Cornell University Press.

Kundera, M. (1986). *The art of the novel*. New York: Harper & Row.

Lather, P. A. (1991). *Getting smart: Feminist research and pedagogy with/in the postmodern*. New York: Routledge.

Leitch, V. B. (1983). *Deconstructive criticism: An advanced introduction*. New York: Columbia University Press.

Lyotard, J.-F. (1984). *The postmodern condition: A report on knowledge*. Translation by Geoff Bennington and Brian Massumi. Foreword by F. Jameson. Minneapolis: University of Minnesota Press.
Mumby, D. K. (Ed.) (1993). *Narrative and social control: Critical perspectives*. London: Sage.
Nichols, B. (1981). *Ideology and the image*. Bloomington: Indiana University Press.
Rutherford, J. (Ed.) (1990). Interview with Homi Bhabha: The Third Space. In *Identity: Community, culture, difference*. London: Lawrence & Wishart.
Shor, I. (1992). *Empowering education: Critical teaching for social change*. Chicago: University of Chicago Press.
Sklair, L. (1991). *Sociology and the global system*. Hemel Hempstead: Harvester Wheatsheaf.
Trend, D. (1992). *Cultural pedagogy: Art/education/politics*. New York: Bergin & Garvey.
Trinh, M. T. (1992). *Framer framed*. New York: Routledge.
Usher, R., and R. Edwards (1994). *Postmodernism and education*. New York and London: Routledge.
Wright, E. (1989). *Postmodern Brecht: A re-presentation*. London: Routledge.

CHAPTER SIX

Reflections on a Dialogue about Education for the Future

Urve Läänemets • Estonia

My African colleague Sid Pandey and I were paired off for the dialogue at the Louisiana conference as representatives of the post-colonial world. We really were in the same boat, considering the need for educational innovation in both of our countries after foreign rule and cultural dominance over a considerable period of time. Although these influences were of totally different origin, representing perhaps West and East in their most characteristic way, post-colonial developments in our countries seem to have a lot in common. These common tendencies could be specified as tasks and problems in the following fields: to lead a life of one's own, to be included and accepted in the global village as a democratic country, and the development of the values and content of learning for the twenty-first century. My contribution here is a discussion of developments and aftereffects in post-socialist countries.

To Lead a Life of One's Own

After the collapse of the Soviet Union, all post-socialist countries manifested innovative programs for their educational systems. This was also accompanied by an upsurge of national identity (Thom 1997). Despite nationalism's bad reputation in the West and its history of dangerous effects, the majority of sociologists consider it a positive phenomenon in the post-socialist world if understood as a factor for preserving and developing ethnic identities and diversities within a common cultural heritage. This creates a kind of defensive nationalism, which contributes to the survival of languages and cultures of small nations and in which education is one of the most powerful factors and curriculum development for general education of the whole population has a particular meaning.

Any curriculum in the broadest sense of the concept has to convey and develop values that strengthen an individual's capacities and capabilities to become included in the society in which s/he lives as well as develop or preserve society at large, establishing and maintaining its cohesion. According to research and educational practice, curriculum also has to contribute to the preservation and development of culture. In a changing world, the need for a reformulation of curriculum periodically appears, and under the new circumstances of the twenty-first century, the tempo of expected and relevant educational change has accelerated. The post-socialist countries have had to overcome considerably greater tensions which are still present between current curriculum prescriptions and perceptions of emerging new educational expectations for society. These tensions and developments in the post-socialist countries offer a lot of food for theoretical thought.

In order to be on one's own, special identity-building fields of curriculum deserve particular attention: namely, the learning of languages, history, and civics. Although the initial position for the change in Estonia and Botswana was more or less similar, developments have progressed in different directions.

For development of a national curriculum, some have studied Western educational literature on curriculum theory and design; some have followed and copied the educational experiences of different countries; some have tried to keep a more balanced approach and have preserved traditional versions of the content of education. Several post-socialist countries have considered it fashionable to ignore the development of educational ideas in Russia. Following or directly copying the examples of the West actually means that aspirations for being on one's own cannot be implemented without considering common internationally created theoretical knowledge and experience in the field. Accordingly, developments have been extremely different and the so-called "opening-up" period of the recent decade has produced results as well as problems. Although the content of education as well as the processes of learning have changed, there are still several national curricula that should be classified as atheoretical or ahistorical.

Being on one's own, as a principle, could find better implementation if the traditional and efficient elements of an educational culture of a country could be preserved but also developed and enriched by new and acceptable ideas of different origins. This is particularly true regarding learning as a cultural phenomenon supported by instructional psychology. Another factor in curriculum development and its practical implementation is its openness regarding the content of learning and school management. Several countries in the world (e.g., France) offer no particular choice of subjects or in the design of educational processes. However, some post-socialist countries, including Estonia, have introduced considerable freedom, allowing high schools to decide the educational content for about one-third of the study time (*Estonian National Curriculum* 1996). This, in its turn, has offered good opportunities for individual learners to make better choices while at the same time it has created undesirably great differences in educational quality, as shown in the results of national examinations.

A totally new factor influencing education directly is the transition of post-socialist countries to a market economy. First, it provided new educational content with the introduction of new subjects and courses offering basic economic and business knowledge and skills in general. At the same time, it offered new opportunities for learning in better educational environments, as private fee-paying educational institutions became available for those who could afford them. The transition of market economy principles to education during the past decade has greatly influenced implementation of the aforementioned aspirations by development of both a more flexible access to education and a greater stratification of society.

To conclude, we have to admit that it has not been particularly easy for any post-socialist country to achieve the aim of being on one's own, and in the globalized world of today we have to understand the role and limits of such aspirations. Cultural diversity can be best preserved in balanced educational environments, which can support educational progress towards lifelong learning, inclusion, and cost-efficient use of available material and intellectual resources in the society.

To Be Included and Accepted in the Global Village as a Democratic Country

Post-socialist countries in their aspirations to be included and accepted as a democratic country have to develop a new approach, that of open discussions, to all educational problems and to those of curricula in particular. The selection of any learning content remains culturally and politically coloured and its relevance to learners' needs can be objectively evaluated only over time. For international cooperation and professional discussions, however, we need some common ground and understanding. It is no easy task to decide about the content or processes of learning in spite of the fact that we all have access to and the opportunity to develop different forms of the organization of knowledge and skills usually specified as general comprehensive education.

Christopher Wynch (1996) writes:

> The selection of subjects to appear on the curriculum is a complex matter influenced by many factors. The question of the worthwhileness of different subjects is a matter of negotiations and compromise between different groups. At first sight, it would appear that the question of integrity of standards within subjects would be far easier to resolve. There are two aspects to intra-subject measures. The first is the diachronic aspect and relates to whether or not performances and the standards used to measure them change over time. The second is the synchronic aspect and is to do with whether or not they vary from educational institution to institution. The notion of educational standards is a fairly restricted one that does not encompass all aspects of educational achievement. In particular, it does not encompass a concern for values or long-term outcomes that some see as important aims of any worthwhile educational process. Those who focus on worthwhileness of education and, in so doing tend to emphasize levels of achievement in fairly tangible forms such as acquisition of skill, knowledge or understanding, will generally accept that there is a range of educational processes that are morally acceptable but will, within that range, advocate those that produce the highest educational performances. Those who make process rather than product the main focus of concern do not necessarily fall into the confusion of thinking that an educational process need not have an outcome, but will emphasize the intangible and long-term nature of educational outcomes and their process dependence. The key points are that what can be assessed should be assessed, and it should be clearly indicated, which aspects of education cannot be assessed so that the public understand the limitations of accountability and can make proper decisions to those forms of education which they wish to support. (63–64)

For curriculum development for the future I would suggest the following fields of inquiry:

1. Development of a core curriculum, offered as a necessary aspect of democracy, "establishing publicly known and acknowledged agreements about the substance of universal schooling" (*OECD/CERI Report* 1994). However, the content of learning as well as its organization must be periodically redetermined if we consider intellectual flexibility to be the main object of education. The perspective is to make academic sense to all young people by clarifying a common core of knowledge and moral values, to prepare their

minds for constant adaptation as well as to help them understand the meaning and inevitability of lifelong learning in their own lives.

2. Development of cross-curricular contents with the development of personal competencies in various fields for building different identities. These aspirations can be identified for consistent treatment in some or all subjects, which can result in new cohesive content or in particular subject cycles in the curriculum. The use of a series of topics as the basis for cross-curriculum studies—including international and (multi)cultural studies, civics, environmental issues, consumer awareness, health, information technology, entrepreneurship education, and so on—can be considered meaningful for change regarding the globalization of human communication as well as regional peculiarities. Although economic development has always been dependent on providing the latest knowledge that could lead to success in the global marketplace, education still remains a moral enterprise, entirely concerned with the development of the minds of learners of different age groups and different socio-cultural backgrounds. It has already led to the emergence of new strategically important content areas as well as the development of new school subjects.

3. For the development of individual identity building, particular knowledges and skills are needed (communication, math, critical and creative thinking, technology, comprehension of social values) which can lead to personal independence, civic responsibility, and the ability to modify oneself (by finding appropriate social roles for a particular time) and one's environment according to developmental needs. It also is important to develop an ability to recognize and avoid undesired developments locally as well as globally, preparing people for wider participation, and social mobility, ensuring loyalty and the capability of sharing common values. These competencies can be developed in different ways, gained by various learning experience offered not only by school subjects. However, all personal competencies developed by formal and informal education will remain individual and integrated according to the diversity of personal learning and life experience. These competencies should also help people avoid unemployment as a structural property of post-modern society in the twenty-first century by allowing them to reconstruct themselves so that they can be included a professional society or other social organizations by the acquisition of different identities. It also is important to influence the development of positive attitudes towards human and natural surroundings.

4. Structural models for selection of the content and specification of

frameworks for designing school curricula in which special educational needs and cultural and social tensions caused by the changing world can be developed. Two models of curriculum design for implementation in school practice have been devised:

- Hilda Taba (1962) called curricula "plans for learning." She suggested some ways of organizing particular activities which could lead the students to consider their capabilities to comprehend the world around them, to see possible causes behind social developments, and to participate in everyday life as responsible citizens. What kind of plans for learning should we work for today? More or less the same is expected of people today, in the beginning of the twenty-first century, and we, educationists, try to compile the best plans for learning for the young people who we expect to make our world a better place. How to decide about these plans and about the future at the same time requires a dialogue between all concerned about education at large as well as on the individual level.

- The European Commission issued in 1995 a White Paper on Education and Training with the title "Teaching and Learning—Towards the Learning Society." This document manifests three major trends or "factors of upheaval in society": internationalization of trade, the dawning of the information society, and the relentless march of science and technology, all with their different impacts. The European Commission also offered two answers which education and training can provide in eliminating the pernicious effects of those factors, namely, reintroducing the merits of a broad base of knowledge and building up employability. Among guidelines for desired actions are five suggested objectives, which are meant primarily to provide food for thought and which in no way set out to impinge on national responsibilities. These objectives are the following:

- Encourage the acquisition of new knowledge, i.e., raise the general level of knowledge;
- Bring school and the business sector closer together by developing apprenticeship in Europe in all its forms;
- Combat exclusion: offer a second chance to complete school by a complementary system which has been successfully tested in the United States;
- Promote proficiency in three Community languages, as language proficiency has become essential for getting a job and for mobility of the labour force in general;
- Treat material investment and investment in training on an equal basis

making education and training a priority (The European Commission 1995: 5–11).

That is how Europe expects to prove that it is not only a free-trade area but a coherent political whole capable of coming successfully to terms with internationalization while preserving traditional values and cultural identities. However, our constantly changing world has influenced curriculum developments in all countries, although educational innovation has proceeded under various economic and political circumstances. One of the basic truths recognized by researchers and practitioners is that of the globalization of education, which, in its turn, has led to the search for a common core of general education in particular.

Problems of curriculum design became especially important in many post-socialist countries after the collapse of the socialist empire when innovational change in education was unavoidable. The development of new curricula for different educational levels and types of schools started almost immediately, and soon first- draft versions appeared.

Constant change in our contemporary world has become somewhat overexploited, and the keyword "flexibility" has triggered extensive debates on what is actually worth learning and what could be considered meaningful in education at large. Attempts have been made to specify dimensions of education, such as regional education, e.g., a European dimension, and others, relevant on a smaller scale of applicability. In this period of change it has become evident that those responsible for state systems of education should develop an improved ability to read and learn from theories, practices, and proposals and to acquire a surer understanding of the cultural and philosophical roots of issues in curriculum design, which, in turn, could create educational options for managing the change on the level of an individual, group, or nation.

Different countries have different cultural values and traditions, and smaller countries, in particular, have to be conscious of and caring about their human resources. This is probably the main reason why general education and its outcomes that affect both academic knowledge and social skills deserve special attention. Systems of compulsory general education are supposed to guarantee some kind of educational minimum which would enable students to meet the needs of society, not only in regard to the demands of the labour market but also in the management of their own lives. In observing educational developments in different countries, we cannot fail to notice that in some places (e.g., Norway and others) the period of compulsory schooling has reached ten years (eighteen years of age). Society at large has recognized equal access to education as a social benefit every country has to provide if development and social stability are the acknowledged common goals. School reforms of recent years in several countries constitute a cultural reform, which, for example, will "help provide good conditions for children and adolescents as they grow up with a wealth of impulses in varied learning environments and where creative activities and forms of expression will become an important part of everyday life of the school, in collaboration with local cultural institutions" (Norwegian Research and Church Affairs 1997: 1).

We should bear in mind that educational reforms, including curriculum reforms, are planned and implemented developments, and the governments of respective countries have the power and responsibility in these processes. Educational reforms also reflect the change of values in a society and consensus about new goals, that take into account the more distant future of the country. The new social agreement about changed values means innovation and change in curricula in different educational institutions within the country, but it may also have a broader effect and influence educational change globally, for instance, with the influence of new info-technologies.

How to Develop an Adequate Curriculum?

There are different approaches to curriculum planning and design which may lay stress on different aspects and extend over different periods of time. All of them have their positive as well as negative characteristics. If there is to be a balance among educational objectives, content of education, processes of learning, and desired social and individual outcomes, all of them have to be managed. Priorities have to be specified, and those aspects of curriculum development which could be labeled as secondary should be compensated by relevant measures, e.g., teacher training or systems of social benefits, motivating the acquisition of education on a particular level. Still we have to consider which approach to use and in what way we can contribute to the development of curricula. Considering the globalization of problems, some common core of curriculum which could be considered globally acceptable and meaningful has to be developed.

Sharing the Common: Building the Core Curriculum

Development of a core curriculum, offered it as a necessary aspect of democracy, could be characterized as "establishing publicly known and acknowledged agreements about the substance of universal schooling" (OECD/CERI Report 1994). Generally recognized ideas for this are usually expressed by such educational aims as development of the capabilities to manage one's life and to be able to adjust oneself to the changing world. It is not very easy to specify this due to different cultural and social values. However, we should think first of what we need for the development of intercultural communication. Z.T. Hasanow (1998) has established theoretical and methodological principles for development of this particular type of culture with relevant personal social skills, which deserve particular attention in designing the content of civics as a school subject. All societies need this culture for the development of social cohesion and integration of the population for identity building within the state.

Accordingly, we can establish some vital fields of knowledge which would enable us to develop the above-mentioned intercultural communication skills. This probably has been the reason for special attention being given to learning regional and community languages, history, and civics in all societies in the East as well as the West.

Language learning has become one of the educational priorities in the European Union (EU) as different language skills can foster and support international communication, personal identity building, labour force, mobility, and social stability. Multilingualism is represented in different forms and linguistic combinations in various countries. According to national language strategies, new approaches can be developed in the field of general education for all the population, considering both the longitudinal research data characterizing the tendencies in societies and political aspirations. Comparison of the social demand for different languages and particular language skills in various countries has been carried out for the first time. The research methodology used in these studies might be of interest for further and more specific language research, including possibilities for improving the processes of language learning.

Political changes always have their impact on practical language use. A political colouring of language use can be observed also in relations between the new Baltic states. Peeter Vares (1993) summarizes this as follows:

> It has always been difficult for the Baltic states to reach a linguistic understanding: unlike the Nordic nations their national languages do not have anything in common. The situation became more complicated after the re-obtained independence: Russian has ceased to be a common language for communication, whereas efficient use of

English, not to mention other foreign languages, still seems to be a matter for the distant future. (23)

Small nations are destined to be multilingual. That is the case for Estonians, who have been influenced by their geopolitical position as well as by various developments of history. The same could be said about the representatives of larger nationalities living as immigrants in foreign states, far away from their native places. Every subsequent language acquired after the native language makes the person not only bilingual but also bicultural, even if the other culture is very different from the language learner's native culture. A person speaking another language cannot avoid development of a kind of cultural awareness, which grows proportionally with the level of competence in the target language. German, for instance, has left its mark on nearly every sphere of culture in Estonia—architecture, language, music, arts—and influenced people's values and way of life in general.

There is a new type of hidden agenda to be considered. As mentioned before, multilingualism develops multiculturalism. New languages bring information about new values and unavoidably influence the people involved. Multilingualism creates wider linguistic and cultural awareness but also will create problems with self-identification and the acquisition of new multiple identities in Estonia. (Allardt 1979: 39; Byram 1989: 38). New barriers have emerged in communication which deserve at least open discussion. Research has shown new tendencies to both integration and disintegration (Kirch, et al. 1992; Proos and Pettai 1994).

As T. Skutnab-Kangas (1995) has pointed out, "nice phrases about the worth of everybody's mother tongue, the value of interculturalism, etc., serve little purpose, unless they are followed up, in how schools are organized" (13). Language education in general comprehensive schools has proved to be the cheapest means of offering language education and also the most reliable, as practically everybody has to attend these schools. Proficiency in globally and regionally important languages also plays an important role in the development of understanding and tolerance as it enables access to the cultural heritage of different countries.

Effective Civic Education with Learning History and Culture

Informed decision making in this particular field for content selection can contribute most to the development of tolerance and social and political stability in the world. Many curriculum developers have tried to include various socially sensitive and culturally relevant themes in new curricula. Developments in Estonia have been quite similar to those in other post-socialist countries, and maybe our experience can help explain the change of educational content in a period of great political fluctuations.

Curriculum development for general comprehensive schools started in 1989 after Gorbachev's *perestroika* had reached the republic, a few years before independence was regained (in 1991). The main aspirations were directed towards changing the approach to the social sciences, especially history and civics. At the same time attempts were made to preserve the encyclopedic content of general education and the high academic levels of math and science. However, new political values also became clearly reflected in the rearranged content of history and civics. New ideas of democratic society building brought new viewpoints for organizing social studies altogether. Changes such as the following were suggested:
- Civic education should be required at every level of the school curriculum, and it should become a central goal of education.
- Civic education should be interdisciplinary and of high quality and sufficient quantity, with the emphasis on how to think rather than on what to think—historical as well as contemporary topics should be included.
- Civic education should reflect community realities and a balance between conflicting social values and political viewpoints and enable participation in the community life.
- Civic education methodology should be primarily interactive. (Valdma 1996)

The result of a declared priority of civic education gave rise to the establishment of a large number of separate small subject courses, all related to human studies. Students began home environment studies, family education, health education, communication, psychology, civics (lower-level course for grade nine at the end of compulsory school and for grade twelve at the end of upper secondary school, etc.), human rights, and street law as optional subjects, which were all considered necessary and important in their own right as well as new and innovative. Unfortunately, in Estonia they have remained up to this day separate subjects and have not yet developed into a meaningful and integrated course of social studies (*Estonian National Curriculum* 1996), although amendments to the existing national curriculum were completed in 2002.

Social studies as an integrated school subject or a cycle of related subjects of human studies has to belong to the core curriculum of all educational systems, as it is the most powerful mechanism for enabling socialization of the people in their environments.

Another field of knowledge has recently gained importance, especially considering the globalization of economy and of business in particular. This field is usually represented in curricula as economic geography of the world (e.g., German *Abiturgeographie*). This subject has to be based on general geography, which can develop a broader comprehension of the world as a social, cultural, ecological, and economic system that has to be kept in balance if we want to survive.

Therefore, a core curriculum could serve as a central axis of global educational content. Its perspective is to make academic and practical sense to all young people by clarifying a shared core of knowledge and moral values and to prepare their minds for constant adaptation as well as to help them understand the meaning and inevitability of lifelong learning caused by constant changes in their own lives. However the content of learning as well as its organization must be periodically revised and redetermined, considering intellectual flexibility as the main object of education. The core curriculum can construct the shared identity of every person as belonging to mankind and as a human and social being in our controversial world.

Development of Cross-curricular Content and Personal Competencies for Building Different Identities

According to Oskar Mader (1979), all theories for developing national curricula as documents of educational content and learning should be dedicated to fostering the development of the culture, society, and the individual person. It means that in addition to globally accepted values and contents, there has to be a special area of developing one's individual characteristics and identities. For cohesion in society a series of topics as the basis for cross curriculum studies usually include international, (multi)cultural, civics, environmental, consumer, health, information technology, and entrepreneurship education. These can be considered meaningful for constantly changing life and globalization of human communication of different kinds as well as regional peculiarities. Although economic development has always been dependent on how widely and rapidly the latest knowledge that could lead to success in the global marketplace can be offered to people, education still remains a moral enterprise, entirely concerned with the development of the minds of learners of different age groups and different socio-cultural backgrounds. Every new global challenge has inevitably led to the emergence of new strategically important content areas (e.g., Sputnik's shock in the 1960, the implementation of computers, etc.) as well as the development of new school subjects.

The more related people become through interactive technology, the more information they get, and accordingly, there will be more and more opportunities to discover the acceptable and meaningful in numerous fields of human communication. These, in turn, may develop for people different feelings of belonging to some particular values or fields of knowledge, as education can make them comprehensible and acceptable. In addition to traditional family and ethnic identities, new identities of belonging to rather different and often international social groups and organizations can be established. The more identities the person may find it possible to take, the quicker s/he has to establish a hierarchy of identities, and the final result is usually a personal priority list of belonging; some identities become accepted and some rejected. These processes, in their turn, may develop intolerance and even conflict, which can endanger social stability on any level of social organization.

Accordingly, for organizing learning, for developing the three aforementioned identity fields, development of a particular curriculum area or cross-curricular contents and activities can be identified for consistent treatment, which can result in a new cohesive content or particular subject cycles in the curriculum and new fields of integration. This might be called a culture-specific aspect of curriculum development, which meets the demands of a particular region, and considers the value and meaning of specified knowledges and skills required for everyday human activities, as well as for the establishment of a basis for future development.

Culture specific aspects are always regionally coloured, according to the geopolitical position of the country and its demographic situation. In Estonia, with its 1.5 million people about one-third of the population speak Russian in their everyday communication, and about 120 different ethnic groups are represented. All these matters tend to be rather delicate and often over-politicized. However, the acquisition of education still remains a moral enterprise, entirely concerned with the development of the minds of learners of different age groups and different socio-cultural backgrounds. It has already led to the emergence of new strategically important content areas as well as the development of new school subjects and individual curricula for learners, especially relevant for the preservation of ethnic cultures. Flexible regional and local curricula will also enable the development of personal competencies in various fields leading to personal independence, civic responsibility, and the ability to modify oneself by finding appropriate social roles for a particular time and for one's environment according to developmental needs. However, all these competencies develop by different contributions from formal and informal learning as a lifelong process and will remain individual and integrated according to the diversity of personal learning and life experience. Integration as a means for the learner's own interested enquiry and the disciplining of one's thinking (Pring 1976: 110) also develops meaning for particular curriculum areas and school subjects. Each of these will also develop a particular value and a personal recognition of the limits of implementation of particular knowledge and skills. In order to foster learning with comprehension, Razumovskij (1997) proposes special cognitive courses for different school subjects, which would introduce different cognitive techniques for the development of general as well as specific study skills.

Education for identity development will always remain an individual and moral enterprise in which education plays a crucial role in establishing the hierarchies of different identities. Identity building on a personal level will decide the possibilities of preservation and development of ethnic cultures. Development of individual and integrated competencies according to formal and informal education and relevant curricula can also help people avoid alienation and unemployment as a structural property of post-modern society in the twenty-first century and included in social activities. It also influences development of positive attitudes towards people's human and natural surroundings.

How to Develop Models of Curriculum Design for Implementation in School Practice

Curriculum design in post-socialist countries, in particular, has, during this period of educational change, presented special problems. The ever-changing world and the keyword "flexibility" have caused heated debates on what is actually worth learning and what could be considered meaningful in education at large (Walsh 1993). The problem of the twenty-first century seems to be not what to include into the content but just the opposite—what to exclude, as, due to unmanageable amounts of information, it has become more and more complicated to decide what we can do without.

In order to design curriculum as an integrated and meaningful whole, some basic structures are needed. The development of national curricula and their implementation programs have created a certain imbalance between the new democratic freedoms of open options within the presented frameworks regarding both the selection of the content and the organization of the process of learning. Considering the ever-growing amount of information, it is becoming more and more difficult to make a good choice of the content for studies that would meet the needs of the learners of today in their future life. There is an acknowledged need to develop flexible curricula, which would allow us to react and make changes in them according to developments in technologies and culture, in the broad sense of the word. However, the selection of the content for general comprehensive compulsory schools is still expected to meet the requirements of equal opportunities regarding access to the available content of education in different schools. For the design of these frameworks in the New Curricula and their practical implementation on the school level (subject syllabi primarily), some structural models could be used which would allow one to choose and develop a meaningful and more integrated content of learning (especially within a subject cycle—languages, science subjects, etc.). This would help to enhance the students' comprehension and to develop their autonomy at organizing their learning, as well as offer more precise information about the expected attainment (achievement) of students for all parties involved (students, teachers, parents, publishers, teacher-trainers, employers, etc.). Two basic models for the development of subject syllabi and their implementation on the school level will be presented. They have been developed considering a European context of curriculum development with the main emphasis on key concepts, development of structured, integrated, and operational knowledge, specification of educational standards as minimal expected achievement, and meaningful evaluation. These also allow a more rational use of the available time, and they enable teachers to develop their own plans of action regarding the implementation of the New Curriculum, they are responsible. Although these structural models have been designed for and field-tested only in general comprehensive schools, similar models could be developed for other types of schools and courses of learning.

The first model offers a structure for selection of the subject content and specifies the basic skills required for its acquisition. The model tries to unite the different approaches: the main stress is laid on the content, but elements of other approaches have also been included. The process of writing a curriculum document consists of the following stages: (1) establishment of consensus about the basic values in society from which the curriculum ideology and the main objectives of general education will be derived, considering cultural context and geopolitical position; (2) specification of the list of subjects which could allow achievement of those objectives; (3) establishment of subject syllabi and educational standards as minimal requirements for operational knowledge and skills; (4) specification of evaluation.

When designing models for curriculum development and implementation, the previous stage of educational organization of the system has to be considered as well as the traditions of pedagogical culture in the society. Considering the educational change in post-socialist countries, the problems of establishing a balance between the traditional and innovational deserve special attention. It is particularly important to distinguish between the old and valuable and the old and outdated. If we fail to make this distinction, it may happen that some traditional human values get lost and this loss would influence social stability within the country. When again the lost values become desirable, their restoration means new efforts and spending resources (time, finances, and human resources) which could be used in a more meaningful way.

It would be of crucial importance that the politicians and the society at large quickly start to comprehend the complexity of the reform and coherence of educational and social developments. Equally important are the specifications of different resources, the cost efficiency of the planned changes, and the various constraints for the reform and development of groups of those who would be possibly disadvantaged. Education is the means of offering opportunities to interpret and reinterpret culture, thus the development of attitudes towards any change creates a value shift.

What are the Social Perspectives on Educational Change in Post-socialist Countries?

Any policy is a mix of political ideals and power; it means an attempt to choose between competing values, and in post-socialist societies great value conflicts can be observed, especially in the period of transition. Several new values have become accepted, usually unquestioned. Therefore, it is particularly important to differentiate between democratic policy developments and policy based on power, which happens to be the heritage for many of the former socialist republics.

There will always be a gap between manifested ideals and policy implementation in reality. It could often be compared to walking in many directions at the same time, lacking any common road map, much less itinerary (Cibulka 1995: 23). This may make change into an endless trying of new things, starting with open-ended exclamations with little follow-through or evaluation. One has to consider the inevitable resistance to change, but at the same time there is no justification for starting with innovation built on nothing but optimism and expectations about practicing teachers, somehow managing on their own.

Further differentiation of schools considering the quality of education as well as controversial and uninformed decisions about the reorganization of the network of schools may lead to further undesired stratification of society, urbanization, and other regional developments. School innovation in many different directions unavoidably becomes eclectic in its results, especially considering the various directly copied experiences or information when they are not analyzed from the point of their implementation under local and regional circumstances.

Despite great aspirations towards integration with European and other international structures, it is also important to think about the achievement-oriented school tradition of Estonia and other post-socialist countries, which has served as the main basis for the survival of ethnic identity and national culture. It would be most necessary to distinguish between the old and valuable, worth keeping for future generations, and the old-fashioned and inefficient.

Every citizen would envisage his educational relations to the state as adjustment models, practically oriented and personally relevant for the development of one's social and economic mobility. Accordingly, educational change should find solutions and alleviate tensions between balance and coherence, as well as between choice and diversity, which is of special meaning for small societies like Estonia. Social perspectives of educational change have to be considered in much broader fields, and in the context of interactions in society, rather than in terms of the changes in the system itself. Educational change in a small country offers opportunities for a considerably faster implementation; on the other side, if managed in the wrong way, these changes may cause devastating effects on the whole system.

In Estonia, regional developments of economy and education have not yet been studied enough, but we have to acknowledge the growth of regional differences within Estonia, and we have to start to study processes of globalization in education similar to those carried out in the sociology of economics. The mutual influence of globalization and local development offers new opportunities for the specification of different identities and new associations. Progress in education can be similarly expected as it is in economy—

by development of new resources, these being new skills and means of communication (Raagmaa 1999). Specification of identities on different levels, starting from local and moving to regional and then to global, allows the development of stability in educational innovation and the avoidance (i.e., educational pollution) of inadequately prepared experimentation with seemingly fashionable ideas. The implementation of the New Curricula cannot be expected to be a success without their further development on the regional level, specifying different regions and identities of educational culture, content, and management.

And still the questions and problems remain. Let's ask just a few of them:
- How diverse can diversity be?
- What must the common core and aspirations of the knowledge society be?
- Can the European dimension really unite the nations although language learning is difficult to implement?
- What can be organized as regional educational management across state borders, in specific regions, or for transition countries?
- What kind of content could create balance between different social and cultural values?
- What is the desired educational quality, considering both the process and the content, especially the operational knowledge?
- What kind of basic education could be considered adequate and flexible, capable of meeting the challenge of a changing labour market (Rifkin 1996), and what kind of new activities could be meaningful for people in information societies?

My good colleague Sid Pandey as well as others participating in the session considered them worth thinking about and hoped some ideas could crop up in our international research community. There are always more questions than answers. But still, let us remember that unasked questions will never be answered.

References

Allardt, E. (1979). *Implications of the ethnic revival in modern industrialized society.* Helsinki: Societas Scientarum Fennica.

Byram, M. (1989). *Cultural studies in foreign language education.* Clevedon, England: Multicultural Matters.

Cibulka, J. (1995). The evolution of educational reform in the United States: Policy ideals or

Realpolitik? In *International Perspectives on Educational Reform and Policy Implementation*. Edited by D. Carter and M. O'Neil, pages 15–30.
Estonian National Curriculum (1996). *Riigi Teatahja* [in Estonian], pages 20–22.
The European Commission. White Paper on Education and Training. (1995). *Teaching and learning: Towards the learning society.* Luxembourg: Office for Official Publications of the European Communities.
Hasanow, Z. (1998). *Education towards intercultural communication culture.* Mahatshkala University.
Kirch, A., M. Kirch, and T. Tuisk (1992). *The non-Estonian population today and tomorrow. A sociological overview.* Preprint. Estonian Academy of Sciences.
Mader, O. (1979). *Fragen der Lehrplantheorie. Berträge zur Padägogik Band 16.* Volk and Wissen Volkseigener Verlag.
Norwegian Research and Church Affairs (1997). *Reform 1.* Oslo: Royal Norwegian Ministry of Education.
OECD (Organisation for Economic Co-operation and Development)/CERI report (1994). *Changing identities in Estonia: Sociological facts and commentaries.* Tallin: Estonian Science Foundation.
Pring, R. (1976). *Knowledge and schooling.* London: Open Books.
Proos, I., and I. Pettai (1994). Non-Estonians in Estonia. *Hommikuleht: Kuulisa* [*Policy Review Monthly Issues*]. November–December: 4–6.
Raagmaa, G. (1999). *Global change in economic environment and regional developments.* Located at http://www.e.2010.ee/teemad/raagmaa 1htm # 1.
Razumovskij, V. G. (1997). Teaching and scientific cognition [in Russian]. *Pedagogika 1*: 7–13.
Rifkin, J. (1996). *The end of work: The decline of the global labor force and the dawn of the post-market era.* New York: Putnam.
Skutnab-Kangas, T. (1995). *Linguistic human rights: Overcoming linguistic discrimination.* Mouton de Gruyter.
Taba, H. (1962). *Curriculum development: Theory and practice.* New York: Harcourt Brace.
Thom, F. (1997). The rise of nationalism in the former Soviet Union. *Uncaptive minds.* Special double issue, Summer–Fall *9* (3–4): 11–20.
Valdma, S. (1996). *About civics and curriculum development.* Tallinn, Estonia: Jaan Tonisson Institute.
Vares, P. (1993). Dimensions and orientations in the foreign policy of the Baltic states. In *New actors on the international arena:The foreign policies of the Baltic Countries.* Edited by Pertt Joenniemi and Peeter Vares. Tampere: Tampere Peace Research Institute.
Walsh, P. (1993). *Education and meaning. Philosophy in practice.* London: Cassell.
Wynch, C. (1996). *Quality and education.* Cambridge, MA: Blackwell.

CHAPTER SEVEN

What Knowledge Is of Most Worth?

Ajeet Mathur • India

Introduction

The presumptuous borrowing of the title of this chapter[1] from Herbert Spencer (1859) is not limited by his scope. This question of questions, *"What knowledge is of most worth?"* has perplexed humanity a long time. It had arisen in mankind's oldest works of philosophy, *Veda Samhitas* (*Vedas*).[2] The present inquiry into this old question is prompted by two considerations. First, the study of knowledge (epistemology) and the study of value (axiology) are central to the purpose of life and everyday living and affect everyone. Yet, the relationships of knowledge to its value are not at all clear. Second, with the proliferation of alternative media, occasioned by the growth of telematic connectivity, educators who do not think through this question risk placing themselves on the list of endangered species if the institutions of knowledge and markets where knowledge is created are replaced by transactions of information. Throughout this paper, the term "data" is used to signify given or received observations or evidence. By information, reference is to the meaning given to data. Justified beliefs in any fact or working hypothesis are considered knowledge. Insight as perceptive or intuitive discernment is distinguished from knowledge. It is obvious that under certain conditions it may be appropriate to recognize insight as a valid source of justified beliefs. If data, information, knowledge, and insight are understood this way, wisdom may be defined as the capacity to act with knowledge or insight or both.

This chapter first traces how the conflict between knowing and thinking has turned the notion of a "university" into an oxymoron in section 2. The agency question of who values knowledge in section 3 is a step towards examining the dynamic interaction among three potential referents—learners, knowledge, society—and the matrix of intended and unintended consequences generated thereby in section 4. Some methodological difficulties of internationalizing curriculum within post-modern discourses are noted in section 5. Spaces that people relate to are pictures-in-mind about spaces inhabited, and in this context the chapter analyses the juxtaposition of real and virtual spaces in internationalising information societies in section 6. Differences between (a) global information conduits and international knowledge networks, (b) individual identities and collective identities, and (c) organisation systems and institutions are thus noted. These distinctions constitute critical points of departure for interpretation of post-modernist conceptions of understanding educational curricula and perils of "one world" oversimplification in section 7. In section 8, problems concerning treatments of plurality in internationalization of curricula are viewed as cathexis and discourses around consensuality of social and intellectual illusions of a time. This is followed up by treating international business studies as a specific case to tentatively formulate some generic premises about the locus of knowing in section 10, and metaphors of illusion are briefly recapitulated in section 11. This chapter concludes that the capacity to be perpetually surprised and to wonder enables authority to remain constantly sensitive and conscious of transcendence in the process of creating, holding, and valuing new illusions while shedding (or hoping to dispel) previously treasured illusions as false or useless or irrelevant or non-existent by the sciences and values we cherish.

Interest in this question was also evinced by early Greek philosophers at a time when Sanskrit, Greek, and Latin as languages with common Indo-European roots bore a similarity to each other. Scholars like Pythagoras and Aristotle concerned themselves with this question in their quest for harmony. However, these early Western philosophers were unwilling to treat knowledge, theological virtue, and morality as distinct spheres as their Indian and Chinese counterparts had done. Greek logicians were further contextually constrained in being almost clueless on where they were located, and remained unable to ascertain the time of the day for the entire period of Greece's Golden Age. The first Western systems of formal logic thus lacked internalisation of two significant boundary conditions: space and time. A virtue was made of this necessity by developing mathematical logic as a formal system divorced from reality in a search for universal and eternal truths.

During the medieval period, theology permeated natural philosophy under the imperatives of governance and security, raising warfare, statecraft, and divinity to knowledge of most worth. With the decline of the Judao-Greco-Roman civilisations and the disintegration of the Holy Roman Empire in the west and fragmentation of the Nile Valley, Babylonian, Confucian, and Indus Valley Civilizations in the east, normative aspects of behaviour gained ascendancy in the design of education in what have been called the Dark Ages. This occurred with respect to three boundary coordinates (sentience, artefacts, technology) from among five (which would include space and time) on which open systems are conventionally distinguished (Lewin 1936, 1951; Miller 1978). The question assumed fresh significance in the fifteenth century when the Age of Navigation altered the conception of lands and seas and natural life including human habitation, with consciousness of "space" being the driver as an expansive vision catalogued the natural and man-made artefacts which terrestrial space contained. With European colonisation of Asia and America and the Industrial Revolution circa 1760, technology became the driver of power in inhabited spaces.

When the Age of Exploration was layered over by the Industrial Revolution, everything that could be brought under the authority of production as resource in the most efficient manner came to be valued on the criteria of exchange. This encouraged slavery and other forms of forced labour. It also legitimised the conversion of human raw material resource into a labouring and exploitable resource under the authority of production. The allocation and use of labour left the question of what knowledge is of most worth to factory owners who owned land, labour, or capital or belonged to the set that discharged administrative functions in emerging governance units. When the skill of the artisan was marginalized, a new division of labour required by the factory system reinforced the division of educational streams into vocational, general, and professional, the last two for those who would not be called upon to work in the new industrial system and could practice the liberal arts or professions, including the new professions of entrepreneurship and management in local, national, regional, and global space.[3] Industrialisation was associated with colonisation over access to raw material resources, and scholarship was mainly viewed in Western European utilitarian terms. Thus, all three notable attempts to consider what knowledge is of most worth occurred in the annals of European tradition (Spencer 1859; Steiner 1924/1982;

Hollins 1968). Alfred Whitehead was interested in this question to the extent of his interest with education as the art of the utilization of knowledge (Whitehead 1929). An abiding interest in this question in a post-modern American tradition is found in the revolutionary work of William Doll (1993) and in its nascent international dimension in the pioneering work of William Pinar (1995: 792–843, 2003).

Herbert Spencer claimed "science" is knowledge of the highest worth. He devoted considerable time and attention to penning his "scientific" hierarchy of races.[4] Spencer's methodology was dictated by utility and the ratio of required labour to probable benefit for maintaining social order.[5] Spencer's hierarchy of activities assigned the highest importance to self-preservation, child-rearing, maintenance of proper social and political relations, and sensory gratifications, in descending order. He placed great emphasis on duties of parents, which he regarded as higher than duties of citizens, on the grounds that the family came before the State in order of time, and bringing up of children would be possible even in States that ceased to be. Spencer ridiculed curricula for the neglect of the knowledge and skills needed for raising families. He criticised educational curricula for prioritising the ornamental over the useful and maintained that it was lack of knowledge of science that led localities to throw away money in impossible projects. If that were the main reason, some projects of the 1990s—like London's Millennium Dome—would not have been undertaken and projects like China's Three Gorges Dam could never be sanctioned. Spencer believed that arts and aesthetics were conducive to human nature but inessential and best left to be acquired in leisure time. Spencer's emphasis on utilitarian science and scientific determination of utility led him to the circular logic that "general happiness is to be achieved mainly through the adequate pursuit of individual happiness, while happiness of individuals is to be achieved in part by their pursuit of the general happiness," providing ethical underpinnings to the aims of education (Spencer 1879).[6] The notion that development of self-interest needs to be visualised individually as well as collectively through reasoned curricular discourse struck a balance between egoism and utilitarianism, between utilitarianism and altruism, and between freedom and responsibility.

T.H.B. Hollins disagreed with Spencer. Relying on the significance of social utility, he concluded that "the arts" are knowledge of the highest worth and argued that splitting professional and liberal education would disconnect the rational and irrational human elements which ought to be nurtured and understood holistically. Labouring under conceptions of a naturally hierarchic social order, he acknowledged the importance of occupational usefulness but constantly referred to John Dewey and Jerome Bruner to emphasise knowledge as a journey and languages as the great technology that make us human (Hollins 1968). In contrast to Spencer and Hollins, Greek philosophers thought a balanced curriculum to be of the highest worth, with the Delphic Oracular admonition "nothing in excess," and Rudolf Steiner believed that reading of nature, self-expression, and a knowledge of the whole person in relation to other persons are needed for a true education, and visualised, growth phases in seven-year periods corresponding to physiological transition markers such as teething (0–7; 7–14) and puberty (7–14; 14–21) as signals of threshold transitions for the design of quite different educational needs and curricula (Steiner 1924/1982). With such a developmental perspective, it would be useful to take into consideration, as David Kirshner (1997) does (in the context of semiosis of situated cognition) with an insightful case study, that cognitive development is not the child's cumulative experiences with objects and actions, but is culturally constructed within established social practices.

Curricular studies generally tend to limit their scope to the design of school education systems and structures, catering mainly to children with a modal age range of seven to twenty-one years of age in formal education. Meanwhile, two important changes have occurred that need to be internalised into the frame. The lowering of the voting age from twenty-one to eighteen by reclassifying young persons as "adults" at eighteen implies their autonomous right to exercise all kinds of choices over their lives, including choices concerning the design of social systems and social structures of which educational curricula are a part. Second, in an age of specialisation and with exponential growth of new knowledge, the gestation period required for every kind of education (general, vocational, professional) has increased because knowledge needs to be bundled together with skills when societies shift away from manufacturing to services, and the pace of change forces more and more people to look at part-time work and lifelong education as norms.

Knowing Versus Thinking: An Eternal Dilemma

The emergence of post-school advanced studies sets universities apart from schools for higher general education and also for educational specialisations, thereby broadening the scope of our question. A university, as the name suggests, may be considered organised on the basis that knowledge is universal (whole) and functioning on the basis of integrity of parts of the whole offered as studies to its students (Newman 1999). Knowledge is called by the name of science when it is organised, acted upon, or informed by logic. To limit this logic to reason, thereby excluding the passions and the experiential, is to separate questions of identity that make us human from products of intellect that flow from the reasoning mind. Newman, in his nine discourses delivered in Ireland, was among the few who recognised the importance of enlarging mind-sets through experiential learning as knowledge; dominant Western traditions did not, with some exceptions, do so until recently (when the discourse tradition became fashionable towards the end of the twentieth century). Traditionally, universities had two major functions: research into forms of knowledge, and the education of elites to prepare them for responsible positions in governance. A third function of catering to the superstructures of businesses and professions was added later. Phenomenally, universities may also be viewed as stocking flows of potential entrants for a delayed labour market entry with a view to increase knowledge and skills or to disguise unemployment. There also arise difficulties in conveniently classifying existing and emerging fields of study into science, arts, humanities, commerce, etc., and not only because of the gulf between dichotomies like "pure" and "applied" (impure?) or "hard sciences" and "soft sciencies," "aesthetics" and "empiricism." Serious methodological and didactic problems remain of locating and structuring fields of study like mathematics, music, management, governance, education, economics, war, law, and philosophy into the conventional taxonomy because each of these has a claim to science with its scientists and a claim upon it from the creative practitioners of its arts. Different education policies, systems, structures, and processes have treated these matters in different ways.[7]

The collective understanding of the human condition and the spaces persons relate to changed dramatically after the reconception of our habitat as a global village with the advent of the space age of the 1960s. Big corporations have since coined slogans like IBM's *"solutions for a small planet"* to replace *"Think."* There is a degree of implied pretence in this. Recall the adage that a knowing being does not think and a thinking being does not know. A phantasy is being nurtured that humanity has been elevated to a level where man *knows* and does not have to think anymore (The CEO of a multinational firm, Oracle, was quoted by the *Economist* in a recent ad campaign as saying "I used to think...now I just read the *Economist*," with pride.) Humanity's adventures in space exploration since the moon landing in 1969 appear to have heralded a transcendent vision just a year after Hollins exhorted the virtues of the arts in the 1968 Bulmershe Lecture.

Is it reasonable to expect that paradigm shifts such as this change to planetary scope of consciousness (altering our contingent and contextual horizons) will always affect answers to our question? If we answer this in the affirmative, the question would need to be cast and considered solvable only within a defined temporal or spatial dimension. However, if we assume that all contextual and contingent horizons offer choices and our preferences may be ordered normatively as well as positively, then it becomes possible to answer this question in the negative. In the latter case, the changing contextual and contingent horizons would be treated as so much a part of lived experience of humankind that it could justify formulating questions about the question as an eternally relevant existential or phenomenal inquiry into questions of life and continuity. In either case, the question is far from trivial. An educator's responsibility cannot be limited to operational considerations on the supply side. Satisfactory functioning of an education system depends on how robustly the system is designed. Digitalisation of information and depersonalisation of data have not altered this fundamental proposition. Acquisition of a data-processing system confers neither information nor knowledge. Any contract of consideration-based sale between suppliers and customers is essentially different from a contract of interactive participation, because the former does not require empathy and commitment from parties to the contract. It follows that participants interacting within institutions cannot be treated analogously with suppliers and customers. Juha Salonen (2000) in his recent doctoral dissertation at the University of Tampere made the point that acquisition of a data-processing system is a distinct kind of composite contract which is not governable by any one law. Any information system that depends on empathy and commitment is robust only to the extent that its notions of space are consistent with the boundaries of solidaristic containment provided by law.

A macrocosmically valid inquiry into the question cannot be initiated even on behalf of the reflexive me or myself without primacy to questions of reason over the illusions of identities I carry in my mind in managing myself in the course of my own life. Such an inquiry may hardly be conceived as an exploration of potential trajectories of orbits on behalf of you, the reader of this chapter, or be legitimately conducted with curricular rationale on behalf of any learner or group of learners or even knowledge itself. Rather, I am inspired by the faith implicit in the vedic suggestion that were we to solve the ontological problem of whether knowledge exists independent of the knower in the affirmative or if a knower could be known, then this question would theoretically or experientially become solvable in any and every context, provided we are able to contingently formulate questions and interpret transformations actualised from cathexis and assign values to such knowledge in terms of absolute or relative worth.

What Is Knowledge Worth?

Questions of worth are regarded tractable with reference to assignment or measures of cost and value. Also, notions of sunk cost and opportunity cost are widely used, as are concepts of externalities, social cost, cost-benefit analysis, and surplus value. The worth of anything is hard to know if knowledge of that worth is to be obtained from preference orderings of rational economic agents, which is usually the case. Further, since preference orderings depend on others' preferences and can never be completely known with certainty, the so-called self-reference problem of situational logic remains unsolvable.

The difficulties of constructing a universal or bounded social preference ordering of what knowledge is worth more may be gleaned from Amartya Sen's (1977) critique of linkages of use and welfare to value in his seminal paper, *Rational Fools*. Sen observes that the economic theory of utility assigns a person a preference ordering, and as and when the need arises this preference ordering is taken to represent his interests; this same preference ordering is also assumed to represent his welfare, inform us what he would normatively wish and still manage to describe his actual choices and behaviour. If any one preference ordering could do all of these, and if the same person could hold on to the same preference ordering for all of these purposes consistently, economic theory regards him as rational. However such a rational person "must be a bit of a fool" if he doesn't understand these subtle distinctions, and so we need to separate the measures.

An example may clarify this point. An expensive business school in Europe recently advertised its MBA programme with posters showing a picture of badly tied shoelaces accompanied by the suggestion, "If you think education is costly, try ignorance." This positioning of ignorance and education as opposites implied the existence of a rational binary choice in favour of this MBA programme compared to the cost of going about the world ignorantly. There was no reference to the value or advantage of education or knowledge to be gained from this programme versus other programmes of education that might introduce questions of relative worth such as "value of participating in an educational programme" or "this curricula" versus "that curricula." In this case, the programme was advertised by relating the worth of knowledge to the nature of a potential learner. But it is also possible to relate the worth of knowledge to two other referents—to the constituents of society and its institutions or to relative worth of knowledge of different kinds to one another and the relative worth of parts of the whole to the universe of human knowledge, recognising limitations imposed by subjective knowability or objective verifiability.

The question of worth is also affected by where knowledge is located and how easily it is convertible from one form to another, whether it is articulable or tacit, and the costs associated with transfers from one domain to another or simply one person to another or one location to another. Thus, the question of worth is concerned with how the matrix of dynamic interaction of these three elements of personal and social coherence acquires meaning from the logic imposed by the economics of education. The notion of education as fostering collectively valued purposes is fairly universally present in many cultures over time and across space. However, education as an institutionalised public activity has essentially been local, sub-national, regional, or national in its scope. Widespread indulgence in public subsidies and grants to educational institutions as a generic pattern arose from the compelling need of Fordist national industrial societies to assure themselves of skilled white-collar and blue-collar labour at public cost (Pinar 2003).

Learners, Knowledge, Society, and Their Interactivity

Knowledge, learners, and society are inseparable in conceptions of educational design (See table 1), in which each row indicates the decision-frame outcome for each referent as a stimulus upon itself and upon two referents in the columns.)

It is well known that learners can carry pictures in their minds about the world they experience from womb to tomb without teachers. The development of tacit knowledge (consciously and unconsciously) occurs all the time that cognitive processes make meaning of perceptions, dreams, and thoughts. The earliest experience of a baby in exchanging or transacting noise with gratification (e.g., mother's milk) or coping with frustration in its absence (pacifier training as discussed in Kirshner 1997) sets the tone for diffusion of tacit knowledge and for exchanges an individual makes with society and its institutions throughout life.

Our second referent, knowledge in its articulable forms, impacts human consciousness, engages the intelligence, and lodges in the memory of a learner through processes of parenting and education. This diffusion of articulable knowledge is achieved through increasingly fragmented offerings as knowledge gets more and more specialised. The percolation of knowledge to an individual or to large numbers of individuals may be regarded as bringing about transformative experiences for individuals and collectivities at various thresholds of diffusion.

Table 1: Interactivity Matrix of Knowledge Referents

	LEARNER (1)	KNOWLEDGE (2)	SOCIETY (3)
LEARNER	Illusion of Identity (1,1)	Diffusion of Tacit Knowledge (1,2)	Exchange Values (1,3)
KNOWLEDGE	Diffusion of Articulable Knowledge (2,1)	Fragmentation and Specialisation (2.2)	Transformation Imperative (2.3)
SOCIETY	Division of Labour; Division of Opportunities (3.1)	Inclusion vs. Exclusion; Proprietary Knowledge (3.2)	Conflict, Competition, Collaboration (3.3)

The transformations referred to here do not happen to inanimate containers like books or compact discs, or magnetic tapes. They occur in the consciousness of learners themselves. To the extent that such learners in formal education systems are able to satisfy curiosities of examiners, the transformations become validated and verifiable learning. Learners function within the constraints of divisions of opportunity and division of labour imposed by structures of society and its institutions. This produces inclusion and exclusion for learners as persons and for accessibility to knowledge for all when the exchange between learners and society and its institutions is regulated and characterised by three concurrent, endemic, enduring, and ubiquitous processes of conflict, competition, and collaboration that characterise human society. Nowhere is this more strongly visible than in management education and education management. Through management education, private and public social organisations acquire and develop talent to reap the greatest profits from the "solutions for our small planet" for themselves. Through education management, whole nation-states compete to create the greatest well-being for their own numbers.

To speak of internationalisation in management education or education management is thus a contradiction in terms, except when we mean it in the restricted sense of using the term "international" as a qualifying adjective for the space beyond national borders that is the object of local or national attention, or unless we use the expression "international community" to refer to the subjective consciousness of one collective unit. Management education has always been designed to be specific to locations, and education management, usually a national ministry, caters, first and foremost, to the well-being of its own citizens. This may seem justified if representative governments guided by the economic self-interest of *homo economicus* within their jurisdictions require such measures as their best (or only) means to promote economic prosperity based on rational self-interest. However, the reference to "well-being" is more expansive than "consumption" or "welfare," because the notion of "well-being" would certainly include a sense of identity, cultural consciousness, intergenerational transfers of knowledge, skills, and behaviour, and so we may expect that inward-looking educational policies may arise or persist on weakly understood (or, unconscious) motivations even if economic self-interest could be shown to be sub-optimised by them. The idea of internationalisation of education presupposes the desirability, willingness, and capacity to transcend or to transform national frames by striving for openness and porosity of national borders and mind-sets. And so it becomes important to examine whether the preference orderings chosen in actual decisions on education policies, systems, and curricular designs for internationalisation correspond to the normative logic of national well-being, or, consistent with the rationale of Amartya Sen's "rational fools," the decision makers favour internationalisation and are convinced about its desirability but refuse to commit adequate resources for the well-being of future generations.

Internationalisation of Education Designs: Some Methodological Difficulties

It is difficult to consider the world as an open system for all its inhabitants. Yet, this remains a solidaristic ideal, utopian for now. American educators like William Doll (1993) envision educational curricula that would maintain a healthy tension between the need to find closure and the desire to explore at every level. Are we to see in this an invitation to a curricula-designing world which would function as a creative container or transformative space involving semi-closed and closed countries and educators with closed mind-sets that periodically open only to snap shut? Doll's postmodernist conception of his ideal curriculum departs from the three Rs (reading, 'riting and 'rithmetic) and instead comprises four new Rs: rich, recursive, relational, and rigorous.

In my understanding, openness and tentativeness could en*rich* curricula like a never-ending magic book; recursiveness in curricula, like the spiral structure introduced in experiential learning designs of group-relations conferences, could enable curriculum to reflect like a magic mirror on itself for reflective transformation of experience; relationality in curricula would be predicated in the quality of "here and now" that would enable human contextuality to be continually examined and heal wounds, injuries, sicknesses, distortions very much like a magic herb; and, finally, rigor in curricula is essential because the purposeful seeking of what is valued being our holy grail or magic sword would enable alternative relations and connections, including alternative hypotheses that may be examined and accepted or rejected, or simply treated as undecided or even undecideable on this razor. I return to the magic book, the magic mirror, the magic herb, and the magic sword later in this chapter as our four metaphors or symbolic artefacts around which an international business management curricula metaphor was created in an inter-university educational programme involving nine European universities in the 1990s to demonstrate the potency of the four new Rs in projective identification in a curricular design exercise visualized by the author to let our question answer itself discursively. Methodological difficulties may yet arise from a number of sources, and the so-called post-modern condition is itself one of them.

Dystopian tentativeness is not a *sine qua non* of post-modernism.[8] Doll himself points out that transformative praxis "need not be a screen for a grand metanarrative." However, in reinterpreting educational views, Doll prefers to cast Dewey's concepts of exchange, Piaget's concepts of development and reequilibration, and Bruner's spiral transformations of learning into strands of post-modernism linked together by growth rather than stasis on the grounds that they are better understood this way (Dewey 1938/1963; Piaget

1978; Bruner 1960, 1986, 1990). This gives rise to an implicit assumption that humanity has reached or is on the verge of, for the main part, transcendence of thresholds of consciousness that would render non-transformational frames with their attainable certainties redundant or irrelevant or impossible. Might this be a case of moving between two polarities or angularities, i.e., modern tradition versus post-modern condition, in exercise of rational binary choice? Does discovering a pre-existing world or dealing with an emergent one constitute our only two choices? What about pluralities and intermediate states? Such binary construction oversimplifies the problems dealing merely with teleological elements in some selected spaces without due regard for or adequate consideration of the pictures-in-the-mind of the world and its inhabitants nor to interventions, facilitations, or time needed for transformations of these pictures into other patterns or modes of thinking.

Pictures in the Mind and How Spaces We Relate to Connect with Spaces We Inhabit

Using the matrix of three referents in table 1 discussed earlier, we may relate learners to society through pictures-in-the-mind, carried consciously and unconsciously. Limiting our attention to consciously carried pictures of the world, let's take a look at figure 1, a map of the world.

Much of the population of Europe and decolonised Asia and Africa have grown up believing this to be the only way the world looks and is mapped. This picture, based on the centrality of Greenwich, a historical legacy from the primacy of Imperial Britain and the significance of Western European powers, suggests that there is an ocean to the West across which but close by is North America (the Atlantic is colloquially referred to as "the pond") and then there are the "Near East," "Middle East," and "Far East" regions. The very concept of East varies as we move eastwards because every country—from England to Turkey, from Germany to Slovenia, from Denmark to Bulgaria, and from Portugal to Greece—sees itself at the centre as a gateway between East and West.

However, pictures of the world are carried by different people in different ways. Let us take another look at the world in figure 2. Children in Canada and the United States of America have grown up with this different conception of the world bounded by two oceans on either side. For them, there is an Atlantic side, across which lies Europe, and a Pacific side, across which lies Japan and the rest of Asia. From school geography to foreign

Figure 1

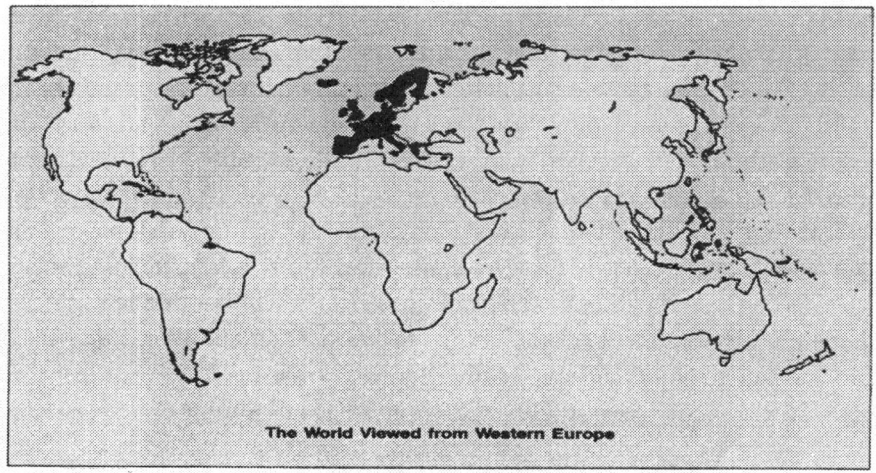

From: STRATEGIC ATLAS:COMPARATIVE GEOPOLITICS OF THE WORLD'S POWERS, REVISED EDITION BY GERARD CHALIAND and JEAN-PIERRE RAGEAU
© 1990 by Gerard Chaliand and Jean-Pierre Rageau.
Reprinted by permission of Harper Collins Publishers Inc.

Figure 2

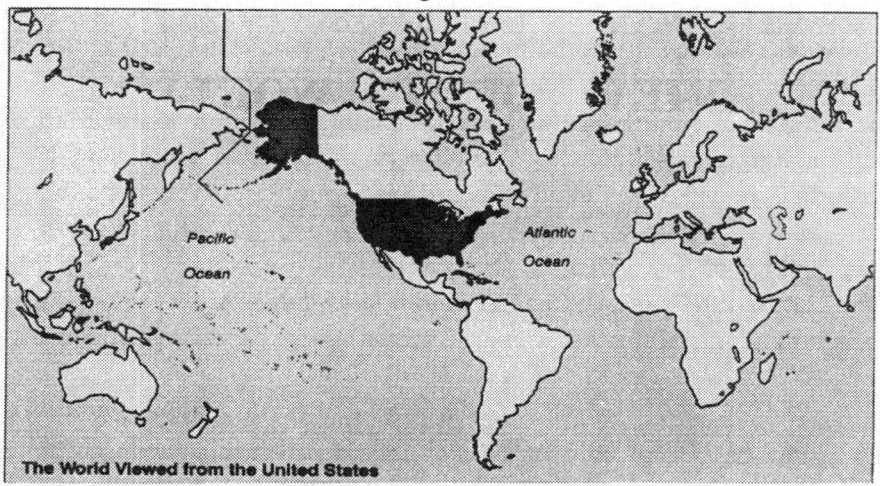

From: STRATEGIC ATLAS:COMPARATIVE GEOPOLITICS OF THE WORLD'S POWERS, REVISED EDITION BY GERARD CHALIAND and JEAN-PIERRE RAGEAU
© 1990 by Gerard Chaliand and Jean-Pierre Rageau.
Reprinted by permission of Harper Collins Publishers Inc.

policy to business policy, the design of curricula has reinforced this picture. We could similarly take other views of the world from Scandinavia, Russia, Japan, China, India, Brazil, North Africa, or Australia. With the possible exception of Australia (with its split Anglo-Asian identity), questions of identity, affinity, and interests are well settled in the "neighbourhood" in the Southern Pacific and Antarctic regions. Similarly, in and around the Arctic, Nordic countries are especially concerned about the northern dimension from where Germany and the Baltics and the Hansa trade, Via Baltica and Mare Balticum and St. Petersburg appear more important.

The recurrence of this orientation is reflected in the geographic centrality that attaches itself to our three referents of table 1 from the way the world is inhabited. This influence which may be called the influence of proximate cognition affects perceptions not only about what knowledge is of most worth but also struggles about which picture of the world is the right one and whose knowledge is of most worth, not to speak of which education design is of most worth. This may seem paradoxical in an age in which the media or multimedia or hypermedia, as it increasingly calls itself, bombards our sensibilities of locatedness in spaces, every day and every moment when we log on to a browser or a television channel, by reminding us that our "one world" connects us all through nets, webs, links, and their representations in sounds and images.

Perils of "One world" Oversimplification

From the preceding discussion, with the emergence of multimedia and hypermedia, three questions arise in the context of globalisation:

1. Does telematic connectivity imply a new notion of multiple spaces?

2. Do identities of human consciousness recrystallise around new collective dimensions?

3. Are virtual systems organisable as open organisation systems and institutions?

The perils of "one world" oversimplification are brought home in a startling way by Noel Gough (2000). Gough narrates his experience of reading an announcement of a new series called "One World, Ready or Not" in his local Melbourne newspaper's electronic version while he was away from home. He tells us that the announcement made no reference to the locality where it was published and where the vast majority of its readership resided:

The main graphic element was a globe viewed from a position above the equatorial plane with Australia at bottom centre (Australia's position in this image being the only clue to location other than the newspaper's name)...a second aspect of the announcement that reinforced its dislocation was that it was not written by a member of the editorial staff or a local journalist...the article itself...from America, written by an American...was sub-titled "America's defining challenge is to prevent globalization from becoming a monster." (333)

Gough questions what he calls "globalization, global village and other transnational imaginaries" by citing Turnbull (1993, 1997), who claims that all knowledge traditions are spatial because they link people, locations, and skills. Defending Turnbull's distinguishing of representational knowledge from performative knowledge (reminiscent of Spencer's ornamental knowledge and useful knowledge), Gough claims that the real bridge to the future cannot be constructed from abstractions like globalisation but rather from deliberate choices, decisions, and actions people take in matters like food, family, social security, and sex, again reminiscent of Spencer's activity hierarchy.

Gough (1998) asserts that the social activities through which distinctive forms of knowledge are produced are local. However, the global reach, first of European imperialism and later American hegemony have given the appearance that universal truth and rationality as a characteristic feature of science exist independent of locality and local traditions. Gough maintains that concepts like photosynthesis, entropy, and closed systems cannot be acultural. What might happen to knowledge frames when power shifts occur? Gazetas (2000b), referring to Homi Bhabha's concept of politics of difference (Bhabha 1994), reminds us that "all cultures are in the process of hybridity where spaces carry both content and its transformation and where the power of late capitalism attempts to turn all cultural constructs into perpetuating myths or master narratives while high-tech forces of the internet implicate everyone into forms of cultural hybridity."(10)

An inherent ambiguity arises in the simultaneous anchorage in real and virtual spaces, such as when talking on the telephone or when surfing the Web. Yet, mere access to a telephone or the World Wide Web can hardly be construed as having conferred membership of any international knowledge network in any sense other than as Benedict Anderson's "imagined community" (Anderson 1991).

There is a clear need to distinguish between:
- international knowledge networks and global information conduits

- individual identities (a matter of choice, growth and transformation at a personal level) and collective identities (a legacy of the residues we were born into or live by)
- institutions (any significant arrangements that are created or which evolve to fulfil human wants for which demand exceeds supply at a non-zero price) and organization systems (designed inventions to regulate conversion or value addition for profit to the stake-holders).

The connectivity introduced by the World Wide Web (WWW) is like magically conferred power. The Web as a tool is simultaneously a means and a cathecting object through which self and the world are cast into new spaces, raising euphoric fantasies and deep fears. However, the transformative powers of the web are based on its virtual reach, not on the quality of tactile bonding that natural proximate communities are capable of creating and which the Web lacks. For this reason, the anti-democratic implications and trajectory of hypermedia ought to be examined carefully. According to McChesney, the Web is "dominated by a few big commercial firms and advertisers spinning a hypercommercial frenzy with little trace of public service" (McChesney 1999, 2000). McChesney further reminds us that every new electronic media technology in the twentieth century—film, radio, television, cable, satellite broadcasting—spawned similar fantasies. In each case the claim that existing monopolies on media would be replaced by more egalitarianism was wrong.

The frenzy for connectivity is inspired by electronic commerce, epitomized in the phrase "I consume therefore I am." That capital overcomes the friction of space with time, conjectured once upon a time by Karl Marx, has come true in a manner he did not visualise. We live in "a world divided between placeless power and powerless places" (Castells and Henderson 1987), which is another way of acknowledging that real and virtual spaces claim our attention simultaneously.[9] Media and cyberspace pundits have been quick to introduce communal notions such as "public" and "civic" and "domain" into virtual spaces. However, the governance of cyberspaces and of human activity in cyberspaces cannot be accomplished from cyberspace itself. A global information conduit enables data to be transferred in meaningful patterns (the very definition of information), and it enables information to be speedily accessible, but it does not create any knowledge network until consciousness of human identities is introduced to engage with the load of that information in a mode of cathexis underlying a communal commitment of dynamic interaction as a community.[10]

All information that a human being possesses cannot possibly be articulated, leaving each one of us with a considerable reservoir of what Ikujiro Nonaka calls "tacit information" which cannot be easily formulated (Nonaka 1998). How identities of human consciousness in ferment may recrystallise around new collective dimensions is not clear. Distinctions may be drawn between *being identical*, *sharing an identity*, and *identifying with a particular group* (Sen 1999).[11] Neither the World Wide Web nor the post-modern condition has solutions to reconcile plurality of identities. The need to distinguish between individual and collective identities remains a critical point of departure for interpreting our reasoned consciousness of identities. An interpretive synthesis of inner and outer worlds involves introjective and projective processes at the individual level. Simultaneously, these processes are capable of triggering transference and counter-transference at a collective level in and between groups.

The Web does not meet the criteria to qualify as public domain because norms of universality, inclusivity, equality, and reciprocity that govern communities are absent. In the use of the Web as an information resource, it is noteworthy that the Web proliferates not only information but also rumour, propaganda, conjecture, misinformation, opinion, guesswork, supposition, claim, myth, fallacy, gossip, viruses, and pornography. Consider the media transition from the printed form to Web-bytes. The content of newspapers is organised on the basis that readers pay for the news, and advertisers pay for the attention they claim on readers. If hypertext literacy is to replace print literacy as valid pedagogy in classrooms, the reliance placed on zapping our way through hyperlinks must be able to provide equivalent or superior content or form. The biggest drawback is that tacit knowledge cannot be shared through the Web, and cultural accumulations involving intergenerational transfers and transmissions of experiences, learning, and memory through tactile interactions are impossible.

In the past decade there has been enormous pressure on libraries to unsubscribe from expensive journals and stop buying books. Suppose we dispense with the investments made in libraries after building up net subscriptions of equivalent material and do away with books, journals, tapes, and cassettes of sound and image and then encounter "Error 404":
- The object you requested could not be found on this server
- Directory listing denied
- This virtual directory does not allow contents to be listed
  For all the comfort provided by "I click hyperlinks, therefore I am,"

Moulthorp (2000) warns that the Web may turn out to be a diversion to hold the attention of people while the masters of capital lock down the gates of information control. Rather than dismiss Moulthorp outright as another cranky conspiracy theorist, let us examine the implications of Error 404, because it is about issues of accessibility which any new technological innovation need to consider. Terry Harpold (1991) makes a good case when arguing that hypertext is a space of illusions and detours and that no link ever runs true, because, phenomenally speaking, hypertext reading is unlike reading a book since it takes us to places which we did not anticipate. And this, based on our own clickings! Nobody can be held responsible for Error 404.

The last of the perils of "one world" oversimplification concerns the rejection of ethnocentrism and its replacement with a post-industrial and post-modern formulation of American or West European experience. This is particularly embarrassing when Sweden, Finland, Japan, China, India, Korea, and Brazil—some of the significant knowledge-producing countries—have to be taken into consideration. They have significant influence on the coexistence of plurality of traditions and diversity of paths thus amply disproving the Anglo-American or Continental European experience as the only valid *currere* to knowledge creation and diffusion.

Internationalization of International Curricula

William Pinar's call for creating a worldwide field of curriculum studies (Pinar 1995, 2003) is timely, yet conservative. Pinar recognises the structural limitations that divide curriculum theorists into national groupings. For learners, university education towards a first degree has become what high school education used to be a generation ago.

The French writer Alain Corbin (1994) notes how the lure of the oceans expanded the reach of societies over the past five hundred years, but the experience of the seaside did not reach the bulk of human consciousness until the twentieth century. He compares the igniting of the spark of desire for knowledge to an invitation to a baptismal font, which is just the start of a journey of discovery and expression. Space has since provided a new frontier to ignite our imaginations.

The conference in Louisiana at which this chapter was presented, as a paper, placed paired presenters alongside each other as conversants. My conversant, Peter Ninnes, analysed how space science is represented in school science textbooks in Canada, Australia, and New Zealand and reached the conclusion that internationalisation of curriculum is difficult even in hard sciences because curricula remain a vehicle for fostering or sustaining hegemonic knowledge relations (Ninnes 2000). This was independent confirmation of the notion developed in section 6 that understandings of spaces we relate to are connected with spaces we inhabit. Also, here was evidence that questions about universality, neutrality, and specificity need to be addressed in internationalising curricula from the perspective of learners and society.

NASA's recent scaling down of distant expeditions like the ones to Pluto and Charon or to Jupiter's moons despite the flurry of new discoveries of about fifty new objects including eight new planets, three quasars, and four brown dwarfs is mind-boggling. It appears that NASA is inspired by Comenius, for whom mirroring the founder of the divine plan was enough. So NASA supports manned space station spectacles of doubtful scientific value costing a hundred times more than an unmanned probe to Pluto,[12] which begs the question: If earth looks the same from space and space looks the same from earth, why does earth look different from earth? With reference to the central box at the intersection of the two diagonals in table 1 in section 4, one possible answer is that when the human mind moves from questions of unity to questions of difference, something is lost in the resulting fragmentation that has to do with the nature of knowledge itself. Yet, academia, as a competitive career system, discourages breadth of vision in favour of depth of focus in order not to imperil the precarious relative position of one's own discipline relative to others. This is devastating in times when specialisations have proliferated.[13]

Knowledge typologies remain connected to local spaces because the desired intergenerational continuities differ from place to place. Thus, the question of what knowledge is of most worth becomes solvable in local contexts, but if our frame of curricular design itself is to be truly global or international or multi-locational, problems arise. Internationalization, as the term implies, refers to the phenomena of relatedness of nation-states to one another that may be studied either in itself or as a point of context for something else.

At an individual level, the question "What knowledge is of most worth?" could be answered in terms of what, in a person's estimation, is likely to satisfy her inter-temporal well-being as a function of her aspirations. The answer could vary depending on her talents, preferences, opportunities, and constraints. At the level of a group or a community, the answer could vary depending on whether members of that group or community consider the world as their arena of action or only a part of the world as their habitat, considering that the labour market remains fragmented by national borders where mobility of persons is regulated.

Knowledge has a transcendental quality in the sense that it is neither diminished by consumption, nor does it cease to have significance beyond its holders at any particular location. In this sense, it is impossible to distinguish global knowledge from local knowledge. For instance, would we call knowledge local because it is locally owned or locally developed or locally disseminated or locally treasured or locally transmitted? Does local disowning by one location of local knowledge of or at another location render it local? Does local recognition of local knowledge by one location of local knowledge of or at another location make it global?

Space travel in the 1960s opened new perspectives for earth. Soon after the "moon landing"[14] of 1969, there was a mad scramble for power that brought about the collapse of the international monetary system, unleashed an oil crisis, and created a profit squeeze from rising wages—all at about the time when a new time and space perspective had arisen and replaced resource management with response management as the new paradigm. The lack of realisation that a planetary time scale had quietly replaced the hitherto unquestioned rationality of quarterly planning cycles of corporations, annual, biannual, and quinquennial planning cycles of governments and international organisations wreaked havoc on time preferences reflected in interest rate structures with consequential fallouts in inflation and unemployment on a scale not experienced since the Great Depression of the 1930s. Solutions to this human tragedy on a global scale were sought in adjustments of balance of payments and cyclic explanations that raised hopes of a return to normalcy. While there may still be some diehard adherents to such cyclic explanations, it is now widely acknowledged that human actions on a global scale caused structural changes of magnitudes that transformed our understanding of factor markets, microeconomics of firms, macroeconomic management of economies, and governance of international regimes.

A part of the problem lies with globalisation of science education, which has been hegemonic. The problem is compounded when we consider other disciplines. Neither economics nor the multidisciplinary field of management is an exact science. Herbert Spencer's question raises positive and normative dimensions. It cannot simply be answered as he did by proposing the uniform solution: Science. Academic scholarship traditions and business practices constantly challenge each other in these disciplines as part of recursive processes. There also arises a conflict between intellectual leadership and civil authority which can be considered represented in the post-modern epoch by democratic governance and market-based management. Science is also a source of power, and scientists work with the resources provided by large firms and governments on mega-projects that are capable of transforming things, ideas, and people's consciousness. Ready or not, this is the "one world" that generations now inherit and bequeath. It is this last part that concerns educators and curricula. Bronowski, in his famous work, *The Ascent of Man* (1973), warns that the very existence of science is dependent upon its relating to the moral imagination.

Much has changed since Charles Darwin's time, but there is one aspect of his work that concerns us here when we examine Bronowski's warning. Darwin avoided attention to the evolution of the human species in his seminal work *On the Origin of Species* (1859) but focussed special attention on the origin and history of our own species in a subsequent work, *The Descent of Man* (1871), in which he pointed out the lowly origin of man in his bodily frame. I refer here to animal behaviour, to psychology of aggression and defense to limbic system responses, and also to ways in which the body-mind duality has been used in greed for collectively valued purposes. Adam Smith (1991), immortalised for his classic *The Wealth of Nations* in 1776, is hardly remembered for having also authored *The Theory of Moral Sentiment* in 1759, which according to him was the guiding principle for what was then regarded as the emerging discipline of political economy and what continues to remain as the elusive context of management as well as governance. Real-life situations differ from computer simulations because there may not always be precise solutions, and real life involves taking into consideration what others may do. Just as different parts of the brain interlock, minds interact to render plans, procedures, and tactics probable but also vulnerable. Neither the lives of persons nor of business firms are tractable by any definable computer scheme of problem-solving. Science is merely the Latin word for knowledge. And knowledge and rigor of observation and logic may transcend the rational. If knowledge is not to be limiting, it could not possibly be discretely bound. Indeed as already noted the concept of the Vedas was focussed around how to delimit with explicit assumptions about the impossibility of articulating all that we may experience and the boundlessness of knowledge and enquiry. Bronowski (1973) regarded knowledge as our destiny, where the ascent of man depends on being able to take the next steps in a never-ending journey involving personal, emotional, and intellectual commitment toward working together to produce knowledge in a never-ending stream.

The feasibility of designing curricula to enable knowledge to be created for more than one set of national constituents may now be examined with reference to an activity that is truly international in scope. An obvious choice is international business management education. Action-research studies into internationalisation of curricula concerning international business management were begun by the author in India in 1988 and continued at the School of Business Administration, University of Tampere, and Helsinki School of Economics in 1994. After the first biennium period 1995–97, when the concept of curricular internationalisation of international business studies was first introduced, the coverage was extended in 1998 to bring together nine European universities for a common international curriculum in international business studies for the first time. This possibility was enabled under the auspices of the project "European Integration and Internationalisation" financed by the European Union.

Curricula Design of International Business Management

Business practices are frequently ahead of derived concepts. The attempt to grasp what is at variance with curricular contents by more tools and more data is *ab initio* doomed because of constraints to information processing and costs. Flowing from modernist industrial conceptions of the manufacturing mode, business schools take in "raw material" and put out "finished products," whose worth is judged by the prices they command in the "free market" and for which reason the saying "He who pays the piper calls the tune" is acted out. Management education is in danger of deteriorating into adult day care of a waiting pool of talent being drilled into the social and symbolic representations by which business firms seek to channelise their creativity and aggression for more profit. The solidaristic elements in this remain generically within management as a competitive career system and specifically with alumni associations. Under conditions of diasporic dispersal, both of these may be classified as what we called information conduits rather than global networks. Management education lacks any notion of solidaristic ethics in the Pinarian sense (Pinar 1995) because it has not been expected to do anything other than mirror the requirements of international business firms without at all concerning itself with diverse ways of factoring in governance of nation-states and international regimes.

Business firms may be characterised as a nexus of treaties held in the minds of stakeholders and as tools designed for the pursuit of objectives. Management as a process for setting boundary conditions of response for resources is a universal process even though it needs to adapt itself in the fragmented real world of nation-states to the requirements of international business when the scope of activities encompasses parts of the world beyond one country. For much of the twentieth century, business management education was primarily driven by the requirements of business conditions in nation-states and by the requirements of multinational firms operating within their preferred arenas of action with resource management paradigms. Management education was constructed as a special category in higher education for agricultural, industrial, technological, informational, and military management. This evolved into forms of graduate and post-graduate multi-disciplinary education for the private purpose of being useful to business firms.

In the search for rigor and wider relational prospects, international business education has generally been designed to the neglect of layers of meaning and recursive processes. There are three mainstream approaches to the design of international business studies curricula which may be categorised into:

A. The Techno-structural Imperative Model, where the primacy of technology determines organisation structures emphasising leadership, modelling of systems, and role-modelling and mentoring.

B. The Management Systems Model, where performance imperatives determine imposition of control systems and incentives emphasizing problem-solving using more data and more (faster) tools or through case studies to compare and contrast the actual from the idealised state.

C. The Cross-Cultural Manipulative Model, where adaptations based on game theory and bargaining predominate where principal-agent frameworks and group relations perspectives emphasise the significance and characteristics of dynamic interaction of participants.

The last of these deserves special mention. In the name of internationalisation, a popular default solution is to push whatever is jarring for prevailing local constructs into a black box called "cultural differences." Instead of learning about management of differences, educational curricula as well as business practices encourage both cultivation of instrumental skills to get around cultural differences and learning how to beat a system from roles in other systems. The popularity of "How to..." books on management and the violence triggered from sanctioned aggression against enemies remains the hallmark of strategy paradigms, and the killer vocabulary in warfare has consciously and unconsciously been adopted with pride by management education.[15]

My first experience with curricula design for internationalisation of management education arose in India when I chaired the committee of professors for the revision of the post-graduate programme in management at the Indian Institute of Management, Calcutta, and then in Belgium as visiting professor at K.U. Leuven during 1992–93. In Finland, I got involved at just about the time the internationalisation need arose, after the Cold War ended, and the Soviet trade constituting a quarter of all Finnish business collapsed. In all three countries, the 1990s witnessed the development of curricula from very different starting points. In India, a virtually closed economy with a large domestic market (comparable to the United States and China in terms of the proportion of the economy exposed to foreign trade and investment), the spurt in demand for management graduates came mainly from large domestic businesses seeking export markets and from foreign multinationals expanding foreign direct investment across a range of products, notably international brands and financial and IT services. In Belgium, a small continental European economy, the curricular needs were driven by the sharp increase in the demand for new positions in the financial sector in banking, insurance, and financial markets, making international business very much equated to learning international finance. In Finland, a small open Nordic economy, membership of the European Union, pan-European consolidations, the recovery from recession, and the technology diffusion imperatives created a demand for international business education on a massive scale.

Predictably, the easiest course for Indian management educators was to choose a combination of B and C above (page 160) for Belgian management educators to choose B, and for Finnish management educators to choose a combination of A and C. There was considerable experimentation in these countries involving many educators working in different institutions. My understanding of curriculum needs as phenomenological text and as international text in the Pinarian sense (Pinar 1995) enabled me to visualize some departures from conventional taxonomies and to propose a fourth way.

The fourth way consisted of engaging in a process. Conversations with my counterparts (in the United Kingdom, Belgium, France, the Netherlands, Germany, Australia, Sweden, the United States, in addition to Finland and India) confirmed that all of us were in the same boat, struggling between American textbook approaches and eclectic local traditions in a state of ferment. I considered the possibility that the "empty" curriculum could be tentatively filled with "content" by examining basic elements representing four kinds of attributes that higher education provides: knowledge, skills, sensitivity, and anticipation. My Concept Note prepared as the basis of what went into the "Curriculum Guide" of the University of Tampere (Tampere Yliopisto, 1995), explicitly stated how and why the courses proposed intended to provide one or more of these attributes. This was openly discussed with colleagues and worked with for over half a year before it was finalised. In content terms, the intended objectives were achieved by organizing the curriculum in three parts: Part A, comprising courses which would cover basic knowledge but emphasize sensitivity and skills; Part B, which would deepen the studies to knowledge and anticipation of sectors within services including product-service linkages; and Part C, which would emphasize knowledge and anticipation relevant for specific geographical business areas like Central and Eastern Europe, the Nordic countries, Southeast Asia, NAFTA, South Asia, etc. Simultaneously, in my work with top management teams in in-house workshops, I began to incorporate a dual primary task design similar to the way Harold Bridger of the Scottish Institute visualised it: There would be a primary task around "content" together with a primary task around "process" concerning the discourse itself. Through my work with large multinational firms and my young students in MBA classrooms, gradually, I was able to associate international business strategy with metaphors around the notion of four artefacts corresponding to the four attributes of knowledge, skills, sensitivity, and anticipation.

Four symbolic artefacts corresponding to these four elemental attributes were conceptualised. These comprised a magic book that contains all the knowledge, a magic mirror in which it is possible to see the future for anticipation, a magic herb by which it is possible to eliminate all suffering (find solutions to all problems) and thereby not have to kill sensitivity, and a magic sword with which all the enemies could be defeated, the ultimate in skill. Top management teams comprising managers in the age group thirty-five to fifty-eight seemed to have no difficulty at all in setting their company curricula around what questions they sought answers to from the magic book, which enemies would they want to kill with the magic sword, what suffering or what problems would they want to solve with the magic herb, and what they would want to see with the magic mirror. Occasionally, this mode of thinking also helped top management teams to get in touch with their painful realities, as when a multinational paper company realized that the company had lost its magic mirror, and the magic mirror was with a technology consulting firm on which they had become utterly dependent.

The next step was to visualize learning tasks so that knowledge, skills, sensitivity, and anticipation were explored and endowed with meaning by studying how participants in an education process would see themselves in relation to the world in a classroom, rather than in a firm. The idea of such a learning task was first tested at the University of Economics in Bratislava, where the necessity of internationalizing a common curriculum for international business studies among nine universities from nine different European countries enabled such experimentation in 1998, 1999, and 2000. The learning task assigned to students was to create a story while in the process of locating and formulating the uses to which the magic book, magic herb, magic mirror, and magic sword found at the Castle of the Wizard of Kremnica (in Slovakia) might be put and to figure out how to organize the use of the resources. In one of many discursive formulations, students visualized that the magic book was taken over by a Japanese Corporation, the magic mirror by Magic Mirror Inc. in the United States., the magic sword by Magic Sword AB, a Swedish firm, and the magic herb by Magic Herb AG, a German enterprise. Fierce and passionate debates allowed students to consider whether such resources could be brought into the market/public domain under international regimes. Without doubt, there was considerable learning from the different versions and assumptions explored in different groups, but more importantly the process enabled students to experience the responsibility that goes with authority, and to consider what problems are most worthy of being resolved. This, without relaxing any of the realities to be taken into consideration, meant that a by-product of such learning was knowledge about matters like how intellectual property rights arrange themselves, the role of the media, emerging morphologies of industrial profiles in service economies of the post-industrial era, international economic relations, public policies and trade, welfare, disparities in development, to mention just a few.

The elements of projective identification in such meta-designs enable the curriculum to be loaded with content and processed simultaneously when the curriculum resembles a matrix of space from within which more spaces may be created or found. In such praxis, a teacher in the classroom functions as a process facilitator listening to a story at the same time as its creation. The myriad variants provide ambiguity, layers of meaning, and reflections through a common learning endeavour assigned the nomenclature of a temporary learning institution whose boundaries (of space, time, artefacts, technology, and sentience) were partly set and partly negotiable. Variations of this meta-design by interlocking whole systems were also tested. Temporary learning institutions were also created as joint enterprises between business schools and business firms, where content and process could be studied together in the here and now experience.

A startling revelation from these temporary learning institutions was that participants did not see themselves as bound by location, nor did they consider themselves isolated from other happenings in the larger world. They freely imported assumptions and traded pictures of relatedness that contributed to the learning experience. It was also possible to invite different resource persons into the learning space at different times and even to let the learning institution function autonomously, with the role of the facilitator formally dissolved and renegotiated, or abandoned altogether. With such curricula, the group of elements formed by discursive practice remains unknowable and unmeasureable even after the mind-expanding experiential learning is affirmed by participants.

Conceptualisation of the interactive experience led to broadening and deepening of the curriculum, as Doll's notion of the curriculum as a vision may enable. A learning contract was negotiated for every temporary learning institution. The insight that knowledge is personal and institutional and that there is wisdom in linking the personal with the institutional was probably the most meaningful first inference that could be drawn from this shift away from utilitarian packaging around the three traditional approaches to curricula design in this field. The intensely personal nature of experiential learning transformations was not inhibited by the content loading in dual primary task designs. But there arose even more important insights about the illusive nature of boundary conditions that are features of curricular frames. If national boundaries (and other boundaries) are enablers of containment inasmuch as national spaces are containers for individual identities and collective identities, our decision to consciously envision different curricula evokes the manifold possibilities of plurality of crystallisations of human identity around all kinds of boundaries, all of which may be illusory. All that the human individual carries as his sense of continuity and integrity is the incompleteness without which undecidedness cannot be experienced. Thus what is unknowable, unknown, or that which is not-knowledge may also be regarded as a valid means to expand our consciousness of what is knowledge. The next question would obviously be how to distinguish between knowledge and not-knowledge to the extent that we tolerate illusions existentially and phenomenally, and perhaps to consider how to transcend such illusions.

Illusions of Knowing Versus Identities of Knowing

Each of the metaphors invited identification and involved specific expression of identity in at least one of its intransitive and transformative states—of cathecting, feeling, sensing, knowing, or wondering. These expressions of identification arose for creating, sustaining, and dissolving boundary conditions of a process of experiencing illusions of projective identification, which we may also call management. Similarly, we may consider that illusions of knowing and not knowing arise from the illusions of identities when identities are experienced transformatively in relating self to others with respect to boundary conditions of space, time, technology, artefacts, and relationships. I maintain that each of these boundary conditions is also a part of convenience and an illusion.

In initial experimentation, I emphasised meta-structures and conceptions of only one set of boundaries as illusions, namely, those of space, which are of greatest importance for understanding what knowledge is of most worth through visible and abstract representations that have permeated our collective consciousness in unconscious ways. Our insights could also have been enabled by analysing friction of space as an illusion of time, as in the excellent analysis by Daniel Hillis (1998) and Stewart Brand (1999), who raise an important question as to whether time has become more valuable or more disposable and whether intense "progress" makes everything better or more temporary. Alternatively, we could have discussed artefactual illusions, particularly the way in which archives and museums treasure and organise artefacts as "muses" of great worth. A stated aim of the famous Delors (1996) *Report to UNESCO of the International Commission on Education for the Twenty-First Century* was the construction of ethical solidarity to link local communities to a world society. In the same vein, we could also have focussed on illusions of relationships and what some thinkers call "related-ness" and considered the nature of illusions created from the search for hypothetical certitude of object relations discourses, because knowledge development cannot be separated from its human cultural contexts. The main point of understanding *homo economicus*'s valuation of what knowledge is of most worth is that cultures are not parts of economies; it is economies that are part of cultural and social traditions, bringing us back to subject-object relations.

Foucault prefers the French expression *connaissance*, by which he means the relations of the subject to the object and the formal rules that govern it, distinguishing it from *savoir* to imply the specific illusions contingent to a specific transient boundary condition. Both words translate as knowledge into English, but there is a big difference. The *conaissance*-science axis cannot escape subjectivity, and the *savoir*-science axis cannot do without discursive practice and experiential learning. According to Foucault, by this distinction we may differentiate scientific domains from archeological territories. This enabled Foucault to state that the total set of relations that unite at a given point in time (which he termed *episteme*) is not a form of *connaisance* (knowledge), because it manifests the totality of what can be discovered.

Discoveries in our universe yield many wonders, and the human mind, which is part of the architecture of life, is itself one of these wonders. R.G. H. Siu (1957) and Dwayne Huebner (1999) independently use the expression "wonder" in the sense of marvel (rather than inquire) or marvel beyond inquiry and revel in the marvel. Wilfred Bion (1952) extends this sense of wonder when he denotes the enlightened mind by the symbol "O," stating one has to be "O" in the sense of negating duality or transcending psychic reality and thus enabling a state of fusion of micro-cosmic identity (as a reflexive discursion of macro-cosmic identity) with macro-cosmic identity. Konrad Lorenz's (1977) reflexive conjecture that the terms "subject" and "object" have exchanged meanings thus makes profound sense. Biologically interpreting space from the experience of living species with limited sensual capacities causes subject-object illusion, according to Lorenz.[16]

Bion's (1952) interest in identity and explaining "O" for human species is behind the strange title of his seminal work *Seven Servants,* in which he points to exactly six questions, although puzzling through "I" and "Thou" would have made them eight. It is possible to see the "O" state not as the letter "O" but as a geometric circle which is complete and represented by the rational number zero. In sanskrit, zero is *shunya,* and *shunya* is used synonymously with universal space, in the sense of inner space of identity and in the sense of space that is outside of us. Such spaces are neither voidable (in a contract law sense) nor void (in an empty or non-existing set sense).[17] This separatedness of what is inside and what is outside remains as long as the dualistic mode of identification of I and Thou is not transcended. All questions of identity would dissolve when and if the duality or separatedness of I and Thou is experienced as illusory. Indeed this is the definition of a self-realised soul, where there can be no distinction between *atman* and *brahman.* The process of evoking this deeper consciousness by revoking the illusions (called *maya* in several Eastern philosophies such as Buddhist and Hindu theistic, agnostic, and atheistic traditions) through a process of negation rather than denial (for to deny is to remain caught up in illusions) came up in the conversation of Nachiketa with Yama in the *Katha Upanishad*, where Yama explains to Nachiketa:

> That by which we know form, taste, smell, sounds and touch, by that we also know what exists besides. (Verse 2: 3)

Knowing *what exists besides* implies having an identity from which to know what exists besides. In the works of Erik Erikson (1968) and Rudolf Steiner (1982/1924), the formation of identity is discussed in an evolutionary perspective. The explanatory power of Erikson's model freezes the frame in early adulthood, whereas Steiner viewed life in a Pinarian way as *currere* and considered questions of identity as part of a dynamic continuity where formative processes of early childhood affect identity transformations also in old age. An explanatory logic is deductive, but hypotheses may also be raised for consideration in the course of inquiry, and it is this possibility that John Dewey proposed with his analogy of spiral curriculum (Dewey 1963/1938).

Questions of knowability, undecideability, and incompleteness are central to any discussion of identity in its transformative aspects. If I don't know who I am or am uncertain about the illusions of identity I hold, it follows that incompleteness is inescapable. There is merit in distinguishing knowledge from not-knowledge to be able to relate parts to the whole and to each other in any formal system. I quote here from the *Ishavasja Upanishad:*

> *Vidja cha avidja cha jast dwedobhaya sa ha*
> *Avidjöja mrtjum Tiirtva Vidjöja amritam ashnute*
> (Verse 11, note: ja has been used to denote the English phonetic ya)

> Knowledge and not-knowledge and knowing the difference between these two terms is necessary to transcend from the realm of the perishable to the realm of the eternal. This defines the relation of the individual identity to the highest consciousness—that which is manifest (*vyakta*) in us is of the same appearance as the unmanifest (*avyakta*). The part that makes manifest individual identity out of wholeness and the matter of which it are made is by their nature such that the wholeness will remain even when part of it is removed and even though that which was taken away is only a part, it is as whole as the original entity and so mathematical equations of whole

and part do not apply to that which is unquestionable nor to its manifestations. (Translation mine, from the Sanskrit original)

This was the first clear statement of undecideability of mathematical logic, predating Kurt Gödel's theorem by about 2800 years. However, it was derived from experiential learning and conceptualised into this form, and I am not sure whether the mathematical treatises in the *Yajur veda samhitas* offer a mathematical proof of this or not. What is strikingly interesting is that like Gödel, whose theorems of undecideability and incompleteness belong together, the discussion on incompleteness in the *Ishavasya Upanishad* follows in the very next verse, which reads:

Om Poornamadaha Poornamidam Poornatpoornamudachajate
Poornasja Poornamaadaja Poornamevaavashishjate (Verse 12)

That is whole and this is whole. From whole, whole is enabled, yet whole remains. Separatedness is an illusion. There cannot be any movement because there isn't anything else. It is far away because we cannot sense it. It is near because it is present everywhere and it is hidden in every individual's own heart. If we understand this all-penetrating/pervading presence, the separation of ourselves from others will melt away and along with that will disappear illusions. (Translation mine, from the Sanskrit original)

The nature of knowing, knowability, certitude, undecideability, identity, incompleteness, illusions, sounds, and harmony and how these notions relate to one another are vividly depicted as interconnected in Douglas Hofstadter's (1979) work that synthesises Gödel's logic with Escher's illusions and Bach's harmony in a metaphoric fugue on minds and machines. The questions of identity and the illusory nature of duality in phenomenal experience remain the undercurrent in his later collection of papers too (Hofstadter and Dennet 1981). This is consistent with the notion in the *Mundaka Upanishad* that there exist knowledge domains higher than empirical knowledge.

This is an apt place to dwell on the nature of knowledge. No one possesses it any less if every other person possesses the whole of it. By this we refer to the world's store of meaning and not to the per-capita availability of zeros and ones of information. We may conclude this discussion by observing that illusions of knowing belong to the partitioning of proprietary domains. Identities of knowing belong universally to experiential processes of meaning making. Time to return to consider where this leaves us with internationalisation of curricula and how it affects our understanding of what knowledge is of most worth.

Recapitulating the Four Rs

From our discussion on human identity we may be justified in viewing identity as a magic wand to introduce a fifth metaphor to make sense of the other four: the magic book, the magic sword, the magic herb, and the magic mirror. I did not realize at the time (although this memory may have been lodged somewhere in the deep recesses of my unconscious mind) that Indian mythology provides for four equivalent artefacts to the ones I used. In the conception of *Vishnu*, responsible for curricular continuity as the maintainer of the universe, Vishnu is always depicted with a *shankha* (seashell), *chakra* (disc or diskette), *gada* (mace), and *padma* (lotus). The resemblance and correspondence with the functional aspects of Doll's four Rs, as well with the four metaphors used by me, are significant. I derive comfort from the thought, that a rose is a rose by any name.

This is an age where the sword and the mirror are valued greatly. The sword signifies the power of organised violence with which enemies may be vanquished or subdued and remains at the heart of leadership, management, and governance. The myth of the sword is essentially reflected in technology as a prime mover and the battles for the proprietary use of technologies with the belief that technology can solve everything. The millennium cult spawned an industry of crystal-ball gazers because the demand for recursive anticipation is high, and people want to plan for a knowable future even if we cannot know what may happen in the very next moment. It follows that the only books that are valued are those that contain recipes for making better swords or better mirrors. Is there hope for our magic book and our magic herb? *Yrtti* (which means "herb" in Finnish, and which is the abbreviation of the full form *yrityksen taloustieteen ja yksitysoikeuden laitos*), as the business school of the University of Tampere is colloquially referred to, in enabling space for experimentation, for a complex curricular internationalization problem to be resolved, lived up to its name. Appropriate institutions like *Yrtti* that enable nexus and locus of international networking are the *magic herbs* needed for creative curricular internationalisation.

At this point, I am tempted to divert attention to which knowledge is of most worth or what education is of most worth or which teachers are of most worth, but that discussion clearly belongs elsewhere—in sequels to this work. Remaining within the parameters set for the present inquiry, it is pertinent to note that of William Doll's four Rs, only relations and recursion are presently receiving great attention to the neglect of richness in depth, layers of meaning, and institutional solidarity for problem-solving, which the magic herb signifies in our metaphoric schema, and at the cost of rigor of observation, experiential learning, and logic, which the magic book signifies.

Many criteria may be developed to remain alert to destruction of potential knowledge creation for our three referents of learners, knowledge, and society. Here, I propose just one. I prefer curricula designs to be inclusive rather than exclusive. A curriculum design that enables a sense of knowledge as unbounded by favouring an expansive notion of space where there is room for new ideas from every direction must be preferred because it is more likely to nourish wonder. The role of the teacher as a facilitator would then be as a witness to the wonder with which questions are formulated, regardless of whether they are answered or answerable. If there is sufficient wonder, it is reasonable to expect that the questions of most worth will be raised and pursued, and perhaps along the way this would be the surest way to partake of knowledge of most worth as a by-product. If our identities of consciousness are to transcend illusions of knowing, a solidaristic vision of that unity will value harmony. If harmony in the pursuit of knowledge is valued as an aperiodic quality of life, by its very nature such harmony may resemble aperiodic crystals amenable to scientific and aesthetic appreciation in new worlds of meanings and open new worlds of wonder.

Conclusions (New Thresholds?)

Phenomena are encountered at three levels—in abstraction, in psychic and sensory experience, and in interactive experience. Only a small portion are codable in zeros and ones. Knowledge of most worth cannot be located in such a subset unless the flow of meaning can be qualitatively and quantitatively enriched to a degree of harmony where it becomes identifiably self-evident in a universal way and opens new worlds of wonder. Knowledge creation and the enabling of knowledge creation constitute investments for well-being as intergenerational continuities. Our changing conceptions of the meta-structures of spaces we relate to or wish to relate to are difficult to satisfy within frameworks of national curricula. Is this a time of *chronos* (wisdom)? Or a time of *kairos* (cleverness)? The choice between recasting valued education systems and abandoning them is not an easy one, but it is a choice educators must make if we are not to invite the risk of degrading civilization itself.

Notes

1. This is a revised version of the paper presented at the conference on Internationalization of Curriculum Studies, Louisiana State University, Baton Rouge, April 27–30, 2000. The author gratefully acknowledges the generous contributions of Swami Gopal Bhai, Risto Nuolimaa, Albert M. Sammut, Akash Narain, and William Doll to his thinking. Address for correspondence: amras@vsnl.com. The author is Research Professor, Indian Council for Research on International Economic Relations, New Delhi.
2. The *Vedas* are part of the ancient *shruti* tradition of oral discourse–based learning with a teacher from times immemorial (going back thousands of years) from which the word "data" of Sanskrit origin derives. The term *data* refers to the giver/bestower of knowledge through insightful information. The *Vedas* (in four parts) were published in written form circa 800 B.C.E, when they became widely available, and predate the earliest Greek philosophers. The written form came with an important caveat that knowledge is infinite and unbounded, and written representations were never to be considered "absolute" or "complete"; learners (subjects) were to treat *data* (cathecting objects—personifiable and inanimate) as given or received to be endowed with meaning from their lived experience to nurture justified beliefs. The word *Veda* means "limiting to a bound, that which is boundless or unboundable." This caveat was not heeded, and *Vedas* were wrongly interpreted canonically except in a few unbroken traditions of continuity like Adi Sampradaya. The Latin language at the time of St. Thomas of Aquinas did not have words like "data" (*dator* meaning "giver" appeared first), "agenda," "stamina." Such words, originally foreign to Latin, are an anamolous group of words referred to in English dictionaries as "Latin plurals." These so-called Latin plurals have no singular forms in the Queen's English as "she is spoke." This may be so because it is not possible to visualize such words with their meanings intact in a singular form. "Data," for instance, require a series of observations; also, subject and object.
3. It is worth recalling that prior to World War I, passports and visas were not required for international travel in most parts of the world. In this sense, the world was more open to cross-border international exchange of people, information, and artefacts than it is today. Of course, the structural limitations were more severe then. However, as far as businesses were concerned, domestic and foreign investments did not have to be limited to natural national endowments. Foreign investments were not so risky, particularly for those of West European and North American origins because of the gold standard and sovereign patronage and privileges in colonies. Knowledge of languages and subjugating "natives" was knowledge of most worth. It was estimated by economists Naoroji and Gadgil and the mathematician Arun Kumar that without the drain on the resources of colonies in Africa and Asia, Europe lacked the capital to industrialise, perennially suffering from a negative balance of trade and payments until 1805. Events like the Boston Tea Party and the American Declaration of Independence were the reasons why European powers created strangleholds on large parts of Africa, Asia, and South America. This paper is not concerned with themes of drain and deindustrialisation but only their residues to note that local knowledge traditions were suppressed to absorb and to layer specific conceptions of universality of modernism, mainly in Anglo-American terms. Generations in colonies were educated with curricula relevant only to the colonist as exemplified by the reciting

of odes to skylarks by people who had never seen a skylark. The very formulation of questions of what knowledge is of most worth was possible only after first identifying with the aggressors.

4. In Spencer's conception, there was science in constructing a hierarchy of races of mankind, and he carried the white man's burden to the extent of rationalising why "negritos" and "Polynesians" were placed at the bottom of the pile. This aspect of the great educationist Herbert Spencer is usually quietly glossed over (I am personally unsure if this happened because previous studies on the topic were mostly by white Anglo-Saxon Protestants or simply out of neglect). When the relevance of worldviews is examined in section 6 on the question of prioritisation of proximate cognition, it becomes clearer how our three referents, learners, knowledge, and society, relate and how normative assignations of value specificity, value neutrality, and value universality affect pictures in the mind. My working hypothesis that Spencer (like many modernists to this day) saw every difference as hierarchic would then assume significance in understanding the limits of internationalisation if reason cannot precede identity. By his logic, Spencer grouped civilized societies into two kinds: flourishing (English) and decayed (Hebrews and Phoenicians, Ancient Americans); the rest were simply uncivilized societies, and these included the American, Asian, African, Polynesian, and Negrito (Spencer et al. 1880).

5. Such a rationale is similar to a recent World Bank president's memorandum (published to his great embarrassment and subsequent apology) that toxic waste dumps should be located in the neighbourhoods of the poorest African societies because financing the compensation costs for lives lost or disfigured would be optimised at such locations.

6. Spencer used the term "data" in the title in its original connotation of "bestower" or "giver" in an effort to understand the origin and nature of altruism. Rudolf Steiner also uses the term "data" in the same way and confirms that the word comes from Sanskrit and refers to the persona of the bestower (teacher?) because meaningful information arises from data received and integrated into consciousness as knowledge (Steiner 1924/1982, 29).

7. Some universities, in recognition of such dilemmas, offer Master of Arts degrees as well as Master of Science degrees (with different curricula) in fields of study like mathematics.

8. Words with the prefix "post" have come into common usage. For example, post-fordist, post-industrial, post-bourgeois, post-colonial, post-capitalist, post-socialist, post-welfare, post-scarcity, post-civilized, post-modern, and post-911. They signal shifts away from ideas that permeated modern industrial consciousness towards emerging states. Some part of this anticipation arises from the power of the metaphor of the new millennium, as if humanity has crossed some definitive chasm, leaving behind notions that do not belong to our times. The other part arises from the realisation that there is a noticeable difference or departure from how things used to be.

9. When Castells and Henderson presented the paper referred to here at the IILS Conference on High Tech Diffusion and the Labour Market in New Delhi in 1988, there was much discussion on characteristics of marketplaces versus marketspaces. With the emergence of standards of Internet protocol (IP) addresses, some of the argument of placeless power loses its force. Further, physical space is also a space of flows, but the only way to define

human activity is by its marketplace value as a consumed or produced good or service.
10. Schools in some parts of the world now require children to become proficient in surfing the Web to strengthen their faith in the new medium as a substitute or supplement to tactile human interaction. Under the guise of teaching letter recognition and number concepts, taxpayers are now subsidising the covert instruction of children in the art of understanding television and Internet commercials at the cost of basic educational activities such as expression, observation, relating to nature and other humans, developing abstract and concrete skills, empathic sensitivities, and cultivating attention spans for concentrated thinking. A by-product of such curricular choice is to make aggressive behaviour in schools more likely, which, in turn, has a social cost in juvenile delinquency and overdrugging of children to control such behaviour—good news for the profits of drug companies and private custodial institutions.
11. Amartya Sen, Nobel Prize winner in economics in 1998 and Master of Trinity College, Cambridge, was stopped by a British immigration official at Heathrow who suspected there might be some impropriety in his trying to enter the United Kingdom because of his Indian passport. Sen was questioned whether the address "Master's Lodge," which he declared he was proceeding to, was presumptuous on the basis that the master is his close friend. Taking the question reflexively, Sen answered in the affirmative and went on to ask, in his Romanes Lecture to the University of Oxford, whether the way we reason can be independent of our consciousness of identity we carry or attribute to others.
12. Refer to: http://www.msnbc.com/news/404924.asp?cp1=1, http://CNN.com/2000/TECH/space/04/14/space.quasar.reut/index.html, and "Why NASA Should Go to Pluto," *Economist*, September 30, 2000, p. 24.
13. Among economists, there are monetarists, trade theorists, poverty economists, industrial economists, agricultural economists, development economists, labour economists, and institutional economists to mention just a few of the labels; in geology, mineral geologists, stratospheric geologists, and tropospheric geologists to name just three kinds in a growing range; among oceanographers, chemical oceanographers and physical oceanographers; in astronomy, positional astronomers and radio astronomers; in life and environmental sciences, meteorologists, gene biologists, mitochondria specialists, plant breeders, and plain farmers, petrologists (who study rocks and throw away the soil), and pedologists (who study the soil and throw away the rocks), and, occasionally, some of these people, may talk to each other.
14. A deconstructionist controversy about whether the moon landing really occurred was raised recently from the data that, apart from some rocks and pictures of fluttering flags on supposedly airless surfaces, there is no independent confirmation to support such a conclusion. More important than the fact of the moon landing is the representation of that fact and how beliefs about it affect our pictures in the mind.
15. Students learn about how to lock customers with relationship marketing and lifestyles marketing, find captive markets, develop killer products and applications, carry out dawn raids, gather market intelligence, use hidden persuaders, kill competition, gather business intelligence, cannibalise machines, eliminate downtime, hunt for heads, right size with exit policies, subtract people, connect outsourced brains and hands to information-processing machines, use golden handcuffs, gold collars, and tin parachutes, use poi-

soned pills, do hostile takeovers, and find white knights and shark repellants. One could go on adding to the list, but this suffices to make the point that the metaphor of business management is war.

16. Lorenz quotes the greatest expert on protozoa, H. S. Jennings, as saying, "If one observes an amoeba in its natural habitat, not on a slide but moving freely in a petri dish, one is amazed at the versatility of its behaviour and its adaptability. If it were the size of a dog, one would not hesitate to attribute to it the power of subjective experience." I presume that if it were the size of a dog, there would then be amoeba trainers too. For a discussion on how minds are related by the phenomenon of life and a specific discussion "From the Minds of Amoebas to the Mind of Einstein," see Skolimowski (1994). It is worth recalling that Einstein failed in the entrance exam to the Eidgennossische Technische Hochschule (ETH) in Zurich in fall 1895, and John Maynard Keynes failed the entrance exam for one of the two best-known British universities because he was found weak in economics. That these luminaries survived this experience suggests that there may be others who don't, and that is in itself a reason to question the certitude of knowledge which is part of the education tradition of what educators do to minds.

17. The word "yoga" means unity and the practice of *yoga* is a striving for unity. This is supported by interpretations of Patanjali's Yogasutra 48 where a distinction is drawn between absolute (*ritam*, which can be translated as "rhythm" or "harmony") and relative (*satyam* or "truth") aspects of creation. I equate *ritam* with rhythm or harmony because of the notion that the sound of a *shankha* (*shankha dhwani*) falls silent when consciousness attains the highest vibrations in the state of *shunya*. This idea is behind a number of meditation traditions, including the *pranahuti* vibrations meditation system of Sahaj Marg and Zen Buddhism. See Chattopadhyay (1999) for an insightful discussion on the illusion of identity, which is close to but not identical with my views. I am grateful to Gouranga Chattopadhyay for sending me his paper in June 2000, and it is with an acute sense of wonder that I derive comfort from the support his independent observations provide to my understanding of the matter presented at the ICS conference in April 2000.

References

Anderson, B. (1991). *Imagined communities* (revised and extended edition). New York: Verso.
Bhabha, H. K. (1994). *The location of culture.* London: Routledge.
Bion, W. R. (1952). *Seven servants.* London: Tavistock.
Brand, S. (1999). *The clock of the long now.* London: Phoenix.
Bronowski, J. (1973). *The ascent of man,* pages 436–8. Australia: Angus and Robertson.
Bruner, J. (1960). *The process of education.* Cambridge, MA: Harvard University Press.
——— (1986). *Actual minds, possible worlds.* Cambridge, MA: Harvard University Press.
——— (1990). *Acts of meaning.* Cambridge, MA: Harvard University Press.
Castells, M. (Ed.) (1999). *Critical education in the new information age.* Introduction by Peter McLaren. Lanham, MD.: Rowman and Littlefield.
Castells, M., and J. Henderson (1987). Techno-economic restructuring, socio-political processes and spatial transformations: A global perspective. In *Global restructuring and territorial development.* Edited by J. Henderson and M. Castells. Beverly Hills, CA: Sage.

Chattopadhyay, G. (1999). The illusion of identity. *Socio-Analysis 1* (1): 1–23.
Corbin, A. (1994). *The lure of the sea.* Cambridge, MA: Polity.
Darwin, C. (1859). *On the origin of species.* London: Collins.
—— (1998). The descent of man. New York: Prometheus Reprint (original work published 1871).
Delors, J. (1996). *Learning, the treasure within: Report to UNESCO of the International Commission on Education for the twenty-first century.* Paris: UNESCO.
Dewey, J. (1963). *Experience and education.* New York: Collier (original work published 1938).
Doll, W. E., Jr. (1993). *A post-modern perspective on curriculum.* New York: Teachers College.
Erikson, E. H. (1968). *Identity: Youth and crisis.* London: Faber & Faber.
Gazetas, A. (2000a). *Imagining selves.* New York: Peter Lang.
—— (2000b). Reconstituting pedagogies: the (im)possibilities for inter/nationalizing curriculum studies. Paper presented at Internationalization of Curriculum Studies Conference, Baton Rouge, April 27–30, 2000 (mimeo).
Gough, N. (1998). All around the world: Science education, constructivism and globalisation. *Educational Policy 12* (5): 507–24.
—— (2000). Locating curriculum studies in the global village. *Journal of Curriculum Studies 32* (2): 329–42.
Harpold, T. (1991). The contingencies of the hypertext link. *Writing on the Edge 2* (2): 126–38.
Hillis, W. D. (1998). *The pattern on the stone.* New York: Basic Books.
Hofstadter, D. R. (1979). *Gödel, Escher, Bach: An eternal golden braid.* Hassocks, Eng.: Harvester.
Hofstadter, D., and Dennet, D. (1981). *The mind's I: Fantasies and reflections on self and soul.* Harmondsworth: Penguin.
Hollins, T.H.B. (1968). *What knowledge is of most worth?* Bulmershe Lecture, Reading University. London: W.H. Smith.
Huebner, D. E. (1999). The capacity for wonder and education. In *The Lure of the Transcendent,* pages 1–9. Edited by Vikki Hillis and introduced by William F. Pinar. Mahwah, NJ: Lawrence Erlbaum.
Kirshner, D. (1997). Situated logic in infancy. In *Situated cognition: Social, semiotic and psychological perspectives,* pages 83–95. Edited by David Kirshner and James A. Whitson. Mahwah, NJ: Lawrence Erlbaum.
Lewin, K. (1936). *Principles of topological psychology.* New York: McGraw-Hill.
—— (1951). *Field theory in social science.* New York: Harper.
Lorenz, K. (1977). *Behind the mirror.* New York: Harcourt Brace.
Lyotard, J.-F. (1984). *The postmodern condition: A report on knowledge.* Minneapolis: University of Minnesota Press.
Marx, K. (1973). *Grundrisse.* New York: Random House (original work published 1859).
McChesney, R. (1999). *Rich media, poor democracy: Communication politics, history and scholarship in dubious times.* Urbana: University of Illinois.
—— (2000). So much for the magic of technology and the free market. In *The world wide*

web and contemporary cultural theory, pages 5–35. Edited by Andrew Herman and Thomas Swiss. New York: Routledge.

Miller, J. G. (1978). *Living systems.* New York: McGraw-Hill.

Moulthorp, Stuart (2000). Error 404: Doubting the web. In *The world wide web and contemporary cultural theory,* pages 259–75. Edited by Andrew Herman and Thomas Swiss. New York: Routledge.

Newman, J.H.C. (1999). *The idea of a university.* Lanham, MD: Regnery.

Ninnes, P. (2000). *Representing space: Complicity and counter hegemony in science curriculum materials in Canada, Australia and Aotearoa, New Zealand.* Paper presented at the Internationalization of Curriculum Studies conference, Baton Rouge, April 27–30, 2000. (mimeo).

Nonaka, I. (1998). The concept of "Ba": Building a foundation for knowledge creation. *California Management Review.* Spring, pages 40–54.

Piaget, J. (1978). *Behaviour and evolution.* New York: Pantheon Books.

Pinar, W. F., Reynolds, W., Slattery, P. and Taubman, Peter (1995). *Understanding curriculum,* pages 792–843. New York: Peter Lang.

Pinar, W. F. (2003). Toward the Internationalization of Curriculum Studies. In *Internationlization of curriculum studies: Papers from the LSU Conference.* Edited by Donna Trueit, William E. Doll, Jr., Hongyu Wang, and William F. Pinar. New York: Peter Lang.

Salonen, J. (2000). *The organisation of processing information flows.* Tampere: Tampere University Press (*Tietojenkäsittelyjärjestelmän Hankinta. Tummavuoren Kirjapaino Oy, Vantaa*).

Sen, A. (1977). Rational fools: A critique of the behavioural foundations of economic theory. *Philosophy and Public Affairs 6*: 317–44.

——— (1999). *Reason before identity: The Romanes Lecture, 1998 at University of Oxford.* New Delhi: Oxford University Press.

Siu, R.G.H. (1957). *The Tao of science.* New York: John Wiley.

Skolimowski, H. (1994). *The participatory mind.* London: Arkana.

Smith, A. (1759). *The theory of moral sentiment.* Full text is available online at http://www.adamsmith.org.uk/smith/won-intro.htm

——— (1991). *The wealth of nations.* New York: Knopf (original work published 1776). Full text is available online at http://www.adamsmith.org.uk/smith/won-intro.htm

Spencer, H. (1859). What knowledge is of most worth? *Westminster Review.*

——— (1879). *The data of ethics.* New York: A. L. Burt.

———, Duncan, D., Scheppig, R., and Collier, J. (Eds.) (1880). *Descriptive sociology.* London: William and Norgate.

Steiner, R. (1982). *The essentials of education: Five lectures delivered during the education conference at the Waldorf School, Stuttgart, April 8–12, 1924.* 3rd edition. London: Rudolf Steiner.

Yliopisto, T. (1995). *Opinto Opas 1995-97,* Ialoudellis-Hallimollinen Jiedekunta, pages 347–351.

Turnbull, D. (1993). Local knowledge and comparative scientific traditions. *Knowledge and Policy, 6* (3/4): 29–54.

——— (1997). Reframing science and other local knowledge traditions. *Futures* 29 (6): 551–62.
Whitehead, A. N. (1929). *Aims of Education*. London: Macmillan.

CHAPTER EIGHT

Curriculum Reforms in Norway: "To Change in Order to Preserve?"

Lars Monsen • Norway

The new curriculum, Reform–94, has been described in many different ways. Some assert that it represents an attempt to develop a completely new education policy for the next century, a resolute attempt to break with old traditions and create new ones. Others maintain that the reform represents a step in the opposite direction, recreating old lines of division (Trippestad 1997). These diametrically opposed interpretations as to the nature of reform indicate how it is possible to read totally different intentions in the document upon which the reform builds. It is an old adage that knowledge "is in the eyes of the beholder." I shall take as my starting point texts (such as the following) on curriculum reform and explore their intentions and ambitions. When I choose to use the term *ambition,* it is taken to mean something more than intentions; it encompasses some of the wider goals held by people or groups with these intentions. In my opinion the new curriculum, Reform–94, is an ambitious reform. I will try to explain why this is the case.

> To transform upper secondary education schools so that they become comprehensive is a notable Norwegian enterprise. The establishment and development of this type of school was a central element in the work on the reforms and all the political parties were in agreement. In 1986 there were 163,000 applicants, and 71% or 116,000 successfully gained a place. In the course of the last decade this represents an increase of over 45%. In the spirit of teaching reforms, this has also led to an enrichment of the teaching offered. At the same time these schools are highly complex

institutions with many conflicting goals, and they are under pressure from many different directions. It has been said that there is a mismatch between what pupils learn and society needs. (KUD/OECD 1989: 131)

The Reform's Ambitions

In this chapter my concern is with the content of the reform. It is characterised by goal-directed curricula. This central ambition is not new, but compared with earlier curricula the new curriculum is formulated as goals for what the pupils are to learn. The question about how and to what extent it is possible to formulate goals in such a manner that they can influence what happens in the classroom was and still is a controversial issue in educational research and debate (Simola 1998; Elliot 1996; Cuban 1990). In the reform documents it is tacitly accepted that the formulation of goals should form the foundation for planning and implementation of teaching as well as the evaluation of the pupil's performance. In this and several other areas the reform marks itself as *ambitious,* since it either ignores or rises above this debate and expresses a clear desire to initiate a change in curriculum thinking. The question as to if this has been wise in hindsight is something I shall return to later.

The ambitious aspect of the reform is also evident in other important parts of its content. I will mention two in particular: 1) new pupil and teacher roles permeate central documents such as the "core curriculum," the "guide," methodology aids, and more implicitly, in the curriculum for different subjects, and 2) changed conceptions of the upper secondary education schools as educational institutions (van den Berg and Sleegers 1996). There are many testimonies concerning the new pupil and teacher roles, but I will draw attention to an aspect which I regard as one of its central ambitions: to create an equal relationship between pupil and teacher in a democratic organisation, where pupils deliver the premises and make contributions to an educational social environment.

> The teachers at the alternative schools tried to create for themselves new roles which integrated the roles of friend, adult and teacher. There was much confusion in establishing this new kind of relationship. There are costs involved in abandoning the old roles. (Wilson 1976, 80)

Norwegian research, following its international counterparts, has been interested in these questions for several decades. And if the conclusion of this research is not unambiguous regarding new roles, many say that these ambitions, which have left their mark on reform pedagogy[1] in the twentieth century, do, in fact, show some of the path-breaking attempts made by individuals and schools (Tyack and Tubin 1994). With different approaches, theoretical conceptions, and methods, the signal is relatively clear: reform pedagogy's ambitions have been tried in many different forms in many different countries, but after a period of enthusiastic support it appears to be the case that the school as a social institution once again takes the reins and the "normal model" returns to a position of dominance (Cuban 1998).

This leads to the next ambition I will examine. To create new pupil and teacher roles, the assumption is that schools as organisations are transformed into learning organisations, where educational questions have an important position in the daily life of the classroom and in the school as a social community. Existing research on upper secondary education has reached the same conclusion: Schools in upper secondary education have less of the character of uniform organisations and should be regarded as groups of professions with common interests, where their professional interests determine what takes place in daily interactions with colleagues and pupils (Siskin 1994). If we accept that this research shows how difficult it has been to bring about fundamental changes in the school as a social institution, it can lend support to my opening assertion in this section: the content of Reform–94 has had ambitious goals. On the other hand, there exists educational research which has been occupied with how the educational systems in different countries have changed both as a result of changes in society and also as a result of political decisions and policies (Eide 1995). This "long revolution" (Williams 1985) of the education system where the structure is transformed, its scope widened, new subjects developed, administrative relations taken into account, and so on doesn't necessarily mean that "life in the classroom" has greatly changed. There is no automatic connection between what happens on the societal level (the macro-level) and what happens in the classroom (the micro-level). I will look more closely at how the intentions or ambitions in the content of the reform, which represent the decisions made on the societal level, have or have not exerted an influence on the daily life of upper secondary education's "thousand classrooms."

The background for my analysis is my work on the evaluation of the content of the reform beginning in the autumn of 1994. For three years I followed eight schools where teachers, pupils, and heads were interviewed on a number of successive occasions. Subjects my colleagues and I have looked at closely are English, mathematics, and the natural sciences. We have interviewed teachers and pupils, while along with two colleagues I have interviewed the principals of these schools and their superiors at the county level. These interviews were used to devise questionnaires. In spring 1995 we sent a questionnaire to a representative sample of teachers (who taught mathematics and English at the foundation level) and to principals. The following spring, in 1996, we sent a corresponding (but not totally identical) questionnaire to a representative group of pupils who were asked about mathematics and English. The final questionnaire was administered in the spring of 1998 with replies from 790 teachers, 40 principals, and 3,709 pupils. The response percentage was, respectively, 52 percent, 93 percent, and 77 percent. The Central Statistical Office was responsible for the collection of the data, and they took a random sample of 45 schools. Even though the last questionnaire, especially with respect to the contribution made by the teachers, was more comprehensive because we cooperated with the Labour Research Institute (AFI), we repeated some of the same questions from 1995 and 1996 so that a comparison was possible. In the last sample all the pupils studying in secondary year course were included along with all teachers born before 1st October. This meant that nearly all subjects taught were represented and that pupils could themselves select which one they wanted to talk about when asked questions on the curriculum.

Interviews were carried out individually or in groups. The group interviews have been used to follow up views and statements expressed in the opening interviews with individual teachers and pupils. This material has been included in four preliminary reports, in the final report, and in three article collections. No new material is presented in this article, but I will try to develop my analysis in relation to the questions formulated above. My goal is, therefore, to bring to light several nuances in research on upper secondary education and, in a more general manner, to comment on the connection between macro- and micro-levels in the Norwegian education system.

Towards New Pupil and Teacher Roles in Upper Secondary Education?

Within these limitations there was however a majority who wanted to make the A-level high school more "pupil centred": When the profile of attitudes in table 7 is examined as a whole, it shows that most A-level teachers didn't want changes which might threaten school standards—as they traditionally have been defined in terms of exams, or changes which would result in the removal of the A-level college as an independent type of school. Most were against merging with vocational schools, and wanted A-level colleges to remain as an academic school based upon the admission of the most academic talented. With with this revervation they hoped that the school would become less paternalistic and that A-level education should be more suited to the desires of the individual pupil (Lauglo 1972: 300).

Before attempting to answer this question, I will say a little about the concept of "role" I intend to use. In sociological theory, role is defined as the basic element in each and every social system, where interaction between different actors occupying roles is based upon the system's expectation of norms and values. Role theories through the years have been criticised for building upon a deterministic view of Homo Sociologicus (Dahrendorf 1961). They have failed to provide a simple, logical, and empirically founded theory able to account for why so much of institutional life in each society can be characterised by stability, predictability, and continuity. Role theory has problems explaining those "moments in history" when events take an unexpected turn, resulting in swift and unanticipated consequences. This means that it is necessary to use other theoretical perspectives to give meaning to and insight into the course of events (e.g., Reid 1972). If Reform–94 turns out to be one of these "turning points" in the development of the Norwegian educational system, then my theoretical conception will not be able to grasp the significance of the reform. But much of what I have already found about the content of the reform and the effect of its implementation upon the everyday life of the school suggests that role theory is still appropriate. This is because even though I shall now look more closely at the possible changes, what is at issue are gradual and system-maintaining changes which role theory takes up.[2]

In the school's institutional life it is possible to say that the pupil and teacher constitute the school's complementary pair of roles. Around this role pair the educational institution has developed itself to become a complicated national educational system. Over a longer historical perspective it isn't difficult to see how the building of this system has influenced life in the classroom (Lundgren 1979). There have been milestones where new laws have been passed, increasing educational opportunities for a new social strata in the population, and developing administrative structures as a result of the system's differentiation. Reform–94 occupies a position in the long tradition of educational reforms which have tried to meet contemporary challenges and led, as a consequence, to developments and restructuring and, in some cases, to radical breaks with each reform's opportunity for system consolidation.

> A friend of mine once remarked to me that Norway had achieved its structural reform goals only to discover that it has not got what it wanted. Any solution to a problem creates other problems. In the Norwegian case their solution is not yet clear. The country leads the way in terms of general reform, and those who are attempting similar reforms may learn some lessons from the Norwegian case that will overcome some of these new problems as they forge their reforms. (Rust 1985: 216)

What then of this reform? Will it lead to system consolidation or to the development of a fundamental restructuring of upper secondary education? The answer to this question is to some extent dependent upon how pupil and teacher roles develop. Are we to experience a gradual change and a development which creates a more differentiated system but with consolidation around well-known norms and values? Before we make a more detailed analysis I must draw attention to a fundamental difficulty with the time perspective. The type of changes to be discussed can rarely be limited to a period as short as four years. This means that the whole of the analysis must be regarded tentatively in this respect. It should, nevertheless, be a contribution to the research work which can and should continue.

What do My Data Indicate of Possible Changes in the Pupil and Teacher Role?

I will take as my starting point a comparison of the two questionnaires completed by the teachers in 1995 and 1998, where some of the same questions were asked. The samples in the two cases were not totally comparable. In 1995, 440 mathematics and English teachers replied, while in 1998 the number of teachers from most subjects and types of course was 790. But, as was revealed in the analysis of the data, the most important variations in both questionnaires were not between the subjects and the difference between general courses and vocational courses and between the sexes. In relation to variables the two questionnaires are comparable. Besides, there was such a large agreement in the answers in the two questionnaires that there is reason to believe that the most important variations in the teachers are revealed in both cases. In the following, I will look at some examples of both stability and change in replies to identical or comparable questions from the two different points separated in time. The examples are chosen because they can

The Teacher's View of the Curriculum Has Changed Little

aid in the analysis of the influence of the content of the reform on the teacher's role.

We asked teachers in both questionnaires what they thought of the general curriculum, of the methodological guide in the particular subject, and of some of the central principles contained in the curriculum reform. The replies were almost identical. It was somewhat surprising to find such a high degree of agreement between the replies across the different answer alternatives. This supported my assertion above that both the surveys were representative for all the teachers in the schools of upper secondary education. It can appear as if the teachers in schools of upper secondary education changed only slightly their opinion and evaluation of the content in the reform from 1995 to 1998. The group who supported the central principles in curriculum reform was then, as now, between two-thirds and three-quarters of the whole. The evaluation of the general curriculum was generally the same. The same applies to the methodological guide.

How are we to understand this stability in the answers when the questionnaires were separated by three years? The group who evaluated the content of the curriculum reform positively and supported its central principles also existed at the beginning of the reform. At the other end of the scale, there is the group who evaluated the content of the reform just as negatively in 1998 as in 1995. It seems that what has happened over three years has influenced only to a small degree the opinions and evaluations of the group of teachers. This stability in opinions must be seen against a background of the efforts made to persuade teachers about the necessity of the curriculum's content, its legitimacy, and its educational reasoning. Has all this effort been in vain when almost none of them have changed their opinions about the content of the reform? This would at any rate be a far too easy conclusion. It is possible that those who were most positive to the principles in the reform has got a firmer foundations for their views by being part of the reform process. Those who were more negative to these principles might have got something to think about, even if they do not admit it. And not in the least, it is possible that a relatively large group of doubtful skeptics hesitated because they wanted to see how things developed before arriving at a final standpoint. If it is the case, that the changes in the content of the reform represent a more comprehensive and farreaching challenge to existing practice, then it can be expected that the changes have not been immediately realised. But, as mentioned above, the reform *has* led to changes. If there have been generally few changes in relation to perceptions and opinions, we have found changes in relation to what teachers *did* with the curriculum.

The Teachers Have Changed Their Ways of Working

A greater number of teachers in 1998 than in 1995 said they used the reform curriculum, both in relation to planning, implementation, and evaluation of teaching. It has become more usual to do planning together with colleagues, and teachers also say that to a greater extent they include pupils in this planning. Even though the pupils to a lesser extent reported that they participated in curriculum planning, the differences do not undermine the teachers' assertions. If these figures are correct, the curriculum reform has had an effect. The changes are not dramatic, and there is still a large group of teachers who continue to work in a manner more or less uninfluenced by the new curriculum.

How can this change be explained? It must be seen against the teachers' background perception that the curriculum does not appear to have changed over this period of time. It appears that some of the teachers who in 1995 supported the principles but either could not or would not realise them in practice, now three years on were planning with their colleagues. They also involved their pupils in this planning and introduced project work. This change is in the order of 10 percent–20 percent of the whole sample. It must be kept in mind that we are dealing here with different degrees of self-reported realisation of the new ways of working. Even though there was some variation from statement to statement, the pattern was nonetheless consistent enough to allow the assertion that there has been a real change. We were here confronted with an example of a number of teachers who had changed their behaviour while their attitudes had remained the same. In the course of the three years it appears that there was a significant increase in the number of teachers in schools of upper secondary education who followed up the expectations contained in the curriculum reform. In some areas these changes appear more marked, such as in regard to the introduction of talking with pupils and the use of informal types of evaluation. Here the differences lie in the region of well over 20 percent. Pupils also suggested an increased use of the new ways of working, but the difference between 1995 and 1998 was less when compared with the figures for teachers. Several explanations can be given for this divergence. The most actual is the shorter time interval between questionnaires for pupils than for teachers. It can be further connected with the fact that pupils, to a lesser degree than teachers, regard the questions as relevant for them and that they therefore express a greater tendency to assemble themselves around the middle of the scale in terms of replies. Even though this might be the case, it should be possible to measure a change in pupil attitudes and behaviour if this had occurred in the time period.

There is a tendency among pupils to indicate fewer changes with respect to other questions. These changes should be seen against a background in which teachers have not followed up the expectations in the curriculum reform. This concerns, in particular, their participation in school evaluation. Even though teachers report somewhat more activity from their side when it comes to involving pupils in school evaluation, the percentages from the two questionnaires are almost identical, e.g., only 14 percent of pupils are of the opinion that they took part in written feedback both in 1995 and 1998. We find here another anomaly. Even though teachers report that they involve their pupils to a greater extent in the planning of teaching and in its realisation, it seems that a greater number of teachers in 1998 are skeptical about the principle of "responsibility for your own learning." The difference is not great but it is confirmed in the interviews. Also there we find an increasing skepticism to the view that pupils are mature enough to take or interested in taking more responsibility for their own learning.

Before I begin a more detailed analysis of these changes (or lack of them), it can be stated that it appears that the curriculum reform has had an effect on the ways of working in many classrooms and that the changes are in the direction of those expressed in the curriculum. It is also possible to hold the view that following up the curriculum has had an effect (but not a marked effect). Even though it does not look like attitudes to the reform have changed, we find changes in behaviour. The question I will now take up is whether the examples which have been given can be used in a more detailed analysis of possible role changes

"To Change in Order to Preserve?"

Raymond Williams's emphasis on the role of tradition as "an actively shaping force" draws attention to the fact that it also provides some of the most significant symbolic materials for the formation of identity, both on the individual and on the collective level. (Halpin 1997: 7)

How can the percentage increase of teachers who follow up the expectations expressed in the curriculum reform be explained? The most fundamental explanation appears to be that it is the teachers who are in agreement about the principles upon which the new practice rests. In the course of these three years, through courses and different forms of stronger directive, they have arrived at some new ways of working. When it comes to cooperation with colleagues, this has occurred under the direction of the school heads, and in many cases it is the new departmental heads who have had this as one of their most important tasks. In the interviews we see that teachers are somewhat ambiguous about this development. They see the need for more cooperation, but at the same time they are more skeptical about the way it is introduced. They want more time for informal cooperation in small groups of colleagues. It is now the case that a lot of time is consumed in relatively large groups, such as departmental meetings. Cooperation with pupils about planning and teaching appears to be the result of the development of planning models where the pupils can be included through standardised procedures which culminate in reports either to the departmental or school heads.

These models (which to an ever-increasing extent can be found in electronic versions) make it easier for teachers to follow up on the expectation of planning together with pupils. The standardized procedures weaken the arguments made by teachers early in the period of reform that it was all too time consuming. Some individual teachers express the view that such an arrangement allows them to meet the imposed directives without it having too much of an effect upon what they see to be their main obligations: to ensure that teaching covers the "curriculum," textbooks, or other basic expressions for the contract teachers think they have with their subject and society. Other teachers express the view that they have little time for such formal exercises. Even though they also follow up, they do not believe strongly in their educational value. There is also a group of teachers, between one-quarter and one-fifth of the whole, who are hardly influenced by these expectations, following up only those things which are clearly and definitely imposed while at the same time regarding much of this as an bureaucratic exercise. It also appears that in the growing group of teachers who follow up the expectations in the curriculum reform, there is a lot of doubt and skepticism as to the value of planning with colleagues and pupils, questioning the results of an increase in the pupil's responsibility for their own learning.

This can, therefore, mean that the changes in the form of more cooperation with pupils are to be found in a limited number of schools and the follow-up work that has taken place. In the final report index values were developed for both pupils and teachers (Monsen, 1998a: 74), based on statements about pupil cooperation from several of the questions in the questionnaires.[3] It was evident that schools with high index values for pupil cooperation tended to have high average values for a number of questions about the curriculum in the new reform. This indicates that the changes we have found for the sample as a whole are somewhat more than an external adjustment to new demands from heads. In the case of a smaller number of schools in the 1998 survey (5–8 schools, dependent upon the line drawn for "high" index values), it is also the case that cooperation between teachers and pupils is regarded as a central element in the curriculum reform, and even though individual teachers can be critical of some of the forms this cooperation has taken, there is great support in these schools for the importance of developing this cooperation. From the interviews in the schools we found some examples of schools had broken away from a close follow-up from the county level and initiated their own forms of cooperation. It was evident in such cases that teachers had established a more intimate relationship to the work required in the development of more fruitful forms of teacher-pupil cooperation.

The dominant teacher culture at the majority of the schools, both in the 1998 survey and the interviews in the schools, regards increased cooperation with skepticism. In other words, they have only changed their attitudes to a small extent over the four-year period. They admit the necessity of certain forms of cooperation with pupils but are of the opinion that earlier experiences and experiences in the period of reform have shown that it should be given a reduced place, both with respect to the standards of teaching and because they hold the view that pupils are little interested in greater cooperation (a view which many pupils support). The demands made by leaders at the county level and by heads in individual schools for reports to document planning with pupils are met with deep skepticism. To a varying degree attempts are made to avoid the new demands by completing the necessary forms with a shrug of the shoulders.

With respect to the opening questions in this section as to whether it is possible to detect a change in roles, we approach our first conclusions. One, the changes we have registered from 1995 to 1998 in relation to the following up of expectations in the curriculum reform are more than just surface accommodations to demands from heads on a county and school level. Two, it can be argued that in some schools there has been, throughout the whole reform period, work of a follow-up and developmental character, where one tries to take as a starting point the positive attitudes that exist in relation to teacher-pupil cooperation. The number of schools which fall under this category is less than one third of the complete sample of forty-three schools. On the basis of what we have learned from the interviews (with other schools), there are strong reasons for believing that these schools have positive experiences of development prior to Reform–94. In these schools, as well, there will be larger or smaller pockets of teachers who express skepticism towards increased cooperation with pupils. Three, in the majority of schools in the sample, the dominant teacher culture is skeptical of increased cooperation with pupils, especially if this is interpreted as time consuming and/or tied to models or procedures requiring some form of report. Nevertheless, at these schools there still exist teachers who, without asserting themselves, have managed situations where pupils experience active participation.

These three conclusions give rise to the following questions: Are we here witness to an increasing difference among schools in their ability (or opportunity) to follow up the content in the curriculum reform? Has the reform in many schools resulted in an increasing awareness of the value of traditional teacher and pupil roles? Will the teacher culture in its meeting with the new curriculum, after a time of defensive reactions, actively support a more "polished," somewhat modernised, but still traditional teacher role? And will there be a more marked distinction between schools which defend old bastions and schools which use the reformed curriculum? It is too early to arrive at an unambiguous answer to these questions, but the changes we have been able to register and the patterns we can see can be interpreted as a positive indicator. It may be the case that there are increasing differences between schools who use curriculum reform as a motivational force in their developmental work and schools where the traditionally oriented teacher culture, through modernisation, reaffirms the teacher (and pupil) role which has developed over the past two or three generations. If this is so, these differences may be significant enough that there will develop—in time—considerably different teacher and school cultures. Modernisation depends on how the teachers accept and adopt some of the new terminology associated with curriculum reform. If they adopt with caution some of the new working methods such as project work and direct consultation with the pupil, they follow the old conservative slogan "to change in order to preserve." The point for the group of teachers who identify with the teacher's role as they know it from their own schooling is that the traditional teacher's role cannot be interfered with. The central values in the teacher's role are connected with the teacher's authority with respect to knowledge and the understanding of this knowledge, which is a necessary part of this authority of knowledge. Their purpose is to be caretakers of their subjects, to defend their knowledge and transmit their values to the next generation.

Role Change and the Conception of Knowledge

> The traditional understanding of knowledge is challenged.... The traditional forms of school are suitable as we shall see—mainly to communicate simple parts of occupational competence and the cultural tradition. Society's communication of qualified practical knowledge or culture doesn't take place inside the school's traditional form of teaching. (Rolf 1990: 28)

In the traditional conception, knowledge is organised in a universe in which the disciplines decide the differences between true and false, between knowledge and meanings, logic, argumentation, proof and subjective assertions, emotional and interest-based conclusions. In this knowledge universe in which "the better argument" takes precedence, will the person who controls both knowledge and its application in rational argumentation have a natural authority? Pupils must, with the teacher's help and advice, and not in the least through the teacher's example, be led into this knowledge universe. Where such a conception of knowledge exists, common planning of teaching and its implementation can have limited significance. Planning only has meaning if one also has knowledge, and the pupil is by definition lacking in knowledge. It is thus meaningful when the teacher asks pupils about their experience of learning, what they experience as difficult, what they would like in terms of methods, but not about the order and progression of knowledge, nor the criteria for when knowledge has been acquired nor when the pupil changes status from unknowing to knowing. That which in reform pedagogy has been termed, in a somewhat patronising manner, "dialogue education," deals with the view that knowledge requires the efforts of a knowledgeable teacher. It is this teacher authority that we associate with the "the traditional teacher role." My assertion so far is that it is the "traditional teacher role" which comes into contact with reform and can develop into a modernised version of the teacher's role. It can appear as if the majority of teachers have developed a clearer understanding of what they as teachers should and should not do if their intention is to defend their knowledge and also their authority as teachers.

But what about the "extended concept of knowledge" as it is presented in the Government Report no. 33 (KUF 1992)? Does this represent an alternative understanding of knowledge which redefines the authority of teachers and opens the way for a more democratic teaching environment in which teachers and pupils can meet on a more equal footing? The term was an attempt to demonstrate the important connection between curriculum reform and a new perspective on knowledge and learning. What is it that is "extended"? First and foremost the content of knowledge: it will include knowledge which does not have accepted status within established disciplines. The debate about the "extended concept of knowledge" is central in relation to the content of curriculum reform. It draws attention to the central challenge which the curriculum can represent for the "traditional teacher role." Nevertheless, the debate has to a small extent taken up what in my opinion is the greater challenge: Is it possible to develop an equal and democratic teaching environment without breaking with the view of knowledge which has been repeated over several generations under the term the "traditional teacher role"? (Rolf 1990; Monsen 1989).

I believe there are indications of such a break in the teaching practice of some teachers and in their understanding of the mediation of knowledge in what the curriculum can and should contain. I have not observed large and dramatic differences, but a connection does exist between what teachers do and how they understand their own practice in relation to expectations contained in the curriculum reform. After following a number of teachers and their classes through the first three years of the reform and noting how patterns have evolved in answers to the questionnaires, particularly in 1998, I have seen traces of a new teacher role, which builds upon a "break" with the established conception of knowledge.

First, I will attempt to explain what this break involves and then look at some examples in practice (Rogers 1997). I will build upon an interpretation of the general curriculum and its knowledge and perspective upon teaching, where the "handbook" plays an important role. That it is an interpretation means there exist other interpretations and that I see fundamental presuppositions and perspectives that are not necessarily in accordance with those made by the authors of these documents. I would nevertheless assert that my interpretation is the source of a consistent and total view of some of the fundamental principles formulated in the documents. The threshold between a new and traditional understanding of knowledge is based upon the understanding of the nature of the knowledge. Is knowledge first and foremost an ordered set of concepts systematised logically and empirically into disciplines, or is knowledge primarily something we all develop in order to interact with others, to solve problems, meet challenges, and gain an insight into our place in existence? Is there a crucial line between knowledge built up scientifically versus knowledge generated in the course of everyday life, or between knowledge with and without a use value? There exists almost a whole library of books which takes up these and similar questions in the zone where philosophy, psychology, and sociology overlap. I cannot begin to discuss all the intricate questions which have been raised and debated over the centuries, so I will limit my attention to one of these many questions (Greene 1994 gives a useful summary of the debate).

The "Guide" —the handbook for pupils edited by the Royal Ministry of Church, Education, and Research in 1993—gives an example of a pupil who actively searches for knowledge by building upon previous knowledge. This active search for knowledge takes place with the assistance of many aids and with the teacher as guide, supervisor, and ideal. The main point is that the pupil builds upon previous knowledge and that new knowledge comes from many sources, requiring the pupil's ability to ask the correct questions and formulate interesting problems. The point is not for the pupil to follow the well-trodden path to knowledge laid down in each subject's knowledge map. Instead, the pupils are to devise their own map and make knowledge into something that is under development the whole time. In such a process the teachers have a role different from the one in which they have to make sure the pupil follows the correct steps in knowledge acquisition. The teacher becomes like the experienced runner in a cross-country race, providing advice on the choice of route, helping pupils to find out where they are as they move through the "knowledge terrain," providing encouragement and descriptions of future checkpoints on the way to the goal so pupils do not lose enthusiasm but continue to make the efforts necessary to learn how to search for knowledge in an experienced manner. This constructionist system of learning and knowledge is found in both the general curriculum and in the "Guide" (Hedegaard 1995).

> The rhetoric of collaboration alone will not promote shared purpose and self-direction among members. On the other hand, to attempt to develop shared purpose and self-direction through coercion is self-contradictory and can only confirm persons' dichotomous models of reality which identify the organizational sphere as the realm of manipulative work; an ironic kind of leadership and organizational struc-

ture, which is simultaneously educative and productive, simultaneously controlling and freeing, is necessary. (Torbert 1978: 113)

I have earlier mentioned how both the majority of teachers and pupils have difficulty in believing in such a view of knowledge, pupils because they believe traditional ways of mediating knowledge are less demanding and give better results in relation to tests and examinations, and teachers because they believe that such a form of learning only suits the most motivated and active pupils. And, as I already noted, in most classrooms knowledge is communicated to a large extent as before but with some modern elements, where project work in particular plays a central role.

The Practice of Teachers and Their Conceptions of Knowledge

> Even though the problems which both schools and universities now face manifest themselves in the meeting between teachers and students, this doesn't mean that this is the strategic point where changes must be introduced. The teacher-student relationship is founded and dependent upon the tasks addressed by the subjects, together with the criteria for evaluating performance which are relevant and the relationship between the teachers. For its part, the relationship between teachers is dependent upon the relationship between subjects. (Herbst 1971: 379)

I will now attempt to depart from the temptation to divide teachers according to their "willingness to reform," as is the normal practice when it comes to interpreting questionnaires such as these. The results are clear enough in themselves. Less than a third of the teachers are in the "unwilling" group, and this number has remained stable between 1995 and 1998. This provides the support for my preliminary conclusion above about the "traditional teacher role" still existing in many classrooms. But such a conclusion can and should be examined in more detail. It might be the case that a greater number have accepted the ideas contained in the new curriculum, but they have faced difficulties in devising ways of incorporating it into their classroom activity. I have already confirmed that there appears to be a considerable distance between general attitudes towards the new curriculum and reported practices (Monsen 1997a: 95). In the interviews which I have re-examined, I see now more clearly than when the material was used in the preliminary reports how many teachers struggle with maintaining their support for principles such as "responsibility for own learning," "pupil consultation in planning of teaching," and their experiences of trying to implement these principles in practice. Some examples of what teachers say in the interviews indicates this ambivalence, or, if you will, the many dilemmas the reform has given rise to. How teachers come to terms with such dilemmas is dependent upon many factors, such as their personal history and the kind of teacher and school culture in which they live. But the fact that teachers both acknowledge this as a dilemma and that they experience it as a demanding and difficult dilemma tells us from our position on the outside that these conflicts reach deeply into many teachers' understanding of their role, what they understand as knowledge, and their view of teaching. Let us turn to examples.

> I have tried to include pupils in the giving of advice on the selection of literature and material from the textbooks, but I meet little response to taking part and participating. I have told them what they are to go through in the coming year and the year leading up to their exam, but it makes no impression upon them. They are just present and make the best out of it. They believe that it is best that I just decide and plan. (Example 1)

This teacher who teaches natural sciences in a course for mechanics is typical of many who struggle with their wish "...to include pupils in the giving of advice" and the pupils' lack of enthusiasm for such initiatives. Between the lines it is possible to detect this teacher's disappointment over the lack of interest from the pupils: "They are just present and make the best out of it." This is an experience that many teachers of theoretical subjects have had and is reflected in my interviews from the following subjects: natural sciences, English, and mathematics. Teachers experience the gap between the ideal model, where most pupils are involved in the curriculum and want to develop it for their own class, and the normal classes, where the majority of the pupils show little interest in participating. For many teachers this becomes a question of justifying what they can use their time on in relation to their ambitions for teaching the respective subjects. Their somewhat resigned conclusion is that if they could end up devoting a lot of time in trying to get the pupils to participate and achieving the desired result, what effect would this have upon maintaining the standards expressed in the curriculum? The teacher in example 2 (also in the natural sciences, in the health and social studies course), like most others, tries to find a pragmatic solution to the demand for more pupil participation and her experience of what it is actually possible to achieve:

> The curriculum can be a motivating factor. I have handed it out. And I have also taken up the topics we are working on, but that isn't enough. As said [sic] I will look at the curriculum after we have covered chemistry for example. We try it out. We can't use too much time on it either, in an evaluation of the details. There are so many things we ought to do. (Example 2)

The teachers experience a lack of time; there are so many different demands in relation to the curriculum and everything else that comes with the reform that they are forced to consider how they can use their time. The result appears to be, as in this case (and many others) that the teacher follows up some of the intentions. She hands out the curriculum and goes through it with the pupils, creating an opportunity for new ways of doing things—"we try it out"—but she is at the same time aware that she has to maintain control and achieve progression: "We can't use too much time" or "evaluate the details." The majority of teachers try to find a position between the new demands in the curriculum and what they, as those responsible for the subject, consider justifiable in the sense of finding pragmatic solutions. They are completely positive to the greater inclusion of pupils ("the curriculum can be a motivating factor"), but they do not want to give up their teaching ambitions, which they feel will suffer if they were in a position to fully realise the new intentions. Several teachers express the view that as things appear at the moment, they might change. The pupils' opinions, which are used by many of the teachers to argue that there is no point in going any further, might be in the process of changing, as this teacher (of English, in the hotel and services course) indicates:

> Pupils feel I'm sure that they have understood what it's about when the teacher says it is to be such and such. With time this might change. In secondary school responsibility for their own learning is coming in more and more. We must however be honest and say that it is we, as teachers, who often manipulate and ensure that things turn out as we mean they should. The curriculum exists and we have a relationship to it. Pupils have become better when it comes to giving constructive criticism, because among other things we more systematically evaluate what we do. (Example 3)

This teacher also makes constructive criticism of her colleagues' practice. She begins by saying that her colleagues are perhaps correct that pupils hold such views and that they might be in the process of changing, and then she draws attention to an important point: "...It is we, as teachers, who often manipulate and ensure that things turn out as we mean they should." She justifies this by saying, "the curriculum exists and we have a relationship to it." The thing which she has a relationship to in the curriculum is from a logical point of view the standards for the subject. At the same time she points to a second development in the same direction: the pupils have become more adroit when it comes to giving constructive criticism because she and her colleagues now carry out evaluation in a more systematic manner. And a systematic evaluation can include an evaluation of the goals in the curriculum.

A more conscious following up of the goals at several of the schools is carried out, and as a consequence of this, planning with the pupils takes place. In the next example we shall see how the new heads of departments have gained a central role in this task of following up (the respondent is the head of department for the hotel and services course and talks about a part of the course):

> Yes indeed, all are meant to have a plan with periods for the different subjects, and a goal has indeed been to plan together with the pupils. Such as we do in our department on the foundation and post-foundation course, we let the pupils have the curriculum, and try to read it together with them, this is what we do. Of course it is difficult, one almost has problems oneself with what is meant with the goals here, and pupils do indeed find it difficult getting hold of their meaning. We take this up in the department for discussion. We hand out the curriculum, and then proceed a little at a time, taking a month at a time. My colleague, who teaches the foundation course, plans for longer periods, but suddenly something happens and it becomes hard to follow the curriculum. I keep to monthly periods and think that is enough. You know the goal after a year, that is there to see. But, it is important that one doesn't plan for long periods because then there isn't so much to do with the teachers. I am very fond of forms and the like, so last year we tried with lots of them. "New forms today," said the pupils. We have to incorporate it if we are to make it work. And they think this is acceptable after a while, for then they know what to expect. (Example 4)

The difference in evidence here with respect to the pupil's role in planning for purely theoretical subjects such as the natural sciences, English, and mathematics, and practical vocational subjects, is reflected in the questionnaires. This head of the department takes it for granted that he and his colleagues are to plan together with their pupils, but he notes that the curriculum as it stands creates problems for the pupils. Planning must be organised so that the pupils can manage it. And this organisation is so comprehensive that the pupil's real influence is limited. It is hard to detect this from this interview, but the reports from the pupils indicate that there is a difference between vocational and more theoretical subjects with respect to how planning with pupils takes place. This is seen most clearly in the use of the report book, which for many teachers in the vocational subjects is seen as a practical instrument for involving pupils in the teaching, while teachers in the theoretical subjects, both on general and vocational courses, experience it as a bureaucratic hindrance (Deichman-Sørensen et al 1997; Monsen 1997b: 53–4).

Can this difference provide insight into the teaching tradition and thus the conception of knowledge of which these theoretical subjects are guardians? There is good evidence of both guild and academic traditions, which have their roots back to the early Middle Ages, each with its own view of teaching and conception of knowledge (Molander 1996). The core curriculum also highlights these two traditions as the foundation for teaching in the schools (The Royal Ministry of Church, Education, and Research 1993: 12–3). What in our connection deals with the differential involvement of the pupil in planning appears to reflect the different understanding of what constitutes the subject and what it means to be a professional teacher. In the guild tradition a subject is defined by its field of practice with craft methods and skills, which the apprentice has to master. The field of practice, to an increasing degree after the Industrial Revolution, has been defined by the level of technological development, laying down demands for a continual modification of techniques, methods, and skills. Within the subjects there is a built-in understanding that the main part of the subject will change. This means that new methods and techniques will have to be learned to keep up with developments in the subject. There is reason to believe that such a conception with continual changes in the subject will also influence those who become teachers in such subjects, so that they will be on the lookout for methods to simplify and increase the efficiency of the teaching. The report book does indeed come from a tradition of teaching where it has stood for a simplification and clarification of what the apprentice has taken part in and what has been taught. It is also possible to argue that in this tradition, with teaching based upon repetition and instruction, where the master demonstrates what the apprenticed is to repeat, it is natural that the success of the teaching situation will be dependent upon the interaction between the master and apprentice. In relation to everything that is to be produced, work drawings have to be made, and it is necessary to plan how they are transformed into the final product. Everything points in the direction of a situation of instruction where the pupils can be involved in several stages of planning. This is why it seems natural to involve the pupils in the planning of vocational subjects.

Academic teaching distinguishes itself from the guild tradition in terms of what it considers to be a subject, each one developed in a qualitatively different manner. Most of the subjects with high academic status can trace their origins back a long way in history. Even though modern science is seen as the driving force in the development of technology, there is still a clear difference between the school-based subjects of mathematics, physics, chemistry, and their technological application. The school-based subjects attempt to grasp the subject's essence, that which constitutes its fundamental insights and upon which all later development has been based. It is not for nothing that the slogan "back to basics" has surfaced periodically in the course of the last century when some people have attempted to water down what has been regarded as a subject's fundamental essence (Apple 1992; Aronowitz and Giroux 1988). As an educational school of thought, this has been known as "essentialism," and it has been connected with a somewhat elitist conception of who should be able to acquire this essential knowledge. But even without an elitist undercurrent, it is in many senses understandable that it is difficult to give pupils an important place in relation to planning and the implementation of teaching if the intention of teaching is to guide pupils into an almost Platonic knowledge universe of "eternal truths." In this knowledge universe the structure of the subjects and progression through them is to a large extent already given, and what then is the point of having a discussion with pupils about what they are to understand before they have understood what it is all about?

Several of the teachers in the interviews have indeed voiced a deeply felt dilemma on this point, between their support for the democratic principles of which pupil participation is an expression and their subjects, deep insights, which require significant efforts from the pupils before they are even in a position to have an opinion about the subject. The solution to this dilemma, as I have mentioned above, is that many take the pragmatic option whereby pupils are allowed to say something about teaching methods and give the teacher some feedback in relation to responsibility for their own learning, but when it comes to the important decisions, these are made by the teacher, who is in possession of what the pupils lack, a deeper insight into the subject's concepts and structure. For many teachers it often feels as if they must agree to compromises in relation to what they might desire as professionals and that which in practice means more time devoted to the pure teaching of the subject so that the pupils can get closer to the subject's essence.

This "essentialist" view of knowledge still seems to have a hold on many teachers and will therefore form the foundation for how they define their role as teachers. The reform has supposedly had an influence on practice in a number of areas, as I have suggested, but this has been the case because teachers themselves experience the dilemma between principles they support and their view of knowledge, which works against their "accepting the reform without resistance," as some individuals have expressed it. They try to move a little in the direction of the reform, but they are unsure if this really results in more knowledge and learning for the pupils. In the questionnaire as many as 54 percent either doubted or felt the curriculum reform had no positive effect on the pupil's knowledge or learning (Monsen 1998a: 34) There are signs that there is an increasing level of unrest among teachers with respect to what is happening with the following up of curriculum reform and in particular with all the demands for reports and school evaluations. Even those who have been positive about school-based evaluation and see the need for feedback from pupils (they are still in a minority when it comes to practicing it, i.e., less than one-third of all teachers), are increasingly worried about all the "paperwork" invested in the different evaluation exercises which they experience as a diversion from their proper tasks: to teach pupils so that they learn more and understand more about the subject's fundamental concepts. (My argument about increasing anxiety is based first and foremost on my contact with different groups of teachers and principals in recent years in connection with different courses and conferences.)

My conclusion to this discussion of the curriculum reform's importance in the development of a new teacher and pupil role is that the "traditional teacher role" is so strongly wedded to an "essentialist" conception of knowledge that it is quite unlikely that teachers are willing to make further compromises in the direction of a reform, the value of which they doubt. A further development of the teacher's role (and also the pupil's) will require engaging with the teacher's conception of knowledge. This will be a far more demanding task than getting teachers to make compromises.

Notes

1. The term "reform pedagogy" is not lacking in ambiguity; it is used as a common term for the different streams and movements in this century where the common goal is the reform of our time's educational traditions. The term is used here because most reform

pedagogy movements have proposed changes in the relationship between the teacher and the pupil in the classroom, or between new pupil and teacher roles, as is the case in Reform–94.
2. The role concept in sociology is part of a theory about institutions in society. The "school" as an institution and the "school" as an organisation should be distinguished from each other. Society has institutions, and as members of society we participate through roles in different institutions. The school as an organisation is a more concrete expression for a special way (in time and space) of organising institutional life. Schools as national and local organisations have their history with accompanying laws and rules (the formal organisation) and through a dynamic interaction with their surroundings have developed perceptions, ways of working, internal expectations and rules for interpetation. Within the framework of such organisations this can be regarded as an expression of the "school's culture." In this chapter I am most interested in the institutional perspective, and to a lesser degree in the school in the study as concrete organisations (Monsen 1998b).
3. The indexes are calculated on the basis of individual replies to a number of questions where the topic is cooperation between teacher and pupil. It is these individual statements which are used so much in a factor analysis that the number of single answers used is considerably reduced. It is these factors consisting of several statements which are the foundation for the calculation of the index values for these factors. No weighting has been carried out so that all the statements in the index are worth the same. The index value is calculated on the basis of the average value and then recalculated to a z-scale, where the average value for the individual factor is 0. Most scales in the questions were designed so that the scale value 1 was reserved as a rule for the most positive statement. This means that in the final report all the factors with a negative sign stand for more than average positive attitudes to teacher-pupil cooperation. When in this article I use the term "high" average values, I mean more positive to cooperation than the sample average.

References

Apple, M. W. (1992). The text and cultural politics. *Educational Researcher 21*: 4–11.
Aronowitz, S. and H. Giroux (1988). Schooling, culture and literacy in the age of broken dreams: A review of Bloom and Hirsch. *Harvard Educational Review 58* (2): 172–94.
Cuban, L. (1990). Reforming again, again and again. *Educational Researcher 19* (1): 3–13.
——— (1998). How schools change reforms: Redefining reform success and failure. *Teachers College Record 99* (3): 453–77.
Dahrendorf, R. (1961). *Homo sociologicus*. Köln: Westdeutscher Verlag.
Deichman-Sørensen, T., Blichfeldt, J. F. and Lauvdal, T. (1997): Kunnskap, Kvalitet, Kontroll: Kampen om Opplæringsboka (Knowledge, quality, control: The fight over the teaching manual). In *Idealer og Paradokser. Aspekter ved Gjennomføringen av Reform–94*. (Ideals and paradoxes. Aspects with the implementation of curriculum reform–94), Edited by Berit Lødding and Kristin Tornes. Oslo: Tano Aschehoug.
Eide, K. (1995). *OECD og Norsk Utdanningspolitikk. En Studie av Internasjonalt Samspill.* (OECD and Norwegian educational policy. A study of international interaction). Oslo: Utredningsinstituttet for Research and Higher Education.

Elliott, J. (1996). School effectiveness research and its critics: Alternative visions of schooling. *Cambridge Journal of Education* 26 (2): 199–224.
Greene, M. (1994). Epistemology and educational research. *Review of Educational Research, Vol. 20.* Washington: American Educational Research Association.
Halpin, D. (1997). In the grip of the past? Tradition, traditionalism and contemporary schooling. *International Studies in Sociology of Education* 7 (1): 3–20.
Hedegaard, M. (1995). *Tænkning, viden udvikling* (Thinking, knowledge development). Århus: Universitetsforlag.
Herbst, P. G. (1971). Strukturering av kunnskap og utforming av utdanningsorganisajoner (The structuring of knowledge and the formation of educational organisations). *Nordisk Forum,* 3: 371–87.
KUD/OECD (1989). *OECD–Vurdering av Norsk Utdanningspolitikk. Norsk rapport til OECD.* (OECD–Evaluation of Norwegian Educational Policy. Norwegian Report to the OECD) *Eskpert Evaluation from OECD.* Oslo: Aschehoug.
Kirke-,utdannings-og forskningsdepartememtet (KUF) [The Royal Minstry of Church, Education, and Research] (1992). *Stortingsmelding nr. 33 (1991–1992). Kunnskap og kyndighet. Om visse sider ved videregående opplæring* (Knowledge and mastery: About some aspects of secondary education). Oslo: KUF.
——— (1993). *Læreplan for Grunnskole, Videregående Opplæring, Voksenopplæring. Generell Del* (Curriculum for primary and secondary school, upper secondary education and adult education: General part). Oslo: KUF.
Lauglo, J. (1972). Gymnaslærernes Holdninger til Skolereform (Higher Education Teachers Attitudes to School Reform). *Tidskrift for Samfunnsforsnkning 13*: 287–310.
Lundgren, U.P. (1979). *Att organisera omvärlden. En introduksjon til läroplans* (To organise the world. An introduction to curriculum plans). Stockholm: Liber.
Molander, B. (1996). *Kunnskap i handling* (Knowledge in action). Göteborg: Daidalos.
Monsen, L. (1989). Læreren som kunnskapsformidler: Tilbake til basiskunnskapene, eller på vei inn i informasjonssamfunnet? (The teacher as communicator of knowledge: Back to basic knowledge, or On the way to the information society?). In *Læreren fra Kall til Lønnskamp. 250 Års Utvikling.* (The Teacher from call to wage struggle). Edited by Karl Oeyvind Jordell and Per Olaf Aamodt. Oslo: Tano Aschehoug.
——— (1996). Kan vi Målstyre Læreplanreformer? (Can we steer curriculum reform?) In *Utdanning for Alle? Evaluering av Reform–94* (Education for all? Evaluating Reform–94). Edited by Jon Frode Blichfeldt et al. Oslo: Tano Aschehoug.
———. (1997a). *Evaluering av Reform–94. Delrapport nr. 4: Innholdsreform: Skolenes Arbeid med Læringsmiljøet* (Evaluation of Reform–94. Part report no. 4. Curriculum content: The school's work with learning environment). *Arbeidsnotat nr. 37.* Lillehammer: Høgskolen I.
——— (1997b). "Ansvar for Egen Læring": fra Slagord til Klasserom ("Responsibility for one's own learning": From slogan to classroom). In Berit Lødding and Kristin Tornes op. cit.: 31–67.
——— (1998a): *Evaluering av Reform–94. Sluttrapport. Innholdreformen–fra Måldokument til Klasseromespraksis* (Evaluation of Reform–94. Final report. Curriculum reform: From

goal document to classroom practice). *Forskningsrapport no. 42.* Lillehammer: Høgskolen I.

────── (1998b). Læringskultur og læringsmiljø: Videregående skoler I utvikling med R-94 som veiviser (Teaching culture and learning environment: Higher education schools in development with R-94 as guidebook). In *Konferanserapport: En Læringskultur I Utvikling: Videregående opplæring ved et veiskille* (Conference report: A teaching culture in development: Higher education at a junction) *Informasjonsserien nr. 7.* Lillehammer: Høgskolen I.

Reid, H. (1972). The politics of time. *The Human Context 4* (3): 456–83.

Rogers, B. (1997). Informing the shape of the curriculum: New views of knowledge and its representation in schooling. *Journal of Curriculum Studies 27* (6): 638–710.

Rolf, B. (1990). Personlig kunskap och kulturformedlingens villkor (Personal knowledge and the discourse on culture), *Forskning om Utbildning* (Research on Education), *17* (2): 17–33.

Rust, V. D. (1985). Norwegian secondary school reform: Reflections on a revolution. *Comparative Education 21* (2): 209–17.

Simola, H. (1998). Firmly boiled into the air: Wishful rationalism as a discursive basis for educational reforms. *Teachers College Record 99* (4): 731–57.

Siskin, L. S. (1994). *Realms of knowledge. Academic departments in secondary schools.* London: Falmer.

Torbert, W. R. (1978). Education toward shared purpose, self-direction and quality work. *Journal of Higher Educatio, 49* (2): 109–35.

Trippestad, T. A. (1997). Idealisme, Utopisme og Retorikk in 1990-årenes Utdanningsreformer (Idealism, Utopianism and Rhetoric in 1990s Educational Reforms). In, *Årbok for Norsk Utdanningshistorie. Skolen, 1997–1998 (Annual book of Norwegian educational history. The school, 1997–1998)* Edited by Knut Jordheim. Notodden: Telemarksforskning.

Tyack, D., and W. Tubin (1994). The "grammar" of schooling: Why has it been so hard to change? *American Educational Research Journal 31* (3): 453–79.

van den Berg, R, and P. Sleegers (1996): The innovative capacity of secondary schools: A qualitative study. *Qualitative Studies in Education 9* (2): 201–23.

Williams, R. (1985). *The Long Revolution.* Harmondsworth: Penguin.

Wilson, S. (1976). You can talk to teachers: Student-teacher relations at an alternative high school. *Teachers College Record 78* (1): 77–100.

CHAPTER NINE

Co-operative Education, the Curriculum, and Working Knowledge

Hugh Munby, Peter Chin, Nancy L. Hutchinson • Canada

This chapter is one of a series of studies on work-based programs for high school students. Our specific interest is in programs known generically as co-operative education, or co-op education. Typically these programs are available as credit courses with both an in-school and workplace component that extend for half a semester or a full semester. The in-school component is a small part of a co-op education course, so students can spend up to four half-days per week in the workplace component, which is unpaid and is typically during school hours. Co-op education takes its name from the idea that schools and the community co-operate directly in the education of youth through such programs. Co-op education is extensive and growing in the United States and in Canada. About 10 percent of Canada's high school students enroll in co-op education each year (Munby, Cunningham, and Chin 1998). Our early work in co-op education centered on students learning in a veterinary clinic, reflecting our interest in science-related co-op placements––the empirical data here are from those studies. Subsequently, we have explored policy and research issues for the area (Munby, Hutchinson, and Chin 2000a), and we have investigated how accessible co-op education is to all students (Hutchinson et al. 1999). This earlier work led to our determination to view co-op education as curriculum. This allows us to use curriculum frameworks, like the commonplaces of Schwab (1972), to draw attention to features of the curriculum that can influence the learner. This paper exemplifies the power of using such frameworks.

Workplace learning, although conducted apart from schools, is still curriculum, but curriculum commonplaces assume different guises in the workplace. Subject matter, or knowledge, is one of these commonplaces. The purpose of this paper is to show differences in the form, organization, and even purpose of knowledge in the workplace. We suggest that some of the difference can be captured by distinguishing between "working knowledge" and the form of knowledge (science knowledge in this case) encountered in the school curriculum. The journey taken in this chapter begins by considering changes in the meaning of vocational education from 1916 to the present. Our point here is to compare current views of vocationalism with older versions and to explore relationships between the intents of the new vocationalism with the practice of co-op education. Then we move to looking at the separation between school and work in order to highlight ideas about forms of knowledge, about authenticity, and about the potential of the workplace for contributing to a liberal or general education.

Meanings of Vocational Education

Workplace learning is far older than compulsory public education, but we start our journey in more recent history: 1916, the date of publication by the Macmillan Company of *Democracy and Education* (Dewey 1916/1964). The following points from Dewey's chapter on the vocational aspects of education are especially relevant here:

> A vocation means nothing but such a direction of life activities as renders them perceptibly significant to a person. (307)
>
> ...
>
> Put in concrete terms there is a danger that vocational education will be interpreted in theory and in practice as trade education: as a means of securing technical efficiency in specialized future pursuits. Education would then become an instrument of perpetuating unchanged the existing social order of society, instead of operating as a means of its transformation. (316)

So Dewey's expectations of vocational education are broad. According to Scheffler (1995a), Dewey tended to view vocational education as having liberating and transformative potential, but "Construed as trade education, the system of vocational education would relinquish the traditional liberal education to the rich, while allotting the masses a narrow preparation for specialized callings under the control of others" (37). For Wraga (1998), the more liberal view of vocational education took hold in the United States in proposals advanced in 1918 in the *Cardinal Principles of Secondary Education* (Bureau of Education). Yet the envisioned synthesis of civic and vocational education failed to materialize. This should come as no surprise for, as Lewis (1998) has documented, "vocational knowledge is treated in schools and in society at large as low-status knowledge, unlike academic knowledge which is considered high-status knowledge, and which is accordingly privileged and dispensed" (284). Sanderson's (1993) historical perspective yielded virtually the same conclusion: liberal education "gained prestige through connection to church, state and empire" (190) while vocational education was clearly of lowly status. Neither was the lowly status restricted to vocational education in schools. Only rarely, as in France's traditional *grandes écoles*—Ponts et Chausées (established in 1715), École Polytechnique (1794), École Centrale (1828)—do we find vocational or applied education occupying a status "superior to the universities" (191).

To a large extent, vocational education maintained its low-status position over the course of the twentieth century, never achieving the liberal or transformative goals of Dewey's design. Not surprisingly, the situation in Canada was similar. Although secondary schools in Canada (and in Britain) increasingly accommodated technical and vocational education, the classes, courses, or streams tended to be separate from those perceived to be more academic. In Canada and in Europe, the move away from the direct employment view of vocational education could be ascribed in part to the failure of what Nijhof and Brandsma (1999) refer to as the "planning tools approach" of the 60s through the 80s. This approach was deficient because of the implicit assumption that curriculum content could be linearly deduced from job content, ignoring interrelatedness and complexity of tasks. According to Wraga (1998), a discernible shift in the character of vocational education is evident in the United States beginning with the appearance of the Secretary's Commission on Achieving Necessary Skills in 1991 and the School-to-Work Opportunities Act of 1994. As a result

> [the] traditional focus on providing students with entry-level, job-specific skills began giving way to a conception of vocational education, that places greater priority on fostering general competencies that will prepare students for workplaces, is increasingly characterized by high skills and rapid change. (Wraga 1998: 185–6)

For example, the SCANS report lists creative thinking, decision-making, and problem-solving among its general thinking skills. Scheffler (1995b) argued for an understanding of the relationship between the complexity and challenge of work and the need for increased judgment by workers. The crafts and trades, he suggests, are fast approaching the intellectual demands of the professions. Not surprisingly, Scheffler's view of vocational education coincides with Dewey's:

> No educated person is ill equipped to pursue a vocation, that is to say, an activity which is purposive, demands attention, concentration, skill, and intelligence. It is not as if some educated persons have vocations while others utterly lack them. Every education is of necessity vocational in organizing a person's capacity and disposition for intelligent activities. (45)

Although possibly not warranting the title "Paradigm shift in vocational education," the return to a Deweyan view was evident in Canada too. For example, the Employability Skills promulgated by the Conference Board of Canada (1992) are listed in the categories: academic skills, personal management skills, and teamwork skills. These are strikingly similar to the three areas of basic competencies represented in SCANS: basic skills, thinking skills, and interpersonal qualities. Vocational education is assuming a different form if not a different stature. Indeed, Lewis (1998) has argued that the demands upon vocational education for meeting the changing nature of work are too much to place upon vocational teachers and that the burden should be for the whole school: "To approach the Deweyan ideal we need to view vocational education as valid school knowledge belonging not at the fringes but at the core of the school curriculum" (291).

Co-op Education and Workplace Settings

A major provision of the 1994 School-to-Work Opportunities Act in the United States was to make work-based learning a significant part of the education of America's youth. And the school-to-work literature contains many lists of the potential benefits of work-based learning to students (e.g., Hamilton and Hamilton 1997), with the most widely cited being:
- acquisition of occupational, technical, or workplace readiness skills;
- career exploration and planning, which can include learning about all aspects of an industry;
- psycho-social development and preparation for adult responsibilities;
- reinforcement of academic learning, through contextual or situated learn-

ing, and through increased motivation.

Goals such as these are not substantially different from those we have found from our recent analyses of policy statements for co-op education in the provincial and territorial jurisdictions of Canada and in Ontario's school districts (Munby, Hutchinson, and Chin 2000b). Although there is considerable enthusiasm for work-based curriculum experiences (Bailey and Merritt 1997; Olson 1997), there also is little empirical study of the goals achieved by students and the processes for achieving these. In addition to serving goals like the above, co-op education in Canada, especially in Ontario, is viewed as a mode of delivery for academic subjects: students enroll in grade eleven biology and also take a co-op course for credit in biology, for example. Thus co-op education is not restricted to career education or vocational education. Neither is co-op education for the less academically oriented student. In 1996-1997, fully 43 percent of co-op students in Ontario were enrolled in advanced-level high school courses (the "academic stream") as opposed to general or basic level courses ("Enrollment in Co-Operative Education" 1998). And 34 percent of the 1999 first- and second-year B.Sc.N. nursing students at Queen's University had taken co-op in high school (Chin, Munby, Hutchinson, and Steiner-Bell 2000). Given that Queen's University has the highest academic entering average among all Canadian universities ("The Ninth Annual Ranking of Universities" 1999)[1] it is safe to say that co-op education is seen as relevant by students who are destined for the professions.

The expectation that in some way co-op education will ease the transition from school (or university) to work suggests the need to explore the depth of the chasm between the worlds of school and work. Differences between the worlds are profound when one considers the difference between "knowledge at work" or "working knowledge" and knowledge that is static and does little more than move from page to mind, then back to page. Context is everything, then, because working knowledge is deeply contextual. But as we show below, compulsory schooling and adolescence itself have made it hard for high school students to experience what this context might mean, so we first revisit adolescence to better understand the gap between the worlds of school and work. Then we briefly describe the setting in which we studied students in a co-op placement, the vet clinic.

Adolescence, School, and Work

Some of what makes school to work transitions a challenge has its roots in the social movements that created adolescence. Bakan (1971) has developed the thesis that adolescence is a social invention. He argues that the overpopulation of U.S. cities in the late nineteenth century, the high incidence of drunkenness and vagrancy, the threat to American ideals by waves of new immigrants, and the substantial amount of child labor (in 1832, 40 percent of New England factory workers were children) contributed to the redefinition of youth in the late nineteenth century. Three significant social movements contributed to this change: (a) the introduction of compulsory public education, (b) child labor legislation, and (c) special legal procedures for "juveniles." As a result, adolescence was invented as an intervening step between childhood and adulthood. And adolescence was curiously defined: "the period of time between pubescence, a concrete biological occurrence, and ages specified by law for compulsory education, employment, and criminal procedure" (981). Bakan acknowledge that the phrase "The invention of the adolescent" is Musgrove's (1964). Interestingly, the National Film Board of Canada used these words as the title of its documentary film, *The Invention of the Adolescent* (Burwash and Glover 1967), depicting society's changing images of the distinctions between childhood and adulthood.

This account of adolescence shows how society effectively removed youth from the adult world of work, and made the transition from childhood to adulthood no longer seamless. As a result, there are now fewer formal opportunities for youngsters to understand the world of work through immediate contact sanctioned by schools. Work in which students might later wish to pursue careers then becomes remote, with little attention being paid to education about work and its context, but some attention being paid to education for work through vocational education. Co-op education and similar work-based high school programs give adolescents unusual opportunities to enter the world of work and to immerse themselves in its context. But the switch in the context of the curriculum from school to work results in some changes to ways in which we might address curriculum commonplaces like subject matter or knowledge, as we show below.

The Clinic Setting and the Data

We conducted our research as case studies of four co-op students in their placement, a "small animal" hospital (the clinic), specializing in the care of household pets. The veterinarian, Bill,[2] had arranged his practice so that scheduled clinic appointments and scheduled surgeries took place in the morning. We collected data at these times of increased clinic activity in the clinic's preparatory room, the surgery, the surgical ward, or laboratory. Our studies involved more than sixty hours of regular ethnographic observations at the clinic and interviews with the students, with Bill, and with other clinic staff—two veterinary technicians (Kelly and Jill), and an animal-care aide (Sue). Data were subjected to techniques of pattern and thematic analyses typical of qualitative research (Chin, Munby, and Hutchinson 1999). For this paper, we use material from our case studies to draw attention to questions about knowledge within the workplace curriculum.

Curriculum in the Workplace

Through the eyes of Bakan we have seen how school has created a chasm between the world of childhood and the world of adults. Adolescence and school interrupt the historically seamless transition. And education for the workplace—vocational education—is defined as preparation for specific labor within the adult world. In the last decade, vocational education has become more general, even liberal, and programs like co-op education allow adolescents to obtain high school credits for work placements. Although the placements are beyond school boundaries, what is offered in the workplace should be construed as curriculum. Our specific interest here is to identify differences between the curriculum of school and the curriculum of the workplace. We initially focus on three differences: organization, purpose, and knowledge.

Organization

Our collective experience of school suggests to us that the orderly sequencing of instruction is a hallmark of the school curriculum. Generally, simple concepts form the basis for presenting increasingly complex concepts and material, and almost every day provide new knowledge, represented by new units or new chapters. It was particularly striking to us that this relatively even presentation of knowledge in school is not at all how the workplace presents knowledge. Our observations showed that tasks expected of the co-op students were introduced early in the placement and were followed by numerous exposures to these tasks to reinforce them through repetition. Thus students quickly are exposed to the routine of the clinic and to routines within these routines. Then they are gradually introduced to parts of the routines, somewhat in the manner of legitimate peripheral participation (Lave & Wenger 1991). For example, in learning the task of preparing spay packs, the co-op students were introduced to the required cleaning techniques for surgical equipment and to the need for maintaining sterile fields: on the first and third day, students receive detailed instruction and demonstration so that they can learn the many steps associated with the preparation of a spay pack, including ways to remove blood and tissue from drapes. The direct instructions included the following:

> Using cold water it [blood, tissue remains] comes off the drape easier. (Sue, Sept.16, 1997)

> Then you have the cutting instrument that removes the claws. Do you have the instrument that holds the claws so they can be removed? That's your Rongeurs. If you think you are missing something from a pack like this, go through and remember how the [procedure] is done (Sue, Sept. 18, 1997).

Similarly, the students are introduced to the anesthetic machine gradually. At first, they watch, then by degrees they are shown how to monitor various parts of the machine. So the knowledge that is presented may be new, but it is set within a routine that has become familiar because it is a central routine within the clinic's practice. Learning then becomes a matter of being increasingly involved in selected portions of the clinic's work as it is repeated daily. This is surprisingly reminiscent of Whitehead's (1963) spiral curriculum, although the routines of the workplace dictate that the spiral is tightly wound.

But there is more to this difference in how the curriculum of school and workplace is organized. It becomes important to understand that, as our data show, the workplace presents all of its complex knowledge in an order that is determined by the purposes of the workplace.

Purpose

There surely is little question that the primary and overt purpose of school is learning, if not education. Preparation for further schooling or for the workplace becomes an associated purpose, so it can be argued that school also serves to shape the futures of learners if not to directly control futures. But when we study the workplace from an educational perspective and think of it as a site for learning, then we get a quite different sense of purpose. It was evident to us as we observed the routines of the veterinary clinic that these were not established to serve the purpose of learning. Instead, they were established to serve the goals of patient health, care, and comfort. Also, the clinic functioned to maintain itself by creating profit. So where the overt purposes of school are learning, the purposes of the clinic as a workplace are not. Providing opportunities for learning becomes subservient to the goals of patient care, and the learning itself is consistently directed at those goals. The purposes of the clinic do not present a conflict for the co-op students, but it is clear that the difference between the purposes of the workplace and of school turn on authenticity: the learning at the clinic was purposeful in terms of authentic goals. The learning demands stem from workplace goals, and so the curriculum has a natural quality that is quite different from the school curriculum in the sciences. In turn, this leads us to consider the knowledge of the workplace.

Knowledge

In Ontario, and to some extent in other Canadian jurisdictions, co-op education becomes an opportunity to gain subject matter knowledge in a context and form different from school. Co-op education in Ontario is styled by the government as a "mode of delivery." Interestingly, Dewey (1964/1916) argued for "using active occupations as opportunities for scientific study" (201), and he suggested that "Connection of occupations with the method of science is at least as close as with its subject matter" (202). Quite clearly, science underlies the activities of clinic staff. But the kind of science is not clearly related to the science of school subject matter. School science is presented in an order that seems to serve the discipline itself rather than its application to phenomena outside the discipline. Whitehead's (1963) description is recognizably a traditional view of science education: "A scientific education is primarily a training in the art of observing natural phenomena, and in knowledge and deduction of laws concerning the sequence of such phenomena" (76). Even in these words, we can see how the science curriculum seems removed from theatres of practice.

Goodson's (1983) work on academic, utilitarian, and pedagogic traditions of subject matter is helpful in explaining how this drift occurs. His case studies show that subjects in the school curriculum begin in the utilitarian tradition, helping the subject to get in the door, as it were. This is followed by justifications from a pedagogic tradition, which focuses on students' needs and the practical and relevant applications of the discipline. Eventually, as a subject area matures and requires subject specialists to teach it, the academic tradition takes hold and arguments focus on the needs of the "discipline" itself. We could extend this analysis further by arguing that the sequence of material taught in a science curriculum seems more bound to the discipline's needs than to those of practical application. So in chemistry, we tend to expose students to the basics of atomic theory and periodicity before we would even think of involving them in the chemistry of combustion. Not surprisingly, there are calls for authenticity in science learning in the schools (e.g., Edelson 1998).

Differences in the science practiced at school and in the workplace are not the only differences in the knowledge one finds in both sites. Our research into the workplace has compelled us to examine the character of workplace knowledge and to contrast it with classroom or school knowledge. At first glance, knowledge at the veterinary clinic appears to be knowing *how*, or procedural knowledge, in contrast to knowing *that* (declarative or propositional knowledge). The latter is, of course, overwhelmingly prevalent in the school curriculum. Importantly, declarative or propositional knowledge is available in the workplace, yet it is much less visible than it is in school. Typically, knowing *that* in the workplace is in the service of knowing *how*. For instance, there are (propositional) reasons behind the order of packing instruments in a spay pack, and there is considerable medical propositional knowledge behind the veterinarian's prescriptions for care. The contrast between the functions of propositional knowledge in schools and in the workplace raises questions about the point of the propositional knowledge contained in the school curriculum, especially in the science curriculum.

Co-op Education's Challenge to Curriculum

Although our studies of co-op students at the clinic plainly show that there is a curriculum "at work," as it were, our research shows that features of the curriculum are unlike those of the school curriculum. The workplace curriculum fails to fit our customary views of delivering and assessing knowledge, for example. And for the co-op student in the workplace, knowledge is different, too, in its organization, purpose, and character. What we have found is that the distinctions between declarative and procedural knowledge do not quite capture these differences because neither concept carries a sense of purpose. Also the distinction between "inert" and "active" knowledge really does not do justice to the difference in the purposes of school and of the workplace. And although fashionable, "authentic" is somewhat overused, so that school tasks tend to get labeled as authentic even though they are still undertaken in school. In our efforts to find a device for marking the distinctive character of knowledge learned by co-op students in the workplace, we have found it useful to start with the idea that the adult world has a sense of purpose that is not shared in the world of school. For the adolescent, the purpose of school may be long range if it is transparent at all. But the world of work has a more immediate and discernible purpose, and the knowledge underlying the workplace is connected to that purpose. Indeed, it could be argued that knowledge in the adult world of work is usually in the service of an action. (For completeness, we add that the action is rarely in the service of learning except for co-op placements in schools, for example, where the object is learning.)

"Working Knowledge" and Liberal (or General) Education

When used as a curriculum commonplace (Schwab 1972), "subject matter" traditionally gives curriculum theorists problems. When we apply the framework of "commonplace" to the work setting and ask about the knowledge students are learning, we find differences that are sufficient to warrant a reconceptualized view of this commonplace in work-based curriculum. Our determination to underscore the vector of purpose within the knowledge of the workplace leads us to describe it in terms of "workplace knowledge." So when co-op students are observing complex routines or procedures, they are not simply engaging in legitimate peripheral participation. They are also witness to how the routine itself is related to the purpose and goals of the workplace. As students' participation becomes less peripheral, then their learning increases, but always in the context of an appreciation of the workplace's goals.

The earlier part of the chapter made the case for the similarity between the new vocationalism and the vision Dewey had for vocationalism in *Democracy and Education* (Dewey 1916/1964). Our argument is that the setting for co-op education provides an unequalled opportunity for teaching about the world of work because the knowledge would be "working knowledge" in the terms described above.

Conclusion

Our conclusion begins by pointing to an irony in the field of curriculum theory, an irony about the work of curriculum theorists and the knowledge we produce in that role. There are many references in the literature to how practical knowledge—the knowledge of action or skill—is undervalued in society in comparison with propositional or declarative knowledge. Oddly, though, propositional knowledge is the stuff of curriculum theorists—we confer, we write, we publish propositions. This form of knowledge is obviously valued inside the academy, but it is knowledge that presumably is directed toward action outside the academy, and purpose is at issue again. So the knowledge needs to be accessible, and care needs to be taken lest it veer toward the other end of the continuum and be dismissed as indulgence. Wraga's (1999) discussion of the connections between curriculum reconceptualization and practice is germane here, and we do not believe that the discussion has closed: we are mindful that there is no independent non-partisan group entrusted with ensuring that the knowledge we produce is in some way or other appropriate, useful, or relevant. Judgments about what knowledge is "working" remain to be made.

A corollary, of course, is that the knowledge taught in school, also should be appropriate, useful, or relevant. Interestingly, a foundational premise of co-op education is that it permits the community to participate in the education of its youth. Our experiences in our research suggest that the participation is not fully collaborative. We have plenty of evidence that the activities of the workplace influence students, but so far we have not noticed evidence that the activities of the workplace influence the high school curriculum so immediately. Conceivably, it is hard for the version of science that functions in the workplace to influence the version of science that functions in schools. Yet there will be problems if the two versions become vastly different. For example, students will find it hard to recognize science in the workplace, and schools will find it increasingly hard to justify teaching what they teach. Evidently, the "working knowledge" of science for the workplace in question needs to be explicated for students so that they can connect it to what they encounter in the science classroom.

This chapter has shown the promise of construing work-based programs like co-op education as curriculum. One outcome is that we now see important differences in the form, content, and structure of the curriculums of school and work. In the veterinary clinic, co-op students experience a curriculum that is quite unlike the biology curriculum for which they receive high school credit: the knowledge is different, it is organized and revealed differently, and it is offered in a context suffused with an adult purpose quite different from the purpose of school. The difference is captured by the idea of "working knowledge," a term that echoes the difference for the adolescent between the world of school and the world of work. A further outcome is that the character of the curriculum in the workplace invites us to reconsider the new vocationalism, specifically, to rethink the appropriate place for teaching about the world of work: the school or the workplace.

Notes

1. The average final-year grades of freshman students entering Queen's University from high school or Quebec's CEGEP system is 87.1percent, the highest of Canada's universities with medical schools and extensive doctoral programs ("The Ninth Annual Ranking of Universities" 1999).
2. In our research, we use fictitious names to refer to clinic staff and to co-op education students.

References

Bakan, D. (1971). Adolescence in America: From idea to social fact. *Daedalus 100*: 979–95.

Bailey, T. R., and D. Merritt (1997). *School-to-work for the college bound* (MDS-799). Berkeley, CA: National Center for Research in Vocational Education, University of California at Berkeley.

Bureau of Education (1918). *Cardinal principles of secondary education: A report of the commission on the reorganization of secondary education, appointed by the National Education Association.* Washington, DC: Department of the Interior Bulletin. No. 35.

Burwash, C., and G. Glover (Producers), Watson, P. (Director). (1967). *The invention of the adolescent.* [Film]. National Film Board of Canada.

Chin, P., H. Munby, and N. L. Hutchinson (1999). *Co-operative education: Challenges of qualitative research on learning in the workplace.* Paper presented at the annual meeting of the American Educational Research Association, Montreal.

Chin, P., Munby, H., Hutchinson, N. L., and Steiner-Bell, K (2000). Post-secondary students' intentions for participating in high school co-operative education programs. *Journal of Vocational Education Research 25*: 126–54.

Conference Board of Canada (1992). *Employability skills profile: What are employers looking for?* (Report 81-92-E). Ottawa: Conference Board of Canada.

Dewey, J. (1964). *Democracy and education.* New York: Macmillan (original work published 1916).

Edelson, D. (1998). Realising authentic science learning through the adaptation of scientific practice. In *International handbook of science education*, pages 317–31. Edited by B. Fraser and K. Tobin. Dordrecht, The Netherlands: Kluwer.

Enrollment in co-operative education in Ontario secondary schools 1996–1997. (1998 Winter). OCEA Exchange, 5.

Goodson, I. (1983). *School subjects and curriculum change: Case studies in curriculum history.* London: Croom Helm.

Hamilton, M. A., and S. F. Hamilton (1997). *Learning well at work: Choices for quality.* Ithaca, NY: Cornell University Press.

Hutchinson, N. L., P. Chin, H. Munby, W. Mills de España, J. Young, and K. L. Edwards (1999). How inclusive is co-operative education in Canada? Getting the story and the numbers. *Exceptionality Education Canada 8* (3): 15–43.

Lave, J., and E. Wenger (1991). *Situated learning: Legitimate peripheral participation.* Cambridge: Cambridge University Press.

Lewis, T. (1998). Vocational education as general education. *Curriculum Inquiry 28*: 285–309.

Munby, H., M. Cunningham, and P. Chin (1998). *Co-operative education: The functions of experience in workplace learning.* Paper presented at the annual meeting of the Canadian Society for the Study of Education, Ottawa.

Munby, H., N. L. Hutchinson, & P. Chin, (2000a). Co-operative education and the Canadian curriculum. *Education Canada 40*: 20–3.

——— (2000b). "I know how to do it": Research priorities for co-operative and career education in Canada's secondary schools. In *A Pan-Canadian education research agenda,* pages 37–54. Edited by Y. Lenoir, W. Hunter, D. Hodgkinson, P. de Broucker, and A. Dolbec. Ottawa, ON: Canadian Society for the Study of Education.

Musgrove, F. (1964). *Youth and the social order.* Bloomington, IN: Indiana University Press.

Nijhof, W. J., and J. Brandsma (Eds.) (1999). *Bridging the skills gap between work and education.* Dordrecht, The Netherlands: Kluwer.

"The Ninth Annual Ranking of Universities." (1999). *Maclean's.* November, *112*: 70.

Olson, L. (1997). *The school-to-work revolution.* Reading, MA: Addison-Wesley.

Sanderson, M. (1993). Vocational and liberal education: A historian's view. *European Journal of Education 28*: 189–96.

Scheffler, I. (1995a). John Dewey on work and education. In *Work, education, and leadership,* pages 26–43. Edited by V. A. Howard and I. Scheffler. NewYork: Peter Lang.

——— (1995b). Reflections on vocational education. In *Work, education, and leadership,* pages 45–58. Edited by V. A. Howard and I. Scheffler. New York: Peter Lang.

School-to-Work Opportunities Act. (1994). *Public Law,* No. 103-239.

Schwab, J. J. (1972). The practical: Translation into curriculum. *School Review 81*: 501–22.

Secretary's Commission on Achieving Necessary Skills. (1991). *What work requires of Schools.* Washington, DC.: SCANS, U.S. Department of Labor.

Wraga, W. G. (1998). The school-to-work movement in the United States: Policies, problems and possibilities. *The Curriculum Journal 9:* 177–195.

Wraga, W. G. (1999). "Extracting sun-beams out of cucumbers": The retreat from practice in reconceptualized curriculum studies. *Educational Researcher 28* (1), 4–13.

Whitehead, A. N. (1963). *The aims of education and other essays.* London: Benn.

CHAPTER TEN

Creating a Dialogue with Difference
Antoinette Oberg • Canada

Introduction

Last year, when I was a teaching a graduate seminar on curriculum theory, I became intrigued by a structure for class dialogue (Schaeffer 1991) based on Gregory Bateson's thinking about *difference, autopoiesis,* and *metaphor.* According to Bateson, a biologist and philosopher whose thinking I interpret in an educational context with the help of Bowers (1993), ideas are triggered by differences that occur among members of a group as they interact with each other. However, as described by the theory of autopoiesis, people respond not to each other *per se* but to their own perceptions of each other, specifically to each others' ideas. Autopoiesis, literally "self-making," is the theory that our response to anything outside of us is mediated by our own interpretations. Meaning is always self-made (Hoffman 1993). The meanings we make individually are part of larger patterns of understanding inscribed in the culture and encoded in the metaphorical structure of language. We are generally unconscious of the constitutive force of these underlying metaphors. Becoming aware of the metaphors embedded in the language we use loosens their restrictive hold on the meanings we make and creates the possibility for changes in our response to difference.

These constructs (difference, autopoiesis, and metaphor) seemed suitable for theorizing what had already been happening in my course. Our class discussions featured a wide range of student perspectives; students individually took responsibility for how they felt and what they said in class discussions, and we often paused in our conversation to note how the language we were using constructed the meaning we made. So when I found a structure for dialogue based on these Batesonian constructs, I decided without hesitation to introduce it to the class.

The structure I introduced was designed by Joseph Schaeffer (1991), who called it the "Pebble Game." In the game each idea contributed in discussion is a *pebble* that is put into play in the group. Players cannot be invested in their ideas persisting in the form in which they were played but must allow them to be transformed, incorporated, or ignored by others. Judgments are regarded not as statements of relative worth but as personal interpretations. No one is to try to convince or persuade or teach anyone else. The object of the game is not to search for truth but to notice the ways meanings are made in response to differences and, if need be, to negotiate meanings in order to decide what to do when group action is called for.

Class response to the prospect of playing the Pebble Game was different from what I expected. I expected that students would feel comfortable about playing the game and would willingly agree to play. However, when I proposed the game, students were not only willing to play, they were so enthusiastic that they immediately imagined themselves playing the game and were reluctant to rein in their imaginations even when it was time to end the class meeting. Encouraged by their unexpected enthusiasm, I opened the next class meeting with an additional proposal that in addition to playing the game, we foster a practice of reflective awareness by studying ourselves playing and present our study at a local conference. Surprising responses this time included unexpected negativity, not only about the reflective research but also about the game itself. The decision was quickly made to drop the research proposal. Subsequent class discussion focused on whether or not to play the game and what had happened to change students' feelings about playing the game. The body of this paper is a transcription of all of these events.

By good fortune as much as good planning, we had made audiotapes of the three class sessions in which we discussed the possibilities of playing and studying ourselves playing the Pebble Game. The first and third class sessions were recorded at the request of class members who were absent. The second session I asked to tape because I thought it would be the beginning of studying ourselves playing the Pebble Game.

Had we undertaken a research project to study our discourse dynamic, these audiotapes would have constituted our data. When the class decided against the research, I asked their permission to transcribe and use the tapes for my own purposes. This they freely gave, in writing, some with the proviso that they see what I wrote before it was made public.

My ultimate purpose in studying the transcripts was to refine my ability to pay attention to what happens in my classroom and to respond. The events described above threw into question my understanding of my practice as instructor. My continuing engagement with the transcripts focuses on articulating my response as instructor to what happened in those three class sessions. The interpretations shown in this chapter are an early stage of that engagement.

Transforming the Transcripts

I decided to shorten the original transcripts to make them more manageable. By eliminating personal identifiers as well as remarks I judged to be inconsequential or repetitive, I reduced the original forty-one pages to nineteen pages. I did not transpose nor add to students' words, but I did select some and omit others and thus changed the way students were represented in the text. I made them anonymous, though not voiceless, and less garrulous.

As I continued to engage with the transcripts, another transformation unexpectedly occurred. I was moved to shape students' spoken ideas as if they were pebbles and to arrange them as if they were scattered in a conversational flow. I rounded each utterance by reducing the horizontal space it occupied and allowing it more vertical space. I inserted multiple line breaks, which made each utterance look and sound like a poem. I eliminated words but did not add any. I used a change of margin to signal a change in the scatter pattern as the conversation flowed. I gave no particular meaning to any margin, except for the far left, which was always the location of my voice. The resulting arrangement of the transcripts showed visually the play of differences within our class group. (Again, students gave permission.)

I could have used a Batesonian perspective to analyze the events of my curriculum theory course. I could have looked at how response to difference created patterns of ideas, at how cultural metaphors inscribed personal meanings, at the degree of responsibility evidenced in group members' responses, and so on. I resisted such analyses. They would have closed down my engagement with the transcripts. After such analyses, nothing more is called for (although much might be said).

The continued liveliness of my engagement with the transcripts depended on resisting such closure. The truth of this assertion is seen in the experience of nine members of the curriculum theory course who outside of class took up my suggestion to prepare a presentation for a local conference about our experiences with the Pebble Game. Our meetings were lively engagements of the question of what to present and how to present it in a way that would convey the liveliness of our classroom engagements. The only product of these sessions was the conversation we had. As soon as we attempted to theorize the conversation, to summarize or characterize or generalize in order to produce an account of it, we ceased to engage each other and the liveliness disappeared. In the end we decided to do a performance of the transcripts which appear in the following pages of this paper.

The transcripts in their poetic form are offered here as an invitation for engagement by readers. They show an interpretation that stays in the sphere of poetic thinking (Caputo 1987), which is also where authentic engagements between teachers and learners occur. Poetic thinking is not rational and analytic but open and attentive to what happens in a relationship, employing "an acuity that knows its way about even and especially when the way cannot be laid out beforehand" (Caputo 1987: 213).

In the following text, I have designated five possible locations on the page, using five different indentations. There is a left-margin location that is my teacher voice, and there are four other locations at relatively equal distances across the page that student voices occupy. Horizontal and vertical spacing is used to differentiate ideas, not necessarily speakers. Each speaker's words are encapsulated within quotation marks. A change in speakers is signaled by closing quotation marks followed by opening quotation marks.

Invitation I

"I have a brilliant idea.
Let's pay attention
to the patterns of our dialogue
using a structure
called the Pebble Game.

"Each idea is a pebble
put into play.
Each person is responsible for
the pebbles he or she plays but not
for its transmutations.
"The aim is
to keep the play in play
and when joint action is required
to agree on
what to do."

"Do we get to
actually use pebbles?"

"Have rocks, will trade."

"I'll raise ya two pebbles."

"Each of us could have a fund of real pebbles."

"The presence of pebbles might distract from
the ideas."

"It depends on whether you are visual or auditory."

"I don't know if I could play a pebble
and not feel an attachment to it."

"Pebbles are hard
and on their own they don't change.
Water will change them or air
or crushing against rocks.
Changeability attached to a pebble
I find really peculiar."

"My understanding is more aesthetic.
It's not the pebbles as objects.
It's the pattern of ideas.
It's the weaving.
It's the web."

"If we all put our rocks in the middle
it's this open invitation.
My ideas are right
next to your ideas."

"What if I put a rock in
and someone else picked it up
and reinterpreted it?
Would I react?"

"All of the feelings that come up
with that externalizing."

"Pebbles are little stones in a brook
where water brushes them together
changing the texture of each pebble
as ideas are moved around
in relationship."

Invitation II

"I have a brilliant idea.
We could play the Pebble Game
and research ourselves
playing it
and present at a conference.

"Our focus might be
speaking across differences and
the play of power.
Our data would be
the transcripts of our dialogue.

"Something to beware of.
There is a danger of
subconscious coercion
because I am the instructor.
Do you see?"

"As you're describing this
all my joy in the class
is going away.
There's a definition of
what we're going to talk about.
It was so fun
when we came in here
and everyone talked
about different things."

"I have an opposite reaction
because I've done conference presentations
and they've been a joyous thing for me."

"When I listened to the tape
it was an incredible opportunity
to really hear
what people were saying.
I would endorse this
great opportunity."

"I think the research is a good idea and yet
it looks like a lot of work."

"I go home with observations of these kinds anyway
and it would be great to formalize it."

    "If we use any data from the tapes
    everybody in the class is implicated
    regardless of whether
    they chose to participate."

"We have people who are comfortable
to speak in the group and
people who are not.
What does their participation
or nonparticipation
mean?
    "I would like to suggest
    we go down this road
    for two or three sessions."

"I'm not afraid of being recorded.
If you want to quote me,
do it at your own risk.

    "I would be willing to do it
    just to try something new."

"I'm having an intuitive
reaction against structure.
If everything we're doing is
for the purpose of a research project
how will that affect the conversation?

"I certainly would be able
to speak up if I thought
the structure was killing
any kind of creativity
we experienced in the past."

"I have really strong feelings about
what happens to an activity when
you do it for the sake of something else.
I had that misgiving when
I first mentioned the Pebble Game.
Make sure we not regard it as
a set of rules that we follow but rather as
a way to orient our reflection on
what we are already doing."

"The Pebble Game sounded like
a description of a process
we were already engaging in.
Doing a presentation sounded like
a product shaping my experience in a way
not natural
       nor interesting
              nor stimulating
                      nor creative
                              for me."

"Worrying about losing
a certain spontaneity
            and intimacy
                    and creativity
                            in the group."

Discourses of Power

"I would just like to ask the question.
Is it appropriate to discuss
the content of last day's tape?"

"I'm the teacher so
I'd better say something."

"I'm directing the question at you
for the obvious reason.
It's also directed to you personally.
Antoinette, I've always felt a power differential
between you and me as a student.
I'm trying to pay attention to
how that power structure is
disseminated within this environment."

"I'd be interested in what you discerned about
how power relations are structured and
how power moves in the group."

        "The amount of time afforded a person
        generates reinforcement of their ideas.
        And you get to intervene and
        bring us all under control.
        I surrender myself to your power
        prior to walking into the classroom.
        There may also be something inherent in our relationship
        within this institution."

"Even though there is a great deal of freedom
in this class to express,
you are always in control and
I go along with it.
I have felt incredibly frustrated
in other classes when the discussion
goes in wild and crazy places and
no one says, 'Let's come back to the topic,' or
'Let's move on to something else.'"

"I've grown up in a tradition where the teacher is a master,
someone who has great depth of experience and
the ability to pay attention to me.
The teacher can give me a great deal because of her or his power."

"Close on the heels of power
is trust—
how much one trusts
a person who has been designated
institutionally or by the class as
the person who has the power.
I haven't always had the trust
in the facilitation of group dynamic
as I have in this class.
If I say something
that triggers something else
does the power reside somewhere
within the group
to successfully address
whatever has come up?"

        "Last term things flowed
        quite naturally.
        This term we're
        into group process."

"This group has been playing
the Pebble Game for quite a while.
The interactions have been
very honest and straightforward
without somebody trying to
dominate the group.
Your role should be
to make us aware of those things so
I'm free to explore issues
that are important to me and
have my awareness raised about
how we put meaning onto things and
how that affects the way we look
at different things."

"Researching playing the Pebble Game
would be a very credible piece of research—
what people like me are supposed to do.
I don't normally do research like that.
I'm naturally drawn to the emergent yet
feel obligated to the preplanned by
the norms of the university.
As a group we've named the difference.

"I'm inclined to give up the research strand yet
keep the Pebble Game in spite of hesitations that
we might pay more attention to the game than
to each other and our interests.
It could give us ways to pay attention to
what we're already doing.
I'll put that out as a pebble."

"I'm fine with that."

"I'd support that."

"I'm fine with that too."

"I'm really intimidated by the mike.
I think it's because it's right here.
I'm really intimidated.
I go to say something and as soon as
I see that I stop.
I think it's because
it's in my line of sight."

"How do other people
feel about the taping?"

                                        "I forgot about that."

                                        "Me too."

                                        "But it's not right in my face."

"Did you say you were okay with it?"

                                        "Yah, I'm okay with it."

                                        "Oh, it really bothers me.
I talk far less than I would.
No, I'm kidding.
It doesn't bother me at all."

                                        "Maybe it pushes you into a
performance level?"

                                        "No, no. I know why but
I don't want to go into that."

"Shall we turn off the tape?"

                                        "No, no, I'll get used to it."

                                        "You don't have to get used to
it."

"We don't need the tape necessarily."

                                        "Well, see I'm already talking
and it's not bothering me."

"And yet you're talking
to that little machine.
You can turn it off."

                                        "No, it's okay. I just needed
to put that out that
I'm intimidated by it."

Research and Real Life

"What happened with respect to
the Pebble Game?

    "It was tied to presentation:
    doing more work and
    getting up in front of
    a group of people."

        "We were all engaged in a process
        I didn't realize how profoundly
        we valued."

        "If there was any fear,
        which some say is where
        all our emotions come from,
        it was about losing
        that sense of community."

        "I was enjoying discovering
        people here and myself.
        It's difficult for me to move
        from playing to product,
        to leave myself and make a project
        out of a communication skills game.

            "A tape?
            Am I now a research subject?
            When you listen to a tape
            you hear the information as object."

"Pay attention to
objectification.
The abstract thinking
required to formulate a research project
takes us away from
the immediacy of interactions."

        "Was fear the prospect of
        being judged by others?
        Or was it that we ourselves
        didn't want to break open
        and look at what we are doing?"

        "What is the mystery
        we're trying to
        protect or embrace?"

"A mystery is a darkness that
wants to be lit."

"How will we sustain this?"
"The greatest risk we take is intimacy—how much we share ourselves."

"Darkness contains the possibility of
everything you could imagine
and never could imagine. Out
of all you are and all
you are experiencing
at any moment and the weather
some phrase comes out.
You have made sense.
You have created something.
And it is a mystery
where it came from."

"I felt comfortable trying to learn
whatever the Pebble Game was.
I felt this would be a framework
to establish rules around
a new level of intimacy.
It starts to get scary when
one reaches a certain level of knowledge
of other people.
What happens next?
How to stop the interplay of stuff that's going on
below the surface.
I don't know where to stop
how far to go
how much to give of myself."

References

Bowers, C. (1993). *Critical essays on education, modernity, and the recovery of the ecological imperative.* New York: Teachers College Press.

Caputo, J. (1987). *Radical hermeneutics: Repetition, deconstruction, and the hermeneutic project.* Bloomington and Indianapolis: Indiana University Press.

Hoffman, L. (1993). *Exchanging voices: A collaborative approach to family therapy.* London: Karnac Books.

Schaeffer, J. (1991). *The Pebble Game: Achieving creativity in human interaction.* New York: Vantage Press.

CHAPTER ELEVEN

The Project and Vision of Transformative Learning

Edmund O'Sullivan • Canada

It is necessary at the outset to provide the reader with a provisional definition of transformative learning in order to anchor this idea in its complex and interweaving contexts. To embark upon a discussion of a transformative vision of education, it must be kept clearly in mind that it will involve a diversity of elements and movements in contemporary education. A vision statement must attend to these diversities. We are living in a major transitional period of history in which there are many contesting viewpoints. To some extent these trends are operating in a somewhat separate and independent way. What I would like to do here is to name some of those elements because I think they will form part of a weave of a new type of integral education that will contest the vision of education for the global marketplace. What is important, at this point in our treatment, is to name some of those elements that are potentially moving toward a more integral transformative vision. I would then like to couch these elements within a broad cosmological framework, which I believe will be my major contribution to the effort of offering an alternative to our present conventions in education.

What we are now coming to understand is that we are living in a period of the earth's history that is incredibly turbulent and in an epoch in which there are violent processes of change that challenge us at every imaginable level. Humans are totally caught up in this incredible transformation, and we have a most significant responsibility for the direction it will take. The terror here is that we have it within our power to make life extinct on this planet. Because of the magnitude of this responsibility for the planet, all our educational ventures must finally be judged within this order of magnitude. This is the challenge for all areas of education. As we think about education, this realization is the bottom line. What do I mean here by bottom line? For me, the bottom line is that every educational endeavour must address the magnitude of our present moment in its educational priorities. This demands a kind of attentiveness to our present planetary situation that does not go into slumber or denial. This poses momentous challenges to educators in areas heretofore unimagined. Education within the context of transformative vision keeps concerns for the planet always at the forefront. From the perspective that I am calling "transformative learning," the fundamental educational task of our times is to make the choice for a sustainable planetary habitat of interdependent life-forms over and against the pathos of the global competitive marketplace. This perspective shares a point of view with a rising tide of people and communities all over the globe. This emergent vision of life deeply challenges the economic globalization that is moving like a tornado in our world as we enter the new century.

A full planetary consciousness that involves the full extension of our human species will have a dream structure that helps us to understand our awesome gift that comes out of a plenitude that staggers both our minds and hearts. Planetary consciousness opens us up into the awesome vision of a world that energizes our imagination well beyond a marketplace vision. Contemporary education lacks a comprehensive cosmology. When education has drawn from the sciences, its attention has been directed to the social sciences as distinguished from the natural sciences. In most cases, educational theory and practice have borrowed from the sciences of psychology, sociology, and, to a lesser extent, anthropology. What is totally lacking in modern educational theory is a comprehensive and integrated perspective that has in the past been identified as a cosmology. Thus, contemporary educational theory and practice carry the same blinders that have plagued modern scientific specialization coming out of the post-Newtonian period. To be sure, modern Western educational thought has attempted to identify itself with humanism, but it has done so without providing a renewal of an acceptable cosmology. What we are working toward in transformative vision is an articulation and presentation of a cosmology that can be functionally effective in providing a basis for an educational program that would engender an ecologically sustainable vision of society in the broadest terms—what can be called a planetary vision.

The idea of transformative vision starts with the notion of transformation within a broad cultural context. In the larger cultural context, transformation carries the dynamism of cultural change. We say that when any cultural manifestation is in its florescence, the educational and learning tasks are uncontested, and the culture is of one mind about what is ultimately important. There is, during these periods, a kind of optimism and verve that ours is the best of all possible worlds, and we should continue what we are doing. It is also usual to have a clear sense of purpose about what education and learning should be. In addition there is a predominant feeling that we should continue in the same direction that has taken us to this point. Here one can say that a culture is in "full form" and the form of the culture warrants "continuity." We might say that a context that has this clear sense of purpose or direction is "formatively appropriate." A culture is formatively appropriate when it attempts to replicate itself within this context and the educational and learning institutions are in synchrony with the dominant cultural themes.

Even when a culture is formatively appropriate, there are times when there seems to be a loss of purpose or a loss of the qualities and features that appeared to have given that particular culture its florescence. Part of the public discourse during times such as these is one of "reform criticism." Reform criticism is a language that calls a culture to task for its loss of purpose. It is a criticism that calls itself back to its original heritage. This is a criticism that accepts the underlying heritage of the culture and seeks to put the culture, as it were, "back on track." When reform criticism is directed toward educational institutions, we call this "educational reform."

There is another type of criticism, radically different from reform criticism, which calls into question the fundamental mythos of the dominant cultural form and indicates that the culture can no longer viably maintain its continuity and vision. This criticism maintains that the culture is no longer formatively appropriate, and in the application of this criticism there is a questioning of all of the dominant culture's educational visions of continuity. We refer to this type of criticism as "transformative criticism." In contrast to "reformative criticism," this "transformative criticism" suggests a radical restructuring of the dominant culture and a fundamental rupture with the past. I would suggest that transformative criticism has three simultaneous moments. The first moment I have already described as the critique of the dominant culture's formative appropriateness. The second is a vision of what an alternative to the dominant form might look like. The third moment is some concrete indication of the practical exigencies of how a culture probably could abandon those aspects of its present forms that are functionally inappropriate while, at the same time, pointing to some directions of how it can be part of a process of change that will create a new cultural form that is functionally appropriate.

Having looked at the notion of transformative learning in its broad cultural context, it now seems appropriate to look at it from the point of view of the knower and known. For this, I will draw upon general systems theory to give us a specific entry into the world of the individual learner. It is the systems theory viewpoint that the mind is in the process of learning to organize itself by virtue of feedback—that is, by monitoring its interactions with its environment. The key term in systems theory is *monitoring*. The basic assumption is that open systems, like the mind, self-monitor. In the context of learning, monitoring assumes that the mind watches what it is doing and adjusts. The mind initially operates through preconceptions and these preconceptions not only shape our interpretations of the world but also impinge on the world itself, for feedback that extends beyond the subjective realm and circles through the environment, as it were, is "out there." In order to comprehend how the world and the mind shape each other, it is necessary to examine the two main ways that feedback works. The first is "homeostatic," or negative, feedback, a process that brings the world around us in line with our assumptions and goals. The second is "adaptive," or positive, feedback, which leads to change in internal codes or presuppositions. Thus negative feedback indicates that you are on track, with no need for adjustment, and positive feedback signals deviation from objective and the need to correct or alter the course. Positive feedback operates when we act upon our environment to make it intelligible in terms of our presuppositions. Adaptive positive feedback occurs when there is a persistent mismatch between perception and code—that is, when we can no longer interpret experience in terms of our old assumptions. The cognitive system then searches for new codes by which novel and confusing perceptions can be made intelligible. This search amounts to an exploration of new ways to reorganize itself, and it continues until codes and constructs evolve that can deal with the novelty of the new data. In this particular context, we see that living systems adapt, by transforming themselves, and thus learning happens. Therefore, from the perspective of transformative learning, real learning is not something added to a system in adaptation. Transformation means, in essence, the reorganization of the whole system. We see in this process a shifting of ground; the viewed world is different, and so is the viewpoint of the viewer. Thus transformative learning processes are counted as the creative function of cognitive crisis. Creativity occurs within a cognitive system when old habitual modes of interpretation become dysfunctional and demand a shifting of ground or viewpoint. The breakdown or crisis motivates the system to self-organize in more inclusive ways of knowing, embracing, and integrating data of which it had been previously unconscious.

I draw on the distinguished cultural historian and ecologist, Thomas Berry, in a talk he gave to the Transformative Learning Center, to highlight the historical task of cultural transformation in our present historical moment. He sees our present moment in history as a terminal state and also as a moment of grace. In moments of grace we take danger and turn it into opportunity. In moments of grace we take decadence and turn it into creativity. Berry maintains that in order to survive our moment, we must be prepared to take a journey into a new creative story. In the present we are living between stories. Thomas Berry speaks of our present historical moment in a story context. He maintains that our present cultural story, which is exemplified in the technical-industrial values of Western Eurocentric culture, is now dysfunctional in its larger social dimensions, even though we continue to believe in it firmly and act according to its guidance. Berry (1993) maintains that we are in pressing need of a radical reassessment of our present situation, especially concerning those basic values that give life some satisfactory meaning. We need an integral story that will educate us, a story that will heal, guide, and discipline us. The transition between stories will be referred to in the text as the movement from the terminal cenozoic to the ecozoic. It is a movement of transformative learning at both the individual and cultural levels of history.

Integral Modes of Transformative Learning: The Tripartite Distinction of Survive, Critique, and Create

Transformative learning encompasses an education for survival, an education for critical understanding, and an education for integral creativity. In my definition of transformative learning, I say that we must survive, critique, and create. Let us look at these three modes in turn.

Survival Education (Survive): The word "survival" comes from the French verb *survivre*. Basically, survival means creating conditions for the continuance of living. The terminal aspects of our historical moment that I have described above involve educational concerns at the personal, communal, and planetary levels. The sense of all of the locations of survival can be crystallized in the awareness that something is very amiss with the practices of an economic system that has led to both human suffering and environmental disaster. Patterns of devastating destruction, which are neither random nor accidental, have arisen from a consciousness that fragments exist. The matrix of Western culture, originating in modern European culture and transplanted all over the world, which considers human existence and above all human consciousness and spirit as independent from and above nature, dominates the world's imagination. This dynamism, which is now embedded in the onslaught of the global market, is withering away our sustenance at the personal, communal, and planetary levels of existence. We see its effect in environmental devastation, human rights violations, the hierarchies of race, the prevalence of violence, the idea of technological progress, and the problem of failing economies. To understand these complex issues as intricate pieces of our understanding of ecological crisis is the survival task of transformative learning. To continue understanding these complex issues in isolation is a basic consciousness attitude, which presently threatens the survival of the earth.

In terms of facing these profound issues of survival, there are three aspects that one does not ordinarily identify with learning. Here I am thinking about the dynamics of denial, despair, and grief. In transformative learning I deal with these dimensions at length; here they must be discussed all too briefly. Denial is a defense mechanism that prevents us from being overwhelmed by the deeply problematic nature of our times. But in order to solve problems, it is necessary to come out of denial. Once the depths of our problems are allowed in, we must contend with despair. Despair will be one of the major difficulties in facing survival issues. Without the development of a critical understanding and creative vision, despair has the potential to overwhelm. Finally, grieving is a necessary ingredient in the survival mode. The sense of loss at the personal, communal, and planetary levels that is part and parcel of the survival mode demands a grieving process at profound levels of depth. Therefore, transformative learning in the survival mode is a learning process requiring the ability to deal with denial, despair, and grief.

Critical Resistance Education (Critique): In the survival mode, we are dealing with a profound cultural pathology. A deep cultural pathology needs a deep cultural therapy. Part of this cultural therapy involves a transformative mode of cultural criticism. Survival is just one mode of transformative learning. We also need to examine the factors and conditions that have brought us to this devastating historical moment. We need a resistance education that moves in the direction of cultural criticism. We are basically dealing with a transformative learning that includes the moments of resistance and critical pedagogy. A critical pedagogical moment will cover several areas that are in need of deep critical reflection.

The first dimension to be examined is the matrix of thought that provides the frame of reference and worldview for the forces of the modern world. Here we need to be attentive to the deep ontological basis of Western European thinking. In relation to the natural world, the dynamics of the modern scientific-industrial worldview have moved an agenda that has had profound effects on how the modern Western European human views the natural world. What is here being called "modern cosmological systems" starts with the post-medieval Enlightenment period taking us into the mid-twentieth century. This is the apex of what we have referred to as the final phases of the late cenozoic period. What is characteristic of this period is the major cultural re-visioning of thought systems that are now identified as the technical scientific-industrial worldview. The movement into this post-medieval period represents a very profound change in cultural consciousness. There was, at this juncture, a change from the medieval into the modern temper as one of the most far-reaching cultural changes in human history. As with other great historical junctures, the movement from the medieval world into the modern world was a movement that involved a new metaphysical and ideological change involving all major cultural institutions and, in essence, formed a new picture of the cosmos and the nature of the human. The sense of the world that views nature as a mechanism enmeshed in mechanical forces has led to a profound disenchantment with the natural world. There is within these forces of modernism a loss of the sense of a wider cosmology in which human actions are embedded.

Philosopher Stephen Toulmin (1985) in *The Return to Cosmology* gives us a convenient entry point for our discussion of cosmology. He observes that there appears to be a natural attitude taken by humans at all times and in all places when reflecting on the natural world, and there appears to be a comprehensive ambition to understand and speak about the universe as a whole. Toulmin notes that, in practical terms, this desire for a view of the whole has reflected a need to recognize where we stand in the world in which we have been born, to grasp our place in the scheme of things, and to feel at home within it.

A second dimension of critical resistance education is dealing with the saturation of consciousness. Marshall McLuhan once quipped, "I don't know who discovered water, but it certainly wasn't the fish." This image succinctly conveys the problem of submerged consciousness that a critical resistance education must encounter. As with the fish in water, so we in relation to our culture are in what Paolo Freire (1970) calls a submerged state of consciousness. With the incredible saturation of information that our modern consciousness demands we attend to, we are, according to John Ralston Saul (1997), an "unconscious civilization." We are caught up in a situation where our knowledge does not make us conscious. Information, in modern societies, comes to us indiscriminately, and the information is disconnected to usefulness. We are swamped with information and have virtually no substantial control over it. Reflecting on the earlier discussion of a fractured cosmology, we see a loss of coherence because we no longer have a coherent conception of ourselves, our universe, and our relation to one another and our world. Within the context of a broader cosmological background, information diversity is as critical to our long-term survival as biodiversity.

The third dimension of a critical resistance education is in the critical examination of hierarchical power. Our modern Western historical inheritance is deeply embedded in a hierarchical conception of power that comes to us in the structures of patriarchy and imperialism. In its simplest interpretation, patriarchy is a system of power where men dominate. Our culture exists within the matrix of patriarchal power. In reflecting on our Western heritage, we see male dominance in the four establishments that have been in control of Western history over the centuries. The four establishments are the classical empires, the ecclesiastical establishment, the nation-state, and the modern corporation. Historically, women have had minimal if any consistent role in the direction of these establishments. A critical transformative deconstruction of patriarchy is one learning task in the critical mode that will pick up the feminist movement's challenge to the destructive effects of patriarchy throughout contemporary societies. Simultaneously with the deconstruction of patriarchy, the deep structure of hierarchical power and violence needs to be critically examined in such areas as race, class, gender, and sexual identities. The structures of imperialism, which have characterized the expansiveness of Western culture in the modern era, are now being brought into the light of profound criticism. John Willinsky (1998), in *Learning to Divide the World: Education at Empire's End,* notes how the subtle themes of imperialism continue to play themselves out at our present historical moment. He posits that imperialism was, in a certain light, an educational venture that captured and captivated the imagination of the West. This captivation has come to an end, and we are now contending with an emergent post-colonial world of critical reflective understanding as seen in the spirit of multicultural, anti-racist, and feminist initiatives that seek to identify and critically understand the Eurocentric and patriarchal matrix of our European cultural heritage.

Visionary Transformative Education (Create): I will develop the idea of a creative transformative learning by highlighting the themes of education for planetary consciousness, education for integral development, education for quality of life, and education and the sacred. The first theme is education for a planetary consciousness. In spite of its powerful dynamics in our world today, the idea of the global market is a small idea. It was my sense when I was attempting to develop a creative vision for our place in the contemporary world that we must locate our lives in a larger cosmological context that is much more breathtaking than the market vision of our world. Brian Swimme (1996) points out that we can be fooled into thinking that our lives are passed in political entities, such as the state or a nation, or the bottom-line concerns in life having to do with economic realities. He invites us to understand that we live in the midst of immensities. I realize that in presenting a larger cosmological context for our lives, it is not enough to defend a new cosmology in opposition to the cosmology that has underpinned modernity. In a visionary context for transformative learning, we must articulate a planetary context for learning in such a way that it can effectively challenge the hegemonic culture of the market vision and a context that can orient people in practice, in their daily lives, to create an environmentally viable world in our present time. The philosopher Arran Gare (1995) maintains that we need a new grand narrative that helps us to find our way in our present situation in a larger narrative story than the market. He ventures that such a narrative will help us to take up and participate as learners in addressing the momentous environmental crisis we face. We need stories of sufficient power and complexity to orient people for effective action to overcome environmental problems, to address the multiple problems of environmental destruction, to reveal the possibilities available for transformation, and to reveal to people the role they can play in this project. The scope and magnitude of transformative stories brings many cultural pieces together in creative dynamic tension. Gare maintains that:

> In order for such stories to work, to inspire people to take them seriously, to define their lives in terms of them, and to live accordingly, such stories must be able to confront and interpret the present stories by which people are defining themselves and choosing how to live in an environmentally destructive way. It is also important to reveal how power operates and to show why those individuals concerned about the global environmental crisis are unable effectively to relate their own lives to such problems. The new grand narrative must enable people to understand the relationship between the stories by which they define themselves as individuals and the stories by which groups constitute themselves and define their goals, ranging from families, local communities, organizations, and discursive formations, to nations, international organizations, and humanity as a whole. (140)

In my own work on transformative learning, I suggest that we need to expand our horizon of consciousness to the universe itself. The cultural historian and ecologist Thomas Berry (1989) reveals the scope of a vision where the universe is the matrix:

> The universe in its full extension in space and its sequence of transformations in time is best understood as Story; a story in the 20th century for the first time with scientific precision through empirical observation. The difficulty is that scientists have until recently given us the story only in its physical aspects, not in the full depth of its reality or in the full richness of its meaning. The greatest single need for the survival of the earth or of the human community in this late 20th century is for an integral telling of the Great Story of the Universe. This story must provide in our times what the great mythic stories of earlier times provided as the guiding and energizing sources of the human venture. (1)

I would say that it might better be called a "wonderful story of origins." It is grander for me in its scope and magnitude, but it is not a "grand narrative" to replace other stories of origins. I am using Berry's ideas as an entry point into a broader cosmological context. I have found that this point of entry has opened up a system of larger meaning that can help create an organic planetary context for educational endeavors and that transcends the myopic vision of the global marketplace.

I believe that educational vision in the twenty-first century must be accomplished within a planetary context. We live on a planet and not on a globe. When we look at the universe story that we have just depicted, we encounter an organic totality and not a map. We are one species living on a planet called "the earth," and all living and vital energies come out of this organic cosmological context. The globe is a construct of human artifice. Before 1492, cartographic procedures for mapping commerce routes were flat. For Europeans, Columbus moved the mapping systems for commerce from a flat surface to a globe. The globe was made for commerce today, and the language of globalization today is first and foremost for commercial purposes. For all of the major issues that we have discussed under "critique," the language of the globalization was the background context. The major fundamental shift in our time is that of the power structures on the globe from national state business (including the military business) to transnational business. All over the world, at this moment, nation-state governments are delivering their governments to transnational business. We cannot, therefore, dispense with global language, and it is absolutely necessary that it be the subject of deep-order cultural criticism at a world level. At the same time, we cannot be confined to globalization visions even as a sole corrective. At the planetary level, we move beyond geosphere to biosphere.

The second visionary theme is education for integral development. The words "integral" and "development" have been carefully chosen. In spite of the very critical analysis of the concept of development that can be ventured against market-driven development, there is still a very core need to retain a conception of development in a treatment of transformative education. It is one thing to severely criticize our Western conceptions of development; it is another to try to conceive of education in the absence of an overarching conception of development. Visionary transformative education must include a conception of development that will transcend the limitations of our Western ideas on development and the attendant conception of underdevelopment. Therefore, integral development links the creative evolutionary processes of the universe, the planet, the earth community, the human community, and the personal world. It is a development that must be understood as a dynamic wholeness, where wholeness encompasses the entire universe and vital consciousness resides both within us and at the same time all around us in the world. The endpoint of all of this moves us toward a deep personal planetary consciousness that one can identify as ecological selfhood.

The third theme to be addressed within the context of transformative vision is that of concerns about a quality of life as part of the learning frame of reference. We in the minority world (First World) must come to terms with the quality of life that we have created for ourselves and also assume the responsibility for how that manner of living has diminished the manner of living of countless peoples in the majority world and in our own. The bottom line in the global market economy is profit. The singular major goal is economic growth indexed in the gross national product (GNP). We have sold this dream of profit to our world by commodity fetishism. Our Western labor force has bought the notion of "standard of living," but this is only a comparative phrase to tell you whether your buying power has increased or decreased in wage potential to buy market commodities. However, standard of living does not add up to quality of life. Our economic market vision has left our whole culture with a crisis of meaning and a felt sense of homelessness. Michael Lerner (1996) maintains that we hunger more for meaning and purpose in life in the final analysis. Our cultural values, fixated on the marketplace, have caught us up in a deep cynicism that makes us question whether there is any deeper meaning and higher purpose to life beyond material self-interest. The bottom line of all this materialism and glorification of self-interest is where we find ourselves.

We are living in a period when human and earth history is in a state of radical transformation. Some of our habitual patterns from the past have now become dysfunctional for our present circumstances. We are being driven, by necessity, to devise new patterns for living in order to survive in a manner that gives us a sustainable quality of life. I feel that we cannot deal with our present historical moment by surface responses to our difficulties. We are now becoming aware that our Western scale of progress and development is not tuned to the human scale or, for that matter, the scale of the earth. Our task must be to deepen our understanding of development in a manner that takes a much wider spectrum of human needs into account.

One of the core need areas we must concentrate on in examining quality of life issues is related to the deep-seated need for community and sense of place. Rootlessness, transitoriness, and dispossession are the fall-out from globalization in an increasing number of communities all over the world: people move to find better jobs; corporations move to find cheaper labor. Products for consumption, such as food, move thousands of miles to reach global markets; shifts of fashion change with each season, and neighborhoods where people grew up (like my own) shift within a generation. Our sense of belonging to a stable community and our security are lost in the shuffle of accelerated change and mobility. The result is a loss of connection—to where we live, to people themselves, and to the natural world that surrounds us.

Educational institutions at all levels must play a pivotal role in fostering a community's sense of place. This is accomplished by including the curriculum studies of the "bio-region." Bio-regional study encompasses study of the land, the history of the community that has occupied a region, and the histories of peoples in the bio-region. Educating for the purpose of cultivating a sense of history of an area enables people to have loyalties and commitment to the place of their dwelling. In a time when the global economy can no longer be relied upon to provide the basic necessities of life, the cultivation of a sense of locality and place has built within it a corrective to the vagaries of globalization. Educating for a sense of place has not only a history to give, it also has a history to make. In the latter context, locality education encourages each self-identified community to build on the educational goal of encouraging an independent local economy capable of providing goods and services for its inhabitants.

Another feature associated with issues of life quality is the need for diversity within and among communities. In the global world toward which we are moving, there is an educational imperative for all members of the planet to enter communities of greater inclusion. Inclusion does not entail violation of boundaries. Inclusion means openness to variety and difference with a sense of including all in a manner of attending to the uniqueness of each and every member. Thus, educating for an inclusive community is open to the fullest sense of differentiation and also a sense of the deep mystery of each person. What is important to understand here is that inclusive communities operate not on the basis of sameness but on the creativity of difference. Inclusion in today's world is not created in a vacuum. Most groups and communities present themselves at varying degrees of inclusion. Finally, a transformative vision of education should be built on the foundational pro-cesses of the universe—differentiation, subjectivity, and communion. This allows a simultaneous articulation of both the different and the communal. The creativity of the community is grounded in the awe and respect for the larger biotic community, the web of life.

Quality of life concerns also connect in the development of a "civic culture." The responses to globalization, bureaucratic government, and media-driven community disempowerment are intermediary structures that bridge the local community to the larger global structures. We call these intermediary structures "civil societies" or "cultures." The need for these intermediary structures is a response to the exigencies of our present global situation. The needs of an alert, conscious citizenry become clear as we assess our circumstances in the global world toward which we appear to be moving. The notion of citizen comes again to the fore. An alert citizenry is the ultimate check on the activities of politicians and commercial and financial institutions. Effective governance will depend on individuals exerting their rights and responsibilities, so as to monitor the activities of governments and apply pressure to insure that the rule of international law is not violated. Good "world citizens" will refuse to be influenced by the propaganda of governments or the media. They will be sensitive to the need to match consumerism with sustainable development and will use their voting power to ensure that economic and financial policies reflect proper care of the world's resources.

The final theme, which brings to an end this vision statement on transformation, is the "sense of the sacred." I believe that any in-depth treatment of "transformative education" must address the topic of spirituality and that educators must take on the concerns of the development of the spirit at a most fundamental level. Contemporary education today suffers deeply from its eclipse of the spiritual dimension of our world and universe. Spirituality, in our times, has been seriously compromised by its identification with institutional religions. It has also been compromised by the vision and values of the market. There is no place in the world economy governed by the profit motive for the cultivation and nourishment of the spiritual life. Leisure, contemplation, and silence have no value in this system because none of these activities are governed by the profit motive. Peoples who attend to their spiritual life are seen as nonproductive or underdeveloped. Our world economy is geared to total emphasis on material wants and needs, and there is an eclipse of the hunger that people have called the hunger of the spirit. From an educational point of view, our present state is in need of transformation. Our first and foremost task in life is to take hold of our spiritual destiny. This is not a household word in education. Nevertheless, we are beginning to see a concern in education that opens onto considering education as a spiritual venture. The sense of the sacred, from my own perspective, encompasses all aspects of transformative vision. It is a dimension that is integral to all three modes of transformative learning and cannot be separated from any one of them. I bring the discussion of this section to an end with a quote from T.S. Eliot (1943) taken from his *Four Quartets:*

> And the end of all our exploring
> Will be to arrive where we started
> And know the place for the first time. (39)

References

Berry, T. (1989). The twelve principles for understanding the universe and the role of the human in the universe. *Teilhard perspectives* 22 (1): 1.

———— (1993). A moment of grace. Paper presented at the Madan Handa Memorial Lecture

Series. November. Ontario Institute for Studies in Education at the University of Toronto, Canada.
Eliot, T. S. (1943). Little Gidding. In *Four Quartets*. New York: Harcourt Brace.
Freire, P. (1970). *The pedagogy of the oppressed*. New York: Seabury.
Gare, A. (1995). *Postmodernism and the environmental crisis*. New York: Routledge.
Lerner, M. (1996). *The politics of meaning*. Reading, Mass.: Addison-Wesley.
Saul, J. R. (1997). *The unconscious civilization*. Toronto: Anansci.
Swimme, B. (1996). *The hidden heart of the cosmos*. Maryknoll, NY: Orbis.
Toulmin, S. E. (1985). *The return to cosmology*. Berkeley: University of California.
Willinsky, J. (1998). *Learning to divide the world: Education at empire's end*. Minneapolis: University of Minnesota.

CHAPTER TWELVE

The Globalization of the World and the Need for the Internationalization of Curriculum Studies: A Change for the Future

Sid N. Pandey • Botswana

A Change for the Future

The problems of the world today have been brought home to every individual by the media to become intimate realities. In fact, we have learned to live with them by just ignoring them, as if they do not exist at all. We feel helpless before the daily menu of TV shows and newspaper articles on corruption; mass murders; atrocities on children, women, and old men; hijacking; plane crashes; HIV/AIDS death tolls; small and big wars; and the impending doom of a global nuclear or biological war. The list makes us sick. The media report all kinds of horrors, which we have to watch helplessly. No wonder Dr. Andrew Weil's prescription for his patients is to "watch and read less news; schedule occasional one-week news fasts" to reduce stress and regain physical and mental well-being (Kluger 1997: 49).

But this abject situation should not make us lose sight of the prospects which the twenty-first century holds once we have learned to solve our problems. I recall that Herman Kahn, the noted futurologist, forecast at a Texas A&M University conference in 1976 that by the end of the century, no country on earth would have starvation. In the twenty-first, nanotechnology will make the present electronic equipment look like Stone-Age implements by offering "options for the fabrication of sophisticated materials and micromachines opening up a staggering array of possibilities" (Beare & Slaughter

1993: 121). Space exploration will result in the discovery of habitable places and the creation of new habitats for humans. The worst ecological problems, the energy crisis, demographic pressures, etc., will be solved forever. Through the inventions of new medicines, surgical procedures, genetic engineering, and DNA synthesis we will eliminate diseases and give humanity victory over death. These and other claims sound like fantasies mainly because a collaborated global effort has not been made to apply all human energy and resources toward the solution of the problems and the realization of human potential.

It is obvious that while the world is shrinking to a global village through developments in information technology, communication, and transportation, the problems have been increasing progressively in complexity to threaten the survival of mankind. There is no unified vision, purpose, will, and effort at the global level to find solutions. However, one idea has persisted: despite the differences and conflicts, education can be relied upon to create a better, safer, and cleaner world. While some leftists and radicals question the role of education in reforming society educators in Third World countries have always trusted its positive role as a transformer. Can we come to a consensus about using education as a lever to save ourselves from the most imperiled situation in human history? Can we create an international curriculum? Are the conditions favorable, or can we try to explore the possibilities by conversing with those who might have different views and perspectives?

It is the purpose of this chapter, call it a conversational tool, to draw the participants' attention to the context of curriculum in the colonized countries of the Third World as related to post-colonial education and the situation in the post-industrial, post-modern world in order to provide a comparative view of curriculum perspectives. It may be useful in suggesting some guidelines for developing an international curriculum for the global village of the future. Botswana, a new African nation, has been presented as a model and case study to indicate that constructive thinking and planning for the future is going on and as an encouragement for those who want to move in positive directions.

The Curriculum in Third World Countries

Since this chapter is going to converse mainly about the Third World countries of Africa and Asia, we need to recapitulate how the prevalent curriculum originated. Despite the diversities of cultures and geographical boundaries, the new curriculum that was implemented in the colonies by the

European rulers had a major aim. Lord Macaulay's "Minutes" in 1834 encapsulated it for the introduction of English education in India:

> In India, English is the language spoken by the ruling class. It is spoken by the higher class of natives at the seats of Governments. It is likely to become the language of commerce throughout the seas of the East. It is the language of two great European communities which are rising, the one is the South of Africa, the other in Australasian; communities which are every year becoming more important and more closely connected with our Indian Empire....We must do our best to form a class who may be interpreters between us and the millions whom we govern...a class of persons, Indian in blood and color, but English in tastes, in opinion, in morals, and in intellect. (Carnoy 1974: 100)

The aim of colonial education was overachieved in India and all over the European colonies. Adeyinka (2000), speaking specifically about the situation in African countries, endorses similar educational achievements: "The educated elite readily accepted the new culture, because it placed them far above other members of the society, and some of them even became more British or more French than their masters" (6). The colonial curriculum created a class of elite and white-collar jobholders who scorned the poor natives and associated their cultural traditions with superstition and backwardness under the influence of the new knowledge backed by the prestige of scientific rationalism and the promises of industrial and technological advancement. They helped the rulers in further colonizing and thus perpetuated class differentiation by widening the gap between the privileged and the common masses.

The Neo-Marxist reproduction theorists (Bourdieu and Passeron 1977; Bernstein 1977) have disengaged three complex strands in this kind of curriculum: knowledge as cultural capital; the pursuit of different subjects, content, and languages for achieving class differentiation; and the ideological nature of the curriculum. Of course Giroux (1981) and even Apple (1982) became critical of the pessimistic views, but the basic reality is apparent. Holmes and McLean (1989), in their comparative analysis of curriculum, show how the colonial curriculum has continued to survive:

> Above all, the persistence in India of views of worthwhile knowledge associated with the colonial regime in a country which has achieved a high degree of educational autonomy from foreign influence and which has enormous human resources to achieve educational change suggests that the Colonial curriculum philosophy

[British essentialism] may not disappear in other countries simply because external dependence is removed. (167)

The Coming of Globalization

While the Third World nations have still to find ways and means to overcome the problems of colonization, the wave of globalization is approaching fast. The technological revolution has compressed time and space and increased the pace of productivity. Computerization, satellite communication, and fiber-optic telecommunication have shortened the turnover time for goods and services. This process has enabled the economic corporations to cross borders in search of new markets and cheap labor to cut costs and increase profits. Most national governments have liberalized their fiscal policies to entice multinational investments to start industries and create new job opportunities. There are prospects as well as prognoses. To utilize the new situation to their advantage, they have to respond with care and caution. The existence of nation-states as clearly identifiable socio-political-cultural entities is in danger. Ethnic and religious groups in some countries have started resorting to cultural action, fundamentalism, and demands for indigenization in order to overcome the fear of losing self-identity and autonomy. The long-term effects of globalization are unknown. Even the obvious economic benefits from more jobs for the poor cannot be guaranteed in the long run. What Reich (1991) and Aronowitz and De Fazio (1994) said about the American workers could easily apply to those in other areas. The boat containing routine producers will sink faster; even in-person service providers will be drowned later. The new technology and the automations used to cut costs will bore holes in their boats. Only a small number of people with specialized skills and abilities will reap the benefit: "the symbolic analysts—who solve, identify, and broker new problems—are by and large succeeding in the world economy" (Reich 1991: 208).

The Entry of Post-Modernism

But this is not all. Now enters post-modernism to erode the values cherished by modernism. Why did the intelligentsia in the Third World welcome the language and culture of the colonial masters? They hitched their wagon to the engine of modernization. To be modernized and Westernized meant to be civilized, educated, democratic, progressive, rational, objective, and scientific as opposed to being traditional, religious, superstitious, bigoted, communal, reactionary, thus overcoming all the evils that could be associated with the pre-colonial time. The new educational curriculum promised liberation from all that. One is reminded of a great ideal to be achieved in human life that was announced by the Victorian world: "to leave the world better than we found it." The post-modernist has no regard for such ideals and expectations. And the continuity of the grand journey is halted and even likely to be abandoned. McLaren (1994) captures the spirit of post-modernism:

> Broadly speaking, the postmodern critique concerns itself with a rejection of or debunking of modernism's epistemic foundations or metanarratives; a dethronement of the authority of positivistic science that essentializes differences between what appear to be self-possessing identities, an attack on the notion of a unified goal of history, and a deconstruction of the magnificent Enlightenment swindle of the autonomous, stable, and self-contained ego that is supposed to be able to act independently of its own history, its indigenist strands of meaning-making and cultural and linguistic situatedness, and free from inscriptions in the discourses of, among others, gender, race, and class....Further, the postmodern critique has been exemplary in revealing the hopelessness of attempts by empiricists to transcend the political, ideological, and economic conditions that transform the world into cultural and social formations. (194)

"Ichabod!" The glory of being modern has departed! All this combined with the general degradation of human life and morality and the physical environment for which man alone is responsible further aggravates the despondence and puzzlement of the intellectual. Once again, McLaren (1994) describes the present conditions:

> We inhabit skeptical times, historical moments spawned in a temper of distrust, disillusionment, and despair. Social relations of discomfort and diffidence have always preexisted us but the current historical juncture is particularly invidious in this regard, marked as it is by a rapture of greed, untempered and hypereroticized consumer will, racing currents of narcissism, severe economic and racial injustices, and heightened social paranoia. The objective conditions of Western capitalism now appear so completely incompatible with the realization of freedom and liberation that it is no understatement to consider them mutually antagonistic enterprises. (192)

Enough of this jeremiad! The presentation provided a glimpse of the paradoxical situation that may be discussed before any attempt is made toward the internationalization of curriculum. At this point, it is pertinent to turn to those positive happenings which indicate the beginnings or readiness for the type of curriculum that can move us slowly and steadily in the right direction. Now let's look at a short case study of a country which has been called "the jewel of Africa."

Botswana: A Case Study of Experiments in Democracy, Modern Education, and Future Planning

Botswana, a landlocked nation of the size of France or Texas, is situated above the Republic of South Africa. It was known originally as Bechuanaland under the British Protectorate until its independence in 1966. It had a subsistence economy of beef cattle and migrant laborers who worked in South African mines during the apartheid days. The major part of the land is arid; the Kalahari Desert is inhabited by Bushmen tribes in the western region bordering Namibia. Most modern habitations are in the eastern region bordering Zimbabwe, which has some rainfall to provide water and basic resources. The Okavango, a river in the north, dries up there after creating extensive marshy islands, which have become havens for a variety of wildlife, attracting tourists from all over the world. Today the human population is just over one million.

After the independence of Botswana, a miracle happened. A huge deposit of diamonds was discovered. Since then the industry, managed by the Anglo-American Debeers in collaboration with the government, has made Botswana one of the main producers of diamonds in the world. The other important industry is beef, which is exported to Europe. Botswana claims to have the largest assembly-line slaughterhouse in the southern hemisphere. There are other small industries for the daily needs of the local consumers and tourists. Some new industries are likely to come up. A few years ago Hyundai Motors started its automobile assembly here and made a significant profit by selling to all the neighboring countries. Botswana has experienced a mushroom growth of a variety of industries mainly started by foreigners, who find it easier to operate in a country with liberal business regulations. While South Africa supplies most of the consumer goods including food items, it is also Botswana's formidable competitor in business and industry. The nation has considerable foreign reserves to maintain itself through thick and thin and to support promising local entrepreneurs.

What has singled out Botswana from other African countries is its democratic government. The late Sir Seretse Khama, the father of the nation and first president after independence, found the democratic roots of the nation in its own indigenous traditions. He forged and nurtured the democratic tradition of a peace-loving, tolerant people and adapted it to the English parliamentary system. In the 1960s, surrounded by the South African apartheid government and the colonial government of the minority whites in Rhodesia, he always insisted on a democratic and non-racial administration. The nation has meticulously pursued that policy.

From the very beginning the people and the government have been conscious of developing a proper educational system for all citizens. During the pre-colonial days, indigenous education, like in other African countries, existed to enable its various tribes to survive through transmission of culture. During the colonial period, missionaries following the footsteps of Livingstone set up English medium schools mainly to proselytize the natives. Some of these schools developed further to inspire people to start their own community schools, sometimes with support from Britain.

The curriculum of the school system was given a conceptual framework by Sir Seretse Khama, who suggested that an education for creating social harmony (*kagisano*) should be the major aim. To meet the aspirations of his people, he appointed a National Commission of Education comprising some noted local and foreign educators, including the Swedish scholar Torsten Husen as the chairman. The commission toured the country to do the needs analysis and collected relevant data to prepare the report, which was released in 1977 as *Education for Kagisano*.

The Setswana word *kagisano* provides the general aim of education in Botswana. It approximates the concept of social harmony and encompasses the four national principles: Democracy, Development, Self-reliance, and Unity. Two important aspects of *kagisano* are social justice, implying fairness and equity, and the sense of community and mutual responsibility (Republic of Botswana 1977: 23–34). Obviously, this general aim is featured everywhere in educational and curriculum policy and planning. A panel of local experts in 1994 revised the report. The revision emphasized these aims and principles, and for their realization recommended the expansion of provisions for education to provide secondary education to all children. To meet the needs for skilled manpower, to reduce dependence on foreigners, and to be at a level with the advanced, industrialized, and modernized world, new programs and units have been introduced. Vocational education centers, computer education courses, environment education units, special education and education for the gifted sections, and technology and design departments are functioning already. The commitment of the nation to meeting the challenge of development can be witnessed in some relevant areas: research on gender issues started two decades ago and is quite advanced now (Tsayang and Ngwako 1989; Mannathoko 1997). Conferences, seminars, and training workshops in relevant areas are organized every month. The Presidential Task Group on a Long Term Vision for Botswana, appointed in January of 1997, submitted its report after extensive consultations and meetings with all concerned, including people in the remote villages. *A Long Term Vision for Botswana (Vision 2016): Towards Prosperity for All* is in booklet form.

Since this vision lays out aims and ideals of Botswana up to 2016, and all important institutions have been asked to provide their plans and input to make it a reality, it is worth knowing a little more about how Africa, whose records in advanced planning and human care are painted negatively in the media, can respond positively towards creating a better world. Vision 2016 adds a fifth national principle, *Botho,* which is clearly defined and explained in the following quote:

> This refers to one of the tenets of African culture—the concept of a person who has a well-rounded character, who is well-mannered, courteous and disciplined and realizes his or her full potential both as an individual and as a part of the community to which he or she belongs. (2)

Botho defines a process for earning respect by first giving respect to others to gain empowerment by empowering others. It encourages people to applaud rather than resent those who succeed. It disapproves of antisocial, disgraceful, inhuman, and criminal behavior and encourages social justice for all. *Botho* as a concept must stretch to its utmost limits the largeness of spirit of all Botswana. It must permeate every aspect of our lives, like the air we breathe, so that no Botswanan will rest their minds knowing that another is in need. The five principles [Democracy, Development, Self-Reliance, Unity, *Botho*] are derived from Botswana's cultural heritage, and are designed to promote social harmony, or *kagisano*. They set the broader context for the objectives of national development, which are:
- Sustained development
- Rapid economic growth
- Economic independence
- Social justice

Furthermore, *A Long Term Vision for Botswana (Vision 2016)* clearly articulates and defines the following seven goals:
- An educated, informed nation
- A prosperous, productive, and innovative nation

- A compassionate, just, and caring nation
- A safe and secure nation
- An open, democratic, and accountable nation
- A moral and tolerant nation
- A united and proud nation. (5–13)

Here is a general picture of an African nation which may prove to be another model emulating the example of Singapore if things happen in a favorable direction. It must be indicated that only the positive aspects of the educational efforts by a new nation have been highlighted. Obviously, it does not mean that there are no problems. Botswana, like any other developing country, has its share of troubles. The purpose of this case study is to reinforce the idea that a conversation on the internationalization of curriculum in the present paradoxical and puzzling situation of globalization is a uniquely healthy and realistic step by educators of vision, enthusiasm, and optimism, even amidst all kinds of gloomy happenings. Botswana is not alone: nations, peoples, and groups are ready to walk along and provide strong support.

Concluding Reflections

Present dreams and future visions have been featured in this presentation. We have not been talking about wishful thinking or Pollyanna-ish views. We are living in a dangerous situation unprecedented in history. We must move forward or the consequences are waiting. The intellectuals who have delved into the reality of exploitation and its complex operations in the school curriculum have rendered a great service to humanity and the cause of progress. The history of human progress and civilization does not move smoothly and steadily; it has its ups and downs and fits and starts. Apparently, we have come to a point of enormous impasse in human history that needs a quantum leap. We have to move beyond pessimism and the moods of uncertainties described earlier. Educators cannot afford to lose courage, hope, and enthusiasm. Giroux (1992) in *Border Crossing* has developed nine principles around the issues of modernism, postmodernism, and feminism for the guidance of critical pedagogy and radical democratic struggle. His theory shows powerful eclecticism in its attempt to choose the best out of important trends as well as the boldness of imaginative synthesis. And in conclusion he points out how important it is to give up the usual narrowness and isolation:

> We live in a time in which the responsibilities of citizens extend beyond national borders. The old modernist notions of center and margin, home and exile, and famil-

iar and strange are breaking apart. Geographic, cultural, and ethnic borders are giving way to shifting configurations of power, community, space, and time. Citizenship can no longer ground itself in forms of Eurocentrism and the language of colonialism. New spaces, relationships, and identities have to be created that allow us to move across borders, to engage difference and otherness as the part of discourse of justice, social engagement, and democratic struggle. Academics can no longer retreat into their classrooms or symposiums as if they were the only public spheres available for engaging the power of ideas and the relations of power. (88)

When there is confusion and uncertainty, it is the social responsibility of intellectuals to pierce through the fog and provide meaningful visions for life to continue progressively. But it is more important now than ever that intellectuals participate in life and operate, not in the ivory tower, but on the ground among the common people. It is this attitude that singled out the great leaders of humanity: Socrates and Christ in the past and Gandhi, King, and Mandela in the present. To these we can add a class of teachers and philosophers such as Bertrand Russell, Jean Paul Sartre, Paulo Freire, and Noam Chomsky, who fought for the right cause intellectually and were not afraid to be nonviolent activists in the streets. They have contributed far more to humankind than all the kings and politicians together.

The spirit of this assembly, this conference, is similar. Our aim is to clarify, persuade, and prevail through telling what we know and understand in the best interest of all, changing the hearts and minds of those in power and positions to support us in the reconstruction of a better world through the teaching of new and evolving curricula.

References

Adeyinka, A. A. (2000). *Education and morality in Africa*. A paper presented in the series of the Philosophical Association of Botswana Lectures in April at the University of Botswana. Gaborone, Botswana.

Apple, M. W. (1982). *Education and power*. London: Routledge.

Aronowitz, S. and W. De Fazio (1994). *The jobless future: Sci-Tech and the dogma of work*. Minneapolis: University of Minnesota Press.

Ashton, D. N. and J. Sung (1997). Education, skill formation, and economic development: The Singaporean approach. In *Education, culture, economy, and society*. Edited by A. H. Halsey. Oxford: Oxford University Press.

Beare, H., and R. Slaughter (1993). *Education for the twenty-first century*. London: Routledge.

Bernstein, B. (1977). *Class, codes and control (Vol. 3): Towards a theory of educational transmission*. London: Routledge.

Bourdieu, P., and J. C. Passeron (1977). *Reproduction in education and society.* London: Sage.

Carnoy, M. (1974). *Education as cultural imperialism.* New York: David McKay.

Giroux, H. A. (1981). Hegemony, resistance, and the paradox of educational reform. *Interchange 12* (2/3): 3–6.

——— (1992). *Border crossing: Cultural workers and the politics of education.* New York: Routledge.

Hargreaves, A. (1994). Restructuring: Postmodernity and the prospect of educational change. *Journal of Educational Policy 9*: 47–65.

Holmes, B., and M. McLean (1989) *The curriculum: A comparative perspective.* London: Unwin Hyman.

Kluger, J. (1997). "Mr. Natural." *Time.* May 19, 44–51.

Mannathoko, C. (1997). Politics of gender in teacher education curriculum and pedagogy. In *A handbook of research on education:Teaching and teacher education in Botswana, Vol. 1*, 130–57. Edited by P. T. M. Marope and D. W. Chapman. Gaborone, Botswana: Lentswe La Lesedi.

McLaren, P. (1994). Multiculturalism and the postmodern critique: Toward a pedagogy of resistance and transformation. In *Between borders: Pedagogy and politics of cultural studies.* Edited by Henry A. Giroux and Peter McLaren. New York: Routledge.

Nurullah, S., and J. P. Naik (1951). *A history of education in India.* London: Macmillan.

Reich, R. B. (1991). *The work of nations: A blueprint for the future.* London: Simon & Schuster.

Republic of Botswana. (1977). *Education for Kagisano. Report of the National Commission on Education.* Gaborone, Botswana: Government Printers.

Republic of Botswana (1994). *The revised national policy on education.* Gaborone, Botswana: Government Printers.

Republic of Botswana (1997). *A long term vision for Botswana (Vision 2016): Towards prosperity for all.* Report of the Presidential Task Group. Gaborone, Botswana: Government Printers.

Tsayang, G. T., and A. Ngwako (1989). *Gender and education: Proceedings of a workshop, February 27–March 1.* Gaborone, Botswana: Faculty of Education, University of Botswana.

CHAPTER THIRTEEN

Teacher Identity and the Ideologies of Teaching: Some Remarks on the Interplay
Eero Ropo and Veli-Matti Värri • Finland

Introduction

This chapter has two motives. One concern comes from practical experiences that we have as teacher educators and researchers. School development is a common slogan of the day, but we seldom see any major advances in school practices. Changes are slow, even when we make efforts to quicken them with institutional training programs. Those phenomena may indicate that how quickly innovations or innovative practices can be adopted in the schools is not just a question of the teachers' skills or knowledge. Theoretical concerns about the nature of change and the processes behind the change are, consequently, another motive for the chapter.

We want to discuss the relationship between teacher identity and ideologies of teaching and teachership. We assume a close relationship between learning and individual identity (self-) reconstruction. This assumption leads us to another hypothesis. We assume there is a connection, but not a linear or simple one, between identity reconstruction and adoption of innovations or professional ideologies into teaching practices at the school level. We shall first describe what we mean by the ideologies of teaching and then analyze the concept and architecture of self and identity. The processes and interplay between self and ideologies will be described in the last part of the chapter.

Origins of Teacher Identity

Teachers' professional identities are constructed throughout the learning processes along with the initial teacher education and teachers' professional experiences. The identity basis, sources upon which an individual bases identity, can be disclosed only by analyzing the historical and social conditions in which teaching and a teacher's work are conducted.

Traditionally, the concept of a teacher depends on the common and shared social, political, and historical context of the nation or the state. Teaching is the main profession involved in the socialization of the young generation and the nurturance of citizenship towards the nationally determined educational goals. Because of its strategically important status, the teaching profession has been a common object for political control and administrative planning. One indication of political influence of education concerns teacher education and the contents of curriculum, areas regulated by legislation in most societies, but because of their significant impact, the nature and contents of teachers' work, particularly teachers' qualifications and skills, have also been the object of scientific analyses.

In addition to political control of teacher education, there are also moral norms and idealistic expectations among the public concerning the teacher as a professional. All those official and unofficial norms and ideals with the support of scientific knowledge constitute the normative pre-understandings of what should be built into teacher training programs for the purpose of educating teachers who are able to realize the accepted educational values through and in their work. The pre-understanding together with the informal social beliefs and expectations about teachers will work as a precondition and objective determinant during the novice teacher's studies.

Teachers' normative pre-understanding has always expressed the intentions of the state to realize its educational ideals and implement reform policy in the society. In the early years of independence, Finnish teachers were expected to be good citizens with high national, moral, and Christian values. The present ideology of teaching emphasizes the need for teachers who are both teachers and researchers (the teacher-as-researcher movement) or who serve as change agents capable of reforming school and their own work. The essential qualities of teachers also include the ability to distinguish the essential from the unessential and the morally edifying and scientific knowledge from the continuous information flow. Despite its temporal nature, the common ideology of teachership constitutes the normative interpretative basis for every individual teacher's professional identity. We argue that in the earlier modern society the common ideology of teaching used to be closer to the teacher's personal professional identity than at present. In the postmodern or the late modern society, the idea of the teacher is not as clear as it used to be. Ideologies change so often and there are several competing ones at the same time. This makes it more difficult to base one's personal self and identity only on professional identity.

Some Models of Teacher Identity: From an Ideal Citizen to a Change Agent

The roots of the conception of modern identity are in the Enlightenment (see Giddens 1991: 9). According to its main message, people could be emancipated from their wild nature by education. Education became a common interest. It was soon understood that educated people were useful for the cohesion of the nation and the increasing welfare of society. Education was organized nationally, and it became the main instrument in social planning and socialization (see Bauman 1992). To situate the notion of *teachership* in the present, we look to the modernist origins of the teacher's identity.

The present national curricula are and have been based on the educational goals constituted by the government. There has been little doubt about the role of a teacher as the representative of intellectual and moral authority, particularly because the epistemological and moral rationality have been taught as universally valid and augmented by scientific knowledge. Educators as representatives of adult generations were supposed to be preparing the growing young generations for a future of unlimited progress.[1] The nation-state has been the anchor of and the actor in the educational beliefs of modernity. At that time an individual teacher was an organic part of the socialization profession with all of its essential virtues: professionalism, citizenship, and educational expertise.

One of the teachers' main obligations has always been to take responsibility for both educational and ideological socialization of the nation/state. Teachers have traditionally been exceptionally faithful to the mission given by the governments. Teaching as a profession and with the ideal of a good citizen has always characterized the common mindset of the teacher. Actually, during the early years and decades of independent Finland (1917)—burdened with the traumas of the Civil War in 1918, two wars against the Russians, and the political tensions after the Second World War—it was the teacher who was expected to unite the divided nation. Subsequently, the teacher's occupation, shaped by the modernization process, has developed into a modern profession with confidence in scientific expertise. Modern teachership, the present teacher education, and the present school institution have been constructed on the basis of scientific education and curriculum design (see Hargreaves 1994). Teachers have consciously aimed at a professional position by emphasizing their educational expertise. At the same time, however, the traditional ethos of teachers as representatives of good citizenship has retained its importance. This implies that the general ideology of teachership materializes in the synthesis of vocation, ideal citizenship, and expertise.

At present there seem to be more aims, demands, and expectations than ever before focusing on teachers' work. Teachers do not experience those expectations only as challenges but also as risks and pressures threatening their autonomy and personal integrity (see Hargreaves 1992). Our concerns, and the focus of this chapter, arise from the very real situations of teachers' practices: overexertion, marginalization from work, and burnout—Some or all leading to premature retirements among Finnish teachers. We may assume that fundamental changes in the basis of teaching as a vocation, the notion of the ideal citizen, and the concept of teacher expertise are occurring.

The prevailing rhetoric constituting the idea of present teachership use the metaphors of change that come forth from the spirit of modernity.[2] By contrast, in the rhetoric of postmodernism, a good teacher is *a change agent*. This is an indication of the mixed and unclear rhetoric of our time. For the individual teacher, it is increasingly difficult to understand "change."

Postmodern Context

A Disintegrated Social Environment Composed of Competing Ideologies of Socialization and Education

The current ideological changes are connected to more widespread social and cultural changes that can be described as the transition from the modern era to the late modern or postmodern era.[3] To oversimplify a little, postmodernization has meant the demand to dissolve or reinterpret the formerly taken-for-granted knowledge and moral basis. The strong belief in a society that was directed hierarchically and planned rationally, and faith in the institutions that used to determine the collective identity, have crumbled. Traditional collectives and social groups based on work have been losing their educational meanings. Because of the changes in the division of labour and lost employment, people have withdrawn from the earlier collective traditions and the life plans they used to have. In our changed situation we are more dependent than ever on education as a road to a successful life. At the same time we have increasing doubts about its promises. It is a common slogan that one education and one occupation are not enough. You must be ready to reeducate yourself and rebuild your career, probably several times during your life. You must be ready to change and withstand uncertainty. Such changes in the social conditions of our life plans force us into and condemn us to individuality. The traditional institutions (family, church, education, and political institutions) no longer provide a clear and ready-made foundation for identity construction and personal responsibility. The disintegration of the basis has led from the common collective to a more "networked" society and the more unpredictable future. People are doomed to individualisation without the unambiguous "anchors" for identity construction and clear models for identity (see Bauman 1992).

According to Bauman, the intellectuals' (including teachers as professional educators) roles as reformers have fundamentally been changed in the postmodern era. In the modern world the intellectuals as "knowers" were privileged to plan the right lifestyle for the citizens (1992). The government hired some teachers for educational work based on the ideals that were believed to have universal meanings. A teacher's task was to formulate these ideals into the actual meanings of citizens' everyday lives. Present intellectuals have lost their leading roles both in reform policy and culture. According to Bauman, the financial markets have taken on the role of leadership. They generate an increasing fund of lifestyles, tastes, and beliefs that speak directly to the consumers.

Because of the disintegrated socialization environment, the modern teacher exists in a paradoxical situation. The teacher can no longer be the sovereign master of knowledge. However, curriculum design has been brought down to the local level of the individual schools. Therefore the teacher has to be more talented than ever before as an interpreter of educational reality. Simultaneously more and more interest groups are making their claims on the school and demanding teachers to make responses.

We argue that there is no one single right model with which a teacher can identify. A model of a good teacher is impossible because the changing social foundations do not offer any unambiguous frame for it. Instead of one model of teachership, there are a lot of directions for a teacher's identity construction.

The Architecture of Self and Identity Construction

There are two requirements if learning is to happen: 1) the person feels a need to change his/her identity (self); 2) the change in identity becomes real by acquiring new knowledge (skills, attitudes, and behavioral practices). Usually people who don't feel a need to change at the level of self acquire new knowledge at the rhetorical level, i.e., adopting the terms and principles (such as constructive teaching) in their speech, but this learning will not change their practice. We describe this process of adopting the terminology but not changing or even planning to change the practice as buffering the change with rhetoric.

The architecture of self is one of the questions researchers in the field of learning have seldom dealt with. The question is more in the area of personality or philosophical analyses. Self is a hypothetical construct in the same sense as some other psychological constructs, such as intelligence, motivation, and so on. Self is a convenient way of referring to a series of mental and bodily events and formations that have a degree of causal coherence and integrity through time (Varela et al. 1996: 124). We apply the term when describing a person's innermost existence, a subject or ego that acts and thinks, works and learns. Self is supposed to be constructed through personal experiences. We also assume that self is under continuous reconstruction through one's lifetime. We will first discuss the architecture of self and then describe our conceptions of the relationship between learning and the reconstruction of self.

The architecture of self as a networked structure has gained more popularity among researchers lately. In their recent book, Marvin Minsky and Seymour Papert propose that the human mind should be studied as a society rather than a unified simple entity (Minsky & Papert 1987; Varela et al. 1996). Without going into detail, we may assume that this kind of conception of self is getting support from brain research and analyses of human cognition and individual experiences of everyday life. We propose that self may be described as a space which is divided into different sections, each representing a more or less independent part of the overall self. Self can, consequently, be metaphorically described as a map. The subject can wander in the space of self, changing the "place" along the contextual or the physical dimension, moving from one place to another. Physical switching from home to work, for instance, is usually represented in the self space with the move that the person makes from home identity to work identity. Each area of the space of self (home, work) is accompanied by not only identity and role but also knowledge, skills, attitudes, values, and norms. This knowledge may be specific to one area of the self space only, or it can be shared by other areas. Self is more than a spatial structure. It is temporal, including the past, present, and future. It integrates time and experiences. Although it may be divided into areas or parts, there has to be enough integrity to maintain personal coherence.

Learning and self space are related with each other in the way that acquired knowledge is stored into a specific self space. Consequently, the acquired knowledge also changes the person's self and identity. Learning can also start from the need to change one's identity. Dreams of becoming something may be an expression that refers to the creation of a new "area" in the person's self space that starts growing and materializing along with the knowledge that the person is now able to store that specific area in his/her self space. Examples of those cases are, for instance, adults' study projects to switch careers to a different area or an experienced need for identity renewal after a personal crisis such as divorce or disability.

What is important to us is the assumption that identity that reflects the structure and contents of one's self space is related to the learning process and acquired knowledge. We may also assume that if the person is unwilling to change his/her identity, this will prevent all such knowledge acquisition that would affect major changes in the structure of one's self space.

This was supported in a recent study by Mäki-Komsi and Ropo (2000). The purpose of their study was to investigate the process of adopting new instructional technology (IT) in adult education institutions. The results showed that all institutions were in the middle or beginning of the process of changing teaching practices and linking them with IT and the information age. The subject teachers described in the interviews had difficulties in transforming instruction from traditional classroom teaching into multi-media instruction in which the distance education and students' independent work were crucial parts of studying. Teachers' and students' roles and power balance were also taking on new directions due to students' independence in goal setting and individual curriculum. This kind of change seemed to be a major challenge to the teachers' professional identity and previous conceptions of learning and teaching. The teaching culture seemed to struggle with the idea of changing from knowledge transmitting to "midwifery" learning.

Although the purpose of the above study was not specifically to study the relationship between the teachers' identity and adoption of new technology, it became clear that at least some teachers were reluctant to change their practices and ways of teaching because they would lose an important part of their knowledge base in the change. The old model of teaching was well learned, and changing it to distance learning would require new learning and "replacement" of old knowledge with the new. Replacement meant, in this case, a real need for learning, since the teachers would have to apply a new knowledge base after starting to teach through the Internet or some other distance education technology. The results of the above study seem to support the assumptions of this study; however, we need more empirical studies and theoretical analyses of it.

How do Identity and Self Mediate Between the Ideologies and Individual Learning and Change?

It is clear from practical experiences and numerous studies that changes are not easy to accomplish. We argue that the role of the individual self is to mediate in human learning. Learning is a kind of "technical" term for specific changes in the memory and knowledge level. However, learning is not the main purpose of human behavior or action. Information processing studies show that it is a by-product of thinking, reflection, problem solving, etc. What initiates learning is a crucial question for the purpose of this chapter. Is it the context or environment, as the behaviorist paradigm emphasized, or is it the genetical growth originating from our genes or something from inside ourselves? The situational paradigm focuses on the relationship between an individual and his/her social context. Learning originates from the discourse or dialogue the person has with the contexts. If we accept the last framework in the analysis of learning, we may also assume that an individual maintains a balance between the outer demands of change and his/her own dreams and goals of maintaining the integrity of identity and self.

Our identity is composed of our interpretative synthesis of inner experience and outer world in the flow of temporality. As Maurice Merleau-Ponty (1986) points out, utilizing Martin Heidegger's (1926/1984) notion,

> each dimension of time is treated or aimed at as something other than itself and because, finally, there is at the core of time a gaze, or as Heidegger puts it, an Augenblick, someone through whom the word can have a meaning. (422)

The term "gaze" means in this context an expression in which the subject (self) gives meaning to the temporality. We always experience the world as subjective and temporal because as bodily beings, we are fundamentally temporal beings. Also as intellectuals, we are embodied minds. The ever-passing present is our focus where we set all our experiences in the temporal order, referring to it as the past, the present, and the future. Our self-identity will always be based on our subjective temporal experiences. In this way we are changeless.

There are a lot of pressures for change and learning. Teachers have buffered those pressures differently. Some are eagerly studying to learn more and learn something new; some stick to the old and make every attempt to prevent the changes. According to our assumption, both phenomena are mediated by the reconstruction of one's self and identity.

Conflicting expectations and reform pressures devolve onto the teachers—including the expectation that they make educational aims of teaching into a means for their own interests. All those interests and pressures influence the integrity and the resources of the teacher. Compared to earlier times, the teacher is forced into a business situation in which she or he must state arguments to justify her or his teaching and even defend its educational values. At the same time, the teacher as the model of a "dynamic" school and constructive learning concept is forced into everlasting identity work and continuing education.

As a concluding remark, we might say that individual change may not be as much a process of learning knowledge, skills, attitudes, or whatever we may call the objects usually listed in the curricula. Development and change, even adult development, might be described as a qualitative development in the combined self-structure. This change from one level to another requires acquisition of knowledge, but also, and more important, is dependent upon the individual decision to change by reconstructing one's self and identity to a new, psychologically balanced level, whatever it may be.

Notes

1. Henry Giroux (1997: 184) analyzes those beliefs of modernity as follows: At issue here is a definition of modernity that points to the progressive differentiation and rationalization of the social world through the process of economic growth and administrative rationalization. Another characteristic of social modernism is the epistemological project of elevating reason to an ontological status. Modernism in this view becomes synonymous with civilization itself, and reason is universalized in cognitive and instrumental terms as the basis for a model of industrial, cultural, and social progress. At stake in this notion of modernity is a view of individual and collective identity in which historical memory is devised as a linear process, the human subject becomes the ultimate source of meaning and action, and a notion of geographical and cultural territoriality is constructed in a hierarchy of domination and subordination marked by a center and margin legitimated

through the civilizing knowledge/power of a privileged Eurocentric culture.
2. Within this notion of modernism, the unfolding of history is linked to the "continual progress of the sciences and of techniques, the rational division of industrial work, [which] introduces into social life a dimension of permanent change, of destruction of customs and traditional culture" (according to Baudrillard, in Giroux 1997: 184).
3. Postmodernism is the term meant to refer to essential features of our time. There is no consensus on its meaning. However, it is a common view that traditions and the conventions of our Western civilization have been reinterpreted in the postmodern era. This concerns not only aesthetics, social institutions, and political ideologies but also the social roots of individual identity (including sexual identity). The principles of the postmodern era are replanning, reshaping, and reinterpreting (see Bauman 1992).

References

Bauman, Z. (1992). *Intimations of postmodernity*. London/New York: Routledge.

Giddens, A. (1991). *Modernity and self-identity: Self and society in the late modern age*. Stanford, CA: Stanford University Press.

Giroux, H. A. (1997). *Pedagogy and the politics of hope. Theory, culture, and schooling: A critical reader*. Boulder, CO: Westview.

Hargreaves, A. (1994) *Changing teachers, changing time: Teachers' work and culture in the postmodern time*. New York: Teachers College Press.

Heidegger, M. (1984). *Sein und Zeit*. Tübingen: Max Niemeyer Verlag (original work published 1926)

Mäki-Komsi, S., and E. Ropo (2000). *Modern media and instructional technology in vocational education: Some experiences of the diffusion of new technology in the adult education institutions*. Paper presented at the AERA Annual Meeting, New Orleans, Louisiana, April 24–28, 2000.

Merleau-Ponty, M. (1986). *Phénoménologie de la perception (Phenomenology of perception)*. London: Routledge (original work published 1945).

Minsky, M. and Papert, S. (1987). *Perceptrons* (revised edition). Cambridge, MA: MIT.

Varela, F.J., E. Thomson, and E. Rosch (1996). *The embodied mind*. Cambridge, MA: MIT.

CHAPTER FOURTEEN

Action Competence as an Educational Ideal

Karsten Schnack • Denmark

For some years action competence has been a key concept in curriculum theory and curriculum development in Denmark. The notion sums up many of the ideas that have been developed within a humanistic, democratic, and critical pedagogy. It has been very much discussed in the realms of environmental education and health education, though its scope is much broader. (Breiting & Nielsen 1996; Breiting et al. 1999; Breiting & Mogensen 1999; Jensen 1995; Jensen & Schnack 1994, 1997; Schnack 1995b, 1998). In this chapter the idea will be elaborated as a general curriculum approach.

Action competence is an educational ideal. It is therefore neither a teaching method nor an objective to be reached, and for this reason the development of it can be difficult to measure. Individual elements of it can perhaps be evaluated, but, as a whole, action competence is difficult to pin down. Nor is it possible to operationalize the concept by converting it into a set of observable phenomena. This is connected with the fact that it is an ideal within the framework of liberal education. One might therefore be tempted to ask whether it exists at all, which in our day usually means: "Where is it?" or, "Point it out!" The only appropriate answer is that action competence is situated in a non-place, a utopia, where it seems to get along very well in the company of such concepts as liberal education, democracy, human rights, sustainable development, and equal *(herrschaftsfrei)* communication. All of these concepts live for, and indeed off, the fight against violence and oppression.

It has often been discussed whether education, or the German *Bildung*, is a process or a product, and there is a sense in which the answer can be both or and, but in the context of this chapter, liberal education is first and foremost a view from a particular perspective, an approach to teaching and learning.

Action competence is an approach within the recent school of critical education, developed within a tradition where *Bildung* is closely linked to democracy. Democracy without *Bildung* is merely an empty shell, a procedure or form of government, which at all events would never be able to survive for long. Conversely, *Bildung* without democracy is reduced to what the leaders of the hour have defined as highbrow culture and good manners. Thus action competence is political and democratic education.

Political Education

The concept of education that is relevant in this situation may be called liberal education, and it can be defined by using two sets of contrasting concepts: liberal education vs. (vocational) training and liberal education vs. adaptation.

The first distinction emphasizes the general character of liberal education. As opposed to training in the narrow sense, the liberal education approach is not directed towards one or several professional functions. Training means specializing with a particular job in mind: one can train to be a nurse, a baker, a farmer, a shop assistant, a surgeon, a teacher, or a banking consultant. On the other hand, liberal education has to do with what is relevant to all these people precisely because they are people and because they form part of a social community that goes beyond any particular professional function, more or less narrowly defined. Liberal education concerns what is general.

The other contrast concerns the fact that liberal education is by nature political education. We all need to be adapted to our surroundings to some extent; otherwise we simply cannot function. On the other hand, simple functioning is not enough: a machine can purr along happily because it is working, but what is human about human beings is not that they can adapt, but that they can become individuals and develop autonomy, authority, and independence.

In the history of ideas, the Age of the Enlightenment (the second half of the eighteenth century) is given the honor of having emphasized this liberal educational approach. In 1784, the great German philosopher, Immanuel Kant, asked himself the question: "What is enlightenment?" His famous and characteristic answer begins as follows:

> Enlightenment is man's emancipation from the tutelage to which he has subjected himself. Tutelage means not being able to use one's reason without being guided by another. Man has indeed brought this condition of tutelage upon himself, but it is not due to a lack of reason, rather to a lack of the decisiveness and courage needed to use reason without the leadership of another. *Sapere aude!* Have the courage to use your own reason! This is the slogan of "enlightenment." (Kant 1968: 53)

To be a political person means being someone who thinks for himself but not only on his own behalf. One is not only adapted to a system, one adopts an attitude, along with others, to the system itself. One does not just shout, "Heil Hitler!" on command, and stretch out one's arm in the recommended fashion (a perfect adaptation to one's surroundings in certain circumstances), but on the other hand one does not simply withdraw and quietly think one's own thoughts.

In ancient Greece, where people also thought about these things, there was a particular word for a person who lived "privately" and took no part in the affairs of the community. Such a person was called an "idiot." One could thus say that political education is a question of helping people become autonomous persons, who are neither simply adapted to the situation nor "idiots."

The reason why I have used the Nazi salute as a symbol of the negative side of adaptation is to emphasize that the discussion about political education in educational circles was naturally very much in vogue in post-war Germany. When totalitarian regimes break down, major efforts have to be made to (re-)politicize the population. People who think and act politically are a necessary condition for the development of democracy, and a politically aware population is the only real defense against indoctrination. In this connection one can speak of political education or education for democracy, and, in fact, both terms have been widely used.

In Germany, because of the country's embarrassing political past, this topic was the center of discussion. At the same time, the discussion gradually became more radical as it was taken up by the many critical thinkers who in various ways identified the mechanisms of forced adaptation and oppression used by modern capitalism in the so-called free world. The "old hands" in the Frankfurt School, such as Theodore W. Adorno and Herbert Marcuse, were ready to tackle just such a task as this; later, Jurgen Habermas came to play a more and more central role. Among those who have applied critical theory to a discussion of liberal education are such major names as Hermann Giesecke, Klaus Mollenhauer, Oskar Negt, Thomas Ziehe, and Wolfgang Klafki.

Democracy

There are many ways of interpreting the term democracy, and all of them are complicated, but they all involve in some way or other such ideas as freedom, equality, and brotherhood. In this vein, Wolfgang Klafki in his more recent works has often repeated what he considers to be the overall aims of all work with curriculum (or what in Europe is often called *Didaktik*): self-determination, co-determination, and solidarity (e.g., Klafki 1998: 314).

Self-determination is connected with freedom. Not so much the freedom to do whatever one feels like here and now, which is more like self-important egoism, but the ability and the will to take responsibility for one's own life and, in this sense, to be master of one's own house. This is the sense in which thinkers such as Oskar Negt speak of autonomy, maturity, and independence.

Co-determination is linked to equality. A basic characteristic of this conception of democracy is that one strives in principle to equal out the balance of power. The right to participation includes an implicit criticism of all authoritarian structures, which automatically place people in a state of tutelage. The authority that forms part of the concept of maturity, if it is not to stiffen into an authority structure, must include respect for the autonomy of others.

Finally, solidarity with the weak is a directly anti-fascist attitude. Equality and justice can in many situations rebound in a negative fashion on those who do not have the material and/or mental resources to tackle a competitive situation. When the self-determining individual freely exercises his or her right to participation in decision making, solidarity must be in the forefront of her mind.

However, all of this presupposes that there are people taking action. It is not enough that society consists of individuals if these individuals do not involve themselves in matters relevant to society as a whole. For this reason, one can also say that democracy is primarily participation. The members of a democracy are not spectators but participants; perhaps not all equally active all the time, of course, but all potential participants, who decided themselves what to be involved in and when. In this sense, then, education for democracy means being educated, qualified, to be a participator. This is the context within which action competence must be seen.

The Humanist Approach

Behind the set of theories used here lies a humanist philosophy of life. The agents involved are not there for the sake of democracy, and they are not machines, roles, or systems. Individuals are seen as persons, and human beings are assigned values in themselves. If we are to understand and explain the human condition, the fundamental unit of reference must be man as a social, active, emotional, and knowing being. This also means that politics, education, and other forms of outward-looking activity must be judged on the extent to which they can create the best conditions for the development of rounded, autonomous, and mature personalities. The task facing us is to make the conditions we live under more human, thereby creating a better background for people to realize themselves and to unfold those characteristic traits of human nature that are specifically human.

Here we shall emphasize two outcomes of this humanist approach. One is that it contains a built-in, radical criticism of the oppression that always exists to some degree, and which is caused by some people trying to realize themselves at the expense of others.

One has often seen this situation legitimized with reference to the undemocratic idea that there are qualitative differences between people. With this in mind, all the great Greek humanists of antiquity (led by Plato and Aristotle) accepted the idea that according to the order of nature the Greek who is born to freedom shall commands the barbarian who is born to slavery. It is interesting to note that the word "barbarian" originally designated those who could not speak Greek but made sounds which the Greeks interpreted as "bar-bar-bar."

More or less all developed versions of humanism have had drawbacks of this type, and radical criticism of them has always been relevant, as when Erasmus of Rotterdam fulminated against the fanaticism that gripped his contemporaries at the time of the Reformation, the sectarian mentality that led many to proclaim who were real humans and who were just Papists, or vice versa. In a similar reaction, John Lennon and Yoko Ono screamed "Woman is the nigger of the world" into the ears of a public that had generally convinced itself that equality between the sexes and the races had more or less arrived.

The second outcome of the humanist philosophy of life is a warning that we must not reduce our understanding of other people to mechanistic explanations of cause and effect. The point is that if we do this we can no longer see other people as persons who act. We can borrow an expression from the later Wittgenstein and say that it is a question of two different language games: one can choose a language of behavior or a language of action. Behavior consists of movement based on cause and effect, and mechanistic models of explanation are in principle the same for things and animals, or even for people regarded as such. Actions, on the other hand, are specifically linked to people; they are not caused but motivated. It is relevant to ask for the reason (or justification) for why a person acted in such and such a manner, just as one expects to find a meaning behind what a person has done.

Actions may well consist of the same movements as other types of behavior, but what is typical of them is that the agent performs them consciously, with reflection and for a purpose. The shortest way to put this is to say that they are intentional; in fact, one cannot separate action from intention. A killing is not a murder unless there is an intention to kill the person; I cannot be said to teach English if I have no intention to teach anyone English. One cannot see what a person who runs across the road is actually doing unless one can hear or see a sign that indicates whether the person is running away from someone, for example, or running to catch a train. In many cases, the movement might be the same, but the sense or meaning will be very different. Intention helps to define action.

Conscious goal-directed actions are the opposite of habits and other behavior that is routine or enforced. One can manipulate and indoctrinate people to do one thing or another, but in terms of the humanist approach, this is not the educator's task. It is not the task of the teacher at any level to instill a particular form of behavior into the pupils. The main task is not to turn the pupils into something specific, other than themselves, i.e. persons. In this sense, therefore, the task is not, in principle, to change the pupils' behavior but rather to change the whole approach to one based on action.

Taking Issue with the Modification of Behavior

For a number of years now, we at the Research Centre for Environmental and Health Education at the Royal Danish School of Educational Studies (now Danish University of Education) have expressed our criticism of the many campaigns, information projects, and teaching projects that aim to change people's behavior. In fact, the modification of behavior has been the overall aim of perhaps the majority of measures taken in the area of environmental and health education, and this, unlike action competence, is something that can be specified and measured.

It is not surprising that within educational circles where people are worried about the present state of affairs and the way the world is going, many well-meaning efforts are being made to improve the situation. And of course, these efforts have to be made: there are an incredible number of things in the world which we really ought to be doing something about, but this is where it becomes more difficult. For who are "we," and "what" is to be done to "whom?" It may quickly appear that opinions are divided about this, or are perhaps diametrically opposed. And if such unanswered questions, opposites, and conflicts are to be treated within the framework of democratic processes, then "we" have to be more or less politically educated and action-competent participants. As such, we must be involved in making decisions for ourselves and the community about necessary measures to regulate behavior, about prohibitions and help to be offered, about efforts to change bad habits, etc.

Even though there is a sense in which action competence is built up by gaining experience in the practice of it, there are major differences between politics and education. Environmental and health problems are primarily social problems that have to be solved at the political level. It is not the task of the school and teaching to solve society's political problems nor to improve the world through the behavior of pupils. This behavior must be evaluated in terms of its (liberal) educational value using educational criteria. It is a good idea for schools to save energy, collect batteries, and sort waste for recycling. In the educational context, however, the decisive factor must be what the pupils learn by taking part in such activities or perhaps by being involved in the making of decisions to do something else.

One can be so fixed on the idea of changing people's habits and other behavior for a variety of more or less acceptable reasons that one comes to concentrate on the modification of behavior using means that are indoctrinating or manipulatory. We see this in a pure form in advertising but also in propaganda, political campaigns, and many teaching programmes. Indoctrination is the inculcation of incontrovertible truths that are reasserted all the time without any justification, often linked to a social or emotional bind which insulates the recipient against too much doubt. Manipulation is a more or less systematic influence exerted on others to achieve goals that remain hidden either consciously, or simply because that is part of the way the system works.

None of these means are democratic, no matter how elevated the goal. When well-intentioned people make use of them only to discover that they do not work, they tend to sharpen their weapons and seek professional help to make their campaign more effective, which is understandable but highly dubious.

In the case of small children, one can open one's arms wide and say in honeyed tones: "Who gets to me first?" The joy of the race, the hug, or the swing-around can bring warmth, security, and trust, but the whole of life is not like that. The child must develop into an independent person who does not run joyfully after whatever appears enticing or whoever commands her. Who says that those arms are worth running into or that it is a positive thing to come first? What are my own thoughts and feelings?

In connection with an evaluation project for the Development Council for the Danish Folkeskole, a colleague and I visited a number of schools where we observed teaching and interviewed teachers and pupils. At several schools the pupils had collected batteries, but at none of them had the pupils any idea what happened to these batteries. One particular school was proud of the fact that they had won a competition concerning who could collect most batteries, but interviews with some of the boys revealed that their class had achieved this "imposing" result by fetching already collected batteries from chemists and suchlike places in the neighboring towns.

Our immediate reaction was one of indignation, but after this we began to examine more closely in what sense these children had actually "cheated." The boys had agreed to take part in a competition, and they exhibited no mean action competence in terms of initiative, inventiveness, and co-operation with those grandparents who had driven them to the neighboring towns. The point is, however, that the boys' actions have no meaning outside the logic of the competition itself. Those who had organized the competition were certainly convinced that it would lead to good habits, but the boys had at no point accepted such a pursuit. So in a way one could maintain that the boys did not "cheat" at all, but that by their conscious actions, which brought home the promised reward to their class, they indirectly revealed the deceit that is built into so many campaigns and competitions.

Now, of course, it is possible to perform more than one action at the same time. The person who was running across the road to catch a train might, of course, at the same time have been hurrying home to his wife, and connected with this action, in turn, there could be several different reasons or intentions. In this way we generally carry out several actions at the same time, even though only one or two of them will normally be obvious to an observer at any given moment.

Correspondingly, we always learn more than one thing at a time, and in this way there will always be a lot of "hidden curricula" for teachers and/or pupils. One can attempt to bring these to the fore, analyse them, and adopt a position in relation to them, but making central elements in the intended learning into a curriculum hidden from the pupils is manipulation. This is not only unethical, but also inappropriate, because if the aim is that the pupils should develop independent, critical thinking, autonomy, and maturity, then it is no use simply setting up aims for them: they must learn to formulate their own aims, alone or with others.

Alone or with Others

There is a certain sense in which the transition from the small child's innocent, trusting, and symbiotic relationship to (at least) its closest relatives to the independence of the older individual is a process of development and maturation, but one cannot put a date on this transition. It is more or less possible to say when a child is potty-trained, when it begins to walk, or talk, but it is not possible in quite the same way to say when it becomes an individual of independent thought and action or when it sheds its last "puppy fat."

This is connected with the fact that this transition is not simply temporal in nature but is also a kind of dialectical process that appertains to the whole of life. We live all the time, by necessity, in a delicate interaction and balance of dependence and independence, trust, and skepticism. Even though modern society is characterized by a marked sense of individualism, it is still built to a great extent on trust in other people and trust in systems.

Anthony Giddens (1990, 1991), the analyst of neo-modernity, distinguishes between two types of trust connected with what he calls "facework commitments" and "faceless commitments," and he points out how developments have led to an imbalance in the direction of an increasing dominance of anonymous, faceless relationships. Social life especially has become more dependent on trust in experts of all kinds, while at the same time it has become increasingly clear that there are major risks connected with these systems.

We live, to borrow an expression from the German sociologist Ulrich Beck (1986), in a "risk society," in which what threatens us is to a far greater extent than previously the product of human intervention and very often of a more or less global nature. In order to be an active agent and participator in democratic processes in this world, one has to develop a personal identity, a belief in oneself, and a certain degree of confidence in abstract principles and systems. This presumes what Giddens calls an "ontological security" developed early in life, typically established in the intimate relationships of the first years of life, but which ideally speaking needs to be maintained throughout life. This latter aspect is made more difficult by the dissolution of tradition: in a sense, we have not only to build up our own identity and self-knowledge, but also those communities within which there is sufficient trust to carry through democratic processes.

Common Sense

We do not live our lives as experts, and we have to relate to affairs of the common weal as laypersons. In contrast to technocracy, therefore, democracy necessarily consists of respect for common sense. Even though we often need to trust experts and the systems created by experts, this trust must not be blind if we are not to abandon the democratic idea. This entails that in the last analysis we dare leave it to those involved to negotiate solutions to the questions at issue on the basis of their own common sense. We may listen to experts of various hues, but the final decision and the ultimate authority are questions for the common man. One can temporarily leave it to people one trusts and who perhaps have more specialized insight into the matter in hand to reach decisions on particular, limited issues, but once again one has to say that if trust is blind, democracy falls by the wayside.

In other words, the democratic perspective is a lay perspective, and as such in principle a holistic perspective, in contrast to the narrow and specialized way in which experts are duty bound to analyze problems. Liberal education is thus a matter for the common sense of the common man, whereas training calls for expertise. Both these elements are important and have to cooperate: respecting common sense does not mean letting it go unchallenged; the reasonable thing about reason is precisely a rational attitude and thereby an awareness of one's own limitations.

The common sense that is linked to democratic political education does not turn pre-formed opinions into dogmas but is open and willing to learn. One might also say, using an expression that sounds somewhat paradoxical, that it is the task of liberal education to raise common sense to a higher level. This process consists partly in the development of a basic critical and rational attitude and partly in the development of concepts and types of intelligence that make it possible to grasp many of the problems facing us as citizens of the modern world. Finally, it consists in the development of courage and the will alone or in concert with others to make decisions relating to action on the basis of insights and value judgments which are, of necessity, tentative and incomplete.

In other words, respecting common sense and taking it seriously also means challenging it, and to this end we need theories, scientific knowledge, and critical thinking. We need to challenge our preconceived ideas and find the opportunity to reflect on the extent to which our views and attitudes are the expression of an ideology that has been put in deep freeze.

Critical Theory

Learning to ask critical questions is part of the process of becoming mature and responsible. One has to learn not to take everything at its face value. Very small children are not surprised by anything: the ability to be properly puzzled has to be learned; there are certain requirements. Indeed, part of the socialization process involves becoming adapted to the cultural norms for what one is expected to be puzzled by and what is mere idle curiosity. Even philosophers have their own more or less established norms for what constitutes good questioning.

Our starting point for an understanding of the world is a naive realism: the world is as it appears to be to me, and everyone else naturally perceives it in the same way. Often, though, one is given the opportunity to see that the state of affairs can be explained in quite different ways. When water is poured from one glass into a narrower glass, there is not necessarily more water just because the water level is higher. Perhaps milk comes from cows and not from the supermarket? Perhaps it is not just luck that I always get the best Christmas cracker? One cannot always see whether water is clean just by looking at it. Maybe there is a difference between wishes and needs. Maybe "all that glitters is not gold."

If the world actually was the way it seems, then there would be no need either for theoretical science or for teaching. The process of knowledge would simply consist of the identification and collection of data, and explanations of new phenomena would consist of references to the way they related to what was already known. However, this is not the way it works: theoretical knowledge does not explain the unknown by the known but conversely challenges what is known by the introduction of unknown patterns of phenomena. The desk I am sitting at is "in reality" a swarm of molecules; a pencil falling to the floor can be explained by gravitation; a rise in prices may be understood as inflation.

In this respect, all theory is "critical" with respect to naive views. Theories do not accept the world as it appears immediately to the senses but move behind sense impressions, looking for unlikely and sometimes surprising connections. Now and then it may be revealed that certain people have an interest in maintaining particular appearances of phenomena. Critical theory in the narrow sense will involve an investigation of this phenomenon with a dimension involving the criticism of ideology.

In this way it is possible to wish for, or even demand, a critical dimension in terms of reflection on education. This is often what is referred to when people speak about critical pedagogy, and it is with this rationale in mind that Wolfgang Klafki (1996, 1998) calls his approach "critical-constructive *Didaktik*." Here, utopias and visions, such as those mentioned in the first section of this chapter, play a major role. When these are used to reflect reality, one may become aware of aspects which otherwise may be hard to see.

Any educational theory or reflection on education which embraces action competence as an educational ideal must be critical pedagogy. Any opposition to a kind of thinking based on the modification of behavior clearly leads to the criticism of ideology; moreover, ideals relating to responsibility and maturity, liberal education and democracy, are in themselves critical concepts in relation to the forms of oppression that exist.

Concepts relating to oppression and repression that form part of the critical theory propounded by the Frankfurt School are very relevant in this connection. Repression can, in fact, mean both oppression and suppression, so that the concept contains the idea of oppression both in a social and psychological sense. And because of the various attempts made by the Frankfurt School to combine Marxist and psychological insights, it makes sense to try and understand the interaction between these two levels. Social conditions are settled as personality traits in individuals, which, in turn, have an influence on social conditions.

The counterpart to this concept of repression is the equally dynamic concept of liberation, emancipation, which Klaus Mollenhauer (1973), especially brought into the discussion of education. This also illustrates the point that critical pedagogy must be both a form of critical theory and also about the development of people who can think critically. Emancipation is nurtured in the fight against repression—both socially ideological and psychological.

Political education, or action competence, must include critical, independent thinking. "Critical" here means that one does not simply take what is given for granted. The Norwegian philosopher, Jon Hellesnes, when characterizing liberal education in contrast to adaptation, writes that liberal education means working on the conditions determining what happens around you and to you. He continues: "The socialization contained in liberal education emancipates people to become political subjects, and not just the objects of control and guidance exercised by other people" (1976: 18).

This is just what political subjects are: participants, agents, or acting persons. Critical thinking forms part of the competence involved in action competence. If it is to be emancipatory it has to include the trait which the American sociologist C. Wright Mills (1959) has called "sociological imagination." This is a capability of shifting perspective backwards and forwards between the individual, personal level, which is often seen as the purely private sphere, and the social, structural level. C. Wright Mills himself illustrated the relevance of sociological imagination by analyses of such topics as unemployment, war, and divorce (Schnack 1998).

With roots in the Frankfurt School, it was natural for Oskar Negt (1971) to pick up this inspiration in connection with his work in adult education and combine it with the ideas of the German science education theorist, Martin Wagenschein (1968), concerning a principle in curriculum about working with carefully selected examples. In this way, this "exemplar" principle was made politically more radical, becoming a matter of a better understanding of one's own situation in life seen in a social context. In terms of an action approach, this is very relevant if one supposes that one's actions can make a difference, that they help to create or prevent change.

Theory and Praxis

The relationship between theory and praxis has been a central theme within the conceptual tradition dealt with here. Interpreting the world is one thing, changing it is another. We can possess much knowledge that does not affect our behaviour; conversely, people seem to be able to do many things that cannot necessarily be explained as knowledge. Different types of theory can be related to different knowledge-forming interests, which are again connected with various kinds of praxis.

Now and then one runs into the term action competence in connection with the traditional distinction between knowledge and skills. As a teacher, for example, it is not enough to know a lot about the theory of education or be able to formulate theories; one also has to be able to teach. Understanding a chart is one thing, said the old Danish author, Ludvig Holberg, navigating a ship is another. There is obviously an important point here that goes beyond the sphere of education.

The real challenge, however, lies in bridging the gap between theory and praxis as two isolated worlds. Action competence as an ideal in curriculum theory attempts to do precisely this by emphasizing both the potential for action and the competence aspect: the latter calls for a qualified, reflective agent.

For this reason, a particular type of interest is linked to the concept of experience. Experience represents a form of knowledge closely linked to action; experience is the result of actions, which are always carried out on the basis of previous experience, which again is the result of earlier actions, etc. This is what John Dewey (1938) called the continuity of experience.

At the same time, however, experience expresses the categories, symbols, and imaginative representations we use to understand the world at any given point in time. Experience consists of experiences that have been interpreted, and reflected upon, and is therefore neither "pure" nor "neutral." Nor does it in any way offer a "truer" access to the world than does theoretical knowledge; in some ways, in fact, less so. This is because, as we have mentioned, the task of theoretical knowledge is to go behind appearances and ask critical questions about our immediate understanding of things and preconceived opinions, which are often given a lot of free play in connection with experience.

In terms of the relationship between theory and praxis, experience is important because it links the objective and subjective aspects; it is always experience of something: "I have had some experience with...", or, "I have experienced that...." At the same time, this is my experience. I cannot take over the experience of others. I have to gain experience myself, and it is linked to me as an involved, intentional agent. It is for this reason that experience plays such a central role in the development of personal knowledge.

Experience, then, can build a bridge between theory and praxis, but it is so closely related to the aspect of action that the gap referred to may reappear as a gap between formal knowledge and life experience. Inspired by Oskar Negt, this problem has been called "parallelism," and it has posed a challenge for the kind of critical progressive educational theory that has emphasised experience. Parallelism poses special problems, because formal knowledge ("school knowledge") and theoretical knowledge are not able to apply their potentially critical power.

If formal knowledge and life experience constitute parallel lines that do not meet, the life of action will not be satisfactorily informed by critical reflection. Formal knowledge will be acquired as rote learning to be reproduced at the examination table or in parlor games, but it has very little influence on our common sense. Life experience is often gained in such a way that, never questioned, it confirms our rigid attitudes to gender or cultural differences, for example, identifying enemies or supporting in us simplistic ideas.

A pedagogy that wishes to develop action competence will have to combat the tendency to parallelism. Drowning pupils in a mass of information and theories about the world is no use: information in itself is of no value in terms of liberal education, and the acquisition of knowledge and theories will not in itself qualitatively improve the life of action. In relation to many of the problems of the world or of life in general, the transmission of isolated information could, in fact, inhibit action. Conversely, a high level of activity and practical action will not in itself increase action competence. Uncritical "practicism" does not lead to political education and action competence.

The interest in teaching activities characterized by the action aspect must be seen in relation to the opportunities thus offered to gain experience on the basis of involvement and critical reflection on this experience. In this context, schools (in the widest sense) offer opportunities lacking in those computer- and video-guided teaching processes which, no doubt, will take over many of the traditional functions of the school.

The Dissolution of Tradition

Social and cultural developments seem to be constantly accelerating. In recent decades we have witnessed a dynamic apparently unmatched in previous generations. This dynamic consists of many converging factors that can be analyzed in various ways. At all events, globalization is one of them, but the dissolution of tradition and value pluralism are others.

It is possible to maintain both that traditions are crumbling, and that they are multiplying. Both at the global and local levels, our modern, multiethnic, and multicultural society is bursting with traditions and values, but the fact that they exist side by side, in schools, for example, exemplifies pluralism and thus relativism. There no longer seems to be any belief in the possibility of one connected account of an ordered universe.

This can lead to many more or less twisted forms of reaction or even just common or garden-variety defeatism as expressed in one of the graffiti on the wall of a university in Denmark: "God is dead; Marx is dead, and I'm not feeling too good myself." However, there is a dialectical ambiguity concealed in this situation, for the erosion of absolute traditions and value systems can be seen as a liberation from their vicelike grip and repressive power. The German critical theorist, Thomas Ziehe (1989), was one of the first to catch this double bind in his reflections on what he calls "cultural release." Anthony Giddens (1991) has pointed out the mobile, fluid nature of self-identity. The dissolution of tradition leads to an increasing number of choices in all areas, and in order not to be swamped by this complexity, one is forced to make many of one's choices routine by choosing a lifestyle, but here the operative word is "choosing." People no longer simply choose a partner, for example, but also choose the rules that are to apply to their relationship.

Ever since Adam and Eve ate of the fruit of that tree in the middle of the Garden of Eden, human beings have possessed the ability to see themselves from the outside and to reflect on their own identity. One aspect of the development of civilization in Western culture, at least since the Renaissance, is that it has become a theme in art and philosophy to adopt a position vis-a-vis this relation to oneself. The most recent developments seem to have made this self-reflection part of our general culture: one has continually to reconstruct one's own self-understanding and that of the communities to which one belongs.

The democratic arena has become larger, and the opportunities to seize emancipation and the development of autonomy seem only to be limited by confusion and rootlessness. Market forces and the mass media are omnipresent and threaten to close off the arena for good. In one and the same process, the world has become both larger and smaller. We possess opportunities as never before, but at the same time, wars, poverty, and environmental problems have been brought into the centre of our common world in a completely new way.

In a world like this, action competence is called to fulfill a major role. The fact is that the dissolution of tradition opens up new avenues for democracy: as the old authorities are gradually deflated, power sharing becomes possible in principle, and this is an important dimension in all forms of democratization. But if the "release" offered by this situation is to be used elsewhere than in the marketplace, we must once more emphasize liberal education towards democratic participation.

The Content of Liberal Education

These tendencies in the direction of value pluralism and the dissolution of traditions mean a new set of conditions for the work to be done within the theory of curriculum (*Didaktik*) towards a clearer definition of the content of action competence. What values can we take with us into this new millennium? And what in the widest sense are basic knowledge and skills in the light of our particular future? Are some things more important than others?

The special conditions for the discussion of these curricular questions are connected with the dynamics of social development and with democratization. Society is developing so rapidly that it is impossible with any degree of certainty to foresee what will be relevant knowledge and skills in a generation or two, at least not in detail. The more general lines can perhaps be glimpsed, but in teaching one has to work seriously with a lot of details. One may be well aware that in the grand scheme of things it matters little whether the pupils learn these details or not, but it is important that they take an active part in the study of the chosen issues. By working with the specific paradigm you may get an understanding of the general meaning of the ideas the example exemplifies. This is the basic philosophy behind the "exemplar principle," and there is an important point hidden behind the rather paradoxical statement that education is what is left when you have forgotten what you have learned.

The democratization tendency within the dissolution of traditions makes it difficult to decide who shall determine the content of education. It has become more difficult to refer to any instance or criteria that bear any generally accepted form of power or authority. The discussion of aims and content has thus become, to a greater degree than previously, part of the democratic discourse, and this also affects the balance between the centralization and decentralization of decision-making processes. While more and more is left to local decisions, centralism is becoming more and more marked. This pulse is part of the life-support functions of representative democracy.

But it is not only a question of centralism and decentralization; it is also of necessity a question of the direct involvement of pupils in their own process of education. The setting of aims can no longer simply be a process whereby some decide and others obey; the idea that the others must learn to set aims and goals themselves must in itself be part of the goal. In this way, the setting up of aims and the choice of content becomes itself part of the content. What are worthwhile activities? How and why? The central curricular question no longer simply concern the process of education but must itself form part of the content.

The self-evaluation carried out by pupils is no longer simply directed at the question: "Did we learn what we were supposed to?" It must also be directed at another question: "Did we learn what we wanted to learn?" Teaching consists of actions carried out by the pupils as well as the teachers, and active learning processes must be seen as goal-oriented, that is, intentional.

The conditions mentioned here help to make the question of the content of action competence somewhat complicated, but this does not mean that the considerations called for are less necessary or relevant. As an inspiration to such considerations, some academic contributions may be mentioned.

In a Ph.D. dissertation at the Research Centre of Environmental and Health Education in Copenhagen, Finn Mogensen has made a kind of factor analysis of the concept of action competence. This leads to a model for what could be significant elements of content. Among other factors inspired by the American authors of "critical thinking" (Brookfield 1987; Giroux 1989; Paul 1992; Siegel 1988), he includes cognitive, value-oriented, social, and personality factors. He calls them: knowing something about the problem; knowing something about what to do; seeking normative justifications; knowing the opportunities offered by the community; having the courage and feeling the responsibility to act; and having the will and the desire to act.

In a book called *The School of the Future,* Hans Jurgen Kristensen (1987) treats the question from the point of view of what roles the students have to play as adults and what they need to learn in order to shape their own future and those of others. He then creates a model offering a possible structure for action competence understood along these lines. The structure contains the following elements:
- Personal, structural, problem-oriented, value-oriented, and action-oriented insight.
- A number of partial abilities, called linguistic competence, investigatory and problem-solving competence, mastery of central cultural techniques, practical/manual competence, social competence, and creative competence.
- A basic self-confidence and trust in the opportunities offered by the community.

In continuation of this, we are presented with a proposal for an overall curriculum for the whole school. It is divided up into a number of cultural techniques and four interactive groups of what are called "problem and experience areas." These latter are called: nature; nature and man; man and society; daily life, communication, and art.

Another proposal for a structure that has played a major role as a proposal that offers an overall picture for further discussion is the so-called four-field model, developed in co-operation between the Laboratory for Democratic Educational Experiments and a specific school in Copenhagen (Henriksen et al. 1987). This model uses four overlapping fields, called, respectively, the manual/productive field, the scientific/experimental field, the musical/corporal field, and the linguistic/social field.

Inspired by Wolfgang Klafki's theory of "Category Education," Hermann Giesecke (1972) has attempted to list the central categories that must be considered when working with political education. His categories are: conflict, actuality, power, right, interest, solidarity, participation in decision making, ideology, historicity, and human values. These are the categories one should be able to use in order to reflect on, understand, and question the world, but in order to promote action competence, the insights gained must be translated into what he calls "action knowledge."

There are a number of similar structural proposals, and though none of them can be final or authoritative, they can provide positive contributions and tools for curricular reflection, which can help one to consider what elements are more important than others and how one can ensure a degree of generality in the process of liberal education.

From the beginning of the 1980s, I have lectured and written about what has sometimes been called "The Didactics of Challenge" (Schnack 1995a). The main idea is that one of the starting points for curriculum discourse could be considerations relating to what are the most acute challenges facing mankind, or perhaps humanity, in the modern world. If future generations shall have real opportunities to be well-qualified participators in democratic processes concerning such challenges (both large and small), then they must be given the opportunity to construct relevant forms of understanding and try their hand at investigating or involving themselves in central types of social issues.

Since the early 1990s, Wolfgang Klafki (1994, 1996) has written about what he calls "key problems" or "central problems" in the world as a thematic dimension in a liberal education context. He presents the idea that international teaching could be international in the literal sense of the word, meaning a common element in the curriculum of all countries. Perhaps it is not possible to get very far in terms of what such challenges are and how they are to be understood locally, nationally, or internationally. But, by emphasizing such curriculum questions and beginning with the most obvious challenges, e.g., peace education, health education, global education, and environmental education these challenges will be put on the agenda and made radical through a form of educational thinking that places democratic action competence as a curriculum perspective.

References

Beck, U. (1986). *Risikogesellschaft. Auf dem Weg in eine andere Moderne*. Frankfurt am Main:Suhrkamp Verlag. (English edition: *Risk society: Towards a new modernity*, London: Sage. 1992).

Breiting, S., K. Hedegaard, F. Mogensen, K. Nielsen, and K. Schnack (1999). *Handlekompetence, interessekonflikter, og miljoeundervisning–MUVIN-projektet. (Action competence, conflicting interests, and environmental education–the MUVIN project)*. Odense: Universitetsforlag.

Breiting, S., and F. Mogensen (1999). Action competence and environmental education. *Cambridge Journal of Education 29* (3): 349–353.

Breiting, S. and K. Nielsen (Eds.) (1996). *Environmental education research in the Nordic countries*. Publication no. 33 from the Research Centre for Environmental and Health Education. Copenhagen: Royal Danish School of Educational Studies.

Brookfield, S. (1987). *Developing critical thinkers: Challenging adults to explore alternative ways of thinking and acting*. Milton Keynes: Open University Press.

Dewey, J. (1938). *Experience and education*. New York: Macmillan.

Giddens, A. (1990). *The consequences of modernity*. Cambridge: Polity.

——— (1991). *Modernity and self-identity*. Cambridge: Polity.

Giesecke, H. (1972). *Didaktik der politischen Bildung. Neue Ausgabe*. Muenchen: Juventa Verlag.

Giroux, H. (1989). *Schooling for democracy. Critical pedagogy in the modern age*. London: Routledge.

Hellesnes, J. (1976). *Socialisering og teknokrati*. Oslo: Gyldendal.

Henriksen, S. et al. (1987). *Undervisningens demokratisering (Democratisation of the teaching)*. Copenhagen: Royal Danish School of Educational Studies.

Jensen, B. B. (Ed.) (1995). *Research in environmental and health education*. Publication no. 30 from the Research Centre for Environmental and Health Education. Copenhagen: Royal Danish School of Educational Studies.

——— (1997). A case of two paradigms within health education. *Health Education Research 12* (4): 419–28.

Jensen, B.B., and K. Schnack (Eds.) (1994). Action and action competence as key concepts in critical pedagogy. In *Studies in Educational Theory and Curriculum, vol. 12*. Copenhagen: Royal Danish School of Educational Studies.

——— (1997). The action competence approach in environmental education. *Environmental Education Research 3* (2): 163–78.

Kant, I. (1968). Beantwortung der Frage: Was ist Aufklaerung? In *Werke in Jehn Baenden, Band 9*. Darmstadt: Wissenschaftliche Buchgesellschaft.
Klafki, W. (1994). Schluesselprobleme als inhaltlicher Kern internationaler Erziehung. In Seibert, N. and Serve, H.J. (Hrsg.) *Bildung und Erziehung an der Schwelle zum dritten Jahrtausend* (Muenchen).
——— (1996). *Neuen Studien zur Bildungstheorie und Didaktik*, 2. erweiterten Auflage (Weinheim).
——— (1998) Characteristics of critical-constructive Didaktik. In *Didaktik and/or Curriculum. An International Dialogue*. Edited by B. B. Gundem and S. Hopmann. New York: Peter Lang.
Kristensen, H.J. (1987). *Skolen I fremtiden* (School for the future). Glydendal: Copenhagen.
Mills, C.W. (1959). *The sociological imagination*. New York: Oxford University Press.
Mogensen, F. (1997). *Handlekompetence som didaktisk begreb i miljundervisningen* (Action competence as curricular concept in environmental education). Copenhagen: Royal Danish School of Educational Studies.
Mollenhauer, K. (1973). *Erziehung und emanzipation*. Muenchen, Juventa: Verlag.
Negt, O. (1971). *Soziologische phantasie und exemplarisches lernen*. Frankfurt am Main, Koeln: Europaeische Verlagsanstalt.
Paul, R. (1992). *Critical thinking: What every person needs to survive in a rapidly changing world*. Foundation of Critical Thinking. Rohnert Park, CA: Sonoma State University.
Schnack, K. (1995a). The Didactics of Challenge, In *Didaktik and/or Curriculum*. S. Hopman, and K. Riquarts (ed.) Institut fuer die Paedagogik der Naturwissenschaften an der Universitaet Kiel.
———. (1995b). Democratisation, citizenship and action competence. In *Democracy in schools, citizenship and global concern*. Edited by K. Jensen, O. B. Larsen, and S. Walker, S. Studies in Educational Theory and Curriculum, vol. 18. Copenhagen: Royal Danish School of Educational Studies.
———. (1998). Why focus on conflicting interests in environmental education? In *Environmental Education for Sustainability: Good Environment, Good Life*. Edited by M. Ahlberg and W. L. Filho. Frankfurt am Main: Peter Lang.
Siegel, H. (1988). *Educating reason: Rationality, critical thinking, and education*. New York: Routledge.
Wagenschein, M. (1968). *Verstehen lehren*. Weinheim und Basel: Beltz Verlag.
Ziehe, T. (1989). *Ambivalenser og mangfoldighed*. Copenhagen: Politisk revy.

CHAPTER FIFTEEN

The Specific Challenges of Globalization for Teaching...and Vice Versa

David Geoffrey Smith • Canada

> In "globalization"...we have a myth that exaggerates the degree of our helplessness in the face of contemporary economic forces. (Hirst and Thompson 1996: 6)

Introduction

While the language of "globalization" has been in the common air for about ten years, the phenomenon itself, as a vision of empire within the Euro-American tradition, likely goes back at least to the late Middle Ages when papal reforms announced a new eschatological dispensation of heaven now being immanent on earth as a political reality (Loy 2000). Later, through the Renaissance and Reformation, individualism, personal autonomy, and self interest became celebrated as sacred virtues, and foundational to the new science of economics. By the seventeenth century, wealth accumulation had become a sign of divine favor and moral superiority; poverty a mark of personal weakness and lack of self-discipline (Weber 1920/1962; Tawney 1926/1938). However, insofar as empire always rests on a will to dominate, so also do those dominated engage in strategies of resistance with interesting and creative consequences. The future shape of geo-political reality is currently being worked out in the tensions between these forces.

It should be noted at the start that there is an important difference between international trade (trade between different cultures and groups) and globalization, the former having been a practice since the most ancient of days, while the latter, at least when conceived as a planetary unified global trading network operating according to a common set of rules, the so-called "borderless world" envisioned by the World Bank, a more recent and contentious development. Throughout all periods, education and teaching have had their role to play, defined in character largely by regnant ideas and dreams circulating in the political realm as those in power have sought to secure the present into the future through the minds of the young.

In this chapter, I wish to keep the two tropes of globalization and teaching circulating together conversationally, instead of polarizing them, as often happens today. Globalizers, operating in groups like the Organization for Economic Cooperation and Development (OECD) and the World Bank, and even in local and state governments, rarely develop their educational policies with a concern for the experience of teachers. Teachers are simply those civil servants who put into effect what others decide, "delivering other people's mail," as curriculum theorist William Pinar has put it (in personal communication).

Indeed, much of the personal and collective agitation of teachers today arises from a growing recognition of their own powerlessness within contemporary educational decision making. In turn, their voices of opposition against the forces of globalization, especially with respect to the commercialization of the educational enterprise and its technologization, are heard as shrill and irrelevant by the other side, largely under the accusation that teachers both ignore their historically constituted service function to broader orders as well as their complicity in the processes of globalization in their lives as common citizens. As a teacher, if you own shares in the General Electric Company, enjoy the choice and quality of goods at your neighborhood supermarket, and thrill to the growl of your SUV (Sport Utility Vehicle), it is unlikely that your protests against the forces of globalization have much moral or even intellectual authority.

No, what is needed today is a more open and vigorous examination of the historical construction of globalization phenomena, a more profound analysis of how we are all implicated in the web of their operations, no matter what our political stripe. We must formulate a teacherly response that emerges out of the heart of teaching itself, that is, out of that awareness of the conditions of life's possibility that may be the unique purview of teachers in any discussion about a shared future. Such will be the agenda for this chapter.

My argument will be that today teachers and teaching are caught in the middle of both a political and an epistemological crisis, and it is a crisis precisely because the epistemological revolution that has taken place in the Western tradition over the last fifty years or so (the shift from stable-state hard sciences and normatively driven social sciences to relativity-driven paradigms such as postmodern fluidity, chaos theory, constructivism, and ecology) has not yet registered within the last great bastion of Enlightenment rationality, namely the dismal science of economics, at least in its dominant configurations. The consequence is that a profound rupture is evolving between a new deep social awareness of the human world's interconnectedness (and its interconnectedness to the natural world) and hard-line economist interpretations of life which insist on an older rationality that relies on exactly the opposite—on the split between subject and object, on a conception of radical personal autonomy, and, most disastrously, on a split between politics (now conflated with economics) and history. Today, economies may boom while quality of life for the average person declines, and those in power of necessity turn a blind eye, precisely because to actually see the disjunction, to have it land within one's cognitive set, would inspire a crisis of confidence for which the solution is nowhere to be found in any comprehensive sense. Globally speaking, old and new orders are dying and rising coincidentally (maybe even respectively), all the while that there is no one interpretive frame, no common grammar, to hold it all together. Indeed, whether, in fact, there even needs to be such a frame or grammar, and what could be its possible sources, are two of the most interesting questions of the day.

Teachers, however, inevitably feel the present uncertainty and its underlying tensions very deeply, at both conscious and subliminal levels. Teacher preparation programs, situated in academies where the epistemological revolution has been going on for almost thirty years, are increasingly organized around conceptions of intersubjectivity, constructivism, and ecology. Storytelling, multiculturalism curricula, teacher-as-researcher/interpretive inquirer, and group work are now part of the standard preparational repertoire. All this is proposed to be acted out in the context of schools and educational systems that were originally designed to serve a different, older, more clearly defined order, one which remains politically regnant even while its conceptual and practical infrastructures are inherently suspect and devolving in spite of themselves. Serving the stable nation, creating the solid citizen, valuing a commodified liberal education for its own sake—what do, what can, these traditional hortatory imaginaries mean for teachers in the age of economic globalization? If once they served to anchor the teaching profession and provide it with public moral authority, where lies the anchor, and from whence comes moral authority if the nation turns into a dynamic narration while constructing the citizen as nothing but a capital resource, with education nothing more than job training? Teachers thus find themselves living in both the old and new imaginaries at the same time, and it is a difficult place in which to dwell.

The task here, then, will be to briefly profile the historical construction of contemporary globalization phenomena, noting the role traditionally played by teaching and education generally within them. Then an attempt will be made to articulate an understanding of teachers' work that may provide an open space within which pedagogically responsible work can be both considered and conducted in relation to the processes of globalization themselves.

The Construction of the Globalization Phenomenon

A good statement has been made by David Held and his colleagues (1997: 258): "Globalization is not a singular condition, a linear process or a final end-point of social change." This characterization addresses a number of important issues. For one thing, some parties do, in fact, operate as if globalization were a singular condition, if not in actuality, then in imaginal terms, in terms of a dream that drives practices in the now. This is particularly the case with American self-understanding. As U.S. Secretary of State Madeleine Albright declared in her speech to the 1997 graduating class at Harvard:

> Today, I say that no nation in the world need be left out of the global system we are constructing....Every nation that seeks to participate and is willing to do all it can to help itself will have America's help in finding the right path." (Spring 1998: 8; emphasis added)

This dream is a legacy of America's leadership role in the reconstruction of world order after World War II, but today its rhetorical force is largely anachronistic and all the more dangerous for being so. It simply ignores some basic facts: America's own version of economic development is a product of its own time/space configuration as a frontier New World culture that privileges geography over history, seeing the rest of the world in terms of spatial conquest with little regard for other people's historical sensibilities

(Campbell 1992). Also, as John Gray (1999: 2) has suggested, America is the world's "last great Enlightenment regime," by which he means that the eighteenth-century project of proposing Reason as the condition of universal peace is still kept alive within the preachments of American neo-liberal economic theory taken as reasonable science, even though such theory has proven a dismal failure in the new Russia, is denounced as predatory and rapacious by struggling emergent peoples, is completely untenable within the social-contract atmosphere of post–World War II Europe, and contradicts the deep sense of familial obligation that inhabits many Asian definitions of commonwealth.

If globalization is not a "singular condition," then how might it best be described? The different circulating influences at work today are the result of historical evolutions that can be traced briefly as follows.

The "borderless world" idea of the OECD and World Bank is the natural extension of the Euro-American tradition of capital development organized around the processes of production and consumption, inspired especially by the Industrial Revolution of the nineteenth century. It was this tradition that was responsible for the colonization of the world under European and, later, American requirements for natural resources and markets. Education played the role of handmaiden in this process both at home and abroad under specific definitions of progress and development that had their origin and legitimation in the philosophical writing of people like Kant and Hegel, and later, Darwin (Eze 1997; Schmidt 1996).

During the period, say between 1884, when the Berlin Conference of European powers convened to divide up Africa, and 1945, when the pre–World War II structure of world order lay in ruins, education was chiefly organized for the production of elites to run that same order both at home and abroad, coupled with the training of the masses to serve the machineries of both capital and the state in their various particularities of bureaucratic functioning, military development, and technical training (Carnoy 1974). In the colonies, Western-style education for indigenous peoples was reserved for a tiny minority nurtured to take their place in local leadership, with the rest minimally instructed to form the service class for their European overlords.

The period of post–World War II to the 1970s, sometimes called the Long Boom, is marked by many contradictions in terms of educational as well as economic development. On the one hand, the Euro-American experience involved the construction of the "mixed economy," wherein capital development was held to a strong sense of social responsibility as a way of allaying the social disorder that seemed always inevitable under the boom and bust cycles of undisciplined market theory. Under the social responsibility framework, institutionalized, state-sponsored public education flourished at all levels. This was partly a way of securing the West's social strength and stability against the feared enemy of communism. Its offshoot was the creation of appetite for formal education as a way of social advancement. Education became heavily commodified, a purchasable "thing" available to the rising middle class under equal access legislation and other forms of "rights" politics (Meighan 1981). This particular vision of education is now dying.

In the colonies, nationalist independence movements successfully fought to gain political sovereignty, but the various machineries put in place to enact the new conditions quickly revealed the many subtle and profound ways old orders were reluctant to fall away. This was partly due to arrogance, partly to ignorance. Puppet local leaders were often installed in former colonies to ensure continued rights to natural resources. Definitions of "education" were still inspired largely by Western models even though their relevance for solving local problems was suspect (Coombs 1985). They were tied, however, to the development logic of organizations like the World Bank, the International Monetary Fund, and the United Nations Education, Science and Cultural Organization (UNESCO), and could be taken as early signs of a move toward a unified global network of peoples.

This period was also marked by new forms of movement between cultures. Many idealistic young university graduates from Britain, America, Canada, and Europe, for example, taught in the former colonies under such programs as World University Service Commission (WUSC), Canadian University Service Overseas (CUSO), the Volunteer Service Organization (VSO), and the Peace Corps. Such experience often served, for the Euro-American young people involved, as an education into the ethnocentrism of their own received traditions. It was also a time of mass migrations from the colonies to former imperial centres and included many seeking higher education. These parallel phenomena, moving in opposite directions from centre to periphery and back, contributed importantly to the great epistemological revolution that has characterized Western academies since the late 1960s, the so-called "Post" revolution (McClintock 1994, 292), carried on under the various banners of poststructuralism, postmodernism, and postcolonialism.

The "Post" revolution in the West had its intellectual genesis in the work of Algerian scholars like Franz Fanon in the 1950s and early 1960s and later

Jacques Derrida, Jean-Francois Lyotard, and Helene Cixous (Fischer 1992: 55), who challenged the organizing principles and structures of the Western episteme, charging it with responsibility for the continuing hegemony of Western economic, cultural, and political interests throughout the world. They showed how the episteme could only have been constructed and sustained through a dependent but silenced relationship to an Other (other peoples, cultures, groups, gods) and that the time had come for those Others to begin claiming their debts. This claim put into effect an epistemological crisis for Western academic work that continues to this day. It involves a whole host of issues, such as the meaning of Identity, the nature of "Man," the question of authority in knowledge, science as a cultural artifact, racial and gender biases in curriculum, and so on. The future of intellectual work, including teaching, will depend on how these issues are taken up and creatively resolved, perhaps especially within the multicultural environments of the West's urban landscapes.

Understandably, the work of "Post" scholarship was seen as a threat by those who saw the purpose of intellectual labor as serving the technical requirements of state-capital linkage. During the 1980s, under the administrations of Ronald Reagan in the United States and Margaret Thatcher in Britain, universities came under attack for being subversive and anarchic, and for teaching distortions of the narrative of Western culture as the natural and proven evolutionary pinnacle of human progress, exemplary for the rest of the species. The actions of the two administrations marked the beginning of the end for the Western academy as a place of free reflection and autonomous scholarly work, a process of devolution that is ongoing.

The period from the early 1970s to the mid 1990s marks the time when the basic configuration of today's globalization processes fell into place, and this was due to a number of interrelated factors. For example, the move in 1971 of the Oil Petroleum Exporting Countries (OPEC) in the Middle East to control the global price of oil revealed the stark vulnerability of Western industry to non-Western interests. In the realm of education, the failure of American military efforts in Vietnam by 1972 was blamed in large measure on the mobilization of war protests on college campuses. Ronald Reagan, as a law-and-order president pledged to securing the conditions for U.S. domination of world order into the next millennium, commissioned a series of reports, such as *A Nation at Risk,* on the state of public education. These were thinly veiled attacks on public education generally, and especially on teachers and teacher training institutions, as failing to work in harmony with the ideological requirements of true "global competitiveness." "Soft" programs in the arts and social issues curricula concerned with the environment, race, and gender inequity, etc., began to suffer from lack of funding.

All this was happening at a time when the basic infrastructure of Euro-American business was entering a crisis phase. Asian countries like Japan, South Korea, Taiwan, and Singapore, which had enjoyed American military protection under the arrangements of the Cold War, had begun to prosper and pose a threat to Western industry. The ready supply of cheap labor in those countries contraindicated the heavily unionized labor of America and Europe, whose businesses, in turn, began to move offshore to take advantage of an unregulated labor market. The new global economic competitiveness forced American businesses to seek from their federal and state governments new rules of taxation protection, especially since much of their industrial manufacturing was not now being conducted on local soil (Clarke 1997).

The rewriting of taxation rules in favor of economic interests over social and cultural ones has marked the most fundamental and profound change in Western societies since the mid-1980s and has been most largely responsible for the gradual devolution of all those public and social institutions that flourished during the Long Boom under the Bretton Woods Agreement of 1945 (in Clarke 1997). The basic turn was made during the Reagan period under the influence of the Chicago School of Economics at the University of Chicago, whose leader, Milton Friedman, espoused the neo-liberal economic theory of Fredrick von Hayek. The Hayek/Friedman thesis reinstalled The Market as the preeminent concern of government (Spring 1998: 120–57), whereby the function of government was to protect the conditions of The Market over and against social and cultural interests, which were usually and contemptuously derided as "special interests." The logic of "neo-liberalism," as it was often referred to, became enshrined as sacred doctrine after the fall of the Berlin Wall and the end of the Cold War, events which, for free-marketeers, were taken as a sign of "The End of History" (Fukuyama 1993), a true eschaton proving the complete superiority of Western economic theory over all competitors.

Public education, first in Britain, then the United States, New Zealand, and the Canadian provinces of Alberta and Ontario, began to fall to the logic of market rule, with language such as educational "choice," and "education-business partnership," gradually infiltrating the halls of educational decision making under pressure from federal, state, and local political administrations (Barlow & Robertson 1994). The mantra of "global competitiveness" brought into effect in public education new levels of paranoia and uncertainty, especially amongst the teaching profession, along with an almost complete collapse of any older virtue of learning being valued for its own sake. Education must now constantly demonstrate how its various programs serve The Market. The Organization for Economic Cooperation and Development calls this the "human capital resource" model of education (Spring 1998, 159–90). When such service actually shows complicity in the destruction of the common good, any expressed concern is quickly dismissed as irrelevant to the larger picture. This has also been a time of efforts to "harmonize" curricula across national boundaries in an effort to produce a set of commonly held knowledges, skills, and attributes that can feed into the converging requirements of the proposed global system. It is also a way of imposing a common discipline on educational systems (Spring 1998; Barlow & Robertson 1994).

If market logic has become the new rule of governance, nothing has been more instrumental in its habilitation and entrenchment than the revolution in computer and communications technology. This revolution has been well discussed in many quarters and needs only brief highlighting here to show its pertinence to the changing roles of teaching and public education. As writers like William Greider (1997) and Jeremy Rifkin (1996) have so clearly shown in their excellent documentary investigations, the computer/communications technology revolution has resulted not just in a Copernican change in the conditions of work with its attendant restructuring of entire systems of production; it has also precipitated profoundly elevated levels of global instability, both within the systems of production themselves and within the international financial systems that now operate as a kind of virtual manager of the international scene but without visible accountability to anyone or any place, except perhaps to the shadow population of international shareholders.

With respect to systems of production, the technology revolution has broken down the old structures of independent in-house corporate activity and forced new kinds of cooperation and merger. Airplanes and automobiles once built from scratch in a single plant in Seattle or Detroit are now assembled from parts made all over the world through new kinds of production agreements and negotiated labor pacts. Production measures have assumed a form of international complexity which no one company or country can alter without serious consequences to multiple partners, partners representing every ideological and political stripe. The steep competitiveness of the globalized system of production has effected an essential blindness to such issues as the environment and human rights concerns related to working conditions, the feminization of labor, the male infantilization phenomenon (how adolescent males get emotionally stuck in Rambo-like machoism while girls go off to work—a common feature of contemporary low-wage industrial labor societies) (Norberg-Hodge 1993), and child labor.

The computer/communications revolution has also made possible lightening-quick processing of international financial operations and the virtual negotiation of commodity exchanges in such a way that these activities have rendered whole economies, such as those of Brazil, Mexico, Thailand, etc., extremely vulnerable to stock market fluctuation. As virtual operations, they bear almost no responsibility to the peoples and places most affected by them. The chronic instability of international finance has had widespread spin-off effects in the realms of society and culture. The extreme competitiveness it produces for market share, for predatory searches for lowest commodity prices, for speculative ventures in financial services such as insurance and credit, etc., all have an effect at the local level of ordinary citizens, from the deregulation of labor with its effect on family life (in Gray 1999) to chronic instability in most agricultural sectors.

In the educational sphere, the general uncertainty which globalization processes have produced is endemic. Postmodern worry over what may be authoritatively taught is merely exacerbated by the difficulty of understanding what it means to teach authoritatively, especially when, in the so-called new knowledge economy, teaching so often reduces to simply "managing" the educational space, without any special personal qualities being required of teachers other than organizational and planning skills. The relation of knowing to being is of no apparent relevance within the cult of information, except perhaps as a personal side-task over which one labors individually, alone, with no help from the teacher, who, of necessity for survival within the cult, may have already made the split between fact and value or sold out to the heralded belief that the only facts of any value are commercial in nature.

Finally, mention must be made of the dialectic currently operating between the forces of global unification and disintegration. The disintegration of the old bipolar world of the Cold War is giving way to increased efforts to secure national, tribal, and ethnic identities that had been formerly subsumed under the old order. Also, the "borderless world" agenda is producing new forms of resistance, both as religious fundamentalism (Marty and Appleby 1994), and in the form of non-governmental citizens' action groups seeking to recover local control over local life (see the journal *Third World Resurgence*), wresting the local away from the aggressive subsumptive power of global market logic.

Globalization in Summary

The following points can be made about globalization as a contemporary condition:

- As a generative force, globalization is an extension of an approximately five-hundred-year-old development in the thought and action of the Western tradition going back most likely to the papal reforms of the late Middle Ages (Loy 2000), which led in turn to visions of sacred empire eventually underwritten by Protestant-inspired "virtues" of self interest and wealth accumulation. Such virtues became the foundation of capitalist economic theory portended for universal application.
- "Empire" always means an encounter with Others, who at first may be contributive to the empire, but eventually serve to undermine its original character and authority. This is clearly the case today. The Euro-American empire is devolving under the very structures and influences it originally put in place. For example, the post-colonial critique is rewriting the rules of epistemic authority for schools, academies, and curricula. The former colonies of Asia are regrouping after the "Asian Crisis" of the late 1990s to formulate theories of economic, social, and cultural development more in line with their own traditions rooted in Confucianism and other forms of wisdom, not grounded in a myth of personal autonomy (Spring 1998; Asian Economics 2000). It is the essential complexity of global interconnectedness today and its unpredictability, not its univocal character, that is the most striking feature of the globalization phenomenon.
- The privileging of economist interpretations of human life over political, cultural, and social ones has led to the gradual devolution of the power of the state over the public sphere, such that national identity is increasingly assuming a chimerical quality. Given the rapid economic integration of Canada into the United States, for example, what does the future hold for Canadian identity? And if it was the state that once gave teaching its moral and professional authority, from whence will that authority come if the state itself is on the wane? Currently the most influential educational policies are being written not by national or local governments but by international think tanks and organizations like the World Bank, funded by the private corporate sector (Spring 1998; CAUT Bulletin 1999; Barlow & Robertson 1994). Some

scholars suggest that the nation-state system that has defined world organization since its inauguration with the Peace of Westphalia in 1648 is falling away to a new network of global cities (Sassen 1998). The cities will become nodes around which populations gravitate and through which personal identity is constructed. I am an Edmontonian, not so much a Canadian, and I think of my future no longer in terms of being a Canadian but in terms of having a place within a new global network of urban landscapes. Of course, whether this is good or desirable is yet to be decided.

- The communications/technology revolution is rewriting the rules of production in both material and intellectual spheres. Materially, in the West, the new technologies, tied to the mantra of global competitiveness, are reshaping the meaning of labor, with career labor being replaced by just-in-time contractual work suffering diminishing security (Gray 1999). International finance is becoming "virtual," i.e., disconnected from people and places most affected by its operations, accountable only to shareholders dispersed throughout the world. Intellectually, knowledge generation and dissemination are heavily influenced by the fact/value separation consequent to the commercialization of the educational enterprise. Computerized information systems are usurping the traditional roles of universities and schools as primary sites of knowledge and information, such that teachers' work is being defined largely in managerial terms rather than in terms that maintain any fundamental connection between knowledge and being. Knowledge itself is becoming disembodied and virtual, disconnected from the person and place of the knower. Generally, these conditions fall under a condition that can be called "de-localization," to be discussed later.

The radical commercialization of human values on a global scale introduces into the discourse surrounding possible futures the question of human values itself, and increasingly forms of resistance are emerging that may prefigure a global conversation, if not confrontation, regarding what it means to live well, humanly speaking. Clearly a vision of endless, and endlessly variegated, consumption, which is the necessary flipside of endless and endlessly variegated production, is an absurd and futile vision for many people, as well as, perhaps, absurd and futile in its own right. The most radical challenge to this vision comes from religious traditions that do not share the sacred/secular conflation that lies at the Protestant root of Western economic theory. Saying this, however, only means that discussions regarding shared futures must inevitably involve religious questions, i.e., questions about meaning, purpose, and what is truly required to nurture and sustain human life in its most noble and dignified senses.

The intertwining of the world's peoples that is largely the result of the earlier colonial period has produced new forms of cultural interfacing that hold promise for a new kind of dialogue regarding a shared future. But this dialogue will not be possible as long as different parties hold on to the dream of their own singular logic, whether economic or religious in nature, being recommendable for universal application. Far more important may be a careful examination of the effects of our differences on each other, how what you, individually/collectively, assume to be true generally, affects me, individually/collectively—and vice versa—and an honest opening of ourselves to the conditions of our mutual survival.

Implications of Globalization for Curriculum and Teaching

What remains now is to explore more specifically the tensions between globalization processes as described and the conduct of teaching. In particular, interest will be directed to the question of what might constitute an appropriate teacherly response to globalization in the midst of its unfolding complexity. Here, the attempt will be to formulate a kind of pedagogical hermeneutic that honours globalization's complexity while also honouring that pedagogical integrity without which teaching as a form of life practice can neither survive nor be called teaching as such. Indeed, probably the greatest threat to teaching today is the seeming indifference shown to the experience of teachers by those most responsible for framing the educational policies of the contemporary period. Like most other forms of labor today, teaching is being reduced to a commodity in a deregulated labor market, with little interest shown by planners for what teaching is in its own right and with scant concern for the effects of new plans on the quality of life for either teachers or students.

What can teachers say that is constructively contributive to the conversation about a world inevitably "globalizing?" Clearly it is impossible to return to an earlier condition when public education was firmly tied to a relatively unproblematic understanding of the meaning of "public," that is, before the crisis of state control increasingly tied education to the processes of commercialization. Nor is it possible to return to the sensibility existing before the "Post" critique or before the communication and information technologies revolution or the foregrounding of fundamentalism in its various guises, economic, religious, and ethnic guises. Indeed it is virtually impossible to predict what the future will hold regarding the shape and character of public education. But as Asian wisdom teaches us (Park 1996), there is always only Now. So perhaps that is the first challenge for teachers, learning to live Now, although it may not be as easy for a number of reasons.

The first reason is that teaching, at least in the Western tradition, has always operated inordinately in the future tense within a temporal frame that privileges the future over the present as well as the past. "When you complete this (course, grade, assignment, year, etc.) then you can ..." is a phrase that echoes throughout the discourse of all levels of education, from kindergarten through post-doctoral work. This is an orientation that is honestly come by if teaching defines its role as being the handmaid of market logic, because as David Loy (2000) has argued, The Market emerged through a template of Christian eschatology in which future time became now time. Indeed, to paraphrase Loy, the West lives in a kind of frozen futurism in which what was expected to be revealed has been revealed, and that what the revelation discloses is that the future will always be more of this, a perpetual unfolding of more and more of this. In this context education becomes nothing but more and more of what it always was. The details may vary over time, but the essential grammar remains the same: Education seems like a preparation for something that never happens because in the deepest sense, it has already happened, over and over. So built into the anticipations of teaching is a mask of the future that freezes teaching in a futurist orientation such that, in real terms, there is no future because the future already is. Hence the ubiquitous icon of the perpetually smiling young elementary schoolteacher and its analogues in both consumer marketing and evangelical Christianity. All three celebrate "enthusiasm" as a cardinal virtue, which means, literally, "inside god" (<Gk *en,* inside +*theos* god). They are the bearers of a verdict that, in the name of the future, the future is now closed. Loy's point is not that the future is in fact frozen, only a particular understanding of it; an understanding in which the secular and the sacred are conflated within a rationalist schema providing Western economics with its theoretical justifications. The real work of the contemporary period is to recover a future that truly is a future, i.e., a condition that is actually open.

It is easy to see how frozen futurism is a recipe for despair for students as well as for teachers and why public education historically has served the forces of conservatism. If the future is frozen in an anticipatory set through which nothing ever really seems to change, even though all of the language perpetually gives assurance that things are always changing, what could one really come to expect after all? Well, more of the same, including perhaps lots of little changes and variations on a theme but no change in the sense that it actually seems to make a difference in the way one lives. Hence the frequently heard reasoning of new graduate students to the question, "Why did you decide to *do* graduate work?" Answer: "I want to make a difference," one implication being that something is stubbornly resistant to becoming different. Indeed, the trope itself projects difference into the future and is therefore part of the very futility it seeks to address but cannot because the underlying cultural grammar has undergone no fundamental investigation.

One of the most pronounced effects of the frozen futurism inherent in market globalization can be called the phenomenon of de-localization, whereby people and cultures everywhere find themselves being told that all aspects of life are now being defined in terms of a connection to "global" networks, and that the immediately-at-hand only has value insofar as it feeds into those networks. Irony abounds. A friend visiting from India simply could not understand what I was talking about when describing the fact that today in Canada a farming family of five to six persons, living on almost a thousand acres of land, increasingly finds it hard to "make a living" on their farm. From his Indian frame of reference, "one acre could easily support a family of ten."

The most sinister effects of de-localization may be the most ordinary. As John Gray (1999: 45) has put it, "We increasingly cannot recognize ourselves in our work." For us as teachers, this may be especially true. The plethora of technical and curricular innovations and recommendations under the rhetoric of globalization has left teachers alienated from what their experience has taught them over time, which is that effective teaching depends most fundamentally on human relationships, that there indeed is a profound connection between knowing and being, and that any attempted severance can only produce a deep cynicism with respect to knowledge itself. In this context, if knowledge production and dissemination are tied most securely only to events that happen far away, eventually a crisis is precipitated with respect to the value of any knowledge "for me."

The issue of de-localization is also linkable to the language of "global competitiveness," which is often used by globalization planners to whip the imaginal energy of frozen futurism into a frenzy. "Unless we do X, we will fall behind." This is a simple but powerful recipe for the creation of Loser Culture. Winning implies losing, so that any social and educational planning motivated by the sheer desire to win of necessity breeds not only hypercompetitiveness within the social realm but also its adjunct effects of heightened social paranoia and the turning of friends into enemies. Most essentially it makes more and more people feel like they are losers, that the race to "keep up" cannot be won, that the game is for winners only, who by definition must be very few, and that therefore for the rest us, life becomes a race to the bottom. A recent Statistics Canada (1999) survey indicated that 80 percent of small businesses in Canada fail within the first two years of operation. Those that survive after five years then become attractive to larger corporations who either develop their own competitive clone industry or seek a buy out of the original firm. As Canadian philosopher of technology Ursula Franklin (1999) recently remarked, "The language of global competitiveness is the language of war." As teachers we might ask, "Who can survive it, and how?"

The more important work however lies not in laying out further examples of frozen futurism and its effects, which are there at every turn should we care to pay attention. The real work may lie in trying to articulate what the meaning of living Now could mean in the context of the dynamics of teaching and learning. Is there a way of living Now that could address the futility of frozen futurism while honoring the truth of human aspiration and dreaming? A way of living Now that makes possible a radical new acceptance of things, of one another, in the Now, without giving up on the possibility of continual regeneration through our mutual encounter? Perhaps most importantly, is there a way of living Now that can make possible a reclaiming of ownership of the local space—in the classroom, in the community, in the home—in such a way that the best aspects of globalization, especially its inauguration of new forms of cultural interfacing—are not sold out to the formulaic logic of The Market but held in the present as an invitation to consider the grounds of a truly shared future, one filled with that rich diversity of life already everywhere on display but which is now under deep threat from the forces of homogenization which the dominant, conservative interpretation of globalization preaches as inevitable?

Indeed, the first thing we may do as teachers is to make problematic this very belief in the inevitability of the present course, not just in the usual manner of protesting its influence but more creatively in affirming what the wisdom of our experience has taught us to be true of the work of teaching itself. We may begin by asking a simple question: "What makes teaching a livable experience?" and then elaborate the answer through positive and negative examples. Through the negative examples we can identify the various ways that teaching can no longer be called such, and teachers break down, finding themselves in circumstances that clearly are not livable, that is, that cannot sustain life in any meaningful sense. Positive examples in turn identify the ways through which the teaching life is worth living, or, better, life is discovered to be worth living through teaching.

Most notably, teaching cannot be a living if there is no truth told in its enactment, or, more accurately, if the classroom is not first and foremost a place of truth-seeking, truth-discovering, and truth-sharing. This is a difficult thing to say in a time when truth is usually claimed to be "relative" and a matter of "perspective," terms which are themselves relative and **perspectival** especially within the culture of science and rationalism which has been our legacy since the eighteenth century. But there may be a way of speaking about truth more hermeneutically such that in those moments when teachers and students find themselves together saying, "Wow, that was a good class!", they are saying they have discovered a truth for Now, something that provides sustenance for Now precisely because of how coming into truth has its own energizing power. When the veil of lies, duplicities, and happy delusions which I ordinarily hold up to shield myself from the glare of truth is suddenly or gradually or even only momentarily lifted, something happens to me. I feel enlivened, unblocked, ready for life in a new way, more prepared to be open to life as it meets me and I meet it.

What then are the main ways that truth, as truth-seeking, truth-discovering, and truth-sharing, gets blocked in teaching? The vivifying quality of teaching-as-truth-dwelling (as it may be called) gets blocked if teaching is understood primarily as an act of implementation, with the curriculum as a settled commodity emerging from a settled anterior logic headed for a settled posterior conclusion. Teaching itself is reduced in the process to being nothing but a form of procedural manipulation in which the being of the teacher requires no true encounter with the being of the student nor with curriculum as something open and interpretable, something that could show the way to a possible future.

In the spirit of re-localization, and a pedagogy of the Now, let me give an example from my own neighborhood and local school which seems to reveal some of these dynamics in a small but specific way. Billy is my seven-year-old neighbor, and he is having trouble in school, where he is in the second grade. His teacher says that he is inattentive, speaks out inappropriately in class, and disrupts classroom harmony by making jokes, passing rude notes about "bums," etc., and not completing assignments. At first, his behaviour made him a favorite amongst his peers and even amongst students in the upper grades. For a while, he was a kind of folk hero. Eventually however, teachers' perpetual criticism of his behaviour began to rub off on other students. They began to see him as a troublemaker, someone to avoid in order to avoid guilt by association. His sense of isolation and now confusion about identity has only exacerbated his alienation within the school community and made his attempts at attention-grabbing all the more exaggerated, thus, alienating him the more. Indeed, his teacher is upset most of all by this "attention-getting behaviour."

As in many schools today which suffer the pressures of political and financial loss of support, the academic staff at Billy's school has been gradually narrowing and hardening the terms of its pedagogical responsibilities. Tolerance for students' disruptive behavior is increasingly being defined in "zero" terms, with preferential attention being given to the more behaviorally compliant "academically challenged" students.

In Billy's case, the following scenario unfolded. The school principal and all teachers involved met to draw up a plan for solving Billy's behavioral problems. It had to do with Billy reporting to his teacher at regular intervals during the day with a checklist of behavioural outcomes that he himself would check. Any lapses would result in a "White Slip" being sent home to his parents, who, in turn, could "work with" Billy to ensure his compliance. The plan was then presented to the parents "for their approval...and to clear up any confusions or concerns."

The interesting points about this little story for our present purposes include not just its testifying to the new forms of tension within the public school under political and financial pressures, which themselves can be traced to globalization developments. Perhaps more important is the way Billy's problems were addressed by the school authorities. Throughout the process, there has been a singular absence of interest in dialogue between the teachers, Billy's parents, and Billy himself about what the source of Billy's problems might be in the Now. Instead, there has been a unilateral importation of externally derived behavior modification strategies designed to normalize Billy's behavior according to predetermined criteria for future results. The normalization acts to install in the present a future that has already been defined, such that Billy now, in fact, has no future in any way that might be derived from a closer, more realistic assessment of his present situation. So his teachers are also deprived of an opportunity of learning from him in the Now in two ways. They are deprived of learning not just about how their practices may, in fact, be serving to undermine a seven-year-old's future by, in these early years, naming him as a "problem" for which only they, as the alienated Other, hold the solution. The teachers also seem to be depriving themselves of an opportunity for their own practices to be creatively refracted through a lens of failure. As one of the teacher aides confided, after witnessing months of an evolving sadness in a child who once had a twinkle in his eye for everyone but whose twinkle eventually became interpreted in conspiratorial terms as far as the school was concerned: "Why doesn't anyone simply pay attention to Billy for himself? He's only seven years old!"

When it comes therefore to the question of how teaching must first and foremost involve the practice of truth-dwelling in the Now, the following three aspects can be suggested: personal truth; truth as shared; and finding truth as finding home. I will conclude this paper with a brief exploration of these themes in relation to teaching and globalization.

The Recovery of Personal Truth

Our contemporary cultural reluctance, in the Western tradition at least, to speak of truth in any way other than through the privileged, though problematic, terms of science deprives us of the opportunity for appreciating how the very difficulty of truth-dwelling is, in fact, part of its pedagogical genius. Truth calls me to human maturity all the while that I would play games to evade the challenge of its call, knowing that in responding I would have to give up the pretense of knowing its concreteness in advance of what confronts me in the Now. The ancient Greeks understood well the slippery character of truth when they assigned it a word with a double and contradictory meaning. *Alethea* indicates both "unconcealment" as well as "concealment." Just when I think I have discovered something to be true, unconcealed, revealed at last, for all time, something with which to secure myself into the future, suddenly it slips away into concealment, confusion, into the cloud of unknowing. Beware of the fulfillment of one's dreams, truth seems to say, because in the very fulfillment, what has been realized will begin to slip away, to turn into something one could easily regret. In the face of this unexpected result, I must search again, both to find as well as to lose, and somewhere in the space between finding and losing, I find myself for what I am, someone who also is both here and not-here, and find that the truth of my being is not for me to know completely for myself, as a self-enclosed, self-realizing entity. Rather who and what I am appears and disappears both to myself and to others as "I" meet the world and others in a movement of perpetual intercourse.

What does this mean, and how does it play out in the context of teaching? I may begin my teaching career with a very clear idea of how I want to be as a teacher, how I want to present myself. Perhaps I want to model myself after one of my own teachers whom I admired. Or perhaps my self-image is constructed out of a reaction against all the bad teachers I thought I had. Perhaps I am in love with the role of teacher, as I imagine it, relating to kids in a particular way, preparing and teaching lessons I think are interesting and that I think students will enjoy. These kinds of self-constructions can serve for a while, but eventually, left to themselves, they turn to dust. In North America, the statistics are that 50 percent of teachers leave teaching after five years (Statistics Canada 1999). This indicates, among other things, that there is a profound dissonance between what I think I want to find as a teacher and what confronts me in the teaching situation, such that I am faced with a particular challenge, which is the discovery that the true or final identity of the teacher does not rest with me and my self-understandings but that somehow it must be worked out in-relation-to that which confronts me in the Now. Later we will explore how this illustrates the way that truth is alive in a classroom only to the degree to which it is truth-as-shared. But first let us briefly explore this conception of personal truth and its essential fluidity in the context of globalization issues.

The recovery of a sense of personal truth is essential as a counter to the forces of de-localization and personal diminishment that are part of globalization's imprint, an imprint first established by Kant's splitting of reason from experience in 1759 (Schmidt 1996). This became a key to the foundation of scientific rationalism in the modern era, and in which both educational and economic theory find a common ancestry. In the contemporary context, however, teachers' recovery of personal truth must be in a new way, not in the old way of celebrating personal autonomy and self-interest because those qualities remain as the anchor myths of the very logic that is part of the problem for educators. No, personal truth for teachers must now emerge from a careful attending to the experience of truth as it arises in experience, which is precisely the experience of its openness in the tension between concealment and unconcealment. Personal truth arises out of the experience that I can never know it completely but only live within the thresholds of human possibility, defined by the limits of what I know and what I have yet-to-know, what I understand and what is yet to be revealed. So personal truth is not a commodifiable thing that can be applied through diligent training but a way of living in the world that is attuned to the way of the world's actual unfolding. It implies letting go as well as embracing; taking unto oneself responsibility for life with others even while accepting that life is always more than I can claim about it, and that living involves letting-live.

Loving the world, loving others, loving one's students suggests standing in a relation to them that does not determine in advance what they shall be for me but rather accepting them in such a way as to accept the limit of what we can be for each other and not just its imagined possibility. Only then can we arrive at truth as shared. Pedagogical care registers within a dynamic of both embracing and letting go, to find oneself again in a position of embracing and letting go. As both students and teacher we shepherd each other into maturity, each contributing our respective gifts in the Now but never under the presumption of "forever" being a predeterminable construct.

This kind of understanding has both epistemological as well as structural implications for teachers. Epistemologically it attends to the essential fluidity of knowledge well articulated in the circulating discourses of constructivism, enactivism, and ecology. Structurally, it means that schools and classrooms are not things that can be clung to indefinitely in any kind of fixed form. The technological revolution has changed forever the conditions of both knowledge production and the pedagogical requirements for an educated citizenry. Today, the challenge of globalization for teachers is not really about education per se but about the meaning of "public" in a world dominated by private enterprise, and about how there can be any sense of community if self-interest is the defining public logic.

The question then of how there might be community in a globalizing world that celebrates first and foremost the self-interested consumption of the Other, often, but not only "Elsewhere" (the exotic, the exploitable Other, the far away), is too great a challenge for schools and classrooms alone. In the modern period the public school and the public classroom were created not just to serve the public but also to "create a public," as Neil Postman (1996) has put it. Today, they cannot do it; they cannot carry the full social and cultural weight of globalization's demands. They can, however, stand in witness to the fact that if there is to be truth in the world, it is because it is in the nature of truth that it be shared. Schools and classrooms can be places of citizenship and community in a globalizing world that is rapidly losing any comprehension of either quality even while new understandings may be emerging. Can the school be a place where these new understandings can be cultivated and learned? I suspect so, but it will require of teachers a disturbingly profound personal and public relinquishment of those fictions through which they may be unwitting partners in the very logics that are killing them.

Truth-as-Shared

If the recovery of personal truth is a necessity in the age of globalization, so too is its possibility only recoverable in the context of relations. This may be the most important conceptual breakthrough of the postmodern revolution. Claim an Identity, whether racial, tribal, or gendered, and quickly it can be seen how it emerges through a web of relationships. Identity is never a stand-alone phenomenon; it is always constructed through the scaffolding of Others (for a good discussion of this, see Hershock 1994). The Rational Autonomous Self is a mythical being only, the haunted and haunting ghost of Western modernity that relentlessly conspires to rob the world of real human fellowship. In actuality, Self implies Other. If there is to be truth in the world, it will be only truth-as-shared, something between us. Such is the foundation for ethics in the age of globalization.

An understanding of truth-as-shared may not be unusually difficult in local situations where we rub shoulders with one another on a daily basis and continually have to face ourselves in each other. In the context of globalization issues, however, the work is more complicated, with deep implications for both curriculum and teaching. Most especially there has to be a retelling of the historical tales such that the Others who have been silenced under the triumphant narratives of empire are given their just due and embraced as necessarily contributive to any future worth sharing. Aboriginals, women, landless peasants in Africa and Latin America, exploited workers in the New Economy—all these have something to bring to the truth that is yet to be revealed, and the revelation can be expedited most urgently through a showing of the real poverties of those hiding behind the gates of their own self-enclosure.

The poverties arising through the logic of pure self-interest include:
- addiction to private fantasy (such as the construction of recluse culture through Internet addiction)
- paranoia (turning the Other into the enemy)
- false generosity (let me help you to be like me)
- condescension (your problems are because of your personal weakness)
- isolation (ultimately I don't care about you)
- arrogance (claiming power for oneself without justification)

These poverties are best addressed not simply through a blanket condemnation, a gesture which contraindicates the very qualities worthy of support. Instead, in laboring for the recovery of the alienated binary, for that which has been pushed aside in order for the present regime to claim itself, a new common space can be formed. Addiction to private fantasy is ameliorated by making public realms more hospitable. Paranoia dissolves through active friendship. Generosity is real if it is freely given without self-regard. Condescension is rendered impossible through empathy. The barricades of isolation fall to simple presence. The justifications of arrogance can be overcome by showing the face of a deeper, more comprehensive justice.

Unfortunately, the historical record suggests that such changes are not easily wrought and that their delay is an invitation to violence for those who refuse to wait for a better day. Indeed, as the world groans under the forces of globalization, forces that are as irrevocable as they are complex and confusing, increased social, cultural, and political violence in the years ahead may be the only sure thing. Its prospect, however, provides no exoneration from laboring in the Now for truth-as-shared.

Truth-as-Home

If truth-as-shared is difficult, its inspiration arises from the realization that the practice of truth is nothing less than the practice of finding oneself at home in the world. This is not an exhortation to romantic notions of family values or home as idyll. Instead it is an appeal to the kind of understanding expressed by the sage Hui Neng: "The world could not be made more perfect." This is a comment on the perfect adequacy of the world with respect to the human prospect of finding itself at home in it; indirectly, it raises the question of why it is our sense of the world's imperfections that seems to dominate our inclinations. The labor of finding truth-as-home is ultimately the labor of overcoming our primal sense of estrangement from the world. This is at once a religious task (<L *religere,* to tie together again), which in the age of globalization means addressing the specifically religious roots of contemporary economic theory, as well as a pedagogical one, in the agogical sense of taking responsibility for guiding others (<L *agogos,* guide). Teachers therefore have a twofold responsibility: 1) to heal their own estrangements as the necessary qualification for 2) leading others home.

The sense of human estrangement from the world takes many different forms, just as the work of reconciliation must have its own specific addresses. There are political estrangements, familial, tribal, sectarian, and so forth, but they find their genesis in the pre-reflective predisposition to see the other as that which constrains the projections of the Ego and which turns the

Other into something that must be overcome to protect the Ego's self-constructed identity. Or, efforts must be made to turn the Other into a mirror of one's own identity as a way of securing oneself in the world. The kind of reconciliation that is being suggested here arises from an appreciation that the differences between us do not need to be arbitrated or overcome because they are reflective of the very condition by which any identity might be possible in the first place. That is to say, our differences are reflective of our common condition in the world, the acceptance of which is the necessary prefigurement to a world not at war with itself, because there is nothing to fight against, only a deeper truth to be shown.

In the pedagogical situation the discovery of truth as learning to be at home in the world is best understood through the practice of discipline, a word which in the contemporary context has taken on a pejorative meaning but in actuality simply refers to the act of following a task to its true end, a kind of obedience to the call of truth as it speaks out to me from the task at hand. When I respond in a way true to the thing itself, I find my estrangement from it slowly melts away, such that I become one with it, and it with me, and something new is brought into the world from out of us both. This is the experience to which true art bears witness; the thing produced transcends both the identity of the artist and the original material from which it is made. It is a testimony to the fruit of reconciliation between self and other, self and world. The act of composition brings a new composure, if one can follow the discipline of it. In the context of globalization discourses, the discipline of the new pedagogy will require this kind of attention to "the thing itself," that is, to the requirement that the value of learning something cannot be attenuated by facile alliance to something other than itself, such as commercial venturing or the seduction of power. Learning truth-as-home means dwelling in the requirements that the world tells me are necessary for living creatively in it and refusing any cheaper way.

Conclusion

This chapter began with an exploration of how the current construction of globalization phenomena, in their various complexities, came about. Generally they can be seen as an extension of the Western European development of empire, now permutated with the identities and actions of others such that the older logics cannot contain or guide a sustainable way into the future. This situation poses a special challenge for teachers who are caught between the logics of the old order and the requirements of the new. It is contestation over what those requirements of the new might be that is defining not just the tensions within teachers' lives but also the lives of ordinary citizens.

The assumption here has been that the central logic of contemporary globalization, i.e., market logic, is not an adequate one for ensuring a future that is truly open and capable of sustaining human fellowship in any decent sense. It is a logic that requires a profound deconstruction, a task made all the more difficult for it being so deeply embedded in a religious eschatology that freezes a particular understanding of the future such that people are prevented from taking up an examination of their own lives and conditions from within their own experience in the Now. The chapter attempts to examine the requirements for a renewed understanding of what it means to live Now, as an act of human healing, and as a prospect for a world that is not afraid of itself.

References

"Asian economies can be different" (2000). *Asian Times 3* (19): 4.
Barlow, M., and H-J. Robertson (1994). *Class warfare: The assault on Canada's schools.* Toronto: Key Porter.
CAUT Bulletin (1999). *World Bank takes aim at Higher Education.*
Campbell, D. (1992). *Writing security: United Nations foreign policy and the politics of identity.* Minneapolis, MN: University of Minnesota Press.
Carnoy, M. (1974). *Education as cultural imperialism.* New York: Longmans.
Clarke, T. (1997). *Silent coup: Confronting the big business takeover of Canada.* Toronto: James Lorimer.
Coombs, P. (1985). *The world crisis in education.* New York: Oxford University Press.
Eze, E. (Ed.) (1997). *Race and the enlightenment.* Cambridge, MA: Blackwell.
Fischer, M. (1992). Is Islam the odd-civilization out? *New Perspectives Quarterly 9* (3): 55.
Franklin, U. (1999). A comment made during a public address at the conference Universities in the Public Interest sponsored by the Canadian Association of University Teachers, Ottawa, Ontario, October 1999.
Fukuyama, F. (1993). *The end of history and the last man.* New York: Avon.
Gray, J. (1999). *False dawn: The delusions of global capitalism.* London: Granta.
Greider, W. (1997). *One world, ready or not: The manic logic of global capitalism.* New York: Touchstone.
Held, D., Goldblatt, D. McGrew, A., and Perraton, J. (1997). The globalization of economic activity. *New Political Economy.* July 2 (2): 258.
Hershock, P. (1994). Person as narration: The dissolution of "self" and "other" in Ch'an Buddhism. *Philosophy East and West 44* (4): 691.
Hirst, P., and Thompson, G. (1996). *Globalization in question: The international economy and the possibilities of governance.* Cambridge, UK: Polity.
Loy, D. (2000). The spiritual origins of the West: A lack perspective. *International Philoso-*

phical Quarterly. June *40* (2): 28–31.

Marty, M., and Appleby, S. (Eds.) (1994). *Fundamentalisms observed.* Chicago: University of Chicago.

McClintock, A. (1994). The angel of progress: Pitfalls of the term "post-colonialism." In *Colonial discourse and post-colonial theory,* page 292. Edited by P. Williams and L. Chrisman. Minneapolis, MN: University of Minnesota Press.

Meighan, R. (1981). *A sociology of educating.* New York: Holt, Rinehart and Winston.

Norberg-Hodge, H. (1993). *Ancient futures: Learning from Ladakh.* San Francisco: Sierra Club.

Neng, Hui (1997). *The sixth patriarch's dharma jewel platform (8th century C.E.) with commentary by Tripitaka Master Hua* (translated from the Chinese by the Buddhist Text Translation Society). 2nd edition. San Francisco: Sino-American Buddhist Association.

Park, O. (1996). *An invitation to dialogue between East and West.* New York: Peter Lang.

Postman, N. (1996). *The "end" of public education.* An address to the Canadian Teachers Federation, Montreal, Quebec, 21 May.

Rifkin, J. (1996). *The end of work: The decline of the global labor force and the dawn of the post-market era.* New York: Putnam.

Robertson, H-J. (1998). *No more teachers, no more books: The commercialization of Canada's schools.* Toronto: McClelland and Stewart.

Sassen, S. (1998). *Globalization and its discontents: Essays on the new mobility of people and money.* New York: New Press.

Schmidt, J. (Ed.) (1996). *What is enlightenment?: Eighteenth-century answers to twentieth-century questions.* London: Cambridge University Press.

Spring, J. (1998). *Education and the rise of the global economy.* Mahwah, NJ: Lawrence Erlbaum.

Statistics Canada. (1999). New business: A report. Ottawa: Government of Canada.

Tawney, R.H. (1938). *Religion and the rise of capitalism.* Harmondsworth: Penguin (original work published 1926).

Weber, M. (1962). *The protestant ethic and the spirit of capitalism.* New York: Scribners (original work published 1920).

CHAPTER SIXTEEN

Creation of Participatory Public Spaces
Judith J. Slater • United States

I hear the ruin of all space, shattered glass and toppling masonry, and time one livid final flame. What's left us then? (James Joyce 1934: 25)

Construction and Limitations of the Public Space

The public space is like a marble statue: lustrous, smooth, impenetrable, expensive (Taussig 1997: 165), and like faith: stately and serene in its final execution, but a birth as violent and powerful as it is chiseled, cool, and elevated to a position above that of common man. Spaces exist in people's heads, containing the form and practice of the theory of social life within them. There are no limits to this mental space, except those that are set by the occupants. Every public space needs an audience filled with people to legitimize the activities that go on as a public performance. People come to occupy each of the spaces through conditions of participation.

What constitutes the public space, and how is it distinguished from the private space? Lefebvre (1997), a French Marxist theorist who linked the production of space to the rise of capitalism, describes the public social space as an invented, indefinite space. The social space was created as a social product, a political positioning of the players who grabbed the arena as the observers watched and waited, hoping that they would be taken care of and be heard. It has turned into a public space of domination and control. Producers of space act in ways consistent with the representation, while users passively experience what is provided for them. They have had no part in the making, only in the using or observing, but they think they have contributed.

This is manipulation, and it occurs when the observer is lost in the speech of the actor on the stage and when the user is taught to follow and obey the habitus blindly. They ignore the possible. They are blinded by the dazzle. This is ignorance. The silent user allows this to happen. They don't protest since they are not enlightened as to their manipulation. They exist in what Greene (1995) calls the opaqueness of life, which does not let them see clearly how they are separate from the stage actors. The silent users wear the mask of a passive mute, their fate played out in the public space. Taking the stage are the vocal, political perpetuators of the acceptable speech that is believed or not. They are the spokespersons for the bureaucracy.

The creation of public space is a process that does not reflect the public community but is a transformed and surreal representation of their wants, needs, and desires. Space emerges from its creation consecrated (Bourdieu 1993). The space grows and develops, becoming more complex as it sustains itself with surrounding structures. Different social spaces penetrate each other, impose themselves on each other, and support each other's existence. School bureaucracies help ignorance perpetuate all sorts of structures that occupy spaces around it, thus the stronger the surrounding structures, the more difficult it is to change practices within. There are supporting visible boundaries of spaces in education, such as the diploma, titles, structure, order, etc., which create restrictions and imbedded social relationships that solidify the public space of schools. The private space has little ability to permeate the walls of defense of public space which provide the foundation for the perpetuation of its social practices.

Each space has status and the subjects within have status. That status is conveyed by those who hold the space and those who aspire to enter. Communities are distinguished by the style in which they are imagined, not by their genuineness (Anderson 1991). Obviously, the public space has more status than the private space. Those who dominate promulgate their ideas on to the private space. This creates great class distinctions. The established culture of the public space has a specific reference point as it supports its own brand of truth and exploits those events which are congruent. What occurs is a "banal consensus" to the space by the public, for who out there takes issue with the truth? It takes an audience for the person to remain on the stage. Once the audience becomes disillusioned with the status of the speaker, his/her use of the public space as a forum for dissemination of his ideas is in jeopardy. The onus is on the holders of the public space to make the audience believe. They can do this truthfully, building up structures that support the common good, or they can do this by advancing their own hidden agenda of power and position. The guardians of the stage cut off the voice of the audience, and they limit their participation. The speaker exists on a level above that is untouchable. He remains there with the consent of the audience and is protected by his peers since his exposure could be theirs. There are so many others who rise to the stage too quickly, who provide a quick fix to a public that is impatient with problems of right and wrong. They flock to those who offer quick solutions to problems that do not address their underlying causes. Public speech about poverty does not meliorate the fact of living. Public speech about literacy does little to teach the adult and child how to sound out the words. Public speech about equity and vouchers does not deliver competitive programs that level playing fields with elite schools. The public must be schooled so that they understand how to transform that public space into one that hears their voice and lets them participate fully in the public discourse. That is what the rest of this chapter addresses. The public needs to constantly challenge the public space wielders of power to make sure that their intentions are for the community rather than of self-serving interests. Perhaps the greatest legacy of the hippy age is this prescription from Timothy Leary: "Question authority and think for yourself."

What goes on in the public space and the discourse within that space cannot give rise to a knowledge of the space itself. This is a harder task than it appears. The stage is a hegemony of class, a dictatorship held over the community, the culture, and the particular audience. It exercises power over ideas and institutions, practices ingrained in the production of the public space, and over the ability of the audience to know it for what it is. It is a knowledge that serves the power of those who hold the public space as their own, and this must be opened to others if barriers to participation are removed. Knowledge should be transformed into a forum that is operational and instrumental to the resolution of problems of concern to the community audience. This does not always occur. The hegemony uses knowledge and counts on the limited knowledge of the public to keep them on the periphery of participation. The receiver remains passive to the use of the public space, which allows those who hold the stage to remain. The semiotic or personal interpretation of the social space is reduced to a message that is read literally by the observers.

The public space consolidates society since it flattens cultural and social participation as it tries to end conflicts and contradictions about itself. It subverts the will of the audience and transforms them through a co-optation of the mind space. The public space is sold as a given, preached to the people as the law of operation within a society, and it is accepted as a way of life. There is a silent acquiescence of practice as the masses sit in the audience and watch and listen but do not speak. There is little that is transparent to them about the workings of the public space. The codes of action are in place, not waiting to be created. There is little talk about those things that could open the spaces further. The public accepts social practices performed in that public space; they accept political power and restrictions, they enshrine the everyday practice of speaking up and about the issues, and they give themselves over to the stage actors who hold the spotlight on themselves. Lefebvre (1997) intimates that to advance the common good, the space must be read and also constructed and reconstructed by the audience, not just those who hold the power. Each space is interpreted by individuals and by how they have been taught by the prevailing habitus to see and hear within that space. For praxis to occur the contradictions of varied spaces and of the individual moving through them need to be seamlessly experienced and understood. Persons should not have to decipher the rules of each space as they come to them, over and over again. There should be some binding understandings that permeate all public spaces so that the observers recognize the potential to involve themselves in meaningful ways within each while keeping their core of beliefs and enacted positions intact as confirmation of their worldview. When common worldviews come together, the public space becomes transformed by the actions and collective understanding of the public.

Thus, spaces harbor political uses of knowledge that advance a constructed truth. The public space excludes the observer's ideology unless they agree. It includes only specific positions that are indistinguishable from the knowledge it presents as truth. Egalitarian public spaces can be responsive to the public which they say they serve. Spaces can also simulate a future possible state as the actors on the stage represent a fantasy of what reality could be. But, the public space is a theater of the absurd, since it may have no basis in the reality of the observers. The community sits passively as audience to the public space, their participation eroded and deferred to those in control—to politicians and professional bureaucrats, to knowledge makers and scientists who tender their own versions of truth. By not being clearly defined, the public space creates a closed opportunity for public participation. It does this to solidify its own existence, to remain closed and mysterious to the public for which the space was designed in the first place. And how does the public space protect itself from intrusion? Violence is used to keep people away from the stage, a violence to the minds of the public, the unschooled, which keeps them thinking about only what is preached. It allows no one to penetrate who does not proclaim and speak the same words. The public space protects itself from erosion by denying free community participatory access. It is all right to observe but not to question. The public space and the knowledge represented seek to bring all into the fold. This limits opposition. The enactment of correct, compliant knowledge tries to reverse the private space ideas of the audience, defragmentizing them and integrating them through powerful knowledge. This is very difficult. It is hard for our pulpit holders to keep the flock with them through the use of speeches. It is harder still to bridge the gap between the stage and the audience and to incorporate a more global perspective, one that more truly represents the observer's perception, which can be at odds with the dominant ideology of the exalted ones. The execution of such a plan would require a continuing disjuncture between the stage and the audience, one that presented a very compelling need of the observers and of the larger community to, one by one, reform and motivate a change in orientation for the public space. It takes, perhaps, money, a commercial exchange of knowledge, and actors in a drama who are willing to step forward and assert themselves and establish an audience. It also requires an open system, a system freed from bureaucratic concerns of control and perpetuation of the structure and placement of props on the stage. It requires open communication about what is said on that stage and its relevance to the public. It requires opening minds to possibilities beyond the concrete reality presented to them.

Given that the use of space is determined and maintained in a way that is supported by those who stage and govern the organization rather than the observer, what is required for full participation are critical signs that the space no longer serves the purpose of the audience. Most often, however, the followers line up behind the leader, reproducing the status quo along with the limitations of opportunities for action within that space. As long as the transactions between stage holder and audience are satisfactory, there is little opportunity for a transformation to occur. Astute observers must look for the falsity of the current rhetoric in order to create a wearing away of the barriers and gain entrée to full participation in the evolution of that space.

Schools transmit the social space; they consecrate certain actions over others that are part of the transmission of the habitus of the culture that prepares students for adulthood. This is well established in the history of schooling in America. What schools also consecrate is obedience to authority, the scientific proof of test scores and standards, and legally imposed attempts at equality to produce an equitable playing field on which the public can participate and compete. The public, who is the audience for these consecrations, accepts them without question. They have faith in the predictions of success and failure, and they bend to the explanations given by the speaker on the stage that the solution to the crises lie in this voucher, that charter, this or that new program, or worse, a return to the tried and true solutions of the past. The habitus is cemented by the fear and doubt in their own private ability to solve the problems of a more just, democratic community of caring through means other than those which are preached on the stage. Behaviors of educators are conforming to that which is promulgated by the stage actors. Participation is limited as knowledge is secreted and restricted to that which is spoken. Learned societal expectations are reproduced and expounded in the public space (Lefebvre 1997: 36). This is supported by the imagery and symbols, the myths and fears that hold them impassive to the will of the public space.

There is a private space opportunity to participate, but it is concealed from the audience through opacity. There is only the illusion of transparency (Lefebvre 1997: 27). The design of schools creates a mode of thought and serves as a mediator between the stage and the audience, between the thought and the activities that are performed on the stage. Anything hidden or dissimilar is a danger to the status quo; therefore, these dangers must be eliminated as a threat to those in power. An understanding of the space can facilitate a transparency in the operations of the producer. Once the opaqueness of the public space is made clear, the public can come to know the mysteries of its operation and forge an inroad to make it more community-sensitive and participative. This requires the overcoming of the cemented written words which codify, like the Bible, action within the space. The written rules overshadow the spoken word, and the latter is the voice of the people. Speech and voice provide a clarity of communication that creates the opportunity for the unschooled to participate. The illusion of transparency is a trap, though. Revolutions must be preceded by change in people, and there must be the desire and recognition of the public to participate so that they do not just continue to repeat the words of the actor on the stage. The public must create the transparency, obliterate the opacity of naturalized structure and operation, and advance the common good of the community by being aware of the possibilities for personal and collective action.

Erosion and Boundary Breaking of the Public Space

The literature on space uses terms such as border, map, location, and place, all geographic metaphors to convey location and spatial and temporal dimensions of issues. These terms provide coherence and order to something that is elusive and evasive, something hard to concretize. In any case, these terms provide form to the notion that it is the erosion of the boundaries which permits movement between the public and private arena which can cause space to be redefined. The landscape changes and new identities are formed (Mitchell 1994). Individuals form their identity around each established landscape. Those persons at odds with the landscape are at odds with the accepted method of discourse and understanding of the public stage. Privately held landscapes are unreadable unless they become a medium of exchange, become the real expression of value and meaning for communication between and among people. The limitations of space engender the production of perceptions, expressions, and actions that are historically and socially situated which limit freedom of the observer to participate. Perceptions which create new visions, future orientations, new discourse, and communitarian possibilities provide what Harvey (1990: 220–221) calls "dreamscapes of what is possible."

Schutz (1999) describes the conditions which would begin to open spaces and make them transparent. These open spaces can provide an opportunity to engage in collective action and public dialogue. This space requires active engagement from each person, or, as Arendt (1958) calls it, a new beginning, a natality, the unique voice potential which is an embodiment of our social world. This commodification, as Greene (1995) describes, is not a conscious representation in either student or teacher, but it exists outside of the awareness of the ritualistic behaviors that compel everyday actions. These new societal expectations are the public roles that erosion causes to be redefined and overcome as restrictions to individual and common good actions. The freedom created from the erosion of the rigidity of the public space comes from collaboration with others. Only with others is the individual free to choose. Only with others is there the opportunity for the possibility of choice. The coming together in public participation places the individual in a responsive community where freedom of action is possible. There is risk involved and there must be a feel for the game, a conscious awareness of how the rules are played and how to work them for the benefit of the community. Action requires the interpretation of the public space as a potential. When individuals enter the stage, when they participate in a common project with others, they become themselves rather than someone defined by the system. Arendt (Schutz 1999: 81) defines self as the position a person takes concerning a common theme recognized by others. This is similar to Buber's (1970) I-Thou relationships, where the person positions herself in relation to the public space. Greene suggests that the public space actualizes persons through the struggle of discovering that persons have both the ability to act and the choice to comply, or to invent for themselves and with others that which could be. This requires the identification of the public space obstacles and boundaries that limit freedom of participation and the identification of opportunities for action. The boundaries must be exposed through the coming together of diverse forces of alienated groups who share their bits of knowledge with each other and put together a whole picture of the public space as it is enacted to facilitate a vision of a public space as it could be (Sibley 1995). Then there comes a positioning of people in the public space into roles that are not circumscribed by class and status but rather by common ends and common goals.

Examples abound of lost opportunities because parents, community people, students, and teachers are left out of the public space of schools. That is not to mean that they are not consulted, rubber-stamping their attendance as audience participators in the process of accrediting and documenting that they were there, in person, while decisions were made for them by those who held power and the command of the public space. But, they were spectators to the decisions rather than equal participants in the creation of the content.

Euchner (1996) describes the underlying dynamics that generate transformational change, the civic ethos that precipitates activist reform movements which are part of the evolutionary history in this country. Local public spaces can provide such a forum where audiences can come together over issues and experience a shared participation and shared effort toward action. But the public space also engenders unpredictableness with respect to the assertion of a new voice or an attempt to enter the stage. Is this due to the freedom itself or the fear of freedom associated with the participation of the audience? Community building must come first, because the human condition that Arendt (1958) talks about is dependent upon the ability to trust others. The human condition does not naturally engender the creation of a collective public space that is more all-encompassing and tolerant of diversity and respect for other's points of view. The wall of the public space needs to be opened to dialogue from all, not just used as a pulpit to disseminate the views of those who have taken over the stage. The structure itself has lessened the ability to make the stage more open, and it must be transformed through a restructuring from opacity of operation to a transparency for potential action.

Freedom, Greene (1995) says, is understanding the ambiguities, and the charlatans and false g-ds need to be purposefully exposed. The audience must challenge the stage actors. The audience must name the structures which block the way, and purposefully dismantle them so that the space is more inclusive. Power normalizes (Schutz 1999: 83), and the common space, the public space, does not cause freedom. It causes dissemination of the views of those who occupy the public stage. The public space should constantly be challenged by the observers. It is a cultural project in the making and must constantly be renewed. Teachers, students, parents, and university researchers become complacent when they are merely observers. They become rigid in their thinking about the space and about the issues, and the unique response becomes the outlier. There is repetition, sameness of the response to the play on the stage, to the space as it duplicates what is rather than what could be. This condition leads either to splinter groups forming their own space and challenging the dominant one, or the reverse, mass identities where the individual voice is not heard. Action is warranted and through awareness of erosion by private space observers, there is a collective chance for action. They can work together and create new public spaces when they no longer serve the public well. It is hard to get past the thinking of the past. The current habitus fills up the time and the space allows this to happen. Sometimes there are hollow interactions, tokens, and meaningless concessions to the private complaints of the public space. That is not sufficient. The community must be aware of the possibilities for its own advancement through the active opening up of the public spaces so that they are responsive to change.

Creation of a New Public Space

What does it mean to revive a community, to bring the people out of the shadows of the unlit audience and provide them with an avenue to participate in the performance on the stage? Etzioni (1999) has written extensively about community and the spirit of communitarianism that would provide a milieu in which the voice of the public could be heard. Recently he presented the limitations to public participation created through the very structures and artifacts and their concomitant moral and legal questions that have been established as a result of pursuing and serving the common good. These, Etzioni premises, have violated privacy as each instance limits the public's right to private reflection and decision making. While focusing on the common good of public safety and public health, he presents the position that in deference to privacy, the common good is being neglected. There needs to be a balance, he says, between the public and private positions, one that privileges neither over the other. Balance between individual rights and the common good is the problem of good rulers, policy makers, and those who hold the rapt attention of the audience. Without taking into consideration the public wants and desires and balancing this with the public perception of use of the public space, there is autocracy of thought and action that is not translated into sustainable and responsive community. "Societies typically cannot make perfect choices, because often they must sacrifice some measure of one good for the sake of another" (Etzioni 1999: 11). That is fine; if those in power balance their position with that of the public, there is equity in the process, and everyone's voice has an opportunity to be heard. Communitarians seek to balance individual rights with social responsibilities, individuality with community. But sometimes the communities and those in power are misleading.

How can a new humanely fabricated public space be created? Arendt (Schutz 1999) suggests that public spaces be small enough to allow the individual to contribute and be recognized by others in the space. Therefore, school reform of the public space should focus on individual schools or communities of feeder patterns of schools that can form their own identity and methods of problem posing and solution finding. These groups should also attend to what Greene (Schutz 1999) describes as the unplanned and contingent details of production to make them their own so that they can be interpreted in accordance with participants' own perceptions of space and time. Individuals can then be schooled and make decisions for themselves about their own choices and the way to live and interact in their life. Public action must mediate between individual voice and the public mission (78). The public mission is the creation of a common good cultural core that synthesizes society so that it can influence whatever public space of which it chooses to be audience. This is the choice we exercise privately in clubs or in religious affiliations which are culturally unified and represent a coherent position that forms the collective consciousness of participation. True participation is the goal for schools participation of the teachers, parents, students, and community.

Where are the barriers and how can they be lifted so that participation is more open? Students represent an opportunity as they acculturate into the social space. They are a potential for democratic participation (Schutz 1999); therefore, they threaten the stability of the public space and its agenda. Restriction of student participation is the norm in schools. Students learn the rules, and the rules restrict their opportunity to participate in the day-to-day operations of the school, especially in their opportunity to affect that structure in any meaningful way. They suffer a school curriculum with subject matter insulated from each other subject, delivered in closed, ritualistic, boundaried environments with limited input from students and teachers (Sibley 1995). The system is not tolerant of new ideas, and knowledge is suppressed or ignored which does not fit into the organizational goals. Teachers are isolated from each other and do not participate in the curricular decision making. Information generation from the university is alienated and isolated from the public space of school reform and policy making. Parents are told what knowledge is most valued, and this perpetuates the public space and the control of those in power.

Dewey's vision of embryonic community life is long past, as egalitarian opportunities are severely limited. Teachers can play a role in changing this. They can instruct children about the potential of the stage so that they are future oriented. Berger (1977: 7) states that "Seeing comes before words. The child looks and recognizes before it can speak." Seeing establishes the child's place in the public and private space. The man-made spaces are driven by the rules of a mystified past invented by a privileged minority to justify the roles that are taught in the schools and institutions that perpetuate and maintain the status quo. Children learn assumptions about culture, positions of truth, and appropriate acceptable behavior in the public space. But there is power in the moment for children who are taught to recognize that choice is the freedom of participation in the community. Students have no narratives to form a public space that meets their needs. Students are subservient above all groups to the dominant discourse unless teachers present them with possibilities. Instead, school practices keep them in the dark about the possibilities for action and active voices. So the audience is taught to be passive from an early age, and only those who conform have an opportunity to become the elite on the stage.

Traditions for students can be open to new ideas and new spaces. These spaces would celebrate participation, blur the boundaries of curriculum content, and provide opportunities for self-government (Sibley 1995). Habitus can be overcome for students by giving them the skills for communal action and public praxis. Greene (Schutz 1999) suggests that civic learning can provide the skills and desire to form public spaces. Civic learning includes health issues, social awareness issues, drugs, alcohol, political awareness, and technology issues. The teacher must collaborate in the process of liberation from the forces that deny an open public arena by providing students with the necessary abilities, capabilities, beliefs, and values to reflect on who they are in relationship to the collective group. The boundaries between the public stage and the roles and relationships which are tolerated can be made transparent and ready for action when the teacher engenders in students the situationally appropriate opportunities for problem-solving and action on issues that concern their current and future participation in the community.

There are at least four elements needed to create responsive public spaces. The elements are leadership, discourse, nurturance of the public, and imagination. There needs to be leadership that represents not just the best interests of the public but morally understands the elixir of leadership and how easily the vision of those in power strays from that of the followers. Leadership must be inclusive of the private space position. An example of such a shift in perspective is seen in the leader in Hermann Hesse's novel *Magister Ludi* (1949/1996) Armed with the certainty of truth, such as the unquestioning of the Bead Game of Life, rebellion by those who are merely spectators of the game is out of the realm of possibility. In the Hesse story, a community of scholars studies the universal language of the intellect; knowledge is reduced to a single principle, but there is doubt that the community which guards and plays the Bead Game may not satisfy the individual who is chosen to lead. It is the mingling with the common man, the discourse with him, and the contact with him, that is really fulfilling to the intellectual. Thus, it is the intellectual's growth and the application of this knowledge that rise above the scientific truth and the formulas of life. It is humanity that holds the true test of ideas; it is the collective understanding that grows from a changing future—a future of participation and responsiveness to the people. It only takes one person armed with imagination to see beyond the rules and restrictions to escape the confines of the functional established community.

Second, a new discourse must be created, one that is participative and future oriented. That future is one where the public discourse is at the heart of participatory decision making. Then the problems that are most relevant to the people can be mediated through authentic clarification of the issues. Public questions must be raised as to the morality of the greater group vs. the individual voice. Voice needs an audience, and the public space should be recreated so that it engenders authentic dialogue concerning relevant issues. It must raise the issues in public forums concerning the amelioration of the objectiveness of the world and the consumerism of desires that suppress the voices of the individual.

Third, the community must be nurtured actively by the public space actors. It must nurture what Arendt calls the "in between," the renewal of the common world. Dewey refers to the need for a committed public community. The community of voices must replace the inbreeding of ideas and paternalism of opportunities. It must end the dominion and supremacy over the weak, the children, the disempowered, and the disengaged so that there is opportunity for them to participate. Creation of voice is not merely the empowerment of words. An unspoken general sensitivity to needs is required, an outlet and a platform for an exchange of ideas and the reformation of ideals must exist. This requires the understanding of the conditions of the communities of the past that were responsive to the individual voice. This understanding must be carried by new generations so that the community of the future is not stifled or embarrassed. (I went to see the movie *Beloved*. The young adults and teens in the audience laughed in embarrassment at the mores, rituals, and ethical fabric of understanding represented as the past that once held that community together.) Replacing that fabric of support are a host of mandated legal remedies that give individuals redress for opportunity but do little to cement a cohesive network of community access to the public space.

Fourth, there must be a restoration of imagination of possibilities, of "social imagination: the capacity to invent visions of what should be and what might be in our deficient society, on the streets where we live, in our schools" (Greene 1995: 5). This rebirth of community includes a rebirth of serenity, of images and actions that create my worldview, my understanding, which I try to live and communicate to others. It requires an iconoclasm of the consecrated tokens of behavior that are followed mindlessly (Bourdieu 1993; Langer 1997). It requires that the public understand the meaning of emerging discourse that is new and future oriented. It requires soul, vision, and actions that are, as Freire (1970) would say, authentic. It requires spectacles that merge actor and audience. How can people become actors when they traditionally are relegated to the role of spectators? They have neither the skills nor the dispositions to perform in the public space. The spectators become relegated to their role, to the habitus of inaction and passive acceptance, to limited participation. People become alienated or coerced—both dangerous conditions if there is to be action and change. The public must have nurtured a desire for a public space that is free of the spectator role played by the public in the educative discourse which has been removed from authentic participation. The current trends of innovation and policy are removed from participative discourse. Dialogue needs to be opened so that authentic public discourse becomes part of the arena, and there is opportunity to recreate the public space. But, if we can train the imagination—if the dialogue becomes educative, then the public can look outward from the audience and imagine diversion and distraction from the consecrated actions that relegate them to inaction. This discourse should be ongoing about methods creating ways of seeing that are authentic so that they are not ready-made by others. There must be a public dialogue about change, about the public space itself, and how each person can contribute to the continuous evolution of a better society.

Changes in life require a change in society. Both require a public space. There is a need to commandeer social space and physical space and reform them into a mental space that prepares the citizen for action. Then the public space will respond to private needs. Ayers (1998) suggests the creation of public spaces through the building of movements for people to come together, permitting living in the real world and looking for allies, attending to the interests of the poor and disenfranchised for whom the system is not working, being committed to small changes that can lead to larger structural change, being willing to rethink and be open to new narratives for education and for society. Michelle Fine (1998) talks about creating linkages between ripples of change, threads that connect one small innovation to another, so that there is finally the possibility of a redefinition of public discourse, and the spectator has a chance to become an actor.

The effect of breaching and coming to understand the public space is that it can unleash desire, and with true transparency, can encourage people to surge forth and lay claim to the field. Disillusionment leaves an empty space, one filled with incomprehensible words, words devoid of individual and community reflection, a position homogenized, rationalized, and constraining, and concurrently dislocated from the audience. This is a need for the reforming of the public space for boundaries between the public space and the private space to disappear. This is the opportunity for the changing of the guard, for the people, programs, initiatives, standards, and testing to be reflected upon and possibilities to emerge that embody a fabric of interconnectedness within the educational space. The educational space is a public space that needs to be for the common good. This cannot occur without participation by the audience. The rejection of other people's g-ds always entails the adoption of new spaces and systems of measurement (Lefebvre 1997). This must be questioned for authenticity as education is questioned by government and testing-companies who hold power over the student's future.

The new space must also be a global space responsive to the environment which gives it a reason to be. We must "structure our society to sustain community" (Fain 1999), otherwise we face a tyranny of democracy, where selected persons speak for us but do not remain true to the needs of the community and the common good. The process of the breaking-up of a public space when it no longer serves the purpose for which it was created leaves a void that can cause a contradiction of the space as more than one view of reality vies for possession of the stage. Opposition creates a value for the space and its use. It is the success of social criticism that it creates what Greene (1995: 61) refers to as an "effort to overcome false consciousness by rejecting an absolute and static view of reality and its resulting subject-object separation." The new space is a transformation of the worldview. The new space faces questions of value, worth, and usefulness to the community. The creation of an alternative space can create an alternative society, which should strive to produce and maintain a transparency so that the public remains involved in the evolution of the public space. The underpinning of common good will permeate future performances and keep them open to dialogue and evolution as everyone dances round, hands united, ready at every moment to change direction together.

Finally, there are two choices. One is to remain an observer, like Vladimir in *Waiting for Godot,* who says:

> Let us not waste our time in idle discourse! Let us do something, while we have the chance! It is not every day that we are needed. Not indeed that we personally are needed. Others would meet the case equally well, if not better. To all mankind they were addressed, those cries for help still ringing in our ears! But at this place, at this moment of time, all mankind is us, whether we like it or not. Let us make the most of it, before it is too late! Let us represent worthily for once the foul brood to which a cruel fate consigned us! What do you say? It is true that when with folded arms we weigh the pros and cons we are no less a credit to our species. The tiger bounds to the help of his congeners without the least reflection, or else he slinks away into the depths of the thickets. But that is not the question. What are we doing here, that is the question. And we are blessed in this, that we happen to know the answer, Yes, in

this immense confusion one thing alone is clear. We are waiting for Godot to come. (Beckett 1954: 51–2)

Or, we can imagine what could be, as Annie Dillard (1982) says in *Teaching a Stone to Talk*:

> We teach our children one thing only, as we were taught: to wake up. We teach our children to look alive there, to join by words and activities the life of human culture on the planet's crust. As adults we are almost all adept at waking up. We have so mastered the transition we have forgotten we ever learned it. Yet it is a transition we make a hundred times a day, as, like so many less will-less dolphins, we plunge and surface, lapse and emerge. We live half our waking lives and all of our sleeping lives in some private, useless, and insensible waters we never mention or recall. Useless, I say. Valueless, I might add—until someone hauls their wealth up to the surface and into the wide-awake city, in a form that people can use. (22–23)

References

Anderson, B. (1991). *Imagined communities: Reflections on the origin and spread of nationalism.* London: Verso.

Arendt, H. (1958). *The human condition.* Chicago: The University of Chicago Press.

Ayers, W. (1998). Personal communication, during open forum (sponsored by Maxine Greene). Center for the Imagination. December, Teachers College. New York.

Beckett, S. (1954). *Waiting for Godot.* New York: Grove.

Berger, J. (1977). *Ways of seeing.* London: Penguin.

Bourdieu, P. (1993). *The field of cultural production.* New York: Columbia University Press.

Buber, M. (1970). *I and thou.* New York: Scribner.

Dillard, A. (1982). *Teaching a stone to talk.* New York: Harper Perennial.

Etzioni, A. (1999). *The limits of privacy.* New York: Basic.

Euchner, C. C. (1996). *Extraordinary politics: How protest and dissent are changing American democracy.* Boulder, CO: Westview.

Fain, S. (1999). Personal communication.

Fine, M. (1998). Personal communication, during open forum (sponsored by Maxine Greene). Center for the Imagination. December, Teachers College. New York.

Freire, P. (1970). *Pedagogy of the oppressed.* New York: Seabury.

Greene, M. (1995). *Releasing the imagination: Essays on education, the arts, and social change.* San Francisco: Jossey-Bass.

Harvey, D. (1990). *The condition of postmodernity.* Cambridge, MA: Blackwell.

Hesse, H. (1996). *Magister Ludi.* New York: Ungar (original work published 1949).

Joyce, J. (1934). *Ulysses.* New York: Random House.

Langer, E. J. (1997). *The power of mindful learning.* MA: Addison-Wesley.

Lefebvre, H. (1997). *The production of space.* Oxford, UK: Blackwell.

Mitchell, W. J. T. (Ed.) (1994). *Landscape and power.* Chicago: University of Chicago Press.

Schutz, A. (1999). Creating local "public spaces" in schools: Insights from Hannah Arendt

and Maxine Greene. *Curriculum Inquiry* 29 (1): 77–98.
Sibley, D. (1995). *Geographies of exclusion*. London: Routledge.
Taussig, M. (1997). *The magic of the state*. New York: Routledge.

CHAPTER SEVENTEEN

"*El sueño de razón produce monstruos,*" or Deconstructing the Curriculum of Philosophy

Tuukka Tomperi • Finland

In one of his best-known works, the eighteenth century Spanish painter Francisco de Goya y Lucientes portrays a humanistic scholar who has fallen asleep over the desk, beside him a blank sheet of paper and a pen that has slipped from his hand.[1] All around him the creatures of the night begin to gather as the sleep of this man of letters gives them a chance to overcome the otherwise vigilant Reason. The picture can be seen as an Enlightenment painter's way of metaphorically warning us of the dangers of irrationality. The lapse of Reason gives room for sleep, emotions, instincts, and other such states of mind that can bring forth unconscious and uncontrollable forces. The only way to stay safe is by strengthening our vigilance and our ability to practice our rational faculty. This is what the usual English translation of the name of the picture tells us: *The sleep of reason produces monsters*. Thus it has often been used as a pictorial testimony of the need to defend the rational spirit of Enlightenment today.[2]

The original Spanish name of the drawing, however, opens up a possibility for a different translation. In the phrase *El sueño de razón produce monstruos,* the word "sueño" means not only "sleep" but also "dream." Thus there is a chance of reading it as "The *dream* of reason produces monsters."

Having seen some of the monstrous things that can be produced by the most rigorous use of Reason and the rational design of utopian societies, we might now be more willing to consider this alternative translation and interpretation. The dreams of rational control and planning, of scientific and technological progress that would be accompanied by moral advancement, all promises of the Enlightenment Reason, may now in part seem like a bad dream, after the havoc of the twentieth century.[3] Reason was not able to deliver the dream nor redeem the reality. Furthermore, we cannot even say that this happened just because Reason lost to irrationality at decisive points in history. Reason, logic, and sciences, as means or instruments, were very much part of the destruction, in fact, a fundamentally important part, regarding the scope and measure of the devastation.[4]

The Cult of Reason and Dualisms in Philosophy

This is not to say that rational planning, design, and utopia are inevitably and inherently always wrong. In fact, it is impossible to maintain the modern society, with the huge complexity of its institutions and the mass of its citizens, without the benefits of rational, bureaucratic planning, and it would be a bare and hapless world in which utopia in the form of hope of transcending the present institutions would not exist. The point is, rather, that the modes of rationality in Western intellectual history have tended to be more one-sided and less neutral, universal, and objective than were commonly thought.

The horrible material violence that the twentieth century witnessed is partly intertwined with the symbolic violence embedded in certain aspects of the modern modes of rationality. In this case, it is particularly the tendency to construct meanings through binary dynamics that I have in mind. The modern dream of Reason, not only the cultivation of rationality but at times the cult of rationality, is deeply attached to many dualisms within Western thought, apart from the obvious one of Reason set against its Other, non-reason or irrationality. These dualisms go back much further than just the last 400–500 years of so-called modernity, or the 250 years of the Enlightenment, although these have certainly manifested some of the most rigid binary thinking in European intellectual history.

We can express many of these dualisms through the problematics of the mind and body. René Descartes, the thinker who laid the foundations of modern philosophy with his answer to another French skeptic, Michel de Montaigne (as the famous version by Vincent Descombes [1980] has it), is well known for his strict formulation of the mind/body dichotomy. Descartes wanted to ensure the possibility of absolute truth and knowledge. Because of this, he had to draw pure rational thinking strictly apart, on the one hand from the senses, the testimony of which is always suspect, and on the other hand from all the irrational forces and emotions capable of distorting rational, deductive proceedings. He did this by linking epistemology to metaphysics, that is, by suggesting that soul (*res cogitans*) alone was purely rational whereas body (*res extensa*) was the source of irrationality, including senses and sentiments. Mind/soul is the cause of itself; it is self-identical and self-present. Even more, it is I, it is my Self, the one I ultimately am. Body is of its own substance, of course, but as far as the Self is concerned, its being and meaning are secondary. It is not really I; it is something I have, something I happen to own although the case could be otherwise. Mind/soul is essential, body accidental.

It is interesting how this original division into reason and non-reason starts to attract other kinds of dualisms. We can focus on sexual difference as an example of this process. In the version by Descartes, the soul is sexless, of course, and sexuality and sexual difference belong to the material world and take place in the body. This should have meant that there was no essential difference between the rational abilities of the sexes, and thus gender should make no difference in our acceptance as participants in the public use of reason. However, as we all know, this has not been the case.

Obviously, there has always been a strong tendency to equate rationality with maleness and irrationality and passions with femaleness all along the history of philosophy (e.g., the Pythagoreans, Plato, early Christian thought, Bacon, Hegel). However, as Genevieve Lloyd (1993) has pointed out, even the arguments like the one by Descartes, which point to the sexlessness of the soul and reason, have time and again ended up reproducing and strengthening the ideology of their maleness (e.g., Aristotle, Augustine, and Thomas Aquinas before Descartes).

This is the case for at least two different reasons. First, real differences in social positions and very different chances for the public use of reason have existed in history and still exist in present societies; therefore, these create gendered expectations on the role of reason and passions (and public and private spheres) in the lives of real women and men; and second, because the sexlessness and pure ethereality of the soul are set against the material and natural sexuality of the body, which has throughout our Western history of ideas been associated with female symbolism:

> The idea of the sexless soul coexists with the maleness of reason, despite the appearance of tension. For the sexlessness of the soul is set over against the sexual difference which belongs with body—the material aspects of being human which have often been conceptualized as feminine. In the complex configuration of sexual symbolism with the ideas of reason, which has been a feature of western philosophy, the sexless soul takes on a shadowy maleness, in opposition to female sex difference. (Lloyd 1993: xi)

This would be a pressing issue even if reason had something to do only with our abilities and dispositions in reasoning and rationality. As we know, there is more to it:

> There is more at stake in assessing our ideals of Reason than questions of objectivity or relativity of truth. Reason has figured in western culture not only in the assessment of beliefs, but also in the assessment of character. It is incorporated not just into our criteria of truth, but also into our understanding of what it is to be a person at all, of the requirements that must be met to be a good person, and of the proper relations between our status as knowers [as choosers, as decision-makers, also in the ethical perspective] and the rest of our lives. (Lloyd 1993: xviii)

This normative function of the dualisms becomes very clear with the Pythagorean table of opposites (from the sixth century BCE): "limit/unlimited, odd/even, one/many, right/left, male/female, rest/motion, straight/curved, light/dark, good/bad, square/oblong." (3)

Because the sexual difference works here only as an example of a problematics with a larger scope, I present the following chains of signifiers (below) to exemplify the discursive field within which the rational subject and

On one side we have:	On the other we have:
Reason	Irrationality
Soul (Mind)	Body
Form	Matter
Self, Identity	Alterity, Difference
Culture	Nature
Virtues	Passions, Vices
Sexlessness	Sexuality
Universal, Eternal	Contextual, Temporal
Free	Bound
Public	Private
Norm, Normal (Western, European, male, mature)	Anomaly, Abnormal (non-Western, foreign, female, immature)

potentially autonomous ethical agency has often been given meaning, through a binary mechanism of exclusion that produces dualisms.

My point is obvious: it is this discursive field with the dualistic motives behind it that must be deconstructed if we are to avoid the symbolic violence inherent in many modern conceptualizations of rationality. And this is a task that is tied to the question of the curriculum and instruction of philosophy of being either empowering and transformative or repressive and reproductive.

The Curriculum and the Canon of Philosophy

What is at stake here, for me, is that sometimes, as a teacher of philosophy and as a lecturer to future teachers of philosophy, I feel like the divide described above is what the curricula and textbooks expect me to teach. With this, I am referring to the obvious circumstance that "philosophy," as a cultural institution, a social practice, and a guide to individual "critical and reflective thinking," has presented itself as firmly standing within the first of these two signifying chains. Saying so, we have to be careful. I am by no means claiming that *all philosophy* embodies these dualisms and engenders similar inclusions and exclusions. The point is that the canon of the "classics" in the history of philosophy often does so, and this canon is almost hegemonic in the standard curriculum. Moreover, decisions on "what philosophy is" are often guided by this canon.

A short look at the canon will serve for now. The answer to the question "who will count as very important philosophers" more often than not includes:
- the great Athenian rationalists (Socrates, Plato, Aristotle) and excludes Roman rhetoricians (Cicero, Seneca)
- systematic scholasticism (Aquinas, Duns Scotus, Occam) and excludes medieval mystics (Eckhart, Angelus Silesius, Teresa of Avila)
- modern rationalists and empiricists (Descartes, Hobbes, Locke) and excludes Renaissance humanists and skeptics (Erasmus, Juan Luis Vives, Montaigne)

The given picture of the established canon of philosophy can easily be verified by looking at any popular textbook, any general dictionary, or any concise history of philosophy. In all the cases above, the canon prefers those who build the core of philosophy stressing the rigid ideal of rationality instead of providing alternatives that would problematize the distinctness of reason from passions and sentiments. This dominance of the canon has thus streamlined the picture of philosophy overall, and by excluding certain styles, forms, and goals has further petrified the dichotomy between reason and non-reason with all the accompanying polarizations.

In defense of the traditional canon of philosophy it can be argued that these dualisms, and the different ways of describing reason and philosophical thought with dualistic motives, many times take place only in the margins of philosophical works. Thus they are not essential in understanding the basic arguments or philosophical conceptions in question. In addition, it has been claimed that the other dualisms (like male-female) derive from the particular contemporary social and cultural matrix within which the philosophers live, and from which they cannot detach themselves. However, these arguments, appealing to the irrelevancy of certain ideologically loaded conceptions or to the "unfortunate" effects of social and historical contexts on philosophy, in no way undermine the fact that these conceptions have had a strong influence on how the ideas of skillful and rational thinking, ethical deliberation, virtuous person, and good life, etc., have been constructed in our culture, nor do the arguments remove the fact that philosophy still carries the same dualisms and in- and exclusions within itself.

Of course these dualisms are often also metaphorical, as has been pointed out, but this does not make them any more trivial or ineffective. This is exactly what the poststructuralist and postmodern theory intends to make us less naive about. Even our philosophical convictions are necessarily constructed in a metaphorical language, and to believe that we are somehow able to overcome this obstacle by purifying our language is only apt to fool us and to bury us once more under the same binary dynamics discussed above. For this reason, we should perhaps be more interested in rhetoric than logic, more willing to look at the consequences than the origins. The curriculum of philosophy should be analyzed discursively, as an ideologically bound cultural and linguistic construction that will always lean either towards the reproduction or the transformation of society. Many an intention may be good, but we should keep in mind that it is the results that matter in the end.

Curriculum Study as Discourse Analysis

Philosophy has always been one of the most prestigious subjects in the European school curriculum (mainly on the secondary level, of course). In some of the most prominent EU countries—especially France, Germany, Italy, and Spain—philosophy enjoys a high esteem both in the culture generally and in school curriculum particularly. In addition, philosophy has a significant influence on the broader curriculum due to the fact that it is closely connected to the curriculum and instruction in the so-called critical thinking skills, ethics, and the history of ideas (seen to be an important part of learning the European "cultural heritage"). In many European schools, the "critical thinking" skills are among the objectives both of ethics/religion and philosophy/human studies, while "the history of ideas" forms a part of the core content of the curricula of both history and philosophy. All of these are part of the curriculum's contribution to the formation of the students' character and their construction of a learned and refined "worldview," which is often seen as one of the most important general formative tasks the school has. Thus, in the curriculum framework of many school systems in Europe, the teaching of ethics, philosophy, the history of (Western) ideas, and the basic skills of critical thinking form a kind of "curricular cluster" both in form and content.

My starting point is, of course, the situation in Finland, but I hope it has more general relevance. Philosophy has traditionally been studied only at the universities (and art colleges) where one or two courses are compulsory for most students. Big changes occurred during the 1990s when philosophy became one of the compulsory subjects in (senior) secondary school (high school/college) and vocational polytechnic curricula. In addition, European philosophy dominates the curriculum of ethics (or "philosophy of life," as it is sometimes called), which is a compulsory subject for all those primary and secondary school students who do not take courses in religion. This gives philosophy a wider audience and greater importance than its curricular status as a separate subject matter might suggest.

In Finland, institutions and teachers have the possibility of designing the curriculum fairly freely, but a normative national framework curriculum is still provided (the latest in 1994). Although the framework does not define teaching methods and is quite open regarding the contents (and is in this sense decentralized and progressive as is stated in the framework itself), it still defines a certain overall range of basic values, content areas, and general aims (a bit like the German *Rahmenplan* although in much lighter form). The National Board of Education framework (National Board of Education 1994) sets the content range for the very important national matriculation exam. Thus it definitely weighs upon and guides teachers' curricular deliberation. More interestingly, however, I would claim that the objectives and the standards included in the NBE framework curriculum pose a representative model of the established curriculum of philosophy almost everywhere that European philosophy is taught. Thus we have a probable picture of what is considered philosophy or the basics of philosophical thought generally in the Western culture and school system.

It is also essential to note how European philosophy has spread out all over the world in formal schooling, much more effectively, in fact, than Judeo-Christian religious ideas, for instance. A couple of years ago UNESCO conducted a survey to examine the state of teaching philosophy in its member countries and found out that almost everywhere Western philosophy and philosophers had surpassed the local traditions of thought in the formal school system (Droit 1995). When asked to list the most important philosophers in the curriculum, the compiled result of all the answers was tellingly unanimous: Plato (72 entries), Aristotle (71), Kant (68), Descartes (66), Hegel (64), and so on.[5] This creates a real need to critically question the established form of the canon and the curriculum of philosophy.

My approach could roughly be described as "discourse analysis," although I do not claim to be reporting research but, rather, presenting some preliminary observations of a phenomenon that, in my opinion, deserves closer analysis. My intention is not to take part in or try to resolve any debates around the general value of the philosophy in curriculum or the value of rationality in philosophy. My goal, a metaphilosophical one, is to question the effects of the established and canonized philosophical discourse in school curriculum. I see this approach as compatible with notions derived from the so-called "reconceptualization" of curriculum theory: "...from curriculum as exclusively school materials to curriculum as symbolic representation. [...] We can say that the effort to understand curriculum as symbolic representation defines, to a considerable extent, the contemporary field." (Pinar et al. 1995: 15). I understand discourse analysis as an attempt to closely read documents that function as "speech acts" within some particular discursive field and to describe the functions, contexts, discursive prerequisites, and effects of these. It becomes deconstructive if special attention is paid to the gaps and inconsistencies that may lead these linguistic and social practices to say and produce something different from what they claim to be doing. Any written curriculum is not only a normatively binding projection into the future but also a testimony of the ways of thinking in the past and a symbolic representation of practices in the present.

Quotations from the Finnish curriculum for philosophy (National Board of Education 1994), referring to the instruction of philosophy are:

The instruction of philosophy in the senior secondary school helps students widen and clarify their conceptions of questions concerning the nature of reality, themselves, values, and the foundations of knowledge. [...] The instruction of philosophy...focuses on the nature and basic structure of knowledge and the world. It offers cognitive instruments with which students can build their own outlook, on the basis of their experiences and knowledge obtained through school subjects. [...] Knowledge and society, taste and culture, as well as man's relationship to nature change quickly and become more complex. For this reason people need an intellectual link to their cultural inheritance offered by philosophy.

The purposes are stated as follows:

The purpose of the study of philosophy is that students... (1) know how to use concepts precisely, and to give reasons for their opinions, (2) are able to conceptualize and assess knowledge-related, individual-ethical and social-ethical, as well as aesthetic problems, and their alternative solutions, and (3) have some knowledge of the basics of philosophical traditions.[6]

The description of the compulsory course:

The course deals with the basic starting points of European philosophy, and an overview of the philosophical method of enquiry, and it gives and searches for answers to the following questions: What is philosophy? What is the nature of reality? What is man? What is truth? What is good? What is justice? What is beauty?

On the nature of studies it says:

[...] Students will obtain philosophical skills to support their thinking. [...] Philosophy works through its tradition even when it makes topical, even personal questions. The study of philosophy means getting to know tradition.

These quotes sound familiar probably to anyone who has ever studied philosophy—in any institution. They sound almost obvious and thus neutral in a way: What else could the instruction of philosophy be about? Yet this is just the question I propose needs to be asked more critically than usual. The curriculum justifies the status of philosophy as one of the compulsory subjects, basically by three arguments appealing to the effects that philosophy supposedly has on students:

(1) philosophy enables and encourages students to think clearly, critically, and reflectively;

(2) philosophy helps in building a coherent and intelligible worldview;

(3) philosophy as a cultural tradition of its own is a central part of our "Europeanness" and our cultural heritage and thus forms an essential aspect of the so-called "all-round education" (*allgemeine Bildung*) of present-day Europeans.

It is a paradox that the above "effects" are said to be what the curriculum and instruction of philosophy achieve, but the real effects of studying or teaching philosophy have never really been studied (empirically, psychologically, socially, etc.). It may even be questioned whether there is any way of studying the *real* effects. The curriculum may state that these kinds of effects take place, and teachers may believe it, but if we want to do rigorous curriculum study and analysis, these kinds of statements are exactly the kind that cannot be taken for granted. We must inquire more radically into the lived curriculum in order to determine what is really being taught when *philosophy* is taught and to find out what the actual effects and curricular experiences are. In the space of this chapter I cannot venture into that, however. I am content in constructing a frame of critique towards the possible reproductive elements in the curriculum of philosophy in reference to their background in the dualistic tendencies of rationality and the canon of the history of philosophy.

Aspects of Cultural and Ideological Reproduction in the Philosophy of Curriculum

To repeat and reformulate: the basic rhetorical argument that the Finnish curriculum (and the paradigmatic curriculum of philosophy anywhere) makes of the place and value of philosophy in school can be translated into a discursive bloc that links the different connotations together in the following way:

> proper ethical conduct and social responsibility (require)
> human rationality and reflectivity (based on)
> critical thinking skills and philosophical thought (manifested in)
> the history of (European) philosophical thought (presented as)
> the canonized European history of ideas and philosophy

This leads us to ask whether it is possible to build a curriculum of philosophy and critical thinking without reproducing the ideologically biased view that critical, reflective thinking is an activity practiced mainly by the European male population of a Caucasian ethnic background. I will later take a critical look at the curriculum in order to play out other different and contradicting views on what the curriculum of philosophy might consist of. My objective is to ask:

- What are the forms of ideological or symbolic reproduction that might be (most often still unconsciously) at work in the curriculum of philosophy, and how are these bound to the fact that philosophy was born from and still often takes place within elitist, upper-class, male, European hegemony in culture and curriculum?[7]
- What are the alternatives we might turn to in search of transformation in the curriculum of philosophy?

Now the task is to specify some of the different ideological implications that may arise from the dualisms mentioned above. Although in the beginning I used Genevieve Lloyd's (1993) feminist criticism of the history of philosophy to set the stage, this dynamic of dualisms has wider implications, as has been pointed out by many critiques of the conservative Western cultural and ideological hegemony, at least since the 1970s. Whether it is a question of patriarchal power structures, anthropocentric ecological negligence, national chauvinism, or cultural imperialism, all these main targets of criticism have for the most part yet to be accounted for in the curriculum of philosophy, and they are all bound to the dualisms discussed above.[8]

As an example of the totalizing and excluding tendencies present in the curriculum of philosophy, we can think of the established way to teach philosophy, ethics, and critical thinking skills through the lens of the history of European philosophy as a single European tradition. In this case, we run the risks of: (1) concealing the complexities and breaks of European history (in concepts and language, in the systems of meaning and discourse); (2) forgetting the significance of the social, cultural, and political contexts of different philosophical eras, discourses, and thinkers (and thus depoliticizing philosophical practices); (3) unconsciously presenting higher thinking and argumentation as predominantly a male activity (by reproducing the decontextualized patriarchal canon of European philosophy); (4) setting the traditional upper-class European education as the principal model of building rational and ethic virtues (and thus excluding other cultural and intellectual traditions); and, (5) reducing thinking to an activity which has to do only with reason and cognition (thus excluding affects, emotions, sensibilities, etc.). It seems that we have to deal with the problem of reproduction in at least these five different areas mentioned.

The Curriculum of Philosophy as the Reproduction of Humanistic, Anthropocentric, Subject-centered, and Individualistic Ethics

Curricula are very often strongly attached to the tradition of European humanistic and liberal ethics based on individual rights and individual freedom. Some possible ways to form a criticism towards this would include:

- *Biocentric* thinking, where ethical priority is given to nature, to life, or to the planet as a whole (e.g., radical deep ecology).
- *Sentientistic* approach, where human beings are given no privileged ethical position compared with any other living creature that has the ability to feel pain and suffer (as often see in the animal rights movement).
- *Social* or *communal* ethics, where priority is given to some unit larger than a single individual (when teaching ethics and philosophy, the ideal of a good community could be taken as a central objective, instead of having a good individual life or being a good person; analogically, we could stress co-operational learning and thus take a *group* of students participating in a course as a starting point instead of isolated individual students).
- *Subject-critical* approach, where the supposedly monolithic and individual subject is shown to be an effect of power, desire, discourse, etc., and the supposedly autonomous agency revealed as a construction of these. To take this approach seriously would radically change the field of relevant questions we must ask in teaching ethics.
- *Holistic* thinking that would draw from the same sources of critique mentioned above but would try to construct positive ethical alternatives to subject-centeredness.

One possible common denominator for many of the dualisms listed earlier is the metaphysics of subjectivity (of thinking and willing subject) in European philosophy. The critique of this subject-centeredness points to alternative approaches in teaching philosophy as well. For instance, we could stress the need to learn to understand and experience ourselves as parts of the whole as something always dependent on something other than ourselves. This is not just to say that "we need other people" or that "we can develop our human capacities only in human societies," both of which are true but also obvious, but instead something much more radical: that the "subjective inside" and the "objective outside" cannot be drawn apart in any dualistic manner. In this sense, the search for truth from "within" would make no sense. We would have to be seen as made up of the textures of physical matter and biological processes, of the socio-cultural and historical textures of signs, meanings, actions, gestures, speech, stories, and so on. These textures expand without boundaries all around us, and for our own being (*that* we are, *what* we are, and *how* we are) we should be grateful to this whole. I think this is why Heidegger, following medieval mystics, wrote that "thinking" (*denken*), in its authentic mode, is and should still be, "thanking" (*danken*). How about a course in philosophy that would take as its objective "learning to thank" instead of "learning to think"?

The Curriculum of Philosophy as the Reproduction of European Ethnocentrism and Cultural Neocolonialism

The Finnish curriculum takes for granted that all students belong to one unitary cultural "tradition," the so-called "European culture" (the words "European cultural tradition" or "European cultural heritage" are mentioned several times in the Finnish curriculum framework). I am afraid that the case may still be the same in many other European countries too. Some possible criticisms of this:

- There is a single continuous, unitary tradition "behind us" only insofar as we continue to reproduce the historical picture that there is such a thing. Philosophy itself is not a single tradition, the cultural practices that have been given the name "philosophy" during the past 2500 years have been many and varied. There have been insurmountable differences in approaches, contents, objects, and styles, and there have been several historical discontinuities of philosophical discourse. Because of this, we should rather aim at affirming and celebrating this historical plurality of "tradition" and "discipline."
- The students today, even in Finland, which has traditionally been one of the most ethnically homogenous nations in Europe, no longer share any single cultural background. Their lifeworlds are not filled only with phenomena and practices that could be easily associated with some elementary "Europeanness." Instead of emphasizing common ground, we should try to figure out how the curriculum of philosophy could encourage the affirmation of the present plurality of forms of life, cultures and subcultures, and ethnic and national backgrounds.

When critical and reflective thinking becomes associated with the traditionally interpreted canon of the European philosophical tradition, other forms of critical thought and other moral traditions stay absent as if there were none. Against this, teaching philosophy could lead to the recognition and affirmation of the existence of other forms of reflective thinking and other ethical traditions.

The Curriculum of Philosophy as the Reproduction of Phallocentrism and Patriarchy Typical of the "Philosophical Tradition"

Most typically this effect follows when the curriculum of philosophy emphasizes the importance of the history of philosophy without problematizing the established historical interpretations. Probably everyone who has studied philosophy knows that philosophy easily becomes a parade of the "great philosophers," battling along with their great "isms," always detached from their social and political contexts.[9] In this case, "critical and reflective thinking" also becomes a curiously male activity. After all this, it is no wonder that so few women continue their studies in philosophy or end up teaching philosophy.[10] The critical analysis of this has been pushed to the margins of philosophy by maintaining that the universal and perennial questions must be "first-order" topics in philosophy, obviously at the expense of more contextual and time-bound ones. As a result, philosophical anthropology (e.g., problematics of "being human") remains in a central place whereas issues of more sociological, empirical, or feminist interest (e.g., the problematics of "gender") do not. This should be countered by attempts at contextualizing philosophical curriculum and discourse on all levels. Attempts at contextualization could include:

- Microhistorical and genealogical discussions on sociohistorical conditions of individual philosophers, philosophical practices, and intellectual discourses of different times, and the forms through which power functions in them.
- Historiographic discussions on how the history of philosophy has been written, for what reasons, and by whom.[11]
- Discourse-critical discussions on power relations in the present philosophical discourses and institutions.

The Curriculum of Philosophy as the Reproduction of Cognitivistic and Rationalistic Bias in Education and Character Formation

The Finnish curriculum framework sets as a goal that "the student learns to search, process, evaluate, and use knowledge," and it states that philosophy "enhances her/his capacity of constructing and maintaining a rational and coherent worldview." Here we could ask:

- Why does the curriculum not state as an objective that "the student learns to understand, evaluate, and develop the *passions* of hers/his?" What justifies

the constant privileging of cognitions and knowledge in curriculum?
- Why does the curriculum not take into account that we live in an environment that is affective and emotional throughout, that there are no real divisions into different faculties like reason and emotion in us, that when and wherever we exist, we exist as whole persons?[12]
- Why does the curriculum not recognize that this overtly rationalistic and cognitivistic approach not only has serious solipsistic overtones but that it also participates in reproducing the whole symbolic field of the modern dualistic conception of subject with all its corollaries?

The Curriculum of Philosophy as the Reproduction of the Primacy of the Epistemic at the Expense of Other Aspects of Our Philosophical Outlook on Life

Even if we use the traditional division of philosophy into the theoretical and practical parts and, furthermore, the division of the former into ontology ("reality") and epistemology ("knowledge"), and the latter into ethics ("moral values") and aesthetics ("sense values"), we can notice that in itself, every proposition made in any of these areas carries implications of and for all the others. This is often forgotten when epistemology and transcendental analysis of our "capacity of knowing" is taken as the starting point for a philosophical or scientific inquiry, as has usually been done at least since the eighteenth century in modern European philosophy. Alternatively:
- We could set *metaphysics* as the "first philosophy," as was done in Aristotle's system or in almost all of pre-modern philosophy.
- We could follow Emmanuel Levinas (1981, 1985) in his dialogical ethos and the claim that *ethics* should always be seen as the "first philosophy."
- We could yet go back with Philippe Lacoue-Labarthe (1993) and his inquiry into the preconceptual meaning of tragedy in Greek culture as an antecedent of the conceptual analysis in philosophy and admit *aesthetics* (or "arch-ethics") the authentic primacy in understanding our mode of being-in-the-world.
- An altogether different way of seeing the issue would be to undermine the whole notion of "primacy" in philosophy or the idea of "origins" in ideas and thinking. One way of doing this would be to use Derridean deconstruction of notions like "origins" or "primary." Another approach would be to see all theories and "outlooks on life" as eventually ideological. In such case, we could ally with the materialistic critics of philosophy (e.g., Feuerbach, Marx, Lukács, Althusser) and begin to see philosophy either as always origi-

nating in "non-philosophy" or as epiphenomenal or superstructural to the material basis or social praxis.

As we can see, none of the reproductive tendencies above represents the whole picture as such. What is at stake is rather the whole dynamic of inclusions and exclusions, of the tendency to construct meanings through binaries that develop into structures of dominance, as Lloyd (1993) points out in the case of sexual difference: "Our ideas and ideals of maleness and femaleness have been formed within structures of dominance—of superiority and inferiority, 'norms' and 'difference,' 'positive' and 'negative,' the 'essential' and the 'complementary'" (103). In the end, the deconstruction of binaries around rationality and irrationality leads to increased awareness of dualistic tendencies, highlighting the need to strive for the critique of this binary mechanism of exclusion and dominance in philosophy and the curriculum of philosophy.

Philosophy / Pedagogy

There is nothing exactly new in my critique. The basic argument is that the supposed universality of philosophical thought is primarily "white mythology" (written by the European male elite). This point was made by Jacques Derrida in an essay by the same name in *Marges de la philosophie* (1972/1982) and later gained credence and momentum through deconstructive projects of his and others during the past thirty years. What is remarkable from my perspective, however, is how little these critiques have actually affected the way we teach philosophy and conceptualize the curriculum of philosophy.

Yet it seems that pedagogy and philosophy are intertwined more deeply than the talk of curriculum and teaching philosophy might suggest. The history of philosophy is closely linked to the history of ideas in pedagogy. As one reminder of this, the faculties of philosophy and pedagogy still share close relations in many of the oldest universities in Europe: in Germany, Italy, Spain, and France. Western education and especially school pedagogy have been founded on philosophical concepts that serve as the main targets for the post-modern and deconstructive critique (such as "subject," "reason," "progress," even the search for "foundations" itself). Thus the whole issue of crisis in the modern conceptions of rational and knowing subject may affect teaching philosophy profoundly, not only because we can see it as a crisis within philosophy but because it is ultimately a crisis of predominant pedagogical ideology or philosophy of education as well. It should be pointed out that I don't mean to dramatize by using the word "crisis." Instead, I am referring to the word's etymological origin in Greek, meaning "turning point." However, such conservative practices as school and philosophy, which have so many traditional underpinnings and powerful interests behind them, turn very slowly.

Jacques Derrida (1995) sees this theme as very important, and he states in an interview that "questions concerning the teaching of philosophy are inseparable from those concerning teaching and research in all disciplines at all levels." He continues: "And these questions are indissociable from the great question of *democracy to come* (in Europe and elsewhere)" (338). I agree with the first claim, but the second claim, I think, is itself just another example of the illusions of omnipotence in European philosophy, stemming perhaps from the central place philosophy occupies in the French literary culture. I would be more willing to believe Richard Rorty (1996) when he admits that he "doubts that philosophy is ever going to be very useful for politics" (73). Politics can manage without philosophy, but philosophy should not try to manage without politics. Becoming more conscious of the different forms of ideological reproduction in philosophy necessarily means politicizing philosophy in one way or another. Philosophy, and the curriculum and instruction of philosophy, will never be politically innocent.

By politicizing the curriculum of philosophy I don't mean to make it party-political, radical, nor activist—unless the participants want to, of course. "Politicizing" here only refers to heightened social awareness and reflexivity, to curriculum as an object of common reflection, critique, and negotiation by the participants. Almost every written curriculum, either generally or in philosophy, contains a lot of talk on reflection and self-reflection. Yet school is a remarkably "nonreflexive" space. School, class, and curriculum practices are noted for their unwillingness to talk about themselves, to look at themselves. The curriculum of philosophy is no exception, for it does not question philosophy or problematize the concept of "philosophy," but takes the existence of a continuous and homogenous discipline of philosophy for granted. It does not interrogate the distinctions, inclusions, and exclusions that construct "philosophy." Neither does it question the existence of school or the possibility of teaching.

Obviously, in education and schooling, it is not enough just to problematize, question, and deconstruct. We need positive and reconstructive strategies as well. In order for philosophy to be relevant to students in the context of late modernity, teachers must be able to detach and distance themselves from the pre-set curricular boundaries (both written and hidden) and develop ways to support their students' and their own attempts to understand the flux of their lifeworld. Learning to be critical means also adopting a critical stance towards school curriculum and philosophy, including the established picture of "critical thinking" presented therein. In one of his last texts, Michel Foucault (1984) argued that the transcendental analysis of our ways of perceiving and thinking, by that archetype of modern philosophy, Immanuel Kant, already has in Kant's texts as its counterpart a more timely meditation of present forms of life and the different prerequisites and possibilities it sets on our ways of experiencing, thinking, and speaking about the world. This latter sort of analysis, what we might call "the philosophical discourse of modernity," is what Foucault calls the "historical ontology of ourselves." It could lead to relevant forms of philosophical thought and practice when teaching philosophy in an increasingly ambivalent and contingent world. Furthermore, with his discussions on the role of passions in our lives and his descriptions of the different historical "techniques of the self," Foucault (1990, 1992) could offer positive strategies for making sense, reconceptualizing and taking the hold of the *currere* of our lives affectively as well. At this point, these explorations must be left to another occasion.

Notes
1. The drawing is *Caprichos 43*. It is commonly thought that the man pictured is Goya himself.
2. Curiously, while I was waiting for my dialogue session at the Internationalization of Curriculum Conference, spending time at the LSU bookstore (on campus in Baton Rouge), I happened to find an anthology published by the New York Academy of Sciences and called *The Flight from Science and Reason*. It had this very drawing by Goya on the cover. The anthology was written by scientific realists, and it was aimed against the "postmodern relativists" in order to "defend science from its irrational critics." Within such academic battlefields today, as in the so-called "Sokal-affair," the debate about the value and meaning of rationality and the threat of irrationality and relativism seems to be very much alive.
3. As the Swedish historian Peter Englund (1999) notes in the introduction of his book, we have just witnessed a century during which more than 180 million people were killed because of the actions of other human beings—more than during all the previous centuries put together.
4. A forceful testimony of this is Hannah Arendt's *Eichmann in Jerusalem* (1963/1994), where she, through reporting the trial of Adolf Eichmann in Israel, analyses the bureaucratic and thoroughly rational mindset behind the Holocaust.
5. The list continues: ...Hume (39), Spinoza (33), Leibniz (31), Marx (30), Locke (29),

Aquinas (29), Augustine (20), Wittgenstein (20), Rousseau (17), Sartre (14), Berkeley (14), Hobbes (11)....

6. It is worth pointing out that these quotes are from the official English version of the framework curriculum. It differs somewhat, perhaps tellingly, from the Finnish original. For example, the last quoted phrase in the original says: "manages the all-round educative basics of *the philosophical tradition*" (emphasis added.)

7. In the above and in what follows, I do not intend to use the term "reproduction" in the overly rigid way that some of the Western Marxism in the 1970s did. I lean on Pierre Bourdieu's (1990) reservations concerning the concept and the phenomenon that the school system *contributes* to reproducing the structure of the distribution of cultural capital and, through it, the social structure, instead of "the ahistorical view that society reproduces itself mechanistically, identical to itself, without transformation or deformation, and by excluding all individual mobility."(vii). There are constant cultural struggles taking place, there is active resistance as well as active consensus-construction to keep real conflicts out of sight and the dominant system hegemonical (in Gramscian terminology). We will have to look for the place of school and curriculum in these struggles.

8. One of the most active strands of criticism bringing these different forms of domination under common analysis has since the late 1970s been the so-called ecological feminism, or ecofeminist theory.

9. See Rée (1991), "The Vanity of Historicism."

10. School curriculum is strongly determined by academic curriculum and corresponding academic disciplines in all the academic subject matters (for several reasons, not least for the will to build and strengthen the academic image of the teaching profession and the professional concern to guard the criteria of recruiting new teachers). This means that the general disciplinary politics and social psychology that prevail on the professional level and in faculties often do so in school and undergraduate level as well. The following is a quote at the *Philosopher's Magazine's* (Issue 12, 2000, page 31) report from the largest general gathering of British philosophers (Joint Session of the Aristotelian Society and the Mind Association):

> Look more closely, though, and you'll notice some decidedly strange things about this crowd. First of all, astonishingly, there was not a single black or Asian face to be seen among the 150-odd delegates. This may not tell you anything in particular about the Joint Session, but it certainly says something very revealing about British philosophy. For whatever reason, the subject has continued to attract predominantly white Europeans and Americans while few black and minority ethnic students have made it through. Second, count the women. Among the delegates with academic affiliations, men out-numbered women by three to one. On the main programme, of the fifteen speakers, only two were women. Just two out of eight session chairs were women. Again, this reflects the state of the profession, which remains male-dominated, even among relatively young philosophers in their thirties and forties.

However, in this sense the situation (as far as I have seen it) seems to be better in the U.S. than in Europe.
11. For instance, in the manner of Rorty's (1993) "The Historiography of Philosophy: Four Genres."
12. See the criticism against Descartes' conception of mind in Antonio Damasio's *Descartes' Error* (1994) and Mary Midgley's *Heart and Mind* (1981).

References

Arendt, H. (1994). *Eichmann in Jerusalem: A report on the banality of evil*. London: Penguin. (original work published 1963)
Bourdieu, P. (1990). Preface to the 1990 Edition. In *Reproduction in education, society and culture*, Edited by Pierre Bourdieu and Jean-Claude Passeron. Translation by Richard Nice. London: Sage. (original work published in French, 1970).
Damasio, A. (1994). *Descartes' error: Emotion, reason, and the human brain*. New York: Putnam.
Derrida, J. (1982). *The margins of philosophy (Marges de la philosophie)*. Translated by Alan Bass. Brighton: Harvester Press. (Original work published in French, 1972)
────── (1995). Once again from the top: Of the right to philosophy. In: *Points...: interviews, 1974-1994* (Points de suspension, Entretiens). Translation by Peggy Kamuf. Edited by Elisabeth Weber, Stanford: Stanford University Press.
Descombes, V. (1980). *Modern french philosophy* (Le Même et l'autre). Translated by L. Scott-Fox and J. M. Harding. Cambridge: Cambridge University Press.
Droit, R. (1995). *Philosophy and democracy in the world: A UNESCO Survey*. New York: United Nations Educational Scientific and Cultural Organization (UNESCO).
Englund, P. (1999). *Brev Från Nollpunkten: Historiska Essäer*. Sverige: Bokförlaget Atlantis AB.
Foucault, M. (1984). Un cours inédit. *Magazine littéraire*. no. *207*: 35–9.
────── (1990). *The use of pleasure. History of sexuality, Vol. 2*. London: Penguin Books.
────── (1992). *The care of the self. History of Sexuality, Vol. 3*. London: Penguin Books.
Lacoue-Labarthe, P. (1993). *Etiikasta: Lacan ja Antigone* (De l'éthique: à propos d'Antigone). Translated by Janna Jalkanen and the team. Helsinki: Loki.
Levinas, E. (1981). *Otherwise than being or beyond essence (Autrement qu'être)*. Translated by Alphonso Lingis. The Hague: Nijhoff.
────── (1985). *Ethics and infinity. Conversations with Philippe Nemo*. Translated by Richard A. Cohen. Pittsburgh: Duquesne University.
Lloyd, G. (1993). *The man of reason: "Male" & "female" in Western philosophy*. London: Routledge.
Midgley, M. (1981). *Heart and mind*. Sussex: Harvester Press.
National Board of Education (1994). *Framework curriculum for the senior secondary school*. Helsinki: Painatuskeskus.
Pinar, W. F., et al. (1995). *Understanding curriculum*. New York: Peter Lang.
Reé, J. (1991). The vanity of historicism. *New Literary History 22*: 961–83.
Rorty, R. (1993). The Historiography of philosophy: Four genres. In *Philosophy in history*.

Edited by R. Rorty, J. B. Schneewind, and Q. Skinner. Cambridge, MA: Cambridge University Press.

―――― (1996). Response to Ernesto Laclau. In Simon Critchley, Jacques Derrida, Ernesto Laclau, and Richard Rorty. *Deconstruction and pragmatism.* Edited by Chantal Mouffé. London and New York: Rouledge.

CHAPTER EIGHTEEN

The Politics of Moral Education: A Cross-Cultural Analysis

Tianlong Yu • People's Republic of China

Moral education and politics are two important and controversial realities imbedded in public schooling, and very often they are woven together. This is a common scenario in both China and the United States. However, the politics of moral education has different faces. In China, the political influence on moral education is mostly explicit, while in the United States, the same issue tends to be more implicit. The current increasingly popular character education movement in U.S. schools has blinded many educators to its political/ideological underpinnings. There is a need to address this important issue. Reflecting on a personal cross-cultural journey, this chapter will explore how moral education in both countries has been socially constructed and politically charged.

Moral Education in China: Politicized Behavioral Training

In 2000, Chinese President Jiang delivered a series of speeches on school education to guide Chinese educational policies in the twenty-first century. He emphasized moral education as the core of an all-around education and asked schools to reinforce patriotic education, collective education, and socialist education as the central goals of moral education (President Jiang Talks 2000: 2).

The president's speech has become the backbone of the subsequent decisions made by the Ministry of Education. Highlights of the ministry's policies on moral education include strengthening moral education in schools; carrying out the Communist Party's educational principles and setting political education as the priority of moral education; reinforcing patriotism, collectivism, and socialism in curricula; cultivating students' moral virtues, law-abiding consciousness, and civilized behavioral habits; shaping students' scientific worldviews; and building healthy and strong character (President Jiang Talks 2000: 3).

The Ministry of Education controls the centralized Chinese educational system by prescribing a national curriculum for all pre-college schools in every subject, including moral education. Schools across the country comply with the ministry's policies. However, they primarily stress political education by following programs that are already in place. For example, schools continue to use a 1950s framework called "Five Loves Education," which includes love of our motherland, love of our people, love of science, love of work, and love of socialism. The fifth love used to be "love of public property" but has been replaced by "love of socialism."

In addition to the political education content, behavioral training remains a major component of moral education. Schools still closely observe "Twenty Behavioral Standards for Elementary School Students" and "Forty Behavioral Standards for Secondary School Students," which were issued by the ministry in the 1970s. Even the language is similar. Students must be good children in the home, good students in the school, and good citizens in society. In the school, they are asked to work hard and follow the school rules, to get along with fellow students, and to help each other. In the home, they are asked to have reverence for parents, to help parents with housework, and to be economical in everyday spending. In society, they are asked to obey the law and to help maintain public social order. These behavioral standards are rigorously enforced in schools, and students are strictly supervised to ensure their behaviors conform to the standards. Currently in Chinese schools, political/ideological education and behavioral training remain central in the practice of moral education.

This type of moral education has evolved through a short but intense history in Communist China and become part of my personal memory. I remember when I was a little boy during the heyday of the notorious Communist Cultural Revolution (1966–1976) I attended numerous meetings in my community to study the works of our "greatest" communist leader,

Chairman Mao. Similarly, in school, we were led by teachers to recite quotations from Chairman Mao's works every day, both during one whole class period and before regular classes began. We were asked to recite fast and accurately. The memorization was quite effective because even now I can recite many quotations from Chairman Mao's works, although I did not fully understand the meanings of those words until many years later. Chairman Mao's teachings were hailed as our highest political and behavioral standards, and we were trained to listen to his teachings and be his good children.

Some American researchers documented this type of moral education in China in the 1970s. Connell (1976) writes about how moral education and political education were inseparable in Chinese schools:

> Moral education is concerned with developing selected kinds of character traits and forms of behavior preferred by the educator. The basis for selection...is political...The good person is the one with the right political attitude. To be a good soldier, peasant, worker, or scholar, one must first possess the correct political views. Technical knowledge and proficiency are essential for the efficient performance of one's tasks, but having the right political attitude ensures that one's task is directed toward the right ends and carried out in the right spirit. (31)

The death of Mao in 1976 and the launch of the "Reform and Open Door" policy in 1978 brought about changes in the focus of Chinese education. When I was in middle and high school in the early 1980s, for example, we did not study Chairman Mao's works any longer. Moral education in schools was not emphasized as much as it was in the years of the Cultural Revolution. As the country rapidly moved toward economic modernization, academics became the real priority of school education. The extremely competitive national college entrance examination, which was resumed after the Cultural Revolution, occupied the focus of schoolwork and drove the curricula even in elementary schools. Pre-college education largely turned out to be college preparation. While teaching to tests gradually became the actual core of schooling, moral education had lost its lofty status in schools.

In spite of this shift, moral education has always been emphasized at philosophical and policy levels as an integral part of school education. As part of the formal curriculum, moral education, in the form of political education and behavioral training, is taught as a separate subject. Even though it receives much less emphasis than other academic courses, moral education profoundly influences the lives of both teachers and students.

One striking feature of Chinese moral education is its expanded mission.

Over the years, the concept of moral education has been broadened. I define this as a trend toward "over-moralization" of issues. Chinese educators tend to believe that, except for education for children's intellectual and physical development, all other efforts (e.g., citizenship education and psychological education) are the goals and content of moral education. The aim is to produce moral people who will contribute to the society.

The root of such a broad conception of moral education is Mao's theory. Fifty years ago, when Mao formulated educational policy for the new nation, he required schools to give an all-around education to children. As Mao (1957/1977) said, "Our educational aim is that we should have our students develop morally, intellectually, and physically, and become cultivated workers with a socialist consciousness." Mao's vision not only set a theoretical framework for moral education but also guaranteed political influence in its practice.

In reality, under this broad umbrella of moral education, educators tend to moralize all social problems. After the death of Mao, the country entered a great transition period, facing a series of social upheavals and problems, such as unethical business behavior, crime, and increasing divorce rates. People asked schools to prevent these problems through moral education. However, these problems cannot be viewed as mere moral problems. They are the result of the dramatic changes in social structures due to the country's opening up to Western cultures and its own social reform. These problems do not represent a moral degeneration among people; therefore, we do not have a good reason to overemphasize the school's moral mission to deal with these problems. Schools can help prepare more intellectually and morally capable young people, but schools alone cannot solve all social and cultural problems.

Ideologies of Moral Education: Communism and Confucianism

The broadened notion of moral education embraces Chinese politics and allows for ideological domination of its theory and practice. The Communist Party is the "unquestionable" leader in China and it owns all schools. "We are the Party's children," a popular self-identification slogan during the Cultural Revolution years, still reflects the reality today, because what students learn is largely determined by the party through the Ministry of Education, but not by students themselves, their parents, or the local communities. The curriculum of moral education naturally becomes the home of communist ideologies such as patriotism, collectivism, and socialism. Bai (1998) reveals how the Chinese moral education system has been based on the legitimacy of the political leadership of the Communist Party. Under Mao's regime (1949–1976), the legitimacy of the party was expressed simply as "Listening to what Chairman Mao says." Now this legitimacy has been developed into a formula: "Patriotism = socialism = Chinese Communist Party = the needs of the country and people" (Bai 1998: 525–6).

Values favored by these larger ideologies are emphasized, while values conflicting with them are ignored, criticized, or forbidden. As Connell (1976) observed, Chinese schools greatly stressed collective virtues. Behaviors associated with various collectives, such as the school, the community, the party, and the country, share some basic moral elements, including honesty, selflessness, industriousness, respect, and responsibility. Hence, moral education is required to build a collective nature in children.

This reality still pervades Chinese moral education curricula today, despite the changes that Chinese society is undergoing. A diversity of values is actually developing within the society, and this diversity is affecting young people. As Yuan and Shen (1998) have found through their surveys, today's adolescents in China tend to prefer values that are related to competence and personal effectiveness (the high-stakes tests have contributed to this change in values). Nevertheless, moral education in schools, both theoretically and practically, still ignores diversity of values and stresses collective values.

The only "new" initiative in moral education is the recent return to the Chinese moral tradition movement. Some consider it as an alternative practice to communist-controlled moral education. However, the movement does nothing more than reinforce the already-existing collective and conservative nature of moral education. The movement is also a response to the recent social changes in China. Leaders of the movement bemoan social problems as "moral decline" and claim the need to rediscover "the quintessence of Confucian ethics" to address those problems. They especially believe a return to the Confucian tradition will save the young from bad capitalist influences. They view it as a critical strategy for the reform of moral education and conduct active efforts to bring Confucian ethics back to school classrooms. A review of research shows titles such as, "List of Chinese Traditional Virtues" (Chen et al. 1993), and "Stories on Chinese Traditional Moral Virtues" (Luan 1992). There also have been several large-scale experimental projects to teach selected Confucian virtues to students.

Not surprisingly, the Communist Party and the Ministry of Education have overtly encouraged and strongly supported this movement. Their support tells us that Confucianism, under the current social and cultural atmosphere in China, does not contradict communist ideology, rather, it supports it. Confucianism as a non-theistic religion has suffered many attacks by other competing religions or ideologies across history, but it remains dominant in Chinese culture. Communists attacked Confucianism during the Cultural Revolution; now they welcome its return. Because of the anti-religious nature of communism, communists still debase the religious and spiritual component of Confucianism. Nevertheless, they have begun to accept and encourage Confucianism as a moral philosophy.

Communists have found that Confucian ethics are compatible with communism's own collective spirit. For example, Confucianism emphasizes interpersonal relationships to ensure proper social ordering. Confucian moral education highlights the inculcation of community values and the cultivation of character in a collective man. Confucianism condemns individualism, seeing an emphasis on individual rights as an invitation to selfishness. Communists have realized they can make use of this type of moral philosophy and moral education to maintain their educational and social purposes just as many imperial dynasties in Chinese history did before them. In Mao's era, the communists set up Marxism, Leninism, and Maoism as the sole official state ideologies, which were entirely separated from the nation's cultural tradition. Now, the communists are trying to integrate their ideologies into the more profound and pervasive Confucian tradition.

What values are advocated in this return to Confucian tradition? Values such as loyalty to one's country, commitment to serving the people, social responsibility, respect for authority, self-discipline, and self-cultivation represent the conservative ideology of Confucianism and are consistent with communist ideological frameworks. As China's Open Door policy has resulted in the emergence of new ideologies and values competing with the official communist ideologies, the Chinese Communist Party repeatedly calls for strengthening political/ideological education and returning to a reinterpreted cultural tradition. The purpose behind the call and actions of the communists is obvious—to employ moral education for the ends of political control and maintaining communist social hegemony.

Thus, the politicization of moral education in China has been situated in and supported by a cultural tradition that strongly confirms a specific type of moral education of the young. Confucianism, standing side by side with communism, nourishes and shapes Chinese moral education. As a result, one particular framework monopolizes the theory and practice of moral education. Moral education largely becomes a process of imposition of external moral rules and principles endorsed by communist ideologies, a process of behavioral training and character building according to prescribed standards, and a process of socialization of the young to established communist power relations. Guided by larger ideologies, researchers work to make the existing moral education system more effective. Teachers are busy applying the national curriculum of moral education and all other directives, teaching what the government requires them to teach. Very few people have critically examined the fundamental political nature of moral education. This situation remains unchanged today.

Then, what is the connection of Chinese moral education to American moral education? Are there any similarities between these two countries in school moral education? According to Jie Lu (2000), a professor of education in China:

> Chinese moral education still fits in a traditional model, theoretically and practically. The process of moral education is largely a process of imposition of external moral influences, which are mainly prescribed moral principles and rules. Such a process puts its very stress on shaping students' behaviors according to those principles and rules. This is exactly what Kohlberg had criticized: inculcation of values, training of behaviors, "bag of virtues" approach, and traditional character education model. (3)

The Chinese approach to moral education largely falls within the same model as character education programs in the United States. We have seen the political control in Chinese moral education. As Bai (1998) points out, "In the given Chinese context, the 'bag of virtues' has already been 'filtered' by the standards of political preference and blended with political values" (526). Perhaps I lead you to ask, what about the case in the United States? Specifically, what is the political influence in American character education?

Character Education
in the United States: Targeting the Political

Character education is currently the most popular approach to moral education in the United States. According to the well-known leader of character education, Thomas Lickona (1999):

> Character education is the deliberate effort to cultivate virtue. Virtues are objectively good human qualities, such as a commitment to truth, wisdom, honesty, compassion, courage, diligence, perseverance, and self-control. Virtues are good for the individ-

ual...and good for the human community....To be effective, character education must be comprehensive, intentionally making use of every phase of school life as an opportunity to develop good character. (23)

Before any close examination, such claims would seem appealing for many people who are seriously concerned about children's character building and schools' moral mission. There are indeed some strong points in Lickona's definition. For example, responding to the non-directive nature of moral education in many American schools, Lickona argues that a systemic approach to moral education is necessary, and moral education must become an integral part of public school curriculum. Schools have both the right and responsibility to engage deliberately, not haphazardly, in moral education efforts. Children's moral development and character building are just too important to be merely addressed by an informal approach or a hidden curriculum. Also, good values indeed exist and become the characteristic features of human well-being and good society. And good values do not grow automatically in human life; rather, they need to be cultivated through positive environment and effective education. As Lickona argues, education for values and character must be comprehensive, and it might include both direct and indirect teaching. In short, upon encountering this American theory of character education, I was drawn to its merits.

Gradually, however, I became skeptical, especially when I found more and more similarities between American character education and Chinese moral education. First, I found a similar social background of and rationale for character education. Like Chinese educators, American character educators also draw attention to social problems and suggest the responsibility of schools for solving these problems (Lickona 1993). But, like their Chinese counterparts, Americans also tend to moralize social, cultural, and psychological phenomena and overemphasize the role of moral education. For example, a singular starting point of all character education advocates is their conviction about youth deviance as exemplified by gun violence, teenage pregnancy, drug abuse, etc. They characterize these problems as individual ones, reflecting a deterioration of personal morality and character, and therefore advocate character education as a solution (Bennett 1996; Kilpatrick 1992; Lickona 1991, 1993).

This way of thinking is similar to that of Chinese educators and is highly problematic. Both stress the individual's moral responsibility but ignore the larger social and cultural conditions that largely construct and define the individual's behaviors. They both emphasize socialization and enculturation of children by passing on social and cultural norms and inculcating external moral rules, but they significantly discount education for critical citizens and values which lead to social change.

A closer examination helped me find that, like their counterparts in China, American character educators also embrace the traditional "bag of virtues" approach to moral education. Character education is overwhelmingly virtue-centered (Leming 1997; McClellan 1999; Noddings 2002). Moreover, the virtue-centered character education is deeply rooted in certain cultural traditions and carries particular political/ideological influences. American character educators define character as the possession and manifestation of virtues, and character education as the cultivation of those virtues. Virtues are defined non-contextually as objective and absolute existences (Lickona 1991, 1999). Since virtues are presumably objective, character educators assume that a consensus can be reached on the virtues to be transmitted. Thus, the so-called universality of virtues becomes extremely popular in the movement. Character educators create a list of the so-called universal or common values to be taught in their programs. Values on their lists include respect, responsibility, caring, honesty, courage, compassion, perseverance, etc. No matter how the list varies from one program to another, developers of each list claim that all people, regardless of their different religious, cultural, political, and economic backgrounds, universally share values on their list.

Serious questions must be addressed to such a claim of university of values. Moral absolutism stands behind character educators' claims. However, there is little agreement on whether virtue has an objective existence and whether a consensus on the virtues to be taught can be reached. Progressive educators discount absolutism in their understanding of morality and moral education and argue that any ethical behavior is related to a particular situation. Hartshorne and May (1928, 1929, 1930) point out that morality is basically a function of the situations where the moral subject is placed. Dewey (1909) denies the assumption of moral principles as "arbitrary" and "transcendental" (58). He (1934) also argues that the child's moral character must be developed in a natural and social atmosphere. Noddings (1995) argues for the situational and contextual nature of morality. Her analysis reveals that virtues like courage and honesty are always socially constructed.

While discrediting moral relativism and emphasizing universality of common values, character educators implicitly discount pluralism of values. Prescribing a list of values, which is by no means omniscient in scope, character educators inevitably overlook many other values, which may make significant sense to the lives of many people. For example, character education programs seriously ignore any values other than standard moral values. Personality traits, intellectual virtues, and physical qualities, which are important for us to live a good life, are excluded from character education curricula. Moreover, the sources of their moral values are singularly located in one tradition, the Western tradition. Similarly to Chinese moral educators, who overtly embrace Confucian ethics, American character educators explicitly argue for the teaching of traditional American values based on the Judeo-Christian tradition (Bennett 1993; Kilpatrick 1992; Wynne 1989).

For example, in an article discussing the management of effective schools, Wynne (1989) lists a number of traditional moral values and claims that these values constitute the moral element of effective schools. Wynne's list includes: 1) the acceptance of traditional hierarchy; 2) the exercise of strong adult control over children and adolescents; 3) the priority given to immediate good conduct over more elaborate ratiocination; 4) great emphasis on the life of collective entities; 5) reverence for the knowledge of the past; 6) the reservation of a sphere of life for sacred activities, beyond the day-to-day business of buying, selling, and producing; and 7) the quality of all community members as children of God despite their temporal, material, and intellectual differences (129–32).

Wynne clearly states that these values stem from the Judeo-Christian ethic and have pervaded the operation of both private and public schools in the United States. He claims that effective schools in which these traditional values are taught have produced students with "good character." The signs of such good character are varied and many but have the following central qualities: good discipline, obedience to adult authority, strong academic commitment, heightened collective identities, and collective loyalties.

Thus, we see a highly selective and narrow version of character or morality in Wynne's account. Wynne and his supporters may argue that his moral education scheme is well grounded in cultural traditions. However, such religion-based moral education can cause serious concerns. One may wonder whether a public school will still remain a public school if it transforms itself according to Wynne's prescription. It is probably safe to predict that if we applied Wynne's character education scheme, we would radically alter the nature and direction of public education in this country. Such an alteration is, of course, not in the American public's interest. Moreover, Wynne's scheme exclusively embraces one tradition while it ignores the cultural diversity of

American society. The Judeo-Christian tradition by no means represents the claimed universality.

However, Wynne indeed believes those Judeo-Christian-rooted values are or should be shared by all the people in America. As he argues, "It is not surprising that persons reared in the United States, a country with a long tradition of Judeo-Christian commitment, should feel affiliation with such values, regardless of their personal religious commitments" (129). By such a statement, Wynne simply rejects a possible denial of Judeo-Christian values by non-Judeo-Christian people in the country and dictates what he and his Judeo-Christian fellows believe to be universal. The cultural bias in Wynne's arrogant argument for traditional Judeo-Christian-based moral education is unacceptable.

The politicized moral training in China has always been conducted in the name of the people. Similarly, American character educators place a strong dependence on community. They emphasize community consensus on the creation of character traits or moral values to be taught. Usually they do so through a seemingly democratic process—forming a decision-making committee, which is typically composed of school administrators, teachers, and staff (see Character Education Partnership 2000). Sometimes the committee may reach out to include students, parents, and other community members. Then the committee works to create a list of certain traits or values. If they do not claim their list is universally shared, they are definitely proud that it is community based.

Such a process of community-based decision making is troublesome. A community does not always agree upon common grounds. As Noddings (2002) points out, it may be easy for a well-established community—one with recognized traditions, shared life styles and values—to come to a consensus on what it values. However, it might be difficult to reach any consensus in most modern communities. In many situations, people get together just because they send their children to the same school, but this does not mean they share values. Thus, one may ask, which subgroup will control the discussion during the decision-making process? Whose values will be taught? These are difficult but legitimate questions to ask.

In the increasingly culturally diverse American society, any pursuit of community consensus on matters of morality might be too simplistic. And any claim of consensus on universal values might be unjustified. There are already many such claims of the so-called consensus on universal values in the character education movement; thus, we doubt the moral ground of such claims. The voices of underprivileged groups may have been silenced and their values marginalized. For example, the schools researched and praised by Edward Wynne espoused traditional Judeo-Christian values, but what of the voices of those non-Judeo-Christian students and their parents? Are their values stressed or even noticed in such settings? I expect a moral outrage from the minority. If my expectation proves untrue, then the school in question must be either racially segregated or must have successfully suppressed the perspectives of the minority.

There is a potential danger in the extreme emphasis on community. As Noddings (2002) warns us, "Character education requires a strong community but not necessarily a good one" (5). My previous description of moral education practices in Chinese schools shows unequivocally how moral education, in the name of the community and people, was once dictated by the Communist Party and contributed to communist control. One might worry that the emphasis on community in character education efforts in the United States may help create a highly moralistic but not necessarily moral schooling. Any moralistic schooling is entangled with certain political/ideological forces. Purpel's (1999) examination of current character education programs reveals that core values taught in character education reflect a continuation of the Puritan tradition (as Wynne overtly argued). Such a historical tradition bears an uncanny resemblance to the rhetoric of contemporary neoconservative movements in political and cultural arenas. Under the name of universality and community consensus, Purpel argues, character education stems from certain ideological discourses and represents particular political control. Do we not see some parallels here between China and the United States?

What methods are used in the character education programs and what ideologies do they entail? Character educators disregard Socrates' doubts about the possibility of a direct teaching of virtues. Philosophically and pedagogically they embrace Aristotle's virtue ethics and idea of training children in virtuous behaviors. Character educators have always urged schools to directly teach students to know the good, love the good, and do the good. Although they claim a comprehensive approach, their views of virtues and education lead them to prefer didactic pedagogy. Programs with a comprehensive approach are few in number. Traditional methods of character training dominate practice. These include the enumeration of virtues, the memorization and recitation of creeds, verses, slogans, and golden texts; the imitation of heroes and role models; and the reward and punishment of certain behaviors. As one critic of character education, Kohn (1997), observes:

> The great majority of character education programs consist largely of exhortation and direct recitation....Even when character education proponents refrain from using that word [indoctrination], their model of instruction is clear: good character or values are instilled in or transmitted to students. (158)

The choice of didacticism and the allowance of indoctrination undoubtedly speak for certain ideological representations in character education. As Kohn (1997) argues, character educators hold the view that children need "fixing." The entire movement is driven by a stunningly dark view of human nature which is explicitly indicated by Kilpatrick (1992) and Wynne (1989). Because of that, character educators overwhelmingly stress direct training of control (make children do what they are told and work hard) and other distinctly conservative values. Again, the connection of character education with the Judeo-Christian tradition is obvious. The conservative values pointed out by Purpel and Kohn in character education programs are probably taught in many Sunday schools and church sermons within this country. The moral preaching in the church, as many would agree, is legitimately didactic and indoctrinating.

The wide use of exhortation and extrinsic inducement in character education programs also entails the influence of behaviorism. Behaviorism in moral education has drawn fire over time. As Hartshorne and May (1928/1930) revealed in their review of the character education programs in the 1920s, teachers' mere urging of certain behaviors had no necessary relation to conduct. Similarly, Kohn (1997) notes, "The techniques of character education may succeed in temporarily buying a particular behavior. But they are unlikely to leave children with a commitment to that behavior, a reason to continue acting that way in the future" (159).

Making the Hidden Curriculum Explicit and Challenging the Politics of Character Education

The exponents of character education ignore an important reality. Powerful conservative moral training already pervades American schools even if it is often in the form of a hidden curriculum. For example, Anyon (1980) explores the actual curriculum of docility and obedience taught to the lower classes in American schools. Giroux (1988) examines the hidden curriculum that imposes dominant class values, attitudes, and norms on all students. Today, the advocates of character education reinforce this type of conformist moral teaching and attempt to transform it to a more directive and systemic approach. It is indeed difficult to find any emphasis in the character education literature on developing thoughtful critics of society's problems and educating students to engage in social improvement.

Unlike in China, where politics controls moral education, the politics of moral education in the United States tends to be more subtle. Educators seem not to see the possible dangers of certain political orientations embedded in the popular character education movement. Character educators claim support from the American public. As another leader of character education, Ryan (1989), notes, the public's views of the issue were "registered in the 1975 and 1980 Gallup polls, wherein 79 percent of the respondents indicated they favor 'instruction in schools that would deal with morals and moral behavior' (Gallup 1975; 1980). So, concern there is" (4). However, the polls indicate that people only support general moral/character education. The polls do not say that people support any specific character education agenda. As Singer (2000) points out, everyone may agree that people should have good character, but there is no consensus about what good character means and how it is achieved. People may "agree with generalities, the 'character education themes,' not specifics—the substance of character education proposals" (275). The fact is that few oppose character education because few understand its political nature.

The debate over character education was present in the most recent presidential election in 2000. When responding to questions and concerns about the problems of guns and pornography in American society, Democratic candidate Al Gore and Republican candidate George W. Bush differed. While Gore emphasized efforts for stricter laws on gun control and more restrictions on the entertainment industry, Bush argued that schools must teach character education as a strategy. Bush said: "Gun laws are important, no question about it, but so is loving children and character education classes and faith-based programs being a part of after-school programs...and so there's a—this is a society that's got to do a better job of teaching children right from wrong"(Bush 2000).

This seems to support what Purpel (1999) argues: "The public discussion of character education has come to the point where it has become an overtly partisan political issue" (83). Many agree with Purpel. For example, Singer (2000) believes that character education is on the agenda of the Republican Party and religious conservatives. Nucci (1989) also notes that the issue of character education is mostly raised by political and cultural conservatives. "Led by public figures such as former Secretary of Education William Ben nett, the political right has called for a return to the direct teaching of traditional values through what is called 'character education'" (xiii).

Clearly, character education in the United States is preferred by certain political groups and represents specific ideologies. However, it is also true that the issue of character education may blur party lines and cross power boundaries. As Ryan (1989) claims, character education has received support from political leaders both on the left and on the right. Indeed, former President Bill Clinton supported character education in at least two State of the Union addresses. Although the difference in the endorsement of character education between Democrats and Republicans can be identified (for example, the Democrats mostly use the term "character education" generally, without referring to specific religious implications), there indeed exists the possibility that two or more political parties may work together to endorse one conservative ideology represented by the character education initiative. The party lines do not necessarily divide between commonly held ideologies. As Nelson et al. (1996) argue: "Ideologically, conservatives and liberals share basic beliefs" (272). For example, neither the conservative nor the liberal sees democracy as problematic, deserving critical examination. Instead, they both assume the legitimacy of the existing social order and demand schools to maintain the status quo. So, it is not surprising at all that character education that stresses more conformity and less critical thinking may obtain a bipartisan or cross-party support.

Any ethical system is always situated within certain social and political discourses. Similarly, any type of moral/character education is also politically charged. There is no politically neutral moral/character education in the world. Educators must be aware of the political/ideological orientations of any moral/character education efforts in the school and be aware of the nature of the politicization they might reinforce through moral/character education programs. Educators must ask and answer questions such as: Who makes the decisions about curriculum and instruction in character education? Whose values are taught in the process? Whose interests are met through the program? At present, these questions are either not addressed or are addressed superficially (e.g., when character educators claim to teach "universal values" or "community-based character traits"). Yet, these are legitimate questions to address. All educators have a responsibility to make explicit the hidden curriculum of politics in moral education, and to challenge the status quo of established moral education practice.

References

Anyon, J. (1980). Social class and the hidden curriculum of work. *Journal of Education 162*: 67–92.

Bai, L. (1998). Monetary reward versus the national ideological agenda: Career choice among Chinese university students. *Journal of Moral Education 27* (4): 525–40.

Bennett, W. (1993). *The books of virtues: A treasury of great moral stories.* New York: Simon & Schuster.

——— (1996). *Body count: Moral poverty...and how to win America's war against crime and drugs.* New York: Simon & Schuster.

Character Education Partnership (2000). *2000 National Schools of Character.* Washington, DC: CEP.

Chen, J., Luan, C., and Zhan, W. (Eds.). (1993). *Collected works on education in Chinese moral tradition.* Changchun, China: Jilin Culture and History Press.

Connell, W. (1976). Moral education: Aims and methods in China, the U.S.S.R., the U.S., and England. In *Moral education...It comes with the territory,* pages 30–43. Edited by D. Purpel and K. Ryan. Berkeley, CA: McCutchan.

Dewey, J. (1909). *Moral principles in education.* Boston: Houghton Mifflin.

——— (1934). *A common faith.* New Haven, CT: Yale University Press.

Gallup, G. H. (1975). The seventh annual Gallup poll of public attitudes towards public school. *Phi Delta Kappan 57*: 227–241.

——— (1980). The twelveth annual Gallup poll of public attitudes towards public school. *Phi Delta Kappan 62*: 39.

Giroux, H. (1988). *Teachers as intellectuals.* Granby, MA: Bergin & Garvey.

Hartshorne, H. and M. May (1928). *Studies in the nature of character (Vol. 1): Studies in deceit.* New York: Macmillan.

——— (1929). *Studies in the nature of character (Vol. 2): Studies in self control.* New York: Macmillan.

——— (1930). *Studies in the nature of character (Vol. 3): Studies in the organization of character.* New York: Macmillan.

Kilpatrick, W. (1992). *Why Johnny can't tell right from wrong.* New York: Simon & Schuster.

Kohn, A. (1997). The trouble with character education. In *The construction of children's character: Ninety-sixth yearbook of the National Society for the Study in Education,* pages 154–62. Edited by A. Molnar. Chicago: University of Chicago Press.

Leming, J. (1997). Whither goes character education? Objectives, pedagogy, and research in character education programs. *Journal of Education 179* (2): 11–34.

Lickona, T. (1991). *Educating for character: How our schools can teach respect and responsibility.* New York: Bantam Books.

——— (1993). The return of character education. *Educational Leadership 51* (3): 6–11.

——— (1999). Religion and character education. *Phi Delta Kappan 81* (1): 21–7.

Lu, J. (2000). Mutual understanding among human beings: Basis of moral education. *Educational Research 21* (7): 3–10.

Luan, C. (Ed.). (1992). *Stories on Chinese traditional moral virtues.* Changchun, China: Jilin Culture and History Press.

Mao, Z. (1977). How to deal with the internal contradictions among the people. In *Collective*

works of Mao Zedong, vol. 5. Beijing: People's Press (original work published 1957).
McClellan, B. E. (1999). *Moral education in America: Schools and the shaping of character from colonial times to the present*. New York: Teachers College.
Nelson, J., K. Carlson, and S. B. Palonsky (1996). *Critical issues in education: A dialectic approach*. 3rd edition. New York: McGraw-Hill.
Noddings, N. (1995). *Philosophy of education*. Boulder, CO: Westview.
―――― (2002). *Educating moral people: A caring alternative to character education*. New York: Teachers College Press.
Nucci, L. (Ed.). (1989). Moral *development and character education: A dialogue*. Berkeley, CA: McCutchan.
President Jiang talks about Chinese education (2000). *Moral Education Information 50* (2): 1–3.
Purpel, D. (1999). The politics of character education. In *The moral outrage in education*, pages 83–97. Edited by D. Purpel. New York: Peter Lang.
Ryan, K. (1989). In defense of character education. In *Moral development and character education*, pages 3–17. Edited by L. Nucci. Berkeley, CA: McCutchan.
Singer, A. (2000). Response to Milson on character education. *Theory & Research in Social Education 28* (2): 273–7.
The Chinese Ministry of Education (2000). Highlights of moral education policies. *Moral Education Information, 51* (3): 2–3.
Wynne, E. A. (1989). Managing effective schools: The moral element. In *Educational policy for effective schools,* pages 128–42. Edited by M. Holmes, K. Leithword, and D. Musella. Toronto: OISE Press.
Yuan, B., and Shen, J. (1998). Moral values held by early adolescents in Taiwan and Mainland China. *Journal of Moral Education 27* (2): 191–207.

INDEX

action competence, 271, 272, 275, 277, 278, 282–289
adolescence, 140, 142, 351
aesthetics, 209–211
Africa, 12, 71, 77, 92, 101, 149, 151, 172, 250, 254, 256, 297, 314
Althusser, Louis, 98, 351
Antonioni, Michelangelo, 108
Anyon, J., 371
Aoki, Ted, 3
Appelbaum, Peter, 15, 24
Apple, Michael, 199, 251
architecture of self, 261, 266
Arendt, Hannah, 325, 326, 328, 331, 354
Argentina, 12
Aristotle, 62, 63, 138, 275, 339, 341, 344, 351, 370
Asher, Nina, 4
Asia, 139, 149, 150, 162, 172, 250, 303
Australia, 12, 151, 152, 156, 162
autopoiesis, 219
awe, 67, 245

"back to basics", 199
Bacon, 339
Bateson, Gregory, 35
Baudrillard, Jean, 107, 114
Beck, Ulrich, 92, 279
Belgium, 161, 162

Berger, J., 329
Bergson, Henri, 35
Bernstein, Basil, 72–77, 79–81, 87–91, 94, 251
Bernstein, Richard, 62, 63
Berry, Thomas, 237, 242, 246
Bhabha, Homi, 110–115, 152, 175
Bildung, 272, 190, 291, 346
biocentric, 348
Bion, Wilfred, 166, 175
Block, Alan, 20, 27, 28, 30
body, 41, 57, 59, 91, 98, 104, 109, 158, 220, 338–340
Bookwalter, Keith, 35
Botswana, 12, 118, 249, 250, 254–259
Brand, Stewart, 165, 175
Brazil, 12, 151, 155, 302
Brewer, Kevan, 51
British Columbia, 65
Bronowski, J., 158, 175
Broudy, 146
Bruner, Jerome, 46, 141, 149, 175
Buber, Martin, 326

Canada, 2, 4, 12, 51, 103, 150, 156, 176, 205, 207–210, 218, 219, 233, 293, 298, 303, 307, 308, 312, 318
Cardinal Principles of Secondary Education, 207

Carson, Terry, 3
Cartesian, 55, 59, 81
chaos theory, 295
character education, 359, 365–373
Chin, Peter, 205, 209, 211
China, 2–4, 12, 140, 151, 155, 161, 359–365, 367, 369, 370, 372
Chomsky, Noam, 258
cinematization, 104, 105
civic education, 126
Cixous, Helene, 5, 298
collaboration, 4, 124, 146, 147, 193, 254, 325
Colombia, 12, 35
Committee of One Hundred, 12
Communism, 298, 364
communitarianism, 327
community, 35, 46, 77, 79, 92, 106, 108, 125, 127, 134, 147, 153, 154, 157, 181, 205, 216, 230, 242–245, 255, 256, 272, 273, 277, 288, 308, 310, 313, 320–322, 324–323, 348, 360, 363, 364, 366, 368, 369, 370, 373
comparative education, 2
computer, 7, 51, 52, 59–62, 66, 107, 158, 255, 285, 301, 302
computerization, 252
Confucianism, 303, 362, 364
Connell, W. 361, 363
constructivism, 22, 77, 97, 175, 295, 313
conversation, ix–xi, 1, 3, 5, 6, 11, 12, 62, 162, 167, 220, 220–222, 225, 250, 257, 294, 304, 305
co-operative education, 205
core curriculum, 120, 124, 127, 128, 180, 198
Costa Rica, 12
Counts, G. S., 6
critical theory, 274, 282
cultural diversity, 110, 368
cultural studies, 108, 121, 259
currere, 155, 167, 354
Curriculum Theory Project, 4
cyberspace, 154

Dahl, Roald, 20
Daignault, Jacques, 11, 13
Davis, Zain, 71, 92, 95, 98
de Certeau, Michel, 21, 22
deconstruction, 107, 108, 231, 240, 253, 351, 352
Deleuze, G., 54, 68
democracy, x, xi, 6, 7, 85, 92, 108, 110, 120, 124, 176, 271–275, 280, 282, 286, 287, 333, 353, 373
Denmark, 12, 150, 271, 286
Denzin, Norman K., 105, 114
Derrida, Jacques, 4, 5, 53, 54, 59, 64, 65, 103, 113, 298, 352, 353
Descartes, 338, 339, 341, 344
Dewey, John, 6, 141, 149, 167, 175, 206–208, 213, 215, 284, 329, 331, 367
discourse analysis, 342, 344
Doll, Jr., William E., 4, 42, 60, 68, 140, 148, 149, 164, 169, 170
dualism, 350–354, 359, 361
Durkheim, Emile, 72

ecology, 36, 295, 313, 348
Egéa-Kuehne, Denise, 4
Eliot, T. S., 246
Ellul, Jacques, 52, 58, 68
empire, 123, 207, 293, 303, 314, 316
England, 4, 26, 134, 150, 210
Enlightenment, 110, 113, 239, 153, 263, 272, 273, 295, 297, 337, 338
Erasmus, D., 275, 341
Erikson, Erik, 36, 167, 175
Estonia, 12, 117–119, 126, 127, 129, 133
Etzioni, A., 327
Euchner, C., 326
European Union (EU), 125, 159, 161
examination, 74, 90, 240, 285, 294, 305, 361, 366, 367, 370, 373

fantasy, 75, 76, 86, 93, 94, 95, 314, 315, 322

Index

Fassbinder, R. W., 108
feminism, 28, 108, 240, 257, 350, 355
Fine, Michelle, 18, 57, 228, 328
Finland, 4, 12, 155, 161, 162, 261, 263, 337, 343, 349
Foucault, Michel, 5, 10, 103, 109, 114, 166, 354
Francisco de Goya y Lucientes, 337
Frankfurt School, 273, 282, 283
Franklin, Ursula, 308
Freire, Paulo, 114, 240, 331
Freud, Sigmund, 10, 71, 73, 84, 85, 87

Gadamer, x, 56, 58
Gallas, Karen, 31
Germany, 4, 12, 109, 150, 162, 273, 342, 352
Giddens, Anthony, 92, 263, 279, 280, 286
Giesecke, H., 274, 289
Giroux, Henry, 108, 114, 199, 251, 257, 259, 269, 288, 371
global village, 117, 142, 152, 175, 250
globalization, 2, 5, 104, 114, 121, 123, 124, 128, 133, 152, 234, 243, 244, 245 252, 257, 285, 293–297, 299, 302, 303, 305, 307, 308, 310–316
Good, Ron, 4, 246, 291
Goodson, Ivor, 3, 213
Gough, Noel, 152, 175
Gray, John, 296, 302, 304, 307
Greene, Maxine, 16, 193, 202, 320, 325, 327, 328, 330, 331, 333–335
Greider, William, 301
Gundem, Bjorg, 3

Harpold, Terry, 155
Hasanow, Z. T., 125
Hegel, G. W. F., 297, 339, 344
Heidegger, Martin, 52–56, 60–68, 268, 349
Held, David, 296
Hellesnes, Jon, 283

Heschel, Abraham Joshua, 16, 30–33
Hesse, Hermann, 330
Hillis, Daniel, 165
HIV/AIDS, 249
Hofstadter, Douglas, 168, 175
Hopmann, Stefan, 3, 291
Huebner, Dwayne, 166, 176
Hutcheon, Linda, 106, 114
Hutchinson, Nancy L., 205, 209, 211,
hypertext, 154, 155, 175

identity, 6, 9, 19, 41, 43, 72, 75, 76, 77, 107, 110–112, 117, 118, 121, 125, 128–130, 133, 142, 147, 151, 154, 165–169, 187, 252, 261–269, 280, 286, 303, 310, 312, 316, 325, 328
imagination, 158, 234, 238, 241, 283, 291, 330, 331
India, 12, 137, 151, 155, 159, 161, 162, 251, 259, 307
individualism, 59, 279, 293, 364
Industrial Revolution, 52, 139, 198, 297
instrumental, 8–10, 53, 56, 62, 65, 66, 161, 269, 301, 321
International Association for Curriculum studies, 1, 12
International Monetary Fund
internationalization, 1, 2, 5, 12, 103, 122, 123, 138, 155, 157, 170, 249, 253, 354
The Invention of the Adolescent, 210
Israel, 12, 354

Jameson, Frederic, 107, 114, 115
Japan, 2–4, 12, 150, 151, 155, 300
Jouissance, 71, 80, 85, 86, 92, 93

kagisano, 255, 256
Kahn, Herman, 249
Kant, Immanuel, 273, 291, 297, 312, 344, 354

Kilpatrick, W. H., 6
Kilpatrick, W. K., 366, 368, 371
Kirshner, David, 4, 141, 145, 176
Klafki, Wolfgang, 274, 282, 289, 291
Korea, 2, 4, 12, 155, 300
Kristensen, Hans Jurgen, 288, 291

Lacan, Jacques, 5, 10, 71, 72, 75, 80–82, 84, 85, 90, 91, 96, 99–101, 103
Lacoue-Labarthe, Phillippe, 351
Latin America, 108, 314
Lefebvre, H., 319, 322, 324, 333
Levinas, Emmanuel, 351
liberal education, 140, 206, 218, 271, 272, 274, 280, 282, 283, 285, 287, 289, 295
libidinal economy, 72
Lloyd, Genevieve, 339, 340, 347, 352
Lorenz, Konrad, 166, 174, 176
Loy, David, 293, 303, 306
Lyotard, Jean-Francois, 5, 104, 115, 176, 298

Malaysia, 361–364
Mao, Zedong, 361–364
Marx, Karl, 153, 176, 286, 351, 354
Marxism, 355, 364
Maslow, Abraham, 35, 58
Mathur, Ajeet, 137
Maturana, Humberto, 57, 58
McLaren, Peter, 175, 253, 259
McLuhan, Marshall, 51, 60, 68, 240
Merleau-Ponty, Maurice, 268
metaphor, 3, 61, 76, 85, 98, 105, 111, 148, 169, 173, 174, 219
metonymy, 111
Mills, C. Wright, 283, 291
Mogensen, Finn, 271, 288
Mollenhauer, Klaus, 274, 282
Monsen, Lars, 179, 188, 192, 194, 198, 200–202

Montaigne, Michel de, 338, 341
Moore, Rob, 46, 72, 73, 101
moral education, 359, 362
Moulthorp, Stuart, 155
Muller, Johan, 72, 73, 95, 101
multiculturalism, 9, 126, 295
Munby, Hugh, 205, 209, 211
Munro, Petra, 4
mystery, 59, 67, 230, 231, 245

Name-of-the-Father, 79
narcissism, 4, 253
NASA, 156, 173
nationalism, 2, 117
Negt, Oskar, 274, 283, 284, 291
Nelson, Nancy, 4, 373
Netherlands, 12, 162
New Zealand, 4, 156, 176, 300
Nigeria, 12
Ninnes, Peter, 156, 176
Noddings, Nel, 367, 369, 370
North Africa, 151
Norway, 3, 12, 123, 179, 184

Oberg, Antoinette, 219
objet petit a, 80, 82, 84, 86, 95, 96
Oil Petroleum Exporting Countries (OPEC), 299
Ong, W., x
Ontario, 209, 213, 300
Organization for Economic Cooperation and Development (OECD), 294, 301
O'Sullivan, Edmund, 233

Pandey, Sid N., 117, 134, 249
pedagogy, 19, 71, 77, 78, 90, 93, 104, 105, 108, 114, 115, 154, 181, 191, 200, 239, 257, 259, 271, 282, 285, 309, 316, 352, 370
Philippines, 12

Index

phronesis, 63
Pierce, Charles, 35
Pinar, William F., ix, x, xi, xii, 1, 6, 9, 13, 140, 145, 155, 160, 162, 176, 294, 344
Plato, 97, 199, 275, 339, 342, 344
poaching, 15, 21–24, 29–31, 33
poetic thinking, 222
poiesis, 62, 63, 66
Poland, 12
postcolonialism, 108, 298
Postman, Neil, 66, 69, 313, 318
Postmodernism, 106, 149, 252
poststructuralism, 96, 98, 198
power, 27, 28, 30, 40, 56, 62, 63, 84, 84, 90, 94, 99, 103, 105–107, 109–111, 113, 114, 124, 132, 139, 152–154, 157, 158, 167, 169, 173, 174, 205, 224, 244, 226, 227, 234, 240–244, 246, 267, 269, 274, 285–287, 289, 294, 295, 303, 309, 314, 316, 321, 322, 324, 326, 328–330, 333, 347, 348, 350, 365, 373
praxis, 35, 63, 64, 66, 149, 164, 283, 284, 322, 330, 352
Purpel, David, 370–372

rationality, 72, 107, 112, 152, 157, 263, 295, 338–341, 344, 346, 352, 354
reason, 9, 51, 72, 79, 96, 98, 101, 106, 107, 110, 123, 125, 140, 142, 143, 153, 159, 172–174, 184, 198, 226, 169, 271, 273, 274, 276, 280, 284, 291, 306, 312, 333, 337–342, 345, 347, 351, 352, 355, 362, 371
reform, 6, 7, 11, 110, 124, 132, 134, 179, 180, 181, 183–192, 194, 196, 200–203, 235, 259, 262, 265, 269, 323, 326, 328, 329, 332, 362, 363
Reformation, 275, 293
religion, 35, 36, 47, 67, 78, 318, 343, 364, 368

representation, 75, 104, 106, 110, 112, 174, 203, 319, 320, 325, 344
repressive sublimation, 86
Renaissance, 286, 293, 341
Reynolds, William, 2, 6, 176
Rifkin, Jeremy, 134, 301, 318
Riquarts, Kurt, 3, 291
Romania, 12
Ropo, Eero, 261, 267
Rorty, Richard, ix, 353
Rousseau, Jean-Jacques, 16–19, 20, 21, 27, 28
Russell, Bertrand, 258
Russia, 4, 118, 151, 297

Sartre, Jean Paul, 355
Scandinavia, 151
Schnack, Karsten, 271, 283, 289–291
Schwab, Joseph, 205, 215, 218
Schutz, 325, 327–330
Schwarzenegger, Arnold, 106
Siu, R. G. H., 166, 176
Sizer, Theodore, 8, 13
Skutnab-Kangas, T., 126
Slater, Judith J., 319
Slattery, Patrick, 2, 6
Smith, Adam, 2, 6
Smith, B. Othanel, 2, 3, 46, 158, 293
Smith, David Geoffrey, 2, 3, 46, 158, 293
socialist education, 359
soul, 43, 59, 63, 167, 175, 331, 339
South Africa, 12, 71, 77, 92, 101, 254
Spencer, Herbert, 137, 139, 140, 152, 158, 172, 177
spiral curriculum, 167, 212
Steiner, Rudolf, 139, 141, 167, 172, 177, 209
Sweden, 12, 155, 162
the Symbolic Order, 76, 87, 88

Taba, Hilda, 42, 122

Taubman, Peter, 2, 6, 176
technology, 15, 51–62, 64–69, 104, 121, 122, 128, 129, 139, 141, 153, 160, 161, 163–165, 169, 176, 199, 250, 252, 255, 267, 301, 304, 308, 330
tests, 194, 361, 363
theory, 3, 9, 11, 35, 36, 42, 46, 47, 55, 57, 68, 71–73, 80, 99–101, 104, 108, 11, 114, 118, 144, 161, 183, 206, 215, 219, 221, 234, 236, 257, 271, 274, 282–284, 287, 289, 295, 297, 298, 300, 303, 304, 312, 315, 318, 319, 343, 344, 355, 362, 365, 366
Third Space, 112–115
Tomperi, Tuukka, 337
Toulmin, Stephen, 239
tradition, 3, 16, 133, 139, 142, 149, 183, 187, 191, 198, 199, 213, 227, 254, 272, 280, 283, 285, 286, 293, 295, 297, 303, 306, 311, 345–349, 355, 363, 364, 368–371
transformative learning, 233, 234, 236–239, 241, 242, 246
translation, 40, 111–113, 337, 338
transnational, 40, 111–113, 337, 338
Trend, David, 108, 115
Trinh, Minh-ha T., 112, 113, 115
Trousdale, Ann, 4
Truiet, Donna, xi
Turkey, 12, 150

UNESCO, 4, 166, 175, 298, 344
United Kingdom, 162, 173
United States, 1, 2, 4, 6, 9, 12, 15, 122, 134, 150, 161–163, 205–208, 218, 299, 300, 303, 319, 359, 365, 368, 369, 370, 372, 373

Varella, Francisco, 57, 68
Vares, Peeter, 125
Värri, Veli-Matti, 125
vocational education, 206–211, 218

von Trotta, 108, 109

Wagenschein, Martin, 283, 291
Wandersee, Jim, 4
Wang, Hongyu, 3
Weir, Peter, 105, 106, 108
Westbury, Ian, 3
Whitehead, Alfred North, 35, 49, 140, 177, 212, 213, 218
Wholistic Educational system (WES), 36–38, 47, 48
Willinsky, John, 3, 240
Wittgenstein, Ludwig, 107, 276, 355
World Bank, 294, 298, 303
World Wide Web (WWW), 153, 154
workplace curriculum, 211, 214
Wraga, W. G., 206, 207, 216, 218
Wynch, Christopher, 120

Yu, Tianlong, 359

Ziehe, Thomas, 274, 286, 291